D0778772

The Program Era

The Program Era

POSTWAR FICTION

AND THE RISE OF CREATIVE WRITING

Mark McGurl

HARVARD UNIVERSITY PRESS

Cambridge, Massachusetts

London, England

2009

Printed in the United States of America

Library of Congress Cataloging-in-Publication Data
McGurl, Mark, 1966–
    The program era : postwar fiction and the rise of creative writing /
Mark McGurl.
        p.   cm.
    Includes bibliographical references and index.
    ISBN 978-0-674-03319-1 (alk. paper)
    1. American fiction—20th century—History and criticism.
    2. Creative writing (Higher education)—United States—History—
20th century.   I. Title.
    PS379.M344 2009
    808'.042071173   2008050588

for Michael and for Mimi

CONTENTS

Preface

This book argues that the rise of the creative writing program stands as the most important event in postwar American literary history, and that paying attention to the increasingly intimate relation between literary production and the practices of higher education is the key to understanding the originality of postwar American literature. Far from occasioning a sad decline in the quality or interest of American literature, as one so often hears, the writing program has generated a complex and evolving constellation of aesthetic problems that have been explored with tremendous energy—and at times great brilliance—by a vast range of writers who have also been students and teachers. In telling the story of the period I call the

Program Era, my effort has been to describe this constellation of aesthetic problems, the various positions and principles and instances of which it and they are made, in systematic terms. My hope is to begin to make sense of a field that has grown so large and internally complex that few scholars even attempt anymore to gather its splinters together.

And for good reason, some will say, noting that many dimensions of postwar literature are left entirely unexamined by this book, and that its accounts of individual writers, institutions, and texts must necessarily be, at times, brutally simplified. Postwar American literature has indeed been a huge and hugely various endeavor, and my strategic decision to concentrate on fiction to the exclusion of poetry and other genres makes it no less so. And yet one of the most valuable lessons taught by postwar fiction is that the limitations of a given point of view are enabling. Indeed, although it may end up somewhere else, thinking can only really begin with a reduction of complexity, with the imposition of a certain frame of analysis. And so I will demonstrate that, for all its variety, postwar American literature can profitably be described as the product of a system, though one (as it happens) ingeniously geared to the production of variety.

In ways that will only become clear in the chapters to follow, the overriding problem for postwar American fiction has been how to adapt modernist principles of writing, developed in the late nineteenth and early twentieth centuries well outside the academy, to a literary field increasingly dominated by bureaucratic institutions of higher education. For instance, the signature preoccupation of modernist fiction with the technical problem of "point of view" in narration finds new meaning when it is transferred to an institutional environment engaged on many levels with the problem and promise of cultural difference. But this is just one example. For better or worse, colleges and universities are now the central conservators of modernist literary value as such, and they are where most "serious writers" (of which there is now an oversupply) and "serious readers" (of which there can never be enough) are trained.

The literature of the postwar period not only reflects this fact but reflects upon it in a number of ways, leading to a body of work that it is fair to describe as self-involved even when its interests are patently social and historical. Explicitly or not, every work of serious fiction in this period is, on one level, a portrait of the artist. Although this has produced many works of forbiddingly difficult self-enclosure, works that only a coterie could love, it far more commonly has produced works that resonate broadly with the concerns of serious readers everywhere, living, as they do, multiply institutionalized and indeed self-reflexive lives. The exaggerated but telling sense that "everyone" across the land is writing or, even more frequently, not finding time to write "their novel" indexes something more than the wide distribution of a certain kind of literary ambition. Those relatively few, but nonetheless great many, writers who actually manage to produce and publish a novel speak to and for a broader existential urge to be living a significant—literally—life. In sum, the creative writing program produces programmatically, but also in rich and various profusion, a literature aptly suited to a programmatic society.

As the reader will soon see, the project of laying out the system of postwar American fiction need not entail any avoidance of the pleasures of charisma and eccentricity. This is a book filled with enough big personalities, awesome individual works, and interestingly symptomatic oddities to satisfy any reader's taste for the individual case; if the writers of the Program Era are subjected here at times to a somewhat unflattering critical analysis, this is only intended to mark their partiality with respect to the system as a whole. Although this requires us to adopt an unfamiliar, because non-individualistic, mode of aesthetic appreciation, it is at the end of the day that wholeness which is to be admired here. The image of "system" as a gray plane of deathly regularity is an outdated and impoverished one, and bears little relation to the actual vivacity of something like, say, the University of California, a.k.a. the UC System, in which a huge and diverse populace thrives, and out of which a great deal of interesting fiction (not to mention this book on fiction) has sprung. The image of the institution as a prison, or of institutionalization as something that happens at a mental hospital, is obviously a satisfying and perhaps even necessary one, but it threatens to sell us on a very naïve sense of how individuals actually come into being. Postwar American literature provides endless testimony, for starters, of the agonizing importance of the institution of the family in making us who we are—and the school picks up where the family leaves off.

One might in principle prefer less compulsory or rule-bound collectivities than the family or the school—for instance, the kinds of loose associations found in the café scene in New York and Paris in the early twentieth century—but the truth is that formality is only a matter of degree. In their own way, the social patterns that laid the tracks for, say, the fateful arrival of Ernest Hemingway at the door of Gertrude Stein's apartment at 27 rue de Fleurus were as rigid as any underlying the many great teacher-student relations of the postwar period, if not more so. It would in any case be a great loss to literary history if our disrespect for institutional relations as somehow embarrassing to art (in a way that the modernist pedagogical relations were not) made us less than vigilant in remembering and understanding them. Although this book tries as hard to motivate further research into the literary history of the writing program as to actually conduct it, I think it is worth simply saying it outright in the form of a plea: We need to start documenting this phenomenon, moving out from the illustrious cases of the Iowa Writers' Workshop and Stanford University and a few others to grasp the reality of an enterprise that now numbers some 350 institutional participants and continues to grow. This enterprise is our literary history.

Wanting as I do to argue for the importance of educational institutions to postwar literary production, it seems something less than a diversion from my task to thank the institutions that made this work on postwar literature possible. Let me begin by mentioning that one of the better sentences in the foregoing paragraphs was borrowed from a report on the manuscript by an outside reader for Harvard University Press; that act of petty thievery, or rather gift-acceptance, on my part can stand for the dense web of influence and material support in which this book took shape. The key institution here has been the aforementioned University of California, in particular UCLA, which not only allowed ample time for the project's unfolding but was the medium of a thousand meaningful intellectual exchanges along the way. To say the names Mark Seltzer, Kate Hayles, Eric Sundquist, Michael North, Rafael Perez-Torres, and Chris Looby in sequence provides good shorthand for the general richness of the intellectual environment in which this book came into being; and to say the names Melanie Ho, Jessica Pressman, Glenn Brewer, and Kate Marshall—all of whom made helpful contributions along the way—does the same for the sharpness of UCLA's graduate student community. The submission of early drafts of some of these chapters to the scrutiny of the Americanist Research Colloquium of the UCLA English Department was helpful to their development.

Farther afield, I want to acknowledge the Southern California Americanist Group, meeting at places like the Huntington Library, Caltech, and USC, though often enough at UCLA; it was first convened by Michael Szalay and sustained by the efforts of Cathy Jurca, Paul Gilmore, Greg Jackson, Eric Hayot, Sharon Oster, and others. Of the great many gifted minds I have seen pass through that group, I would point to Jen Fleissner, Elisa Tamarkin, Joe DiMuro, and Mark Goble as four whose advice and counsel at various stages of the writing of this book have been lastingly helpful and reassuring. A year-long residential fellowship at the scholar's paradise known as the Stanford Humanities Center really got this project off the ground, and I am grateful to John Bender and the staff at the SHC for making that year possible. Audiences at Chicago, Yale, Stanford, Columbia, Harvard, Iowa, Fordham, Riverside, and Irvine offered, by contrast, a more punctuated sort of assistance in helping me to see what was at stake in my research. As did, in a different way, the efforts of the editors of *Critical Inquiry* and *American Literary History,* where parts of two chapters of this book first appeared in print. Add to this the innumerable bits of wise counsel, timely advice, useful references and the like that I have received over the years, and you have a book that has accumulated more institutional debts than its author can possibly repay.

But more than any other, this book is owed to the institution of Sianne Ngai.

Introduction: Halls of Mirror

> It had to be U.
>
> RICHARD POWERS, *Galatea 2.2*

EROS AND INSTITUTION

"I am sick of teaching, I am sick of teaching, I am sick of teaching," wrote Vladimir Nabokov to his friend Edmund Wilson, desperate to get back to working on the novel whose outsize success would, in fact, free him forever from his teaching duties at Cornell University.[1] In its peevish negativity, the complaint seems perfectly opposed to the famously lilting opening of that same novel—"light of my life, fire of my loins"—and could be offered as a nonfictional counterpoint to its virtuoso verbal music: Lo. Lee. Ta. *Sick of teaching, sick of teaching, sick of teaching.*

1

The irony being that, with a small twist of fictional fate, the school-girl idealized by Humbert Humbert in *Lolita* (1955) might have become a collegian of the sort who packed Nabokov's classes and emitted stacks of exams that needed to be graded before he could turn to more personally rewarding tasks. Humbert's pathologically narcissistic love for Lolita is all but unimpeded by the interests of the real little girl named Dolores who is its victim, but this same girl grown into a college coed would have personified the intractable otherness and obduracy of material necessity as it impinged upon Nabokov's real life as an artist. Throughout the writing of the novel he was, as he put it, in "miserable financial difficulties" with "no way out of academic drudgery (ill-paid to boot)."[2] Not that he ever lowered himself to attending faculty meetings, or sitting on committees, but he met his teaching responsibilities head-on.

Nabokov's fictional European gentleman-scholar, with a steady income inherited from a rich American uncle, has no such money troubles, and he does not need to teach—not even his nubile charge, whom he tries merely to distract. And yet, set free to act upon his fantasies, he ends up in the prison cell from which he narrates his tale of forbidden love. For his well-behaved author, it was something like the reverse. The more powerful fantasy for Nabokov seems to have been one of ideal working conditions, a release from the prison of the classroom into the richly reflexive freedom of artistic expression. This, as much as anything else, is what is at stake in the creation of a narrator like Humbert, whose ethical complexity is a form of authorial defiance. He is unreliable in the usual sense that the reader cannot necessarily trust what he says, but on another level he represents Nabokov's aestheticism, his high-handed commitment to the "unreliability" of art itself, which should not be tasked with the fulfillment of extra-artistic ends—certainly not moral-pedagogical ones, perhaps not even the end of paying the bills.[3] According to his biographer Brian Boyd, Nabokov never dreamed in all the years he was writing it that *Lolita* would make him serious money, assuming instead (correctly) that it would be difficult even to find a publisher for such a work. It was in many senses a labor of love. That an assertion of artistic freedom ended up earning him his financial freedom was from his perspective a miraculous windfall, if a well-deserved and overdue one. Then again, once upon a time, so had the opportunity to escape the deadly chaos of wartime Europe for a life of teaching in the United States seemed a miraculous windfall. The Nazis had been advancing upon Paris. Nabokov's wife, Véra, was Jewish. They had a very small son. There are necessities and necessities.

This book will take up residence in the gap between freedom and necessity—or rather, in the higher educational institutions that have been built in that gap, with gates opening to either side. On the one hand, nothing could be more constrained than the modern American school, which, never mind the plight of émigré authors, is anchored K-through-Ph.D. in the unbeautiful realm of social needs, hemmed in all around by budgets and bureaucracy and demography. On the other hand is the shimmering vision of self-realization-through-learning toward which it bends. We go to school, or are made to go, to become *richer* versions of ourselves, however that might be defined. This doubleness is readily apparent in the educational endeavor called creative writing, whose profound contribution to postwar American literature will be my central concern in the chapters that follow. Conceived, as D. G. Myers has taught us, in the firmament of early twentieth century progressive educational reform, creative writing is surely one of the purest expressions of that movement's abiding concern for student enrichment through autonomous self-creation.[4] What could be further from the dictates of rote learning, or studying for a standardized test, than using one's imagination to invent a story or write a poem? At the same time, and especially to the degree that it would end up linking the profession of authorship with classrooms and committees and degree-credentialing and the like, creative writing cannot help pointing toward the unglamorous institutional practicalities of literary life in the postwar U.S. and beyond. This, as we shall see, is the realm not only of institutions but also of technologies, the hard and soft machines in and by which literature comes into being.

In his classic account of Anglo-American literary modernism, *The Pound Era* (1971), Hugh Kenner mapped the innovative tendencies of interwar writing through the work of the great poet, editor, and all-purpose publicist of high cultural endeavor, Ezra Pound. Taking inspiration from Kenner but turning his methodological investment in the dominant individual inside out, my book traces the fate of U.S. literary modernism after World War II, when the modernist imperative to "make it new" was institutionalized as another form of original research sponsored by the booming, science-oriented universities of the Cold War era. The literature of this period would remain obsessed by individuals and their individuality (and so must this book be, to a degree), but its true originality, I will argue, is to be found at the level of its patron institutions, whose presence is everywhere visible in the texts as a kind of watermark. Arriving in the U.S. in 1940, Nabokov entered the picture too early to profit from what was at that point little more than a twinkle in the eye of Paul Engle, Wallace Stegner, Elliott Coleman, Baxter Hathaway, and the many others who would soon be forging a new place for writers in the American university. This place was the graduate creative writing program, which turns writers into salaried writing professors and students into tuition-paying apprentices. Creative writing had been offered in scattershot fashion to undergraduates since before the turn of the century, but the graduate program represented a dramatic escalation of the relationship between the profession of authorship and the school, a systematic coupling, without (as of yet) a final merging, of art and institution.

Nabokov got a taste of creative writing instruction when he touched down at Stanford University to teach a summer school class in playwriting, his very first teaching assignment in the U.S. But after that it was low-paid Russian language instruction and lecturing on literature at Wellesley College for several years, and then more of the same, minus the language teaching, at Cornell. We can only speculate, but it's hard to imagine that he would have turned down the opportunity to teach creative writing classes, which in the standard form of the workshop consists of a small group of students sitting around a table discussing each other's stories, with the professor sitting in as a moderator and living example of an actual author. On the other hand, once Nabokov had his lectures written, he delivered them year after year, never changing the syllabus and making no pretense of taking any interest in his students (Thomas Pynchon famously among them) as individuals. So perhaps in the end, even with the stacks of exams, that was the less demanding assignment. It is in any case hard to imagine Nabokov genuinely approving of the *idea* of the creative writing program, which begins with a commitment to the importance of individual creativity he shared but immediately surrounds it with the dubious trappings of institutionality.

"I write [only] for myself in multiplicate," he declared in clear violation of the sociable spirit of the creative writing workshop, with its provisional ceding of authority to the peer group which evaluates an unpublished work while its author, by custom, listens in squirming silence.[5] The creative writing program would replicate the spirit of communal endeavor and mutual influence found in the Paris and Greenwich Village café scenes of an earlier era, but Nabokov was not one for that sort of esprit de corps. He was a militant Cold War individualist who did not admire "sticky groups," who did not "write for groups, nor approve of group therapy" (*Opinions,* 114)—to which, sure enough, the creative writing workshop has sometimes been compared. It was after all a thing born (although of course it had many stages of birth stretching back through time) in the thirties, with the founding of the Iowa Writers' Workshop in 1936, and the "group-ness" of that decade could easily be detected in its rituals.[6] But since the founders of Cornell's creative writing program, one of the nation's first, seem to have disliked their notoriously self-delighted colleague, Nabokov was not invited to compromise his distaste for group endeavor for the benefit of his own career. He therefore presents us with the interesting case of a writer famously associated with a university—and a university, in turn, famously associated with the rise of creative writing—who nonetheless missed a date with institutional destiny. Like many of the figures who will make memorable appearances in this book, he is as interesting to us for how he didn't quite get with the program as for how, in a way, he did. Certainly it would have made his life a lot easier if his fiction writing had been defined, as it is for the tenured creative writing professor of the present day, as a kind of "research" for which he needed, like the scholar, paid time away from the classroom.

Not that Nabokov was a stranger to research. In fact, one of his best-known quirks was a scientific passion for a certain family of butterflies, the Blues. If the creative writing professor can be described as a practitioner of a sort of disorganized science of creativity, or the creative process, Nabokov was actually both a writer and a scientist. Between his classes he devoted a lot of precious time to catching butterflies in the wild and even more to pinning them down in elaborate classificatory arrays at Harvard's Museum of Comparative Zoology, making lasting contributions to their study. There is a touch of inadvertent irony in the fact that the linguist Roman Jakobson's witty rebuke to the notion of hiring a fiction writer to teach literature at Harvard—"What's next, shall we appoint elephants to teach zoology?"—came at Nabokov's expense, but only a touch.[7] Nabokov pursued his zoological passion in a proudly scientific but obviously anachronistic spirit, never aligning himself in any serious way with the broader field of professional entomology. Without any advanced degree to his name, a professorship in that field was even less plausible than one in literature.

He was, in other words, an "amateur" in the literal, not necessarily derogatory, sense—a *lover* of the objects of his knowledge no less than Humbert is a lover of nymphets. With its obvious kinship to aesthetic miniaturism, his scientific work on beautiful little butterflies speaks powerfully to the importance of pleasure in study, which had been another of the themes of progressive education. Although it is in some ways the opposite of a campus novel (i.e., a road novel), *Lolita* recalls the many works in that genre—from Robie Macauley's *The Disguises of Love* (1952) to Philip Roth's *The Professor of Desire* (1977) to Joyce Carol Oates's *Unholy Loves* (1979) to John L'Heureux's *The Handmaid of Desire* (1996) to Michael Chabon's *Wonder Boys* (1995) to (and especially) Francine Prose's *Blue Angel* (2000)—that are fascinated by the scandalous persistence of Eros in the social life of otherwise risibly politically correct institutions.[8] The broader point, though, is that to the degree that educational institutions have embraced progressive educational ideals—beginning, let's say, with the revolutionary idea of student "electives" concocted by Harvard's Charles Eliot in the late nineteenth century—they are structured as well by an appeal to Eros that can take any number of forms. An elective course in creative writing is one of these. The frequently "sticky" group dynamic of creative writing workshops is another. Both are distant descendants of Plato's erotically charged symposium, and their leaders, the creative writing teachers, can be counted on to love literature (if not necessarily the teaching of literature, or even the teaching of writing) with a passion. Exemplary in this regard was John Hawkes, a wildly experimental writer who taught at Brown University for many years. His student Rick Moody summarizes his notoriously amorous approach to teaching thusly: "He wanted us to believe in literature. He felt he had done his job if we could explain why *The Real Life of Sebastian Knight* was a masterpiece, from the standpoint of language and construction. Hawkes played favorites, which was bad; and he loved women a lot more than men, which was bad too; and he allowed us to drink wine in class, which in my case was an incredibly bad idea, since I was developing a drinking problem. All these things were inadvisable, but what was not was the idea of emotional commitment to the process, a strong relationship between student and professor."[9]

The author of *The Real Life of Sebastian Knight,* Nabokov, had no strong relationships with his students that we know of, but he did communicate the strongest possible belief in literature, even to the point of descending into a fussy sort of fetishism. Contrary to their reputation for luminous brilliance, the lectures on literature that he delivered for a paycheck were, on the cruel evidence of the notes he never meant to be published, surprisingly dutiful exercises in low-level formal analysis and plot summary. Like his lab work on butterflies, which mostly entailed paying dogged attention to minute differences of anatomy for hours on end, the lectures by design contain a minimum of interesting ideas about literary works and a maximum of what he called the "fondling" of their details.[10] Not that the entreaty to *pay close attention* wasn't delivered with considerable personal aplomb, and not that it didn't speak to a matter of legitimate concern to lovers of literature. Perhaps because the novels leading up to *Lolita* sold so poorly, Nabokov was able to perceive with great acuity what the fundamental threat to traditional literary culture in the postwar U.S. would be: distraction.[11] Consecrated by the charismatic presence at the podium, the university lecture hall was one place where a novel or poem could still command center stage as an object of reverent scrutiny. But Nabokov was not interested in synthesizing his close observations of literary texts to produce a compelling *reading* of any of them.

To perform an interesting reading, we can surmise, would have been to start down a path of critical self-imposition leading to the kind of ego-maniacal insanity we see in *Pale Fire* (1962), where Charles Kinbote woe-fully (but amusingly) distorts the meaning of a long poem he is supposed to be faithfully annotating so that it refers to himself.[12] And true enough, to "have a reading" of a novel, as contemporary literary scholars like to put it, is to lay claim to a successful act of interpretive appropriation that can at times seem competitive with the simplest account we might give of the author's lucidly conscious intentions.[13] But in stark contrast to Kinbote's flagrant nonsense—*Pale Fire* would be a better book if his anno-tations were more disturbingly believable than they are—the success of these appropriations usually stems from their plausibility, from the sense they give us of coming closer to the meaning of the literary work even as it is tied to some larger context (theoretical, historical, or otherwise) that has conditioned the author's intentions without his necessarily being fully aware of it. In this dialectical interplay of text and context the fondling of details begins to have an intellectual as well as experiential payoff for the reader, and the value of the work—even, ironically, when the work is sub-jected to an irreverently "political" critique—is increased.

Although Nabokov was more concerned with satirizing a certain kind of scholar than scholarship itself, it is easy to read this novel as the first broadside in the sneering war between creative writers and scholars in the university, who upon the fading of the great poet-critics of the 1940s and 50s from the leading edge of literary scholarship came to seem divided by their shared object, literature, even as their offices were still often found side by side in the same hallways. As an author Nabokov did not hesitate to produce fictions that uncannily refer to himself, as when the much-abused scholar Krug is saved at the end of *Bend Sinister* (1947) by the *deus ex machina* of his author, or when the fictional Timofey Pnin encounters his fellow émigré Vladimir Nabokov in the novel *Pnin* (1953).[14] Alfred Appel has called the obsessive reflexivity of Nabokov's work an aesthetic of "involution," and it was of a piece with a broader postwar codification and intensification of modernist reflexivity in the form of what came to be called "surfiction" or, more durably, "metafiction."[15] But lecturing on the literature of geniuses (there were only a handful) could only be a process of slowly and respectfully *experiencing* their work in the most immediate sense, not thinking about it for oneself, and still less contextualizing it as part of a broader human drama: "Let us worship the spine and its tingle. . . . The study of the sociological or political impact of literature [is] for those who are by temperament or education immune to the aesthetic vibrancy of authentic literature, for those who do not experience the telltale tingle between the shoulder blades" (*Lectures*, 64).

Although one can credit Nabokov with not forgetting the physicality of aesthetic experience, tingle worship would not cut it as an approach to literature even among academic critics as eager as he was to protect literature from politics and sociology, of whom there were (and are) many. For better or worse, the modern university is predicated on the values of the Enlightenment, on the attempt (however difficult, perhaps even futile) to trade our childish enchantments for valid knowledge, including knowledge of the ways and means of enchantment. Valuing the experience of enchantment above all else, Nabokov's theory of literature short-circuits the pursuit of literary knowledge on behalf of a mystical submission to aesthetic authority felt along the spine. His is the crudest form of what a certain kind of literary scholar calls the "ideology of the aesthetic," and in generally less militant forms it is endemic to the discipline of creative writing, whose ultimate commitment is not to knowledge but to what Donald Barthelme called "Not-Knowing."[16] This is not a commitment to ignorance, exactly, but it does entail a commitment to innocence: the aura of literature must be protected at all costs, and the mysteries of the creative process must be explored without being dispelled. Although literary studies as we know it is probably unthinkable except as built upon a foundation of awe—supplying it one of its strongest motives—Nabokov's scholarly contemporaries were better equipped than he to make literary criticism seem a genuinely intellectual, if not exactly a scientific, endeavor.

In fact, by the time he arrived in the U.S., Nabokov was not much of an intellectual, if by that term we mean someone profoundly interested in the conflict of literary and cultural ideas. If it is easy to mistake him for one, it is because he was such a theatrical holder of opinions. Henry James was a "complete fake . . . a pale porpoise [of] plush vulgarities";[17] Hemingway and Conrad were "hopelessly juvenile" (*Opinions,* 42); the idea that any of William Faulkner's "corncobby chronicles" could be considered a masterpiece was an "absurd delusion, as when a hypnotized person makes love to a chair" (*Opinions,* 57). Proclamations such as those found throughout the aptly titled *Strong Opinions* (1973) are little more than vamping performances of judgment, all the more impressive because unreasonably extreme, if not simply stupid. The same streak of anti-intellectualism is evident in Nabokov's fiction. Its obsessive reflexivity produces an intimidating effect of hyper-cleverness, true, but this is less the working out of an interesting idea than a career-long compositional *reflex:* everyone in the novels, including the person at the source of their utterance, is subject to an ongoing process of figural doubling, division, rotation, and reversal—a sequencing of formal-ontological differentiation along various axes of identity. Humbert is the reverse of his nemesis, the playwright Quilty, and both are versions-in-reverse of Nabokov, the well-behaved author of the autobiographical text *Speak, Memory* (original version, 1951), who in *Pale Fire* splits himself between the married poet Shade and the homosexual critic Kinbote, who may or may not be the same person in the fictional world of the novel, and so on.

It makes sense that he would refer to his writing ability as a "combinational talent" (*Opinions,* 15). And he did not dispute the idea that he was quite repetitious. "Artistic originality has only its own self to copy," he granted, meaning not only that he was doing his own thing as a novelist but that writing those novels was a process of "evolving serial selves" from the unique self at their origin, Vladimir Nabokov (*Opinions,* 95; 24). As he makes clear in his lectures, no matter what a book is about, its "style constitutes an intrinsic component or characteristic of the author's personality," which even in the most impersonal narrative "remains diffused through the book so that his very absence becomes a kind of radiant presence" (*Lectures,* 59; 97). In this sense, even beyond the nonfictional memoir *Speak, Memory,* all of his writing might be described as *programmatic self-expression.* And this too, although he remained mostly an outsider to the new institutional arrangements of the Program Era, makes Nabokov's work emblematic of something central to the institution of creative writing, and of the ends to which its technologies are put.

Even more than self-expression, his fiction could be described as an act of programmatic self-establishment, an elaborately performative "I am." Using his own preferred idiom of fairy tale and romance, it could be described as a way for a king-in-exile to recover his country and reassert his rule on a linguistic-aesthetic plane. Nabokov's lifelong attraction—sometimes ironic, sometimes not—to the traditional romance motif of unrecognized royalty is fabulously evident in *Pale Fire,* where the deranged editor Kinbote has (at least in his own mind) been chased from the throne of the nation of Zembla to his ignominious dwelling at Wordsmith College, U.S.A. As the descendant of Russian nobility cut off from the vast country estate he roamed as a child, and from the language, Russian, in which he first made his name as a novelist, Nabokov had a more plausible biographical claim to a fantasy of royal restoration-in-language than most. But even for him this was essentially metaphorical, a way of imagining a life of uncompromised and exalted individuality. Certainly the fantasy is transposable to the inhabitants of the democratic United States, the immigrant nation where, as it has been well and untruly said, "every man is a king."[18] And it certainly fits quite snugly into the progressive school's commitment to enhancing students' self-esteem. It's good to be king (or queen); and to recover one's throne in the enchanted realm of one's own writing is to bend the arrow of personal experience around until it re-attaches to its origin like a golden Möbius band. Instead of testifying to a permanent condition of disadvantage in the face of physical necessity, or to the relentless humiliations exacted by social institutions, or to a perpetual process of wounding at the hands of history, "personal experience" is redeemed in this manner as a proud and vibrantly reflexive textual presence.

That anyway is the idea. Of course, in practice, time marches on and nothing really comes full circle. And when we pull back from the therapeutic enchantments of literary experience to a wider angle of vision, we see something slightly less mystical than a golden Möbius band: a world in which the category of "personal experience" has over the course of the twentieth century, and in the postwar period in particular, achieved a functional centrality in the postindustrial economies of the developed world. These economies in turn inhabit what Ulrich Beck, Anthony Giddens, and others have described as a "reflexive modernity."[19] The utility of this concept for understanding the metafictional impulse in postwar writing leaps off the page, suggesting that literary practices might partake in a larger, multivalent social dynamic of self-observation. This would extend from the self-observation of society as a whole in the social sciences, media, and the arts, to the "reflexive accumulation" of corporations which pay more and more attention to their own management practices and organizational structures, down to the self-monitoring of individuals who understand themselves to be living, not lives simply, but *life stories* of which they are the protagonists. It would be absurd to deny the large payoff to individuals living in the inherently pluralistic conditions of reflexive modernity, who are vested with a thrilling panoply of choices about how they will live their lives. But it would be equally wrong to deny the degree to which, as Beck puts it, modern people "are condemned to individualization." To be subject to reflexive modernity is to feel a "compulsion for the manufacture, self-design, and self-staging" of a biography[20] and, indeed, for the obsessive "reading" of that biography even as it is being written. And in this project there are a host of agencies, including schools, waiting to help.

One of the many names for the economic forms native to reflexive modernity is the "information economy," which isolates the importance of data and communications in the economic life of our times, and it will be of some help in defining the broader environment in which the system of creative writing moves. Although millions of people in the U.S. and abroad continue to work in factories and in the fields, this term does begin to limn the situation of the enormous and growing segment of the population, most of them college graduates, whom C. Wright Mills called the "white collar masses," and Christopher Newfield simply calls the "middle class."[21] Andrew Hoberek is right, in turn, to remind us that to the extent that these people can be described as middle class, it is a middle class quite distinct from either the European bourgeoisie or the yeoman farmers of the early Republic in that it is not comprised of independent owners of the means of production but of *employees*.[22] On one level, of course, the information in which these employees traffic plays the other to literature. As William R. Paulson has recounted, since the nineteenth century texts have been considered "literary" to the degree that their value does not seem reducible to the information they convey, and an author is in fact distinct from the typical information worker to the extent that she is an independent producer and owner of the fruits of her labor. And yet if we conceptualize literature, as Paulson does, as a kind of "noise" that opens the world of information to its outside—and thus to generation of new and potentially useful orders of information—it can be seen to have a special sort of utility in that world, a job to do.[23]

But even with these or similar dialectical adjustments, the term "information economy" does not adequately register the pleasurable existential narratives and dazzlingly colorful media spectacles increasingly associated with postwar economic life, missing the way it continually solicits from its actors a range of emotional responses, from bemused curiosity to laughter and tears and shame and shock and awe. This limits the term's reach as a descriptor of the environment of creative writing, and threatens to sell us on a set of images of corporate life—in effect, the world of the man in the gray flannel suit—that have been out of date since the 1960s, when (as recounted by Thomas Frank and others) the energies of the counterculture began to be integrated into business practices.[24] What the business authors Joseph Pine and James Gilmore instead call the "Experience Economy" is one in which all commodities are at risk of "commoditization"—the catastrophic deflation of their brand-name value (and per-unit profitability) in the direction of undifferentiated natural resources.[25] As an antidote, they suggest the staging of business transactions as a set of memorable experiences that would in theory be as various as the individuals who enjoy them, and thus immune from the consequences of the encroaching de-differentiation of their material vehicles. Which is really only to say, in a final realization of the logic of modern advertising, that marketing (or, rather, the experience of being marketed to) must in a sense *be* the thing being sold. The experience economy generalizes the affective protocols of consumerism such that they become relevant across all economic sectors.

Providing a compelling critical account of what Pine and Gilmore now offer in the glib spirit of how-to, Dean MacCannell long ago described the world of the experience economy as one of generalized tourism, a world in which the "value of such things as programs, trips, courses, reports, articles, shows, conferences, parades, opinions, events, sights, spectacles, scenes and situations of modernity is not determined by the amount of labor required for their production. Their value is a function of the quality and quantity of *experience* they promise."[26] This, as MacCannell notes, marks the domain of cultural production as the leading edge of modern capitalism, which, in a way that Marx's account of the commodity fetish did not quite foresee, trades more and more in purely symbolic, notionally "immaterial" goods. Instead of reifying the social relations of production in the form of a thing, as Marx had it, these symbolic goods (as it were) flip those relations over, trans-coding labor into leisure, production into consumption, with only a begrudging concession to their material substrate.

One of the jobs of this book will be to illuminate and appreciate postwar American literature by placing it in this evolving market context, examining how the university stepped forward in the postwar period both to facilitate and to buffer the writer's relation to the culture industry and the market culture more broadly. While I have less to say about the nitty-gritty of writer-publisher relations than I might, and even less about such things as the corporate consolidation of the publishing industry and the demise of the independent bookstore, the market is everywhere relevant to the story I will tell, even beyond being something that must be held at bay for the health of literature. A novel is, after all, a very good example of an "experiential commodity" whose value to its readers is a transvaluation of the authorial labor that went into its making, and most often has little to do with the economic value of the pulp upon which it is pressed. This is brought into relief by the even better example of tourism, where the tourist pays simply *to be* in a certain place but hedges the immateriality of his experience by taking pictures and purchasing durable souvenirs. Since reading novels and being on vacation are so often aligned in popular practice, we might well suspect a deep link between the two. Isn't the printed matter of the novel put back on the shelf in a sense the "souvenir" of the quasi-touristic imaginary experiences that were had inside it? For the reader of *Lolita,* this "tourism" is well nigh literal. Escaping from the town of Ramsdale just as Nabokov escaped from his job in Ithaca, New York, in pursuit of butterflies, the novel becomes a narrative of travel into the charming innocence of American fakeness represented by the corny motels and tourist sites that Humbert and his captive visit along the way.

To the extent that it, too, can be understood as an experiential commodity that the student purchases with tuition money, creative writing instruction can be understood in similar, if less artifactual, terms. As an elective element of the undergraduate curriculum, creative writing issues an invitation to student-consumers to develop an intensely personal relation to literary value, one that for the most part bypasses the accumulation of traditional cultural capital (that is, a relatively rarefied knowledge of great authors and their works) in favor of a more immediate identification with the charisma of authorship. Taking a vacation from the usual grind, the undergraduate writer becomes a kind of internal tourist voyaging on a sea of personal memories and trenchant observations of her social environment, converting them, via the detour of craft and imagination, into stories. By contrast, to read and analyze a novel in a regular literature class is to turn around and head back toward the workplace—back, that is, toward the submissiveness of homework. The detritus of this process—the little library of novels, poems, and plays the English major carries with him into life—is both a souvenir of the "college experience" and a materialization of the cultural capital which he worked hard (or not so hard, as the case may be) to acquire there.

This is not to say that the self-tourism of creative writing is necessarily easy. Writing well is by all accounts very hard work, and part of the value of the program for graduate students in particular is in the outsourcing of self-discipline it facilitates, where the artifice of deadlines and grades helps the apprentice push through the quagmire that leaves untold thousands of citizens in the perpetual state of (not) "working on their novel." Indeed it has been argued that one of the benefits of creative writing instruction is an increased appreciation, on the part of the student, of the true difficulty of the achievements of "real" writers. A nicer way to put that would be to say that creative writing makes for "creative readers"—which is to say, more involved readers, which may be true. (But if this is so, then creative writing should be integrated much more widely into the English curriculum and not held in reserve, as it so often is, for students who demonstrate talent. It would likewise be interesting to see what would happen if all faculty in English departments, even the most hardened historicists, were asked to teach creative writing.)

Like all progressive educational initiatives, however, creative writing does have a reputation for leniency, and why wouldn't it? In creative writing more than any other subject, it can seem that the teacher is grading a person, not a paper, or answers on an exam. It is, after all, a therapeutic educational enterprise in a way that, say, a physics class could only inadvertently be. No wonder then if, as poet-teacher Anna Leahy has observed, self-esteem is a "hidden guiding principle in our pedagogy."[27] My sense is that this is true even on the graduate level, where plumbing one's depths as a writer has been defined as a potential occupation. Of course one hears about cases like David Foster Wallace, who was said to have been harshly criticized by his teachers in the M.F.A. program at Arizona for his experimental impulses, but the most reliable source of negativity in the graduate workshop is no doubt other students—the competition—not the teacher. The teacher knows that for the vast majority of her charges the M.F.A. will not in fact function as a professional degree leading to a job but rather as a costly extension of their liberal education. In this sense it is a prolongation of the "college experience," an all-too-brief period when the student is validated as a creative person and given temporary cover, by virtue of his student status, from the classic complaint of middle-class parents that their would-be artist children are being frivolous.

But to speak of creative writing as inhabiting an "experience economy" does not go far enough in correcting the emphases of the term "information." To be sure, as we shall see, making this link begins to explain the deep affinity of workshop fiction (not to mention that curious new thing, "creative nonfiction") to the nonfictional genre of the memoir, but it leaves unexplained the specific role, precisely, of creativity—and relatedly, fictionality—in the enterprise of creative writing. In the fiction workshop the student writer is invited to do something she cannot do anywhere else in her studies except at risk of expulsion: make stuff up. Although the practice of creative writing is grounded in the value of personal experience, it is in theory "set free" by the imagination which reshapes that experience to a greater or lesser degree. Creativity may stem from, but is not finally reducible to, personal experience: this is one thing that Nabokov's complex deployment of narrative unreliability in *Lolita* insists upon.[28] The difference between evil émigré Humbert and his not-so-evil émigré author, or between Philip Roth and the "counterlife" lived by his novelist-character Nathan Zuckerman, or even between the author Richard Powers and the character called "Richard Powers" in the novel *Galatea 2.2* (1995), is the all-important difference made by the creative counterfactual, by fiction as a cipher for freedom. And this, in turn, echoes an understanding of creativity that began to emerge in the Renaissance, where human beings are understood to have the power to exceed the world as empirically given, turning the gift of free will toward the perfection of humankind, the harmony of nations, the invention of the new. The importation of this idea into the rationale for creative writing instruction is sometimes quite direct, as when David Fenza, making the case for his dis-

EXPERIENCE ⟶ **CREATIVITY**

AUTHENTICITY   FREEDOM

MEMORY, OBSERVATION   IMAGINATION, FANTASY

Here I introduce the first of several dynamic oppositions of value embedded in the practice of creative writing as it has been collectively understood and enacted in the postwar period. Its basic terms (in practice always intertwined and hard to distinguish) are inherited from two millennia of thought about art and art making, from Aristotle and Plato to the Renaissance to, perhaps most importantly, nineteenth-century romanticism. In recognition of the fundamental importance of self-reference in and to this practice, I will call the act of authorship in the Program Era the "autopoetic process," and here designate as two of its most basic interacting elements the values of creativity and experience, leaving for later the equally important value of "craft." We can flesh out these terms with the more overtly ideological values with which they have often been associated, and we can furthermore attach them to the cognitive faculties which they typically assume will be brought to bear in the act of writing. To write "from experience" is either to plumb the depths of memory or to engage in quasi-journalistic reportage; in either case the fiction so created will (in theory) have the ring of authenticity. To be "creative" in one's writing is, by contrast, to imagine the world anew, "improving" upon experience so that it makes for a good story, part of whose excitement will stem from the sense that "anything can happen" in the freedom of fictional worlds.

cipline, speaks of how "creative writing classes often demonstrate the efficacy of the human will—that human experience can be shaped for the good."[29]

Hence the irritation one so often encounters on the part of professional authors in the face of what seems to them a limiting biographical reading of their fiction. Alfred Appel notes on Nabokov's behalf how those readers who note some similarities between author and narrator and "immediately conclude that *Lolita* is autobiographical in the most literal sense" have fallen into a cunning trap set by the author, who is much more sophisticated than that.[30] As John Irving's *The World According to Garp* (1978)—the story of an only-somewhat-John-Irving-like novelist—puts it, "Garp always said that the question he most hated to be asked, about his work, was how much of it was 'true'—how much of it was based on 'personal experience.' . . . Usually, with great patience and restraint, Garp would say that the autobiographical basis—if there even was one—was the least interesting level on which to read a novel."[31]

But, contra Garp, readers who go in for the biographical reading of fiction are not only naïve but also savvy, drawing potentially interesting if perhaps inherently indeterminate conclusions from the proper name—e.g., "John Irving"—on the cover of a book. They know that fiction emerges in the most literal sense from the experiences of the author —writing fiction *is* one of those experiences. And they know that in the literary culture in which the fictional author named Garp came to exist, "personal experience" and "creativity" are primary values that relay one to the other in a relation of mutual authorization, distortion, and augmentation. They know that part of the value of the modern literary text, quite apart from the "relatability" of its characters, is the act of *authorship* that it records, offering readers a mediated experience of expressive selfhood as such. If, as in *Speak, Memory,* that story is essentially true to experience, there is still the fascination of the conversion of memory into felicitous expression. If, as in *Lolita* or *Garp*, that expression is dazzlingly ironized, turned inside out and around and folded thrice, all the better. The complexity of the situation can be seen in the fact that there is little doubt that

John Irving shares the opinions of his character on the limitations of biographical reading—little doubt that Garp is in general the author's (as they say) mouthpiece. Furthermore, the novel itself takes considerable interest in the way the raw material of Garp's life experiences is used in the manufacture of his fiction, some of which (oddly enough) was published separately under the name John Irving. The indeterminacy of the relation between author and character is in this case quite real, a matter of pragmatic fact, but to make it a principle (whether by way of prohibitions against the "biographical fallacy," as the New Critics called it, or in the absurd declarations of the "death of the author" that were heard in the 1960s) is to risk missing one of the most basic dynamics of postwar literary production.[32]

The name for the economic world in which the principle of personal indetermination will always be paid flattering respect is the "Creative Economy," which proceeds on the simple theory that anything is possible except the restraint of capital. This is Richard Florida's alternative, borrowed from John Howkins, to Pine and Gilmore's Experience Economy. While his account hits some of the same notes as theirs, it is broader in conception, drawing attention not only to the suffusion of contemporary commerce with experiential fictions, but to the necessity of providing the right social climate (liberal, diverse) for creativity.[33] It also, more simply, draws attention to the increasing importance in our time of research and development as engines of the new, and to the way—this is Howkins's emphasis—intellectual property in the form of new patents, trademarks, and copyrights has become the digital bedrock upon which the contemporary economy is built. There is, in other words, a deep continuity between *creativity* and *R&D,* and nowhere more so than on the campus. While they are also (with museums) our culture's primary custodians of the obsolete, it would be an understatement to say that modern universities have been eager participants in the pursuit of the new. As centers of basic and applied research, they lend aid to the development of the local, regional, and national economies they inhabit, doing their bit for the unending project of capitalist "creative destruction" celebrated by the economist Joseph Schumpeter in the 1940s.

Of course, nothing much is "destroyed" by creative writing, not literally. It remains for the most part a rather low-tech and quaintly humanistic, if increasingly sprawling, affair whose role is rather to give something back to the student which the perpetual displacements of modern life—Nabokov knew more than his share of these—might seem to take away. It is easier, in other words, to see creative writing as one of the forms of obsolescence conserved by the university than as part of its R&D wing. Even so, the remarkably smooth entry of the discipline of creative writing into the U.S. university over the past fifty years or so has been facilitated by the concurrent rise of creativity as a value beloved by American artists and scientists and corporate types alike—by everyone, really, certainly including literary scholars like me.

Who doesn't love creativity? "No word in English carries a more consistently positive reference than 'creative,'" observed Raymond Williams in 1961, and since then its reputation has only improved.[34] The fervor of our lip service to creativity is matched only by the enthusiasm of our paeans to personal experience. If, in the chapters that follow, I seem too willing to discount the enchantments of the first, and question the authority of the second, it is only in the interest of restoring some balance in favor of the claims of the collective life we live through institutions. Or rather, as the systems theorists would less flatteringly put it, the collective life that institutions live through us.

GETTING WITH THE PROGRAM

The American writer's intimacy with the university in our time is not an entirely unprecedented phenomenon. If only as students, and occasionally as teachers, writers have been spotted on campus before now. The gradual conjoining of the activities of literary production and teaching over the course of the postwar period is, however, in the sheer scale of the institutional program building upon which it has depended, and in the striking reversal of attitudes that it suggests, about as close to a genuine literary historical novelty as one could hope to see. Once perceived as the stuffy enemy of modernist innovation in the arts, the last place a self-respecting artist would want, or be welcomed, to ply his trade, the university has with the rise and spread of classroom instruction in creative writing, and with it the creative writing professorship and other forms of writer-in-residency, become perhaps the most important patron of artistically ambitious literary practice in the United States, the *sine qua non* of countless careers. "All this represents a very great change," wrote Alfred Kazin in the mid-1950s, already amazed by the transformation he was witnessing. "When I was in college in the 'thirties, it was still well understood that scholars were one class and writers quite another. They did not belong to the same order of mind, they seemed quite antithetical in purpose and temperament, and at the very least, they needed different places to work in."[35]

Of course there were some obvious exceptions to Kazin's rule—most importantly the New Critics, who had previously convened in the environs of Vanderbilt in the 1920s as the Fugitive poets, and whose later promotion of the practice of close reading of literary texts in the classroom would harmonize conspicuously well with the obsessive concern for "craft" that began to define writing programs at roughly the same time. This can be seen in Jay McInerney's recollection of how, when he submitted his apprentice fiction to Raymond Carver at Syracuse University, "manuscripts came back thoroughly ventilated with Carver deletions, substitutions, question marks and chicken-scratch queries. I took one story back to him seven times; he must have spent 15 or 20 hours on it. He was a meticulous, obsessive line editor. . . . Once we spent some 10 or 15 minutes debating my use of the word 'earth.' Carver felt it had to be 'ground,' and he felt it was worth the trouble of talking it through. That one exchange was invaluable; I think of it constantly when I'm working."[36] The idea is that stories, prose though they may be, and preferably (for a writer like Carver) grounded in everyday speech, should nonetheless be constructed with the same precision and subtlety as the Metaphysical poem, with every word weighed and measured and balanced for meaning and effect.

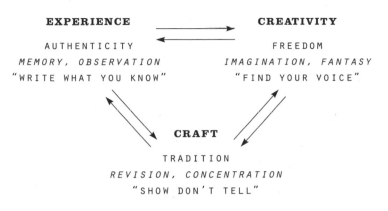

Here I fill out the abstract model of the autopoetic process as the Program Era has understood it, adding the all-important value of craft and its associated elements to the values of personal experience and creativity. This diagram abstracts from the totality of the rhetoric of postwar creative writing the key components of the autopoetic process, separating this specifically literary endeavor from the "writing process" or "creative process" more generally. The values of experience, creativity, and craft can be understood as the psychic and symbolic resources upon which a writer draws in the act of writing, and here they are supplied with the pedagogical imperatives with which they are commonly associated. Craft—also called "technique"—adds the elements of acquired skill and mental effort to the process, and is strongly associated with professional pride and the lessons or "lore" of literary tradition. The imperative to "show don't tell" is, in turn, strongly associated with the disciplining of the "natural" impulse to express oneself as a self, that is, with the classically modernist value of "impersonality."

However untrue, it makes sense that the aforementioned Fenza, in his role as Executive Director of the AWP (Associated Writing Programs, founded in 1967), would claim for his organization the honor of having "rescued literature from the exhumations of the philologists to elevate literature's status as a *living art*"; that was the achievement of the New Critics, many of them poet-critics, who began as relatively marginal figures in academia, with low status even at places like Vanderbilt, but lived to see their ideas lodged at the core of American literary studies in the postwar period.[37] In this they can be taken as emblematic of American writers more broadly, who have gradually, since the founding of the Iowa Writers' Workshop, seen the "extramural" consciousness of their modernist predecessors turned inside out—or, rather, outside in.[38] The handful of creative writing programs that existed in the 1940s had, by 1975, increased to 52 in number. By 1984 there were some 150 graduate degree programs (offering the M.A., M.F.A, or Ph.D.), and as of 2004 there were more than 350 creative writing programs in the United States, all of them staffed by practicing writers, most of whom, by now, are themselves holders of an advanced degree in creative writing. (If one includes undergraduate degree programs, that number soars to 720.) Fenza estimates that the total contribution of this, "the largest system of literary patronage for living writers that the world has ever seen," runs to at least 200 million dollars annually.[39] You don't have to be a dogmatic historical materialist to believe that a transformation of the institutional context of literary production as fundamental as this one might matter to a reading of postwar American literature.[40]

Indeed, one might imagine that the rise of the writing program would have already attracted considerable attention from literary scholars, who have after all been on hand to watch it occur at close range. But in fact—perhaps as a result of its occurring at *too* close range—it is only a small exaggeration to say that the rise of the creative writing program has been entirely ignored in interpretive studies of postwar literature. Discussion of the writer's relation to the university has instead largely been confined to the domain of literary journalism, and to the question of whether the rise of the writing program has been *good* or *bad* for American writing.[41] Whether couched in populist or elitist terms, the suspicion running throughout these discussions is that there may be something inherently wrong with artistic activity being, as critics ominously say, *institutionalized* in such a way. Published to considerable fanfare in *Harper's Magazine* in

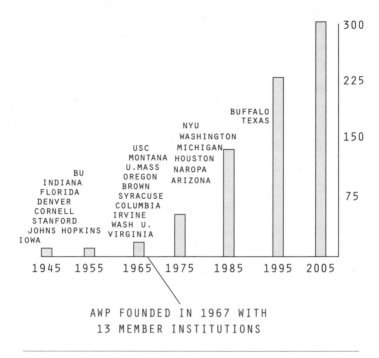

AWP FOUNDED IN 1967 WITH
13 MEMBER INSTITUTIONS

A cluster of creative writing programs appeared in the immediate postwar period, but with the progressive educational revival of the 1960s, the numbers exploded. Note that, while creative writing is a relatively cutting-edge educational phenomenon, its most prestigious or notable instances (indicated by the names superimposed upon the bar graph, arrayed roughly according to the year of a given program's founding) are correlated with relatively long duration. As of 2004 there were well over 300 graduate programs affiliated with the AWP, while the total reported individual membership (faculty and students) in the AWP was some 25,000, according to the AWP website: *www.awpwriter.org.*

1989, Tom Wolfe's "manifesto" for a new social realism, "Stalking the Billion-Footed Beast," is perhaps the most notorious of these critiques, complaining of "writers in the university writing programs" who in "long, phenomenological discussions" have "decided that the act of writing words on a page [is the] real thing and the so-called real world of America" is the fiction.[42] In place of this effete and tedious navel-gazing, Wolfe would have writers return to the robust example of nineteenth-century literary naturalism, where the practices of novel writing partially converged with those of investigative journalism.

Others such as John W. Aldridge have given thumbs-down to the writing program not only for its removal of writers from the manifold stimulations of the real world, but also for the damage it has done to the originality of the individual authorial voice. Demonstrating the continuing appeal of the romantic conception of the artist as an original genius, "assembly-line" writing programs are blamed by Aldridge for producing a standardized aesthetic, a corporate literary style that makes a writer identifiable as, say, an Iowa writer. The claim here is that the collective pursuit of perfectly crafted, workshopped prose has the effect of eliminating the salutary unpredictability of the students in question, ironically reproducing the machine-made quality of formulaic genre fiction on another, slightly more elevated or rarefied cultural level. The result, according to Aldridge, is that products of the writing program become, not writers, but "clonal fabrications of writers" who can only be expected to produce "small, sleek, clonal fabrications of literature."[43]

A nervousness surrounding these issues is evident even in the official history of the illustrious program at Iowa, available on its website, whose rhetorical curlicues are a typical response to the simple but difficult questions that have haunted creative writing programs since their inception:

> Though we agree in part with the popular insistence that writing cannot be taught, we exist and proceed on the assumption that talent can be developed, and we see our possibilities and our limitations as a school in that light. If one can "learn" to play the violin or to paint, one can "learn" to write, though no processes of externally induced training can ensure that one will do it well. Accordingly, the fact that the Workshop can claim as alumni nationally and internationally prominent poets, novelists, and short story writers is, we believe, more the

result of what they brought here than of what they gained from us. We continue to look for the most promising talent in the country, in our conviction that writing cannot be taught but that writers can be encouraged.[44]

Tilling the symbolic ground between teaching and development, teaching and encouragement, this cannily argued document manages on the one hand to pay respect to the "popular" idea of natural individual genius and to communicate a strong sense of Iowa's considerable historical importance and continuing prestige. The point here, indeed, is to make populism and elitism indistinguishable. The same sort of fusion is evident in the creative writer's distinct claim to prestige in the English departments to which writing programs tend to be attached: although typically relatively undereducated for that milieu, such a writer may actually be known to a nonacademic readership. This fact, combined with the spiritual privilege derived from the writer's intimate commerce with the Muse, and with the apparently bottomless desire of undergraduates to take creative writing classes, offsets to some degree the intramural dominance of Ph.D. scholars who largely run the place but who are famous, if at all, only to each other.

Writing programs: pro or con? There is nothing wrong with this debate, but surely it's time for the museless pedants to have their say. What is needed now, that is, are studies that take the rise and spread of the creative writing program not as an occasion for praise or lamentation but as an established fact in need of historical interpretation: how, why, and to what end has the writing program reorganized U.S. literary production in the postwar period? And, even more important for my purposes here, how might this fact be brought to bear on a reading of postwar literature itself? Focusing on fiction at the expense of the equally interesting (and potentially inter-illuminating) cases of poetry and the other arts, this book will take some steps toward answering these large questions and only in conclusion will circle back around to sketch a new and I think more interesting form of appreciation—a *total* appreciation—of what the program hath wrought. The challenge will be to generate concepts and critical vocabulary broad enough to describe an entire literary historical period, but flexible enough to admit that the phenomena they name were in fact gradually assembled over many decades, and continue to transform under our eyes. To facilitate a perception of historical process, I have divided the chapters of this book into three roughly chronological parts: the first tracks the gradual assemblage of the system as we know it across the first two-thirds of the twentieth century, culminating in the founding of the Iowa Writers' Workshop; the second examines the upheaval and elasticity of that system in the pivotal and famously "expressive" period of the long 1960s, when the program really began to multiply; the third analyzes its normal functioning since then as one of the signal educational practices of reflexive modernity.

The first term in my critical vocabulary is therefore the "Program Era" itself. If only for the allusion it makes to Kenner's magisterial account of interwar modernism, this term would be a little risky, setting a standard for critical vivacity and acumen that I cannot hope to match. A more consequential risk is that it can seem simultaneously too broad and too narrow in defining a critical domain. How can I offer this book as an account of an era when that era has evidently not yet concluded—indeed, is perhaps best thought of as having just recently gotten fully underway? How, for that matter, can I all but ignore the genre of poetry that was Kenner's central object of attention? I could try to justify my focus by saying that the postwar period is, in some deep sense, a "novelistic" and not a "poetic" period, and I might even half believe it. Certainly the increasingly multimediated and aesthetically "impure" qualities of postmodern culture have a compelling precursor in the history of the novel genre as described by Mikhail Bakhtin.[45] By the same token, the sheer garishness of postwar image culture has as often been declared the occasion of the "death of the novel" as it has been declared novelistic. Better, then, to admit that a restriction to fiction is simply one of the innumerable limitations I have had to accept in order to lend coherence to the critical narrative I want to construct, which will not come to the resounding conclusion of a post-program era but will trail off into an uncertain future.[46]

That said, one of the interesting side effects of the rise of the creative writing program is the way that it tends to divide its denizens, teachers and students alike, into either a fiction or poetry or nonfiction "track," and the way that this bureaucratic convenience ramifies throughout the postwar literary field. (An even more extreme division is enacted between these genres and dramatic writing, which has over time disengaged from the English department entirely in favor of an affiliation with Drama). For instance, a writer like Raymond Carver may have felt himself to be equally a poet and a short story writer, but his professional identity suggested starkly otherwise. While his plainspoken poetry is mostly ignored, his short fiction has become required reading for students of creative writing, the very model (with Hemingway) of writing as painstaking understatement. The social-professional and patronage networks of fiction and poetry are substantially different from one another, and so is the situation of these genres in the economy at large. In contrast to poetry, which (as a paying profession at least) has been all but entirely absorbed by institutions of higher education, the situation of fiction remains complex, extending outward from the institutionally subsidized high-art experimentation of publishers like Fiction Collective 2 and Dalkey Archive into economically viable domains of serious middlebrow fiction and from there to Oprah-enhanced bestsellerdom and multi-phase movie deals. The Brat Pack phenomenon of the 1980s, when program products like McInerney and Bret Easton Ellis were promoted as a glamorous new Lost Generation, could not have happened if the brats had been poets. More recently, the impressive cultural entrepreneurship of Dave Eggers, with its literary magazines and publishing ventures and community centers, could not have been built on a foundation of poetry. An account of the Program Era in poetry would therefore look substantially different from this one, and not just on the question of marketability. Insofar as literary forms are specific to literary genres, the effort to link forms with their contexts will be relatively specific.

Of course, the residually if inconsistently viable relation of fiction to the market might be another reason to object to the term "Program Era," since it would seem to marginalize all those postwar writers—for instance,

Don DeLillo, John Updike, Cormac McCarthy—who have only glancingly, if at all, gotten with the program. They have instead been supported by book sales, by the healthy per-word rates of a magazine like the *New Yorker*, or by the largesse of non-academic institutions like the Guggenheim Foundation. And yet consider the seemingly banal fact that virtually all contemporary American fiction writers, including the three named above, have attended college, and that the most "out on the range" among them (McCarthy) got his start by publishing stories in the campus literary magazine at the University of Tennessee.[47] In previous generations this would not likely have been the case, both because fewer individuals of any kind went to college before the postwar advent of mass higher education and because a college education was not yet perceived as an obvious, and still less a necessary, starting point for a career as a novelist. Rather, as the uncredentialed, or rather press-credentialed, example of the high school graduate Hemingway makes clear, the key supplementary institution for the novel until mid-century was journalism, which remains importantly "on the map" of the field of literary production to this day. (Think here of the careers of Norman Mailer, Joan Didion, Donald Barthelme, Tom Wolfe, William T. Vollman and the like, or of the obvious importance of the *New Yorker* and a few other reportage-dominated, large-circulation magazines to the fate of postwar American fiction.)

Thus we will want to be attentive not only to the program in isolation and as such but also to something larger, what Langdon Hammer has called the "culture of the school."[48] At its farthest reaches, this might encompass phenomena as broadly spread as, say, the importance of Augie's reading of the Harvard Five Foot Shelf of classics in Saul Bellow's *Augie March* (1953), which reflexively explains that novel's celebrated amalgam of learned and demotic speech, or Eggers's using the proceeds from his best-selling memoir and novels to found a community writing workshop and tutoring center for youth, 826 Valencia. If we were feeling especially expansive, we might note that two of the most phenomenal best-sellers of our or any time—J. K. Rowling's Harry Potter series and Dan Brown's *The Da Vinci Code*—are both in different ways conspicuously "scholarly" fictions, suggesting a deep well of utopian longing on the part of readers for meaningful education and the (alas) hard-won pleasures of erudition. My thesis is not that creative writing programs preclude all other forms of literary patronage or venues for a career, but that these programs are the most original production of the postwar period, its most interesting and emblematic—and, yes, increasingly hegemonic—literary historical trans-formation. Having learned a great deal from the pioneers (Ihab Hassan, Marcus Klein, Tony Tanner, Morris Dickstein, Jerome Klinkowitz, Robert Scholes, and others) who established the viability of academic criticism of contemporary literature, and from the critics (Brian McHale, Linda Hutcheon, Philip Brian Harper, and others) who have most acutely de-fined what we mean when we say "postmodern fiction," I want however to shift the discussion to the actual institutions, technologies, and practices from which postwar fiction emerges. Building upon the work of those (Gerald Graff, John Guillory, D. G. Myers, and others) who have drawn our attention to the function of literature as an institutional value in and of the postwar American academy, and taking what I will from recent work in systems and media theory, I aspire to offer an account of postwar fiction that is at once more concrete and more comprehensive than usual, ranging from close encounters with literary works and their authors up to the flagrant abstraction of the diagram.

By way of introduction to this project, I want to take the two charges most frequently heard against program fiction in literary journalism—that it is *self-involved*, that it is *unoriginal*—as occasions to begin the non-partisan examination of the *reflexivity* and *systematicity* of postwar American liter-ary production which I will carry out in the course of this book. Whatever opinion one may have of the fact, it is true that contemporary literary au-thorship is a profoundly self-conscious occupation, and also true that, un-der the auspices of the creative writing program, the ways and means of literary education have been structured in new ways. As the poet William Matthews put it in his foreword to the 1980 edition of the ever-fattening AWP *Catalogue of Writing Programs:* "What is clear is that the process of literary education has become increasingly formalized, and so perhaps easier to begin to describe, since the propagation of creative writing as a formal study appropriate to universities."[49]

Venturing to map the totality of postwar American fiction, I will describe it as breaking down into three relatively discrete but in practice overlapping aesthetic formations. The first, "technomodernism," is best understood as a tweaking of the term "postmodernism" in that it emphasizes the all-important engagement of postmodern literature with information technology; the second, "high cultural pluralism," will describe a body of fiction that joins the high literary values of modernism with a fascination with the experience of cultural difference and the authenticity of the ethnic voice; the third, "lower-middle-class modernism," will be used to describe the large body of work—some would say it is the most characteristic product of the writing program—that most often takes the form of the minimalist short story, and is preoccupied more than anything else with economic and other forms of insecurity and cultural anomie. These more or less barbarous neologisms are obviously not native to the rhetoric of creative writing and postwar fiction which they seek to describe. They are rather the self-consciously "reductive" instruments of a scholar reviewing the situation from a point of critical remove and trying to organize it afresh, and would ideally be thought of not as separate baskets into which individual works can be placed but as principles around which they gravitate at a greater or lesser distance. This obviates the need to force hybrids and outliers into a false conformity, and dissuades us from turning classification into a parlor game. Theodor Adorno and Max Horkheimer once observed that "classification is a condition of knowledge, not knowledge itself, and knowledge in turn dissolves classification."[50] In that spirit we can take for granted that the whole truth of any given instance of art exceeds its membership in some category; but that insofar as the category might help to make that excess visible, it is all the more useful.

Technomodernism, high cultural pluralism, lower-middle-class modernism: I will describe the variable tendency to "involuted" self-reference in all of these aesthetic formations as "autopoetics." It may be true that the dominant aesthetic orientation of the writing program has been toward literary realism and away from the experimentalism we naturally associate with reflexivity.[51] This is mostly accurate as a description of the programs at schools like Iowa and Stanford, which emerged from the richly descriptive regionalist literary movements of the thirties, and have generally remained committed to some version of literary realism ever since. Still, one can find obvious exceptions to this rule even at these places—for example, Kurt Vonnegut at Iowa, Gilbert Sorrentino at Stanford—and it seems a fairly weak description of programs at schools like Johns Hopkins, Brown, and SUNY Buffalo, all of which have been and remain strongly supportive of experimental writing. T. Coraghessan Boyle recounts how, when he was studying with John Cheever at Iowa in the seventies, "I kept making noises about 'experimental writing' and hailing people like Coover, Pynchon, Barthelme, and John Barth, but Cheever would have none of it. He couldn't make any sense out of *The Sot Weed Factor* and didn't see that it was worth the effort of trying. Further, he insisted that his writing was experimental, too, but I didn't really get what he meant till he published his collected stories five years later. . . . All good fiction is experimental, he was telling me, and don't get caught up in fads."[52]

The struggle between a dominant "conventional realism" and a minority "radical experimentalism" is an ongoing one in the creative writing establishment, but it is a classically dialectical struggle in which opposing sides begin, despite themselves, to interpenetrate. For instance, as we shall see, bodies of realist fiction founded on the experience of racial difference always incorporate, if only as a structural principle, an "outside" observer of that difference. In these works a racial identity, no matter how realistically described, is a reflexive identity, and ethnic realism is a perforce a reflexive realism (as W. E. B. Du Bois could have predicted). So, too, the realism of a Cheever or Carver, while it entailed a rejection of the extreme formal experimentalism of Barth and Barthelme and Coover, and of the influence of important academic promoters of experimental writing like Robert Scholes and Jerome Klinkowitz, is nonetheless rife with reflexive consideration of writing as an occupational and existential condition. The autopoetic processes they exhibit speak to the fundamental non-naïveté of modern literary authorship, which as a product most broadly of reflexive modernity and, more specifically, of the school, cannot help seeing and knowingly announcing itself as authorship of one or another kind. This is literally true in creative writing Ph.D. programs—the latest advance over the M.F.A., opening up a wider range of academic jobs to program graduates—where students write a creative dissertation but typically supply it with a critical preface that, as the University of Denver policy states, "situates it in its literary context."[53] The idea is that, caught up in the systematization of writing in the university, most postwar writers exhibit this autopoetic self-referentiality and most of their work gravitates toward one or another or several of these formations—and that to the extent that they don't, that is interesting.

These terms will be set off in subsequent chapters against some of the indigenous rhetoric of creative writing itself, where the values conveniently designated by the terms "experience" and "craft" and "creativity" have been in more or less constant dialogue across the Program Era. One way to flesh out this dialogue is to look at the familiar set of prescriptive slogans in which they are complexly encoded: "write what you know"; "show don't tell"; "find your voice." To be sure, no self-respecting creative writing teacher of the present day would be caught dead using such hackneyed phrases (except perhaps the last) without heavy scare quotes, but I believe they accurately frame the implicit poetics of the program. This principled avoidance of clichés—"write what you know" goes back at least to the nineteenth century, "show don't tell" to the early twentieth, and "find your voice" to the neo-romantic 1960s—is no doubt admirable in many ways, but it is symptomatic of a general avoidance of systematic reflection on classroom protocols in the discipline of creative writing.[54] "What, after all, is the discipline of creative writing? If we taught it, what would we be teaching?" Shirley Geok-lin Lim asked this question in 2003, when the discipline was some fifty years old, and to a remarkable degree, no one in the field even tries to answer it.[55] The current head of the M.F.A. program at the University of Michigan, Eileen Pollack, could be speaking for thousands of program graduates when she recalls how her teachers at Iowa "commented on what they liked or did not like about a particular story, offered isolated bits of advice about technique, but most of us got through two years of instruction without any formal discussions of theory or craft, New Critical or otherwise."[56]

Partly this neglect has to do with the fact that, as we saw in Iowa's self-description above, many of those involved in the field of creative writing *agree* with their critics that it cannot be taught, though unlike them they believe that writing should be *occasioned* in the classroom nonetheless. Partly it has to do with the fact that historically, as with Nabokov, a teaching job for writers has been an add-on to what they *really* do, which is write. As the protagonist of Karl Shapiro's novel *Edsel* (1971) admits to his creative writing class on the first day of the semester: "'The hard thing to say is that as a teacher I am not a writer; as writer I am not a teacher. Writing is solitary, absolutely between you and your piece of paper. Not an act of self-expression but of self-love, an act of exclusion, so to speak . . . I am just putting myself on record, to introduce myself and let you in on this paradox . . . Why do universities let us writers in? Don't ask me,' I chuckled, 'but it's a fine thing for writers that they do.'"[57] In this way creative writers are somewhat like elite academic researchers in other disciplines, who are good teachers (when they are good teachers) almost by accident. For all the lip service paid to the nobility of teaching, an artist or a scholar (or better yet, "thinker") is a much more revered being than a teacher, and it is hard to fault the wish to be the one more than the other, if possible. The former represent the essence of professional autonomy and cultural authority, while the social position of the schoolteacher, like all feminized labor, tends toward low-paid subjugation to societal need.

The rationale for this disregard of teaching method in the institution of creative writing is, however, unique to itself: it is the notion that the relation between student and teacher in creative writing is one of *apprenticeship* rather than of teaching per se—the idea being that a master craftsman communicates her knowledge informally, in daily practice, not by means of a systematic presentation tied to a formal syllabus. One flaw in this notion is that, in fact, neither undergraduate nor graduate student writers typically sit alongside their teachers all day as they practice their craft, as the anachronistic term "apprenticeship" implies. Rather, they show up in the classroom or office hours at the appointed time, then leave. Moreover, the teacher's own writing is only rarely introduced into the workshop; class time instead is given over to the consideration of works of (more or less) contemporary fiction by name writers or, after students have had a few weeks of classes to generate their own work, writings by the apprentices themselves. As Kelly Ritter and Stephanie Vanderslice have noted, the name for the knowledge disbursed under these conditions is *lore*.[58]

The apparent informality of creative writing pedagogy—in fact it is as systematic in its way as any repetitive human activity—can usefully be contrasted with that other, more utilitarian, and generally non-elective form of writing instruction frequently attached to English departments, composition. Over the many years of its existence, this increasingly autonomous discipline has devoted a great deal of attention to what exactly the process of expository writing is and how it can best be taught; and, what's more, a considerable amount of time is spent teaching its student-teachers how to do this teaching. The pedagogical professionalism of composition puts that of creative writing (not to mention traditional literary studies) to shame, but that shame is on another level a point of pride. No one has ever proved that creative writers make the best creative writing teachers, but that sort of proof is evidently beside the point. What the literary artist is presenting to students in the classroom is a charismatic model of *creative being*. This means that, notwithstanding the ample amounts of testimony supplied here in the form "so-and-so taught me X," the task of tracing the "lessons" of creative writing from the classroom into the literary texts of the Program Era will be a somewhat indeterminate enterprise. Influence of course takes many forms, and the absorption of precepts or rules of literary composition is only one of these. Critics and champions of the writing program have always asked: can it be taught? The scholar of the program era is stuck with a different and equally difficult question: *has* it been taught?

To discover the narrative poetic system latent in the proudly "unsystematic" endeavor of creative writing instruction, and to determine the ways it has structured postwar American literary production, will therefore require some work, and is bound to be elliptical in its conclusions. But it is worth doing if only for the new tools it will give us to read postwar American fiction itself. This, I believe, is as rich and multifaceted a body of literary writing as has ever been, and whether this is so thanks to, or in spite of, the rise of the creative writing program, should be at no risk of seeming less so for our unliterary efforts to understand it.

TECHNOMODERNISM

It's hard to say when exactly the presence of writers on campus came to seem natural—assuming that it ever has. Certainly as late as the mid-1960s, by which time creative writing programs were beginning to multiply exponentially, the sense of strangeness hovering about this juxtaposition of scholars and writers had not yet diminished. This can be seen from the prefatory "Cover Letter to the Editors and Publisher" attached to the long, bizarre comic novel *Giles Goat-Boy* (1966), where John Barth notes that "like most writers these days, I support myself by preaching what I practice."[59]

This, he playfully explains, is how he came into possession of the original manuscript of the work we hold in our hands, brought to his office on campus one afternoon by a curly-bearded, smelly young man he wrongly assumed to be an undergraduate of the aspiring-writer type. Of course, what is more plausibly explained by this apparition "so like a certain old memory of myself," putting him "in mind of three dozen old stories wherein the hero meets his own reflection," is how there could have come to be a novel like this one, subtitled *The Revised New Syllabus,* the entirety of which takes place on a strangely altered modern university campus. On Barth's imaginary campus, divided into East and West, there is little difference between the University and the Universe as such; here all humanity is known as Studentdom, and all of Studentdom is studying for an ominous Final Exam. Indeed, the ingenuity and doggedness with which Barth finds allegorical analogues to world history and the cold war ("Quiet Riot") and reconfigures them as features internal to campus life is impressive. First educating John Barth as an undergraduate, then as a graduate student in creative writing at the John Hopkins Writing Seminars, and now employing him as a creative writing instructor in a "fiction-writing seminary," the university appears in this novel to have captured his imagination entirely.[60]

Much of the plot of *Giles Goat-Boy* revolves around the growing commitment of the smelly goat-boy—sired somehow by the all-powerful West Campus computer system, but raised among the animals at the Agriculture School—to his academic-messianic destiny as Grand Tutor. The crucial technological advance represented by this computer is the addition of an algorithmic Eros, an intuitive and passionate "humanity" that counters and radically complicates its old-hat capacity for calculation. Not only does this make the computer "creative," but it becomes subject as never before to a kind of bio-mechanical lust: indeed its enthusiasm for the act of reproduction, evident in its fervent practice of genetically engineering student bodies, meshes the acts of social and biological reproduction typically distributed to the institutions of the school and the family. This makes the computer called WESCAC seem a sort of condensation and literalization of the social technology of the progressive educational institution, whose pleasures are aimed at the erotic production and reproduction of the social system. At the same time, and somewhat presciently, WESCAC is represented as the materialized principle of what Barth calls the Campus's "informational" (as opposed to industrial) economy, its economy of signs. If, as Daniel Bell has argued, the university is the "axial institution" of postindustrial society, then the computer tape reels of WESCAC are the medium in which it spins.[61]

To prove his divinity, the goat-boy who is the human issue of this desiring machine must depart the pastoral innocence of the Ag School farm, travel with various hangers-on to Commencement Gate, vanquish a devilish pretender to his role, and answer the great riddle of Passage and

Failure. Something like a comic, novelistic version of "The Waste Land," the novel patches together conventional elements from a range of mythic, epic, and biblical-allegorical literary traditions but then, quite unlike Eliot's *noir*-ish, urban poem, projects them into the pastoral scene of American higher education. Hence, in a way, Barth is already working the themes of the novel when he refers in the "Cover Letter" to his teaching duties as "preaching." The link between professing and preaching, syllabus and Bible, makes sense in a novel that will ask the reader not only to think of the university as a universe, and vice versa, but also to see the modern, secular research university as re-imagined by the quasi-sacred literary tradition of which it is now the custodian.

One could also see the novel, somewhat differently, as a dramatized return of the repressed history of the American university. In the United States a fitful transition from religious to modern secular institutions began soon after the Civil War, as the older private colleges, traditionally associated with one or another Christian denomination, were divided into autonomous fields of scientific inquiry and reoriented toward systematic research and knowledge-production. Here, as in so many other institutions, the "modernity" of the university was achieved in its simultaneous outward expansion and internal differentiation. When the Morrill Acts of 1862 and 1890 made resources available for the founding of public universities, these "land grant" institutions were generally of a practical-industrial bent and followed the same disciplinary research model, continuing the drift away from curricular religion.

Even as this happened, however, the Sciences of the university were supplemented by a newly invigorated and expanded Arts (alternatively "Humanities" or "Letters") curriculum, centered on the study of literature, to which fell the responsibility in the new context of disciplinary specialization of "making knowledge cohere." Jon H. Roberts and James Turner have argued that this expansion of the Arts, whatever its intentions may have been, helped to smooth the passage to a modern university system by sublimating the traditional moral-religious emphases of antebellum liberal arts training in the secular values-discourse of humanistic aesthetics.[62] And in fact, while they may have begun as an institutional placeholder for the Unity of knowledge once represented by God, the Arts soon came under the sway of the pluralist regime of disciplinary specialization as well. Bastard progeny of religion and science, the Arts of the university have experienced periodic bouts of schizophrenia ever since.

John Barth began to write *Giles Goat-Boy* at Pennylvania State University, a land-grant institution where, as he later explained, "in an English department of nearly one hundred members" he taught his classes "not far from an experimental nuclear reactor, a water tunnel for testing the hull forms of missile submarines, laboratories for ice cream research and mushroom development, a lavishly produced football program . . . a barn-size computer with elaborate cooling systems . . . and the literal and splendid barns of the animal husbandry departments."[63] Massively infused with federal funding for the support of Cold War weapons technology and other scientific research, but still catering to a regional and state economy (and its large football fan base), the secular university has become, for Barth, comically expanded and diversified in its worldly pursuits, nothing like the pious gentleman's college of yore. In this Barth echoes what was no doubt the most influential and widely read account of higher educational institutions in the early sixties, Clark Kerr's *The Uses of the University* (1963), which proposed the neologism "multiversity" as a description of these institutions that are, as Kerr later reiterated, "pluralistic in several senses: in having several purposes, not one; in having several centers of power, not one; in serving several clienteles, not one." The multiversity, in short, "worship[s] no single God" and "constitute[s] no single, unified community."[64]

In *Giles Goat-Boy* this pluralistic multiverse is re-unified by literature, as the messianic goat-boy sets about synthesizing the fundamental dualities and differences of campus existence, descending into the bowels of the campus computer system and re-emerging with a mystical vision of Unity. Reading the disciplinary allegory he embodies, we could say that the role of the literary goat-boy is to speak for the higher Unities that the experimental sciences have left behind in their pursuit of knowledge of diverse things like submarines and ice cream. In hindsight, what is bound to seem most remarkable in this project is that in 1966, just in advance of the campus cultural nationalisms of the late sixties, this Unity can still be imagined as the synthesis in and of a transnational literary tradition such as was "made new" in high modernism.[65] That is, the Campus of this novel, divided by many things, is not yet overtly differentiated by race, ethnicity, class, or gender (or their bureaucratic expressions), and it is assumed that one literary tradition, one Grand Tutor, will do for the unification of all. As we shall see, the collapse of this assumption inaugurates the regime of high cultural pluralism.

At the same time, since the hero in *Giles Goat-Boy* is "all of us, writ large,"[66] one could argue that the novel represents literature as a mode of appreciation of individualistic agency in an otherwise highly organized, bureaucratic environment. In this it would echo the progressive educational rationale for introducing creative writing into the grade school curriculum earlier in the century. Here, in works like Hughes Mearns's influential *Creative Youth: How a School Environment Can Set Free the Creative Spirit* (1928), the newly dubbed activity of "creative writing" was promoted as an antidote to rote learning and the conformist genres associated with it: the translation, the theme, the report.[67] In this sense, as suggested earlier in the discussion of Nabokov, the heroism of the goat-boy could be understood as a figure of democratized Authorship itself, of the spiritual authority of even the lowliest man or woman to play God in the domain of his or her own imagination, if nowhere else.

And yet—and here one can begin to register the absurdity the novel attaches to the goat-boy's messianic activities—Barth's disciplinary allegory works in both directions. If it re-imagines the secular research university in terms of a spiritually elevated literary tradition, it also strongly associates the "preaching" and practice of literature in the university with the scientific research being conducted in the same institutional space. Clark Kerr had done the same when he began to rationalize the presence of creative writers and other artists on campus by linking them to scientists: "Another field ready to bloom is that of the creative arts, hitherto the

ugly ducklings or Cinderellas of the academic world. America is burst-
ing with creativity in painting, music, literature, the theater with a vigor
equaled in few other parts of the world today. . . . In the arts the universities have been more hospitable to the historian and the critic than to the
creator; he has found his havens elsewhere. *Yet it is the creativity of science that has given science its prestige in the university.* Perhaps creativity will
do the same again for the humanities . . . though the tests of value are far
less precise [than in the sciences]."[68] Updating the traditional term, Barth
echoes Kerr in associating creative writing in the university not with the
dusty workshop but with the modern Cold War laboratory.

Often labeled postmodernist, this literary enterprise would, I think,
be more usefully described as "technomodernist." This term reasserts the
obvious continuity of much postwar American fiction with the modernist
project of systematic experimentation with narrative form, even as it registers a growing acknowledgment of the scandalous continuity of the literary *techne* (craft) with technology in the grosser sense—including, most
importantly, media technology. Seen in the sickly light cast by the latter,
modernist narrative becomes visible not as the antithesis of debased genre
fiction, but as a genre in its own right called "literary fiction"—which rela-
tivization does not, it should be noted, disable the distinction between
high and low (one common account of what postmodernism entails) but
rather situates it in a larger cultural industrial system. Indeed, the high/
low distinction floats everywhere in this system, internally differentiating
"genre-fiction" genres and literary fiction alike along various scales, including those of greater or lesser consumability, originality, and self-
conscious attention to craft.

The potential for such an acknowledgment of kinship between high
literary *techne* and media technology was already latent in an earlier modernist fascination with technology explored by Kenner in *The Mechanic
Muse* (1987), and in the high literary appropriation of low media that one
sees in John Dos Passos's *U.S.A. Trilogy* (1930–1936). And while the term is
most easily applied to those writers like Barth, mostly white males, who
have gained prominence by featuring techno-mediatic themes—Thomas

Pynchon, Don DeLillo, Joseph McElroy, Richard Powers, et al.—works like Samuel Delany's *Dahlgren* (1975) and Karen Tei Yamashita's *Tropic of Orange* (1997), with their simultaneously ethnicized and media-saturated landscapes, and their ethnically marked authorship, suggest a broader reach. Just as modernism's relation to an antecedent romanticism (in some ways continuous, in some ways a break) has been a matter of some debate, so, too, is technomodernism shadowed by what can only be called technoromanticism; this will become clear in Chapter 4, when I discuss the simultaneous emergence of a fascination with the authentic ethnic voice and the tape recorder in sixties fiction. The most literal contemporary instantiation of technomodernism, meanwhile, is found in the emergent field of electronic literature, including foundational hypertext fictions like Michael Joyce's *afternoon, a story* (1987) and Shelley Jackson's *Patchwork Girl* (1995). Strongly associated with Brown University, where the proprietary software used to create hypertext fiction was developed, and with the pedagogy of Robert Coover, an English professor and writing instructor at the same institution, electronic literature remediates the values and practices of textual modernism (the fragmentation, difficulty, and general "literariness" still so abundant in Coover's own print productions), replaying the venerable modernism/mass culture dialectic in its status war with a non-literary commercial variant, the video game.

Electronic literature's literalization of "program fiction" is prefigured in one of the paranoiac conceits of the novel *Giles Goat-Boy:* formally divided not into parts but into magnetic computer tape "Reels," it may have been written by the all-powerful WESCAC itself. In that case it would seem, alas, that Unity and individual heroism are merely generated by the campus computer system as some of its narrative effects:

"GILES, SON OF WESCAC"
   Milk of studentdom; nipple inexhaustible! I was the Founder; I was WESCAC; I was not. I hung on those twin buttons. I fed myself myself.
   "DO YOU WISH TO PASS"

I the passer, she the passage, we passed together, and together cried "Oh, wonderful!" Yes and No. In the darkness,
blinding light! The end of the University! Commencement
Day![69]

Here it appears that Graduation from the all-engulfing University can only
be imagined as self-annihilating sublimity, figured here as the unification
of the ultimate division in humankind, the division of sex.[70] Like the high/
low binary to which it is often attached, but even more pervasive and various in its uses, the male/female binary floats throughout the system of
higher education, the creative writing program, and postwar fiction alike:
one can point to the division between the (hard) sciences and the (soft)
humanities, or to the division between the low-status "schoolmarm" and
the high-status "professor," or, perhaps most interestingly, to the distinction between feminized "caring" institutions (e.g., the hospital) and mas-
culinized "disciplinary" ones (e.g., the army). The school is neither a "feminine" nor a "masculine" institution per se but is rather the scene of
countless micro-struggles between "maternal" love and punitive "paternal" judgment as two different forms of institutional authority. This reflects at long distance the advent of large-scale coeducation in the postwar
period, and the related entry of (some) women into the professional-
managerial stratum of the corporate workforce.

The merging of the "feminine" and the "masculine" technological
institution as a threat to male autonomy is easiest to see in the persona of
the steel-breasted phallic mother of Ken Kesey's *One Flew Over the Cuckoo's
Nest* (1962), Nurse Ratched, who is an agent of what the novel calls the
Combine. It is more subtly implicated in Richard Powers's *Galatea 2.2*, in
which a novelist named Richard Powers becomes involved in an effort to
create an artificial intelligence whose answers on an M.A. exam in English
Literature can be passed off as the work of a female human graduate student. As this undertaking becomes intertwined with the narrator's recol-
lections of a failed relationship with a woman who had been his student,
the gendered making (man makes woman) referenced in the novel's title is

set alongside, but ultimately against, a more threatening idea of biological reproduction and mothering (woman makes man). In Neal Stephenson's engrossing science fiction work *The Diamond Age; or, a Young Lady's Illustrated Primer* (1995), the ultimate in intelligent, interactive textbooks is designed by a man, a nanotechnological engineer, but it is "staffed" from afar by an empathic woman, a thespian who becomes a virtual mother to the neo-Dickensian gamin into whose hands the textbook falls.[71] The best-case scenario of the merging of different forms of reproduction, however, was imagined in the M.F.A. program at Brown, where Shelley Jackson's feminist hypertext fiction *Patchwork Girl* was conceived and executed for credit toward a master's degree.

A compendium of various linked elements including diagrams, samplings of feminist theory, and the instruction manual for the hypertext compiler, Storyspace, with which it was made, this work is most importantly a rewriting of Mary Shelley's *Frankenstein* that draws the novel's allegorical meditation on the complexities and contradictions of female authorship to the surface. For Katherine Hayles, Jackson's hypertext is most interesting for the way it attacks traditionally "male" notions of literary originality, privacy, and copyright, confessing everywhere that it is a patchwork of previous works and attesting to the socially occupied nature of the individual who scripted them. Not only this, but in drawing attention to the technology with which it is executed, the work refuses the virtual transparency of the medium of print, which after centuries of use has become too familiar even to be noticed. For Hayles, the novelty and reflexivity of Jackson's hypertext enacts a critique of the exaltation of the mind over the lowliness of a corporeality aligned, in the cultural imaginary, with the maternal body of the woman: "In *Patchwork Girl,* the unconscious of eighteenth-century texts becomes the ground and surface for the specificity of this electronic text, which delights in pointing out that it was created not by a fetishized unique imagination but by many actors working in collaboration, including the 'vaporous machinery' that no longer disappears behind a vaporous text."[72]

Another way to read this text, however, is as a testament to the possibilities of systematic creativity—creativity authorized and sponsored by erotically technologized institutions like Brown. And here it is the creative writing program, the institution, the social technology, that too easily plays the part of "vaporous machinery," receding from our view even as we become interested in the properties of print and pixels. It is the university that provides the technology for hypertext, and it is the university that doles out the cultural capital and technical expertise that Jackson puts on display, never more so than when she mashes feminist *theory* into her creative work. While it only rarely leads to genuine acts of collaboration—literary authorship remaining, unlike scientific authorship, an overwhelmingly individualistic enterprise—the conviviality of the workshop and the direct involvement of others in the writing process are no less a threat, for some, to the "fetishized unique imagination" of the mythical heroic male artist on the craggy mountaintop than the materiality of the text.

In one of *Patchwork Girl*'s most readable clusters, the various body parts that have gone into the making of Mary Shelley's / Shelley Jackson's female monster "speak for themselves," suggesting rather vividly how a corporate body might retain, and not cancel, the individualities it subsumes. "I don't want to lose the self," writes Jackson in an essay on her work, "only strip it of its claim to naturalness, its compulsion to protect its boundaries." She "would like to invent a new kind of self which doesn't fetishize so much, grounding itself in the dearly-loved signs and stuff of personhood, but has poise and a sense of humor, changes directions easily, sheds parts and assimilates new ones."[73] This is the self as "team player," and for all of Jackson's commitments to the avant-garde, it is not hard to see it as the model of an unresisting employee, the office worker willing and able to learn the new software.

AUTOPOETICS

Giles Goat-Boy is only one of the odder of innumerable examples of a conspicuously flourishing genre in the postwar period, the campus novel.

Typically written as satire, this genre usually registers not the metaphysics but, more humbly, the ironies of institutionalization. Unlike works from earlier in the century, like Owen Johnson's best-selling football romp, *Stover at Yale* (1911), or throwbacks to that earlier era like Tom Wolfe's *I Am Charlotte Simmons* (2004), the postwar campus novel is most often written from the perspective of the faculty, taking as its focus one or another ludicrous dimension of departmental life, and almost always portraying literary scholars as the petty, cynical idiots we are. At its best, the genre of the campus novel capitalizes on the resemblances between a college campus and a small village, deploying its relative social coherence and richly articulated social-professional hierarchies in a revivification of the gossipy comedy of manners.[74] "Furness adored, as he frankly confessed, reversals and sudden shifts of fashion—the life of a small college charmed him as a microcosm of high society": Mary McCarthy's send-up of a progressive college in *The Groves of Academe* (1951) is one of the better known of these, and the sentiments of her character indicate how the genre's typical smallness of concern might open it to the charge of triviality and banality.[75] This is why one finds defensive blurbs like the one on the dust jacket of Saul Bellow's *The Dean's December* (1982), which assures its readers that this "extraordinarily vivid book" is "anything but a campus novel," as though these two things are fundamentally at odds.[76] In this sense, since virtually every novel would be a "vivid" one, the implicit subject (or project) of every campus novel is the existential triumph, by satirical objectification— this may be true even of *Giles Goat-Boy*—of the writer over the institution that would institutionalize him.

The proliferation of universities as settings for novels is, in other words, what we might call a thematic symptom of a larger shift in the institutional arrangements of postwar literary production as such. The question is whether and to what degree all novels aspiring to the honorific status of literature must be considered campus novels of a sort. Beyond the question of a novel's setting, for instance, how might we see the metafictional reflexivity of so much postwar fiction as being related to its production in and around a programmatically analytical and pedagogical environment? That, certainly, was Wolfe's implication in "Stalking the Billion-Footed Beast." Pursuing this line of inquiry, but setting aside Wolfe's negative evaluation of the phenomenon, we could read the reflexive prose experiments of academic creative writers such as Nabokov and Barth and Shelley Jackson not as radically "deconstructive," as they sometimes are, but as radically conventional, as testaments to the continuing interest of literary forms as objects of a certain kind of professional research.

At least one contemporary strand of theoretical endeavor, systems theory, would insist that we understand reflexivity not as an invitation to the abyss, but as a necessary component of any system's self-constitution, its "autopoiesis."[77] Self-reference in this view is perfectly routine, not impeding but participating in the making and organizing of things, including literature, whose reflexive construction of autonomous fictional realities serves, according to Niklas Luhmann, to make visible "the inevitability of order as such."[78] While reflexivity, as systems theory sees it, is the general condition of reflexive modernity—this is why Mark Seltzer can produce such a powerful diagnosis of what he calls the pathological public sphere from a reading of the lowly true-crime genre—an aura of intellectual sophistication still attaches to overtly reflexive (that is, reflexively reflexive) projects like Nabokov's and Barth's and Jackson's, inviting critics to take them seriously as participating in the modernist/postmodernist high literary tradition.[79] Holding up a flattering mirror to the critic's own sophistication, these invitations are of course often accepted, but at the risk of a tiresome redundancy (who needs criticism when literature adopts a critical relation to itself?).

What this means is that, in the modernist tradition, the portrait of the artist is not only an important single book and an important genre, but also a name for one of the routine operations of literary modernism. For the modernist artist, that is, the reflexive production of the "modernist artist"—i.e., job description itself—is a large part of the job. Flouting the strictures against personality proposed by T. S. Eliot in "Tradition and the Individual Talent," works like Joyce's *Portrait of the Artist as a Young Man*, or Thomas Wolfe's *Look Homeward, Angel,* or—looking ahead to a pro-fusion of postwar examples—Maxine Hong Kingston's *The Woman Warrior* stage the autobiographical drama of heroic self-authorization that accounts for their own existence. Taking the suggestion of Barth's notionally computer-generated heroism in *Giles Goat-Boy,* we might understand these acts of authorial self-making not—or not merely—as the feats of radical individuation they often represent themselves to be, nor as evidence of a final dispersal of subjectivity in and across social institutions and the mediasphere, but as moments in the operation, the autopoiesis, of a larger cultural system geared for the production of self-expressive originality. The name for this overall project is "technoromanticism," and taking advantage of a common Greek root in autopoiesis (self-making) and poetics, and forcing an obvious but helpful pun, we can call the routinely reflexive operations it calls for "autopoetics."[80]

The campus novel and the portrait of the artist are, then, two of the signature genres of the Program Era, each of them allegorizing, in complementary ways, the autopoetic agendas they also enact. But they are after all only thematic symptoms, and do not exhaust the characteristic genres of postwar writing, which also include the workshop story collection, the ethnic family saga, meta-genre fiction, and various forms of prison narrative, including a form I will call the meta-slave narrative. A more complex mode of reflexivity than the thematic representation of authorship is enacted at the level of narrative form in the dynamics of what is popularly known as "point of view." The systematic concern for what critics, after Gerard Genette, now tend to call "focalization" made its first appearance on the American scene in Percy Lubbock's *The Craft of Fiction* (1921), which was essentially an expansion and codification of the narrative theory developed piecemeal across Henry James's prefaces to the New York Edition of his novels. Its most basic lesson—that the technical question of narrative perspective has profound aesthetic consequences for the work—is one that would reverberate throughout the rest of the twentieth century and beyond.

Indeed, whether in the form of "stream of consciousness" narration in Joyce or Faulkner, or "unreliability" in Nabokov, experiments with point of view would become one of the earmarks of modernism. If, as Franco Moretti has argued, the quintessential narrative form of nineteenth-century realism was free indirect discourse, which systematically coordinated the perspective of the individual character with that of his community, the modernist tradition markedly disintegrates this relation into its component parts.[81] In the twentieth century, point of view would become both an object and a vehicle of cultural politics, a matter of explicit debate: is it wrong for a white writer to write a first person narrative from a black point of view? Will the student who makes her way through all of the many selections in a short story anthology (another key genre of the Program Era) called *Points of View* (1959/1995) be a better person, as well as a better reader, for having exercised her sympathetic imagination so many times?[82] Debates about these sorts of questions typically encode two competing conceptions of the narrative point of view. The first would ground it in personal experience, and sees the point of view as a virtual claim to intellectual property in a certain domain of experience; the second sees the inherent mobility built into the artifice of point of view as a lever with which one is pried loose from the determinations of identity and allowed to see the world differently. The chapters that follow will give plenty of airtime to these and related questions. Here I want simply to step back and notice how, beyond the question of one's mobility (or not) between narrative positions, the dynamics of narrative focalization project a simplified model of the modern pluralistic society as an assemblage of different and sometimes conflicting, but always aesthetically redeemable, points of view.

The ways and means of interwar literary modernism have been modified in the postwar period, where they have been codified in the pedagogy of New Criticism and then disseminated to a range of student populations previously underrepresented in the writing profession. Among other effects, the institutionalization of modernism has conspicuously strengthened and broadened its social functionality by coupling it with the educational system. Once the product of urban coteries, circulating in the tiny sphere of little magazines, now the texts of the modernist tradition reside helpfully on the syllabus as objects of study; its canon of literary practices, including a demand for self-conscious attention to technique, is pursued across the land in classes in creative writing; and its latter-day practitioners attend faculty meetings. For a small percentage of these practitioners—Kingston, Toni Morrison, Sandra Cisneros, Tim O'Brien, and others—this coupling has created a significant student market for their wares. The rest exhibit the same more or less vexed relation to the publishing market as their modernist forebears did, selling relatively modest numbers of books, not intentionally, exactly, but by design. Meanwhile the autopoetic thematization of authorship in the various projects of postwar literary fiction has continued unabated.

Consider the case of Philip Roth, who between 1959 and the present, even as he has frequently associated himself with colleges and universities (including, briefly, the Iowa Writers' Workshop) as an adjunct faculty member, has published some thirty novels and other books. In that period he has developed what it seems fair to call a singular authorial persona, where an unmistakably forceful and mostly invariant writing style—a "foaming confluence," as he puts it in *The Anatomy Lesson* (1983), of "diatribe, alibi, anecdote, confession, expostulation, promotion, pedagogy, philosophy, assault, apologia, denunciation"—is matched with an obsessive attachment to a small constellation of patently autobiographical themes: masculinity, sexuality, family, Jewishness, and authorship itself.[83]

Even beyond the explicitly interrelated Zuckerman novels, the internal coherence and serial continuity of this autopoetic enterprise over so many years and so many novels are astonishing, and Ross Posnock is wholly justified in interpreting Roth's oeuvre as "one vast text with each book to be read within and against the larger whole."[84] Roth can seem by turns endlessly inventive in finding new ways to manipulate its few terms, and to be without any imagination at all, a nasty narcissist lost in a highly polished hall of mirrors. The hall of mirrors effect is most forcefully introduced into the system by the Zuckerman novels, which provide a kind of running commentary on the life and career of a Jewish American novelist named Nathan Zuckerman, who, we are given to understand, has written his own versions of Roth's non-Zuckerman books, including most importantly the controversial National Book Award-winner, *Goodbye, Columbus* (1959; Zuckerman's *Higher Education*) and the hugely best-selling *Portnoy's Complaint* (1969; renamed *Carnovsky*).[85]

With Zuckerman, Roth is able to record and redeploy as fiction the response of readers to his best-known works, incorporating into his own serially-renewed discourse the voices of the rabbis who have found his representations of Jews unflattering, the feminists who find his work misogynist, the literary critics who find his work crude and repetitive, and the mass audience that, with the publication of *Portnoy's Complaint,* began to find him fascinating, a celebrity. It's impossible to say, encountering this process, whether it suggests the radical openness of Roth's fiction, constantly overtaken by its own discursive outside, or its radical closure, an imperial absorption of that outside. Beginning with *Zuckerman Unbound*'s crazed Zuckerman fan Alvin Pepler, the cybernetic circularity that produces this ambiguity is exemplified in the appearance in the novels of a certain kind of character. Approaching Zuckerman in public places, these accosting strangers assume an immediate familiarity with the famous novelist who they assume (not any more unreasonably than we do when we think of Zuckerman as some form of Roth) has been speaking for and as himself in his fictions. But if these characters therefore seem, on one level, to personify popular (pepler) "reader response," they don't only do that. Routed back through the narrator, this response becomes intertwined with Roth's own voice such that the character projected into the fictional world seems a curious amalgam of other and same—that is, a double. Their manic verbal energy—Pepler speaks uninterruptedly for pages on end—and their childhood connections to Jewish Newark are always strongly reminiscent of Roth's own well-known versions of the same thing.[86]

Reflexively enough, this "critical" understanding of the accoster-as-double, as well as the possible seed of the very novel we are reading, is already provided in the pages of *Zuckerman Unbound* itself when we are shown the journal notes that Zuckerman is scribbling even as he is trying to slip away from Pepler by stepping into a crowded funeral home: "But: the bullying ego, the personal audacity, the natural coarseness, the taste for exhausting encounters—what gifts! Mix with talent the unstoppable energy, the flypaper brain . . . [the] brute strength, the crazy tenacity [and you get] The Jew You Can't Permit in the Parlor. How Johnny Carson America now thinks of me. This Peplerian barrage is what? Zeitgeist over-spill? Newark poltergeist? Tribal retribution? Secret sharer? P. as my pop self? . . . Book: *The Vrai's Revenge*—the forms their fascination takes, the counterspell cast over me."[87] The very oddness of this journal-keeping activity, attended to when Zuckerman is literally on the run, makes an important point. Henry James's famous injunction to aspiring writers to be "one of those on whom nothing is lost!"—embodied in James's own life-long practice of note-taking—is shown here to be at one and the same time a handmaid to literary realism and to a vertiginously "postmodern" reflexivity: encouraged to "write what you know," the novelist eventually is driven to represent his intimate knowledge of the writing process and its consequences, to address the fact of fiction making.

This lends another level of irony to a moment in *The Anatomy Lesson* when Zuckerman learns that the student editors of the University of Chicago newspaper want to "interview him about the future of his kind of fiction in the post-modernist era of John Barth and Thomas Pynchon" (280). Sent to him in writing, one of their questions reads, *"Do you feel yourself part of a rearguard action, in the service of a declining tradition?"* (281). "Yes," mumbles Zuckerman to himself in response, but his sense of the "declining tradition" is not necessarily the same as theirs. Rather, the systematic reflexivity that produces both the "realist" Zuckerman novels and Barth's technomodernist *Giles Goat-Boy* has devolved here into a kind of sickness of circular self-consumption: "My life as cud, that's what I'm running out on. Swallow as experience, then up from the gut for a second go as art" (196)—and then down again, we might add, as the biographical consequences of that art. Zuckerman has dreamed of curing himself of his illness by quitting writing altogether and going back to school. This time, however, it will not be English literature that he will study, but medicine. This is not quite the novelistic journalism called for by Wolfe, but its effects would be similar. Attaining scientific knowledge of other bodies will, Zuckerman hopes, give him access to "the real thing, the thing *in the raw,* and not for the writing but for itself" (204). Ultimately, though, he cannot escape his fascination with the body most closely at hand, his own, and so in more senses than one he cannot "escape the corpus that was his" (291).

The first point to mention here is that the pervasive reflexivity of Roth's many novels, however dizzying the spirals it makes, however spiritually sickening it may have become, has been anything but disabling of his writing, but is rather the motive principle of its serial continuance. The constantly troubled interplay between "fiction" and "autobiography," creativity and experience, in Roth's corpus is what in systems theory is called the cut—the primary distinction—that initiates its very existence. At the same time, the making of this distinction implicitly posits a third position, a point of remove from which the initial distinction is made, from which its operations will be observed, and in which its terms do not necessarily apply. Observing this third space from yet another point of remove (call it the literary-historical perspective), Roth's fictions can be seen for what they obviously, in one respect, are: real. They are real not because they are "true" but because they are the real products of a writer situated at specific positions in an evolving literary field.

The second point, then, is simply that however claustrophobically self-enclosed Roth's autopoetic enterprise might seem—such that even a historical novel like *I Married a Communist* (1998) is legible as a blow-by-blow allegorical account of Roth's tumultuous relationship with the actress Claire Bloom[88]—it is in fact a series of events that take place in a larger system that constantly produces reflexivity of various kinds and degrees and is ultimately a trans-individual enterprise. Indeed, the unmistakable singularity of Roth's voice and persona and the continuity of their presence on the scene of American literary fiction for the last forty years can make his career seem, paradoxically, among the most contextually determined the system has produced. This is why his project is subject to being skewed in the direction of hyper-experimentalism, as in Ronald Sukenick's *Up* (1968), or replicated, as in Joyce Carol Oates's "Roth novel" *The Tattooed Girl* (2003).[89] Those accosting doubles in Roth's fiction are not, or not only, evidence of the solipsism of his diegesis; they also record the discovery of the systemic contextual-environmental other *in* himself, and are evidence that he is part and product of his own externality. Call it the Roth ecology.[90]

This conspicuously "networked" feature of his individualistic auto-poetics is recorded in other, simpler ways as well—for instance, in the prideful Jamesian literary professionalism that Roth began to assume in college and graduate school. From his earliest short stories, Roth has been intent to show the high stakes, high drama, and high difficulty of group membership. Excepting the "community of writers," familial, ethnic, religious, and especially heterosexual romantic ties are placed under awful pressure in his work. But Roth makes a comparatively effortless identification with, first, the modernist masters (James, Kafka, et al.) whom he learned to appreciate in school, then the Eastern European writers (such as Milan Kundera) whose wide exposure to English-speaking audiences owed a lot to his editorial efforts, and finally the warm friendships among writers, mostly male, that make their way (as in *The Ghostwriter* [1979]) into his fictions. This identification produces volumes such as the well-nigh Portnoyan orgy of professionalism, *Shop Talk: A Writer and His Colleagues and Their Work* (2001).

Yes, for all the self-involvement and "individuality" of his fiction, Roth is very much a man of the system. He cares for literature, teaches it to students, worries about its fate, and is frankly snobbish about the cultural encroachments of television (which he only rarely deigns to appear on) in a way that younger academic writers might find anachronistically touching. In a 1996 interview Roth spoke of a "drastic decline, even a disappearance, of a serious readership" in the United States that is "inescapable, given the pressures in the society," and is "a tragedy."[91] The plot of *The Human Stain* (2000), a campus novel that could be said to be all about various forms of illiteracy, is founded on the irony that even elite liberal arts colleges now endorse poor reading skills, as the scholar-protagonist (a Newark-raised African American passing as a Jew) is held responsible for his students' misunderstanding of the word "spook."

HIGH CULTURAL PLURALISM

Another way to get at the impressive typicality of the figure of Philip Roth would be to note how, seen against the forty-year backdrop of the field he has inhabited, he can seem to figure either as a culturally conservative white male writer, staunchly upholding high modernist literary values, or, as was more plainly the case in the 1960s, as a conspicuously "ethnic" writer ("The Jew You Can't Permit in the Parlor") who introduces cultural difference into that system. Braiding these roles together, he could be said to hold in suspension the elements of the form of postwar literary fiction that I will call high cultural pluralism, which combines the routine operation of modernist autopoetics with a rhetorical performance of cultural group membership preeminently, though by no means exclusively, marked as ethnic. Paired with and against the complementary aesthetic of technomodernism, and (as we shall see) supplemented by the inverse aesthetic of lower-middle-class modernism, high cultural pluralism has governed the production of a very wide swath of postwar American fiction.

"Cultural pluralism" is of course a term historically associated with figures like Randolph Bourne, Alain Locke, and especially Horace Kallen, the American pragmatist philosopher and Zionist who began in the early twentieth century to transpose the philosophical pluralism of his teacher at Harvard, William James, into the domain of cultural identity. I prefer it to the more recent and essentially synonymous "multiculturalism" for the way it helps to return us to first principles unburdened by accretions from the so-called "culture wars" of the 1980s and 90s, in which the mass media took a brief interest in the "scandal" of differentiation, making hay with what was in fact the orderly appearance of new subfields in the humanities, new writers on the syllabus, and so forth. This will allow us to link it more soberly than we otherwise might to the institutional context of its emergence, and facilitate our seeing how its dominant association with race and ethnicity does not begin to exhaust its meaning. Decades later, but with no mention of race or ethnicity, Clark Kerr would also trace the intellectual origins of his conception of the multiversity back to James's philosophical pluralism, presenting it not as an ethos but as a matter of fact: in the modern world everything, including universities, grows more complex. No wonder, then, that cultural pluralism and the multiversity have coupled so nicely. Both are driven by the logic of expansion and differentiation, and the continual birth of new scientific subdisciplines is echoed, on the other side of campus, in the emergence of Ethnic and Women's and Cultural Studies, and, within English departments, in the demarcated study of alternative literary canons.

High cultural pluralism enacts a layering of positively marked differences: in the modernist tradition, it understands its self-consciously crafted and/or intellectually substantial products as importantly distinct from mass culture or genre fiction, although in practice—for example, when Joyce Carol Oates flirts with low genres, or when Roth produces a best-seller on the titanic scale of *Portnoy's Complaint,* or when Toni Morrison's *Beloved* (1987) or Cormac McCarthy's *The Road* (2006) is read by Oprah's Book Club—this distinction is often blurred or intentionally put at risk.[92] The high cultural pluralist writer is additionally called upon to speak from the point of view of one or another hyphenated population, synthesizing the particularity of the ethnic—or analogously marked—voice with the elevated idiom of literary modernism.[93] Thus, while one path to literary distinction in the postwar period has been to assert the themes of techno-modernism, another, though sometimes overlapping, path has been to forge a career in literary cultural pluralism, from the Jewish American writers who emerged in force in the early postwar period, such as Saul Bellow and Roth; to the Native American renaissance that began with N. Scott Momaday's *House Made of Dawn* (1968) and continues through the novels of Leslie Marmon Silko, Louise Erdrich, and many others; to the appearance of a growing number of celebrated Asian American writers from Kingston to Chang-Rae Lee; to the distinctly theory-inflected field of Chicana/o literature most prominently represented by Sandra Cisneros and Ana Castillo; to—and all along—the African American experience as it has been represented by writers working in the modernist tradition, from Ralph Ellison to Ishmael Reed to Morrison. All of these writers are widely taught, and all were or remain significantly connected to universities.

Describing his own initiation into the modernist tradition at a largely Protestant liberal arts college in the early 1950s, Roth notes how at first it "did not dawn on" him that the "anecdotes and observations" of his boyhood in lower-middle-class Newark with which he entertained his highbrow friends "might be made into literature." Instead, the "stories I wrote, set absolutely nowhere, were mournful little things about sensitive children, sensitive adolescents, and sensitive young men crushed by the coarse life. . . . The Jew was nowhere to be seen; there were no Jews in the stories, no Newark, and not a sign of comedy."[94] This would soon change. Like so many other writers of the postwar period, Roth would learn to join the modernist literary sophistication of his higher educational training with the ethnic experiential specificity of his upbringing—the late modernist version of writing what you know.

Occurring in the broader context of the rise of mass higher education in the U.S., high cultural pluralism is the product of a certain institutional history, the most important feature of which has been the partially overlapping institutionalizations of elitist high modernism and cultural pluralism in university English departments of the postwar period. The result could be described either as a partially democratized modernism, which would emphasize the conditioning effect of a liberal-progressive (at least as compared to other American institutions) institutional context on an elitist aesthetic discourse, or, because universities are still a long way from offering unrestricted social access to the masses, as an elitist pluralism in which the lucky ones, among their other privileges, are taught to savor their own open-mindedness. Declining to choose between these two understandings, for now I will simply observe that, associating the *individ-*

ual writer with a *group* from which she draws a claim to personal literary distinction, high cultural pluralism becomes one model, in the university environment, for the productive mediation of "group-think" and "individual genius."

While the privileged marker of difference here is a racial or ethnic one, it would be a serious mistake to think that writers with no strong ethnic associations have been shut out of the high cultural pluralist enterprise; they are merely (and ironically) minoritized to a small degree, even as the category of "difference" easily includes them and motivates the interest of publishers and readers in their work. Most writers of literary fiction have "their subject," which is to say, a signature set of preoccupations stemming (typically) from one or another aspect of their biography. Not that all identities are equally claimable; an identification with female experience alone, to take the most important example, will not typically succeed in finding a place for a given writer in the high cultural pluralist system, and this is perhaps because, as detailed by Sandra Gilbert and Susan Gubar, "woman writer" was precisely the category against which modernist authorship had originally defined itself.[95] Without the affective intensities of race and ethnicity, or the prestige associated with aggressive experimentalism as we see it in *Patchwork Girl*, women's writing is a majority, not a minority, phenomenon and is apt to be perceived in terms of the middlebrow sentimentality of "daytime" culture. Categories that more obviously split the national culture into smaller units are an easier sell for high cultural prestige leading to inclusion in the syllabus of postwar literature.

Indeed, as has been suggested by Werner Sollors, it may be that the original version of cultural pluralism was regionalism.[96] And though it is a typically less fraught form of identity in the postwar period than an ethnic or racial one, a regional identity still enables a form of alignment by analogy with the dominant form of the aesthetic appreciation of difference. Regionalist fiction has always been cultural pluralist in the sense that it is a form of appreciation of diversity within a larger national whole, and as we shall see, regionalism was crucial to the emergence of the Iowa Writers'

Workshop. Certainly the most important form of literary regionalism in the twentieth century has been the Southern variant; a white Southerner like Flannery O'Connor, for instance, returning from the workshop in Iowa to her home in Milledgeville, Georgia, associates her fiction with a cultural entity understood to be significantly different from American culture as such. In doing so, she achieves the logical equivalent of an ethnic difference within the system. In one of her essays, echoing Roth's assessment of his own earliest collegiate fiction, she notes disapprovingly how she "read some stories at one of the colleges not long ago . . . [and] with the exception of one story, they might all have originated in some synthetic place that could have been anywhere or nowhere."[97] In another essay she establishes the importance of Southern cultural difference for her fiction in strong, if negative, terms, noting how Southern writers "are all known to be anguished. [And some editorialists] suggest that our anguish is a result of our isolation from the rest of the country. I feel that this would be news to most Southern writers. The anguish that most of us [feel] has not been caused not by the fact that the South is alienated from the rest of the country, but by the fact that it is not alienated enough, that every day we are getting more and more like the rest of the country, that we are being forced out, not only of our many sins but of our few virtues."[98] Written during the civil rights era, when the South was beginning to be pressed into conformity with federal law, O'Connor's anguished appeal to and for the maintenance of difference would reinstall Southern culture as one of the terms in the developing cultural pluralist aesthetic program of the 1960s, promoting Southern writing as, in effect, a white minority discourse that resists assimilation into the American mainstream.[99]

Equally important to the emergence of the writing program, although somewhat harder to conceive as a minority "culture," is the difference made by a personal experience of war. Sitting in the Quonset huts erected in Iowa City where her classes were held, Flannery O'Connor was on hand to observe the literary after-effects of war at close range. When the first graduate writing programs were being assembled in the 1940s, the first several cohorts of students were made up of recently returned veterans studying on the G.I. Bill. For these men, Hemingway's conversion of war trauma into graceful literary understatement would prove a powerful example, even as his avoidance of the university was being reversed. The process they underwent on campus was one of "softening," a subtle transition from the silent suffering of trauma into the controlled pathos of literary recollection. In a 1996 article on the mysteries of creative writing instruction, Elizabeth Tallent asks us to imagine the situation of one of her predecessors as head of Stanford's creative writing program, its founder Wallace Stegner: "Imagine a classroom crowded with clean-shaven young soldiers newly returned from a war. Imagine these young men unable to slouch or sprawl . . . but sitting in straight, starchily attentive ranks because military discipline has owned them for so long, and is reluctant to let go. Moreover, they don't know who they will be when it does let go. Imagine reading their eyes for proof of damage. . . . You know they have *seen things* . . . each young man has *stories to tell* as surely as he has a heartbeat. . . . You look away, out the window, you have to confront another new fact of your life: California. You've come to Stanford fresh from Harvard. In a profound sense, you're not sure what you've done. This is the fall of 1945."[100]

Like his fellow Iowa graduate O'Connor, Stegner's own claim to cultural difference in the literary field would be regional: having grown up on the Great Northern Plains, he would circle back to that experiential datum to become the dean of a conservation-minded Western literary regionalism that would include writers such as Larry McMurtry and Edward Abbey, both of whom were his students. What Stegner witnessed in his first classes at Stanford was something else: the emergence of a virtual cultural identity emanating from an authoritative experience of war. It is thus that we can speak of Tim O'Brien, author of *Going after Cacciato* (1978), *The Things They Carried* (1990), and several other Vietnam-themed works, as a *Veteran-American* writer, in the sense that the psychic wounds inflicted on him in his year of combat have become foundational to a career in the same way that Roth's Jewishness has. The "Things" carried by the soldiers in the title story of O'Brien's 1990 collection are what we might also call "burdens," and they are both quite literal (C rations, ammo, socks) and spiritual. But as the self-reflexive story "Spin" makes clear, their weight is also the weightiness of a certain quantity of experiential capital. Making our terminology of the "autopoetic process" seem especially apt, the writer-narrator notes that "You take your material where you find it, which is in your life, at the intersection of past and present. The memory-traffic feeds into a rotary up in your head, where it goes in circles for a while, then pretty soon imagination flows in and the traffic merges and shoots off down a thousand different streets."[101]

At the very limits of the high cultural pluralist enterprise, where the space it inhabits begins to curve, one encounters technomodernism, its unmarked dialectical reversal. Whereas high cultural pluralism represses the technologies that contribute to its performance of authenticity, technomodernism identifies with the "emptiness" of pure formality—that is, with the systematicity of the system itself, drawing the machine to itself in a form of ontological prosthesis. One sometimes hears of a postwar literary field divided cleanly into postmodernist and ethnic realist traditions. Apart from the descriptive weakness of this notion—as though there could be either a more "postmodernist" or a more "black" writer than Ishmael Reed—this way of conceiving things misses the profound complementarity of high cultural pluralism and technomodernism, each of which contains, in latent form, the other's primary term.[102] If we apply interpretive pressure to overtly pluralist fiction to make visible the machinery involved in its production of difference, with overtly machinic technomodernism we can apply it in the opposite direction. Doing so, we see how even the "whitest" technomodernism can function as a discourse of difference, producing a symbolic placeholder for a paradoxically non-ethnic ethnicity that might as well be called (with apologies to John Guillory) "technicity."[103] Put baldly, what Roth knows about the Jewish experience, and Morrison knows about the African American experience, writers like Powers, DeLillo, and Pynchon know about the second law of thermodynamics, cybernetic causality, communications and media theory, and the like, and it is on the basis of this portfolio of technical-cultural capital that they, too, are put on the syllabus.

That technicity, no less than ethnicity, might be imagined to be prosthetically lodged in the body is suggested by Pynchon's *Gravity's Rainbow* (1973), where it is the distinction of the character Tyrone Slothrop, who imagines inscribing his name on a missile, to become sexually aroused at the sites of future rocket blasts. In Don DeLillo's campus novel, *White Noise* (1985), as suggested by recent readings emphasizing the double signification of the titular term "white," the ethnic specificity of the techno-saturated Midwestern family of Professor Jack Gladney is secured by the presence of the "outsider," Murray Siskind, a visiting professor from New York City: asked what "type" of person he represents among the others at his boarding house in town, Siskind answers, "I'm the Jew."[104] Similarly, when Gladney struggles with the obscurely racialized drug-dealer antagonist, Mink, at the novel's conclusion, he pointedly calls Gladney "white man," and then, though he could simply be observing Gladney's sickly pallor, seems to convert the question of whiteness into an existential-epistemological quandary: "You are very white, you know that?"[105] The "white noise" in *White Noise* can thus be understood either as the "static" pumped into the lives of the U.S. middle class by the mass media, obliterating cultural differences in favor of national brands, or as technicity, the displaced representation of a paradoxically ethnic non-ethnicity.

LOWER-MIDDLE-CLASS MODERNISM

Sitting at the keyboard to produce fiction, aspiring writers in greater and greater numbers in the postwar period have done so under the auspices of creative writing instruction. But in an even more basic sense, where does the individual's recognition of the value of literary experience come from? Where for that matter do readers—in particular, readers of the kinds of writing that ask to be called "literature"—come from? They come from many places, no doubt, not least from an upbringing in an identifiably "bourgeois" or upper fraction of the middle class that has long oriented its children toward the appreciation of high culture. This group had formed the social substrate of interwar literary modernism, the source both of the conventionalities it sought to outrage and of most of the personnel— the T. S. Eliots and Gertrude Steins and James Joyces—who did the outraging, and it still exists. By far the largest number of serious readers in the postwar period, however, have been produced through the agency of the school, where millions of students were first introduced to the refined pleasures of the literary and convinced, to some degree, of its worth as a mode of experience and body of specialized knowledge. These students were as likely as not to come, as Gordon Lish described the scene of his own upbringing on Long Island, from a "home that was empty of books."[106]

The information economy calls forth a great number of highly skilled professionals and experts whose domain of experience is reflected in the work of writers like Barth and Pynchon and Powers—the kind of writers whose work circles within or gravitates toward the aesthetic formation I am calling "technomodernism." But that economy also calls forth a vast body of workers to fill jobs in the lower and middling orders of the corporate and public sector workforce, college graduates all, who comprise the bulk of Mills's "white collar masses." A more familiar term for this group is the "middle class," but a more accurate one might be the "lower middle class," since that would emphasize the degree to which the independent bourgeois of yore has been downgraded to a condition of insecurity and dependency akin to proletarians of the past. Indeed, while many members of this class would not readily recognize themselves in the images of mass-produced respectability or encroaching seediness evoked by the term "lower middle class," Rita Felski is surely right to claim that this "widespread yet indeterminate, important yet under-analyzed class stratum" has grown tremendously in the postwar period, when "the lives of ever more individuals in the industrialized West are defined by occupations, lifestyles, and attitudes traditionally associated with the lower middle class."[107] She is also right to note that this domain of experience has been the least susceptible to any kind of simple conversion into literary or cultural capital, since nobody is proud to be associated with the lower middle class. It is the class designation, above all others, that tends to be taken simply as an insult. The social entity designated by the term "lower middle class" is, for this reason, bereft of class consciousness in the sense of communal solidarity, but constitutively possessed of and by "class awareness"—the measurement of oneself and one's social surround in terms of various markers of status.[108]

It would not be true, however, to say that lower-middle-class experience has been unimportant to postwar U.S. literary production, and any account of the Program Era that failed to find it on the map would have fallen prey to a kind of blindness. Consider the case of Raymond Carver, about whom his first wife observed: "Nobody in Ray's family had ever gone to college, so there was no tradition for it. . . . But [then he realized that] it was important that he get started in school as soon as possible, and he did," enrolling in classes at Yakima Community College in 1957, transferring from there to Chico State, where he studied creative writing with John Gardner, and from there to Humboldt State, where he published his first stories in the college literary magazine. After years of struggle, holding down various low-status jobs, he broke through with a collection of short stories, *Will You Please Be Quiet, Please?* (1976), and became the very emblem, for some critics, of a "program writer." And then there is Jayne Anne Phillips, who grew up in modest circumstances in West Virginia but found her way to the Iowa Writers' Workshop, where she met Carver, and from there to a series of teaching jobs at universities. Her breakthrough collection *Black Tickets* (1979) is structured like Hemingway's *In Our Time* (1923), with short stories interspersed with somewhat inscrutable vignettes.

It would be hard to overestimate the influence of Hemingway on postwar writers, and, though he himself would have nothing to do with college, too easy to forget that the medium of his influence has been the school. Easier still, because they are not themselves typically included on a syllabus of postwar American fiction dominated by the likes of Pynchon and Morrison, would be to forget the empirical centrality of the more or less "nondescript" white followers of Hemingway in the institutional structures of the Program Era. Their medium of greatest achievement has been the minimalist short story—itself, because of its brevity, the key genre of creative writing instruction—and the most common way of insulting these writers has been to associate them with creative writing programs. In a generally admiring review of *Black Tickets,* Phillips's fellow Iowa graduate John Irving spoke of how his pleasure in reading it was interrupted occasionally by reminders of "what total praise she must have received in any creative writing class," "little oddities too precious to the author—or perhaps to her memory of [that] praise—to be thrown away."[109] A later reader would note that "many of the stories, especially the shorter ones . . . could almost be the product of assigned tasks at a creative writing course."[110]

The careers of Carver and Phillips and a great many other postwar writers would have been unthinkable except through the agency of the system of higher education, which in the postwar U.S. expanded to include a larger segment of the population, approaching 50 percent, than ever before seen in human history. Part of the reason the lower middle class has been so hard to account for in cultural historical terms is that college attendance, established as a social norm across a broad swath of the population in the postwar period, was understood to release the individual from any particular class designation into the amorphous potentiality and mobility of the American middle class. To say that the pointedly low-rent world of Carver (sometimes anachronistically described as a "proletarian" or "working class" writer) is emblematic of the middle class as such is therefore a strategic generalization on my part of the condition of dependency, economic insecurity, and anomie his stories so often represent.

Interwar modernism had shuttled between the extremes of high and low, between the values of "aristocracy" on the one hand and "primitivism" on the other, in its delineation of the anti-bourgeois bourgeois aesthetic we call modernism. In the social class imaginary of the postwar period, the social distance traversed by the modernist dialectic is substantially narrowed: the crucial distinction here is between an upper middle class, for whom economic security is a given and higher education is understood as a virtual birthright, and the ethnic or post-ethnic traditional working class, which instead of individual advancement through education offers its members the benefits of belonging and communal solidarity. The version of modernism that shuttles between these class positions, unable to come to rest in either of them, is what I am calling a lower-middle-class modernism. As such, it can be seen either as a lower technomodernism, where high-tech knowledge is downgraded to a "craft" skill, or as a marginal—because largely post-ethnic (in Carver's case, post-Irish)—high cultural pluralism. While the heights of postwar literary prestige are reached elsewhere, in the precincts of technomodernism and high cultural pluralism, lower-middle-class modernism can claim a kind of centrality to the enterprise of creative writing in that it is probably the most characteristic, or numerically "normal," product thereof.

Just as bourgeois modernism was an anti-bourgeois enterprise, lower-middle-class modernism defines itself largely against the cultural forms actually consumed by the lower middle class from whom it struggles to separate itself—sentimental literature, genre fiction, and television—even as it positions itself against the flagrantly intellectualist experimentalism of technomodernism. Among myriad other effects, this has meant that the heavy existential drag of an unliterary upbringing, the shame associated with lower forms of cultural consumption, would often become the *content* of lower-middle-class modernist forms. We see this when the narrator of Phillips's story "Home," returning to her mother's house after years away, takes deadpan, sardonic note of the preferred reading material of the woman who "sent me to college . . . paid for my safe escape," as Phillips's own mother had done when she sent her daughter to West Virginia University: "My mother gets *Reader's Digest*. I come home from work, have a cup of coffee, and read it. I keep it beside my bed. I read it when I am too tired to read anything else. I read about Joe's kidney and Humor in Uniform. Always, there are human interest stories in which someone survives an ordeal of primal terror. Tonight it is Grizzly! Two

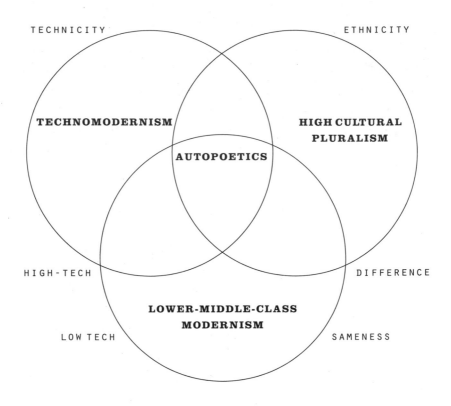

Aesthetic formations of postwar American fiction. These categories correspond roughly to what is more casually called "postmodern-ism" (technomodernism); "ethnic literature" (high cultural plural-ism); and "minimalism" (lower-middle-class modernism); in each case the new term is intended both to draw the three fields into con-ceptual relation and to draw attention to an important feature of each one that otherwise tends to be missed, whether that is a relation to media technology, to the elevated discourse of modernism, or to the question of socioeconomic class. At the core of all three is the ordinary literary reflexivity called autopoetics, while some of the rough distinctions between them occur around the periphery. But note the high degree of overlap in all three.

teenagers camping in the mountains are attacked by a bear."[111] Hence the cruel irony of the fact that it is these writers, more than any others, who have been stigmatized by their association with the writing program, made into poster children of what Aldridge called the "small, sleek clonal fabrications of writers" coming off the program "assembly-line."

To describe these writers in this way, or to apply to their work the insulting term "Kmart realism," is to negate the exquisite "ordinariness" of lower-middle-class modernist writing and to find it *merely* ordinary, the product of a system. The truth in these obnoxious observations, which it is fair to see as conducting a kind of low-level class warfare, is in their apprehension of the iterable and modular nature of the minimalist mode, which can be, and was, reconfigured along various axes to accommodate the expression of various kinds of experiential injuries, not all of them the injuries of class. Phillips, Ann Beattie, and, perhaps the purest instance, Amy Hempel are three prominent minimalists who pointedly reverse the seeming affinity of minimalism with silent masculinity, making it work to record and manage the trauma of female experience. In Andrea Lee's *Sara Phillips* (1984), this becomes the refined, ironic voice of the bourgeois African American, unable to make a "proper" identification with African American oppression on the maximalist model of writers like Toni Morrison. In Susan Minot's *Monkeys,* from the same year, minimalism seems to come full circle, wielded here as the appropriate idiom in which to represent the experience of wealthy, but emotionally repressed and alcoholic, New England WASPs. It is, in other words, not wrong to see in the aesthetic formation I call lower-middle-class modernism the workings of a system, but it may be wrong to assume that this systematicity is something to be ashamed of.

I, ROBOT—OR SYSTEMATIC CREATIVITY

We love to blame the system, and so does the system. And so do postwar institutions blame themselves for their "institutionality" and attempt to correct it. Consecrated to the value of freedom, and disturbed by the idea that they might be occasioning the conformism of their inmates, American universities began in the 1950s to set their course by the polestar of "creativity," softening the rigid boundaries of educational tradition to make way for the new. The great irony in what Hoberek describes as "postwar intellectuals' shared dislike for the institutions . . . of intellectual life"[112] is that these institutions, often enough run by these same intellectuals, shared this dislike. As the dean of the New York University School of Education, George Stoddard, put it in 1959: "Inside the school, many teachers and textbooks (refrigerated versions of teachers stamped and sealed) pay homage to the same god of conformity. It used to be thought that this made little difference in mathematics, physical science, and grammar, but we were wrong even there. Three hundred years of standard instruction in these disciplines have produced populations whose chief reliance is on the conditioned response, the repetitive act, the voice of authority."[113] Striking a blow against conformity on behalf of the creativity of art and science alike, Stoddard hits a note that had already been sounded by the National Science Foundation, which in the mid-1950s began to fund large-scale studies of creativity and the "creative process." They hoped by these means to identify the unusually creative students in a given scientific field and to provide the right conditions for their work. It was, after all, only by staying "creative" that American scientists could outdo the group-thinking communist enemy in the ingenious design of weapons technology—"creative destruction" of a rather literal kind. And it was only by staying creative that the United States could pride itself, unlike its relentlessly drab ideological competitor, in satisfying desires that consumers might not even have realized they had. The critique of the communist war on originality and individuality in a novel like Nabokov's *Bend Sinister* is not subtle, showing us, among its other horrors, how thuggish adherents to the pseudo-communist ideology of "Ekwilism" use a mechanical device that replicates an individual's handwriting, thus proving "the fact that a mechanical device can reproduce personality, and that Quality is merely the distribution aspect of Quantity."[114] This was the context of Stoddard's hope that, "counteract[ing] the drab effects of generations of mass conformity in the arts," universities might finally be transforming themselves into places where "creative art, music, and writing are no longer alien." In turn, with any luck, "the campus will eventually reproduce itself in the American community," turning this nation of crass materialists and Bible-thumping religionists into a more cultured bunch. "Slowly we are becoming a nation of college alumni," Stoddard observes optimistically, "as we are already one of high school graduates."[115]

But could colleges really be counted on to champion freedom from the conformities of Cold War life? For Clark Kerr these suddenly swollen, sprawling public spaces were veritable temples to the worship of creativity, ceaselessly whirring engines of the new, but student radicals of the sixties saw them otherwise. Weren't the universities really just one more agent of social conformity, a bureaucratic stand-in—*in loco parentis*—for their hopelessly square parents? Weren't they more or less reinforcing and reproducing the hierarchical social structure from which they emerged? Even more troublingly, weren't they, too, heavily invested in the dirty business of destruction in Vietnam and elsewhere? Weren't they doing everything they could to grease the war machine?

They were. And the fact that they were, and still are, might well inspire some ambivalence on our part toward all of their products, including their human products, ourselves. Almost the first decision I made when beginning to research this book several years ago was to resist the strong pull of opinion that hangs around the program—what I referred to earlier as the "pro and con" of it—which seemed anathema to the scholarly disposition I wanted to adopt. Not only would the platitudes of pro and con impede the fascinatingly complex history I wanted to relate, but they could not begin to address what seemed to me the true and deepest irony of the creative writing program, one that would reassert itself again and again in various forms throughout the writing of this book. The version most obviously germane to an inquiry into creative writing is the one that saw a discipline concocted as a progressive *antidote* to conformism instead charged with being an *agent* of that conformism on the literary aesthetic plane. A more abstract version, however, is condensed in the very idea of *systematic creativity* which the proximity of "creative" and "program" in the term "creative writing program" brings to mind. Is such a thing possible? Or is it, rather, perfectly normal? Is it an ideological delusion, a way to make us feel better about our captivity, or is it simply a description of what is? To have an opinion on the creative writing program before having an answer to this question seemed premature, and so I determined to replace the platitudes of pro and con with a studious neutrality.

Once upon a time "systematic creativity" would have seemed a contradiction in terms, and wherever an unreconstructed romanticism holds sway it still does. The mythology of scientific creativity is one of inexplicable "Eureka" moments and, in the arts, of the mysteriously pleasing effluence of unpredictable personalities. Thomas Kuhn's *The Structure of Scientific Revolutions* (1962) is perhaps the most brilliantly counterintuitive rebuke to these notions, observing that, historically, most scientific progress has been made in times when there is a near-total commitment to a consensus "paradigm" in a given subfield. Rather than wasting time debating first principles, Kuhn explained, scientists engage in these periods in the continuous or "normal" production of new knowledge. At the same time, because their research inevitably discovers inexplicable anomalies in the paradigm under which they faithfully work, they set the stage for the paradigm-shift of scientific revolution. For Kuhn, in other words, conformism is the shortest path to creativity on *both* an incremental and a fundamental scale.[116] But this in essence absolves institutions of the charge of conformism from the outset. Most developments of the idea of systematic creativity in the postwar period have paid more heed to the problem of conformism than Kuhn did, seeking ways to systematically combat it.

An example is the heady intertwining of romantic and programmatic themes in a work like Edward de Bono's best-selling *Lateral Thinking: Creativity Step by Step* (1970), which reads as though it were written by a New Age robot. As his "step by step" implies, de Bono argues for the conscious adoption of "formal techniques" for generating new ideas, even recommending that problem solvers engaged in a task establish a "quota" or "fixed number of alternative ways of looking at a situation," rather than leaping immediately to an obvious solution. Since the spatial orientation suggested by the term "lateral thinking" turns out to be beside the point, this process might less confusingly have been called *non-linear* thinking: in contrast to the linearity of the "vertical thinking" to which it is opposed, where each step of a proof must be valid in sequence for the conclusion to be valid, lateral thinking permits intuitive leaps. The lateral thinker is allowed to be wrong, silly, irrelevant, and even "deliberately perverse," all in the interest of a pure intellectual fecundity that might end up fundamentally "restructuring" a problem rather than merely solving it. Of course, eliminating the deceptive spatiality of de Bono's terminology would eliminate the populism it subtly wants to communicate. Very much in the spirit of its time, lateral thinking would counteract the "arrogance" of vertical thinking, which "involves being right all the time," with the playful humility of the horizontal multitude. It is finally the multitude, the aggregate of inhabitants of the social system, that is systematically creative.

The research psychologist Harold H. Anderson championed an even stronger version of this progressive creativist populism. Indeed, "naturalism" might be the better term for it. In his introduction to a collection of essays called *Creativity and Its Cultivation* (1959), Anderson assured his readers that "creativity, the emergence of originals and of individuality, is found in every living cell. . . . We are just beginning to think of individual differences in a moving, changing, progressing, interacting way, a way we are beginning to call *dynamic*. This *flow* and interweaving of individual differences is, by definition as well as by discovery the process of emerging individuals, creativity. Creativity is in each one of us."[117] This is to align creativity with the fundamental principle of biological evolution and sociology alike, *differentiation*. The law of differentiation holds that the diversity of life as we know it evolved from a simpler state, and that modernity is characterized by an ever-increasing complexity of social organization. To argue for the "creativity" of the cell is to align human creativity with the life force, with the restlessness of need and the will to thrive. It is to reclaim the artwork as an instance, however remarkable, of the general creativity of humanity, which is creative not only because it must reproduce itself, but because it must try to adapt itself to an ever-changing environment. That this collective struggle is so often experienced as beautiful is obviously to our benefit as a species.

I confess I find this idea appealing, and much more interesting than the therapy of enchantment, or the aura of rarity, or even the supposed benefits of sympathy-training, that have clung to and justified literature for so long. To the degree that creative writing embodies this concept, to the extent that it attempts to realize a diverse aesthetic democracy, I find it appealing, too. That is why the appreciation of postwar American fiction conducted in this book, even against my aspirations toward scholarly neutrality, is less an appreciation of individual writers and works than of the aesthetic-institutional totality they comprise. I admit that my examples are chosen as much for their evidentiary and entertainment value as for their not-infrequent excellence and occasional awesomeness. But that is also why, to the degree that the usual insults hurled at the creative writing program stem from the rejection of the value, even the possibility, of a general human creativity, I find these insults unpersuasive and finally boring. If literature as we know it does not survive the Program Era, it will not be the fault of the program, which is doing what it can to make literary experience relevant to a world that has many other things to attend to. In the meantime, it has bequeathed to us more interesting reading than one person could do in a lifetime. By the same token, to the extent that creative writing represents a further incursion of consumerism into the academy, a ballooning enterprise of mass vanity and anti-intellectualism, it needs to be described as such, and will be, though we can be sure it is no worse in this regard than many human endeavors.

PART ONE

"Write What You Know"/"Show Don't Tell"
(1890–1960)

1

Autobardolatry:
Modernist Fiction, Progressive
Education, "Creative Writing"

> The affinity between a pianist and a waiter, which Marx had
> foreseen, finds an unexpected confirmation in the epoch in
> which all wage labor has something in common with the
> "performing artist."
>
> PAOLO VIRNO, *A Grammar of the Multitude*

BIG MODERNIST ON CAMPUS

Among the prolonged series of climaxes that conclude Thomas Wolfe's autobiographical first novel, *Look Homeward, Angel* (1929), there is one that strikes us as being somewhat out of place. Knowing the period's strong commitment to the poetic potential of prose and prepared by the bouts of rapturous elevation encountered throughout this novel in particular, we might well expect this story of the coming of age of the young literary genius, Eugene Gant, to gear up for one last wave of poetizing before falling silent, and we are not disappointed: "Star, night, earth, light . . . light

. . . O lost! . . . a stone . . . a leaf . . . a door . . . O ghost!"[1] Nor should we be
surprised (though here it takes an unusually visceral form) to find young
Eugene, "touched with the terrible destiny of his blood" (490), meditating
conclusively upon his well-nigh eugenic superiority, as an artist-aristocrat,
to the mass of mediocre men: "The web of my flesh is finer . . . the hair of
my head, the marrow of my spine, the cunning jointure of my bones, and
all the combining jellies, fats, meats, oils, and sinews of my flesh . . . is
mixed with rarer elements, and is fairer and finer than their gross peasant
beef" (488). The idea of the artist as a self-authorizing genius may have
had its heyday in romanticism, but we know that it easily survived the
onslaught of arch Eliotic impersonality-theory, with its countervailing emphasis on the authority of tradition, to become an important feature of
the self-conception of modern artists like Thomas Wolfe and his protagonist Eugene.[2]

The climax that seems out of place, odder than either of these ironically quite conventional, if comically exaggerated, assertions of the awesome originality of the modern artist, is one of a more *conventionally*
conventional kind. This is the one that sees the gangly, smelly boy-poet
Eugene, once a lowly freshman at the state university at Pulpit Hill, arriving at last at an unassailable position atop the campus social heap. Now
"Eugene was a great man on the campus of the little university," we are
told, as springtime of his senior year comes around. "He joined everything
he had not joined. He made funny speeches in chapel, at smokers, at
meetings of all sorts. He edited the paper, he wrote poems and stories—
he flung outward without pause or thought" (487). Footing the bill for his
education, Eugene's parents are gratified at year's end by the graduation
of their "great man on the campus," for whom so many "prizes and hon-
ors were announced." F. Scott Fitzgerald's similarly autobiographical *This
Side of Paradise* (1920) had tempered the early success of his young "Romantic egotist" at Princeton, first with personal failures, then with the
large-scale historical ruptures of the First World War. But here in Wolfe,
almost a decade later, it is as though that novel were rewritten in reverse as
a tale of the steadily accumulating triumph of the collegiate will.

In the "Autobiographical Outline" that Wolfe made as a guide for writing the novel, he called it the "flowering of the joining spirit"; at the University of North Carolina this had brought him membership in no fewer than four literary societies, a fraternity, and the student council, as well as the editorships of the yearbook, the school magazine, and the school newspaper, the *Tar Heel*. True enough, and importantly, the novel made from this outline denies that Eugene was an indiscriminately conscientious scholar, since he had "simply performed brilliantly in all things that touched his hunger, and . . . indifferently in all things that did not" (501). Not for him the anxious grade-grubbing of the scholarship boy. But the fact remains that in *Look Homeward, Angel,* as in no other major American novel of an otherwise militantly extramural modernist period, we encounter the self-portrayal of the modernist author as a successful collegian, celebrated as a "genius" by his fellow students, admired by his professors, launched with "wild ecstasy" toward his future as a graduate student in English literature.

The decades since his death in 1938, when he was widely believed to be among the few greatest American writers, easily the equal of contemporaries like Hemingway, Fitzgerald, and Faulkner, have not been good ones for the reputation of Thomas Wolfe. Although *Look Homeward* is still in print, these days Wolfe is likely to be confused with his near-namesake Tom Wolfe, dapper New Journalist and popular novelist of a later generation, and is no more likely than the younger Wolfe to be found on any college syllabus. But while Thomas Wolfe is well on his way to becoming a footnote to American literary history, the intense identification of his protagonist with the university does begin to indicate how even now he can stake a significant claim on our attention. It is not simply, as David Herbert Donald points out, that he was perhaps the most educated American novelist of his time, with lots of Latin and even more Greek, and with an unusually comprehensive knowledge of the English dramatic, poetic, and narrative tradition.[3] More important for my purposes here, Wolfe is a clear precursor to artistically ambitious American novelists of the post–World War II period in his prolonged intimacy with institutions of higher education.

After Chapel Hill came three years as a graduate student in playwriting at Harvard University. Although it focused on what would prove to be a marginal genre in the postwar writing program establishment, George Pierce Baker's Drama 47 Workshop was among the first creative writing classes ever offered at the graduate level, and during his years in Cambridge Wolfe was a faithful, if darkly disgruntled, attendee. Finally, with a Master's degree under his belt, he was for the better part of a decade an adjunct teacher of composition and literature classes at New York University. Describing it as a kind of racial soul murder, teaching was nonetheless the only form of salaried employment he could imagine taking, and, needing the money, he rose to the task. Set against the tendency to avoid the stuffy conventionality associated with the university on the part of most of his contemporaries, these facts suggest that Wolfe might be a useful figure for drawing attention, near its source, to one of the organizing elements of American fiction in the era of the writing program. In Thomas Wolfe the "autopoetics" of modernist fiction, as I called it in the Introduction, takes its most obvious form, *self-expression,* and a rather extreme species of that. We can think of his writing by analogy to the cybernetic model of positive feedback, where a system's output is fed unaltered back into the system as input. In the form of praise, positive feedback is something we all look for—a sign that we are doing okay and should continue to be as we are—but in Wolfe's case it begins to cycle in his prose until at points it begins to approximate the deafening wail of the self-amplifying microphone.

Never mind that the careening decline of Wolfe's reputation soon after his death can be traced to his brazen flouting of the idea of painstaking craft that the postwar creative writing program would do so much to institutionalize. Never mind that he was often mocked by those associated with writing programs, and held out to students—it is the young, above all others, who have proved most susceptible to his self-aggrandizing charms —as an example of bad writing. The monstrousness of his literary ego, the way it vibrated in every word he wrote, makes his writing useful as a kind of tunnel into the darker corners of the program's soul. Indeed, his writing is the reductio ad absurdum of the familiar call to *write what you*

CREATIVITY
"FIND YOUR VOICE"

CRAFT
"SHOW DON'T TELL"

SELF-EXPRESSION

SELF-DISCIPLINE

EXPERIENCE
"WRITE WHAT YOU KNOW"

We can most accurately locate Thomas Wolfe in relation to the process-ideal of the Program Era if, building on the simple model set out in the Introduction, we now chart how its terms combine to produce the composite ideals of "self-expression" on the one hand, and "self-discipline" on the other. While we can safely assume that all the elements of the autopoetic process are always present to some degree in any act of literary authorship, we will be interested in the way this structure of relays becomes activated as an opposition between different ideals of literary composition, with a given school of thought hewing to one or another of these ideals as supreme. Note that while the poles of self-expression and self-discipline meet directly on the value of personal experience, which they share, they stand at a distance between creativity and craft. For the champion of self-expression, "craft" is likely to be seen as a cipher for conventionality and timidity, while for his opposite number, paeans to "creativity" invite the production of half-baked fantasy (the true meaning of the call to "write what you know" for this camp is "don't write what you don't know"). Craft and creativity nonetheless do come together indirectly: no writer or writing teacher could ever completely dispense with either creativity or craft as a value pertaining to literary production; and so too, in some ultimate sense, literary self-discipline is a form of self-expression and self-expression a form of self-discipline.

know, and a dubious monument to the progressive educational value of self-esteem. It's just that, judged by the usual standards of the creative writing program, Wolfe's fiction seems lopsidedly committed to one side only of what ideally would be a harmonious engagement of the compositional values of personal experience, creativity, and craft.

As an apostle of "self-expression," Thomas Wolfe can be understood to have privileged the value of personal experience above all else, but the cluster of values surrounding "creativity" was important, too: while he showed little interest in the act of fictionalizing—making things up—authorized by the rhetoric of creativity, the sense of cognitive self-sovereignty it carries in train was central to his sense of his own genius, and made even ordinary events in his life seem like emanations of an autochthonous artistic design. An adherence to the value of painstaking craft, however, is difficult to find anywhere in Wolfe's work, having mainly been outsourced to his long-suffering editor, Max Perkins. Wolfe was self-disciplined only in the sense that he was a tireless graphomaniac who hewed with dogged fidelity to the novelistic representation of events that he himself had actually experienced, or to the expression of opinions that he himself held. These included, reflexively enough, the educational experiences that prepared and encouraged him to become a writer and, eventually, the experience of being a novelist who writes autobiographically. Reading Wolfe's looping project of fictional self-expression will thus allow us to explore, not only an early iteration of the model of professional affiliation with the university that would later become common for American writers, but some of the deeper conflicts in educational theory and practice from which the creative writing program and Thomas Wolfe alike emerged.

Creative writing as we know it is the product of a historical moment when traditional conceptions of formal education as an occasion either for externally imposed mental discipline or the conveyance to the student of standardized subject matter came under sustained attack. Dating from before the turn of the twentieth century and exerting a strong (if severely embattled) influence in U.S. schools even now, the progressive education movement came of age with Wolfe and contributed dramatically to his intellectual and authorial formation. Reversing the recently installed critical commonplace that all autobiography is "really" fiction, the form of Wolfe's novels as performances of learned and allusive but only minimally fictionalized self-expression can be seen as closely responsive to the conflicting elements of his education. This was a partly traditional, partly progressive education, and it had him alternating, in his freshman year at UNC, between faithful translations from the ancient Greek and composition themes with titles such as "Who I Am."[4]

An explicit allegiance on the part of progressive education to artistic modernism, too rarely discussed, is announced in the first pages of one of the classic texts of the movement, *The Child-Centered School* (1928). Here Harold Rugg, prolific author, professional educator, and intimate of Waldo Frank and other modernist intellectuals, claims that in order "to comprehend the significance of the child-centered schools, one would need . . . to understand the attempts of the [modern] creative artist to break through the thick crust of imitation, superficiality, and commercialism" that she inherits from tradition.[5] Modernism and educational progressivism—one profoundly external, the other profoundly internal to the educational system—were alike in rejecting early twentieth-century schools as they knew them, and in envisioning the artist as the highest form of human being. Born in the collision of these two discourses, and in the confusing interpenetration of previously polarized *campus* and *urban-bohemian* social-institutional spaces, the postwar creative writing program must therefore be considered in part as a product of larger-scale transformations in the U.S. educational system. Responsive to a growing concern that institutions, left to their own devices, make for problematically "institutional" subjectivities, progressive educators worked to re-gear U.S. schools for the systematic production of original persons—more than a few of whom would actually become the most celebrated form of the self-expressive individual, the writer.

I will begin with Wolfe and then will juxtapose him to other, less documented writers of his period who like him were linked to higher educational institutions, and like him wrote autobiographical fiction, but who stood in a substantially different relation to the category of the "American writer" than his strikingly privileged one. The cases of Younghill Kang and Nella Larsen will allow us to give a fairer hearing to the value of self-expression in creative writing than we otherwise might. While Wolfe eschewed identification even with his home region, the American South, as too limiting of his expansive artist-self, these minority writers would deploy the progressive model of self-expression in the context of a nascent ideology of cultural pluralism that placed hard ontological boundaries between the ethnically or racially marked individuality of the artist and the totality of the United States as such. While Wolfe could fantasize himself as a kind of unacknowledged dictator laying down the law for his readership, the most relevant rhetorical analogue for the latter projects is *testimony*, where the authority of the ethnically marked author is contained and conditioned by the looming and potentially violent—though also potentially protective—presence of jury, judge, and State. Their most significant precursor is the nineteenth-century American slave narrative, where the project of self-expression is conducted with obvious political utility against the threat of what Orlando Patterson famously called "social death." No less than Wolfe's auto-bildungsroman, but shadowed by the power of the racial majority, these works frequently reproduce *as theme* the education that accounts for their existence as authentically self-authored, and (in theory) politically efficacious, narrative forms.[6]

The convergence of testimonial discourse (inflected by an "exoticism" specific to its Asian materials) with the creative-writing aesthetic injunction to "write what you know" can be seen in the opening paragraphs of Younghill Kang's autobiographical novel, *The Grass Roof* (1931), written when the highly educated Korean refugee from Japanese imperialism was a colleague of Thomas Wolfe's at NYU, and published by Scribner's at Wolfe's urging:

> At last the truth must be told about my life, and by my own
> pen, without boasting or pride because it has gained some suc-

cess, without hidings or modesty because it has suffered failure. I swear it is true by the Bible, for I have seen in a Law
Court the Americans swearing by this. . . . I shall relate here
plain matter of fact, although it may seem strange to a Western reader.

Yes, the life that I have lived, with all the joys and sorrows,
is an interesting life, and I should be the author of the story,
because this is the one life I know best. I have always believed
in heroes and I have thirsted to study the lives of all great men
. . . but I know my own story better than theirs.[7]

Kang's reference to the "Law Court" links his first person narration explicitly to testimony and in turn, although less explicitly, to the exclusionary
laws that deprived him of the U.S. citizenship for which he lobbied Congress for many years. If this did not cause social death in Patterson's extreme sense, it did leave Kang stateless, and his novels were on one level
an effort to write himself literally and figuratively into a condition of full
U.S. citizenship. This is one backdrop against which to view the "claiming voice" paradigm that would organize ethnically marked fiction of the
postwar period for several decades, envisioning the novel as an act of self-
representation (whether as defendant or plaintiff) in a quasi-legal sense.[8]
Another—both will get a full treatment later in this book—is the practical
aesthetic injunction to "find one's voice" as a writer, which emerged in a
system of higher education that increasingly wanted to understand itself,
not as an agent of cultural homogenization and upholder of tradition, but
as a kind of socio-intellectual "difference engine" that could produce original research and original persons at one and the same time.

CONVENTIONAL UNCONVENTIONALITY

We owe the widespread use of the term "creative writing" to a particular phase of the progressive education movement in the late 1920s, when
the practice of self-expression became paramount in progressive theory.

While it is now sometimes used as a catchall phrase for fiction, poetry, and drama—that is, for what otherwise tends to be called "literature"—this use represents the semantic spread of the term "creative writing" from its dominant referent, which was a new academic course of study, or pedagogical practice, centered on the student's production of these literary forms. Emerging from debates about the elementary and secondary school curriculum, the "creativity" of creative writing was defined in opposition to the notionally uncreative genres with which students had more traditionally struggled—translations especially, but also themes, papers, and reports. Operating in contrast to the two traditional (often competing) accounts of what schooling should be, creative writing was understood neither as the internalization of a specific body of information or subject matter, nor as a process of mental disciplining or training. It was, however, closer to the latter since it, too, called for a certain form of mental exercise. Drawing on the faculty of imagination, and yet strongly tied to personal memory and observation, this new writing practice would minimize the slavish dependence of student writing on the "arbitrary authority" of established opinion, freeing the young person to bring into being, in his text, something original, something that had "never appeared in the world before."[9]

Foremost among the original entities created by creative writing, it was assumed, would be the personality of the student herself, who in a circular process of literary-existential autopoiesis would find and fashion a self—call it a realist fiction of self—in the very act of creative self-expression. While this imaginative writing practice was understood to be *based on* personal experience, it might be more accurate to say that it *completed* the process of "experience" as theorized by John Dewey, for whom "mere activity" in the world does not count as authentic experience until it is "connected with the return wave of consequences" that load "mere flux . . . with significance."[10] Intensifying the feedback loop that transforms actions into meaningful experiences, creative writing contributes to the "continuous formation" of the individual who is the sum of these experiences. It thus took the traditional concern for "character building" entailed in the virtuously unpleasant translation of the Classics and made it an occasion for pleasure. Championed in the publications of the Progressive Education Association, in classics of the movement such as *The Child-Centered School,* and in a successful series of books by Hughes Mearns of the Lincoln School at Columbia University, "creative activity" became all the rage in American educational theory of the twenties and thirties, and an increasingly common feature, thereafter, of elementary, secondary, and undergraduate education. Soon enough, following the early example of Baker's Drama 47 Workshop, creative writing would establish itself as a viable subject for advanced degree credentialing.

The earliest phases of progressive education, dating from before the turn of the twentieth century, had come to be centered in large cities like Chicago and New York and in industrial towns like Gary, Indiana, and had sometimes been understood as laboratory experiments in education (hence the "Laboratory School" at the University of Chicago).[11] As was most evident in the much-documented Gary schools, however, their primary purpose was to re-engineer public education to accommodate the massive influx of immigrant children to the U.S. in the late nineteenth and early twentieth centuries, preparing them to take their places both as fully assimilated citizens and as well-trained workers in a booming, industrial-revolutionary economy. The latter, it was argued, required a fundamental societal orientation toward the new: "One can hardly believe there has been a revolution in all history so rapid, so extensive, so complete," wrote Dewey in *The School and Society* (1899), and that "this revolution should not affect education in some other than a formal and superficial fashion is inconceivable."[12] It would do this, he hoped, through the institution of various kinds of group activity and hands-on learning in the progressive school, activities that would be "practical" in mirroring those needed in the industrial world outside the school but also "aesthetic" in their "liberation from narrow utilities" (13) of the actual workplace. Founded on the bedrock pragmatist concept that "we learn from experience, and from books or the sayings of others *only* as they are related to experience" (12), progressive education would supply the student with a "genuine motive" for learning, thereby avoiding the dreary defects of traditional education. These included, most significantly, the passivity that it was thought to encourage by putting "the center of gravity" of education "outside the child . . . in the teacher, the textbook, anywhere . . . except in the immediate instincts and activities of the child himself" (23).

In Dewey's version, the benefits of "child-centered" progressive education are imagined first and foremost as benefits to modern American industrial society as a whole, mobilizing curiosity for the ends of successful socialization, using even the child's instinct for self-expression—"the art impulse is connected mainly with the social instinct" (31)—as a way to foster the "mutual interdependence" of the future labor force and citizenry. But one can see how his theorizations might easily be rotated toward the far more individualistic emphasis of the child-centered schools of the twenties and thirties, which not coincidently, as Patricia Graham has noted, dramatically shifted the avant-garde of progressive educational practice from urban, immigrant-oriented public schools to private "Country Day" schools or public schools in affluent suburbs.[13] Here, dispensing with both the scientific-experimental and the immigrant–working class orientation of Deweyan progressivism, wealthy parents could demand that an element of "child-centeredness" and a concern for "creative self-expression" be added to the other educational privileges enjoyed by their children. Eventually, as would become obvious in the progressive educational revival of the 1960s, the heightened respect for *difference* evinced here in progressivism's second, "suburban" phase would circle back to alter progressive educational thinking even as it was directed at minority populations, who in the economically and educationally expansive postwar period would be recruited in large numbers into the suburban middle class.[14]

With its concern for the instinctive creativity of all children—indeed of all humans—the first wave of progressivism had envisioned a thorough democratization of the romantic conception of "genius" as pertaining only to the very few who are "nature's elect." The second wave of progressivism did not entirely reverse the democratization of genius as creativity, but it did strongly associate the creative classroom with middle-class privilege and with the unalienated labor of self-making best exemplified by the artist. Thus Stanwood Cobb, organizer of the Progressive Education Association and founder of the Chevy Chase Country Day School, assured the readers of his self-help treatise, *Discovering the Genius Within You* (1932), that "modern psychology has shown us that there is no un-bridgeable gulf between the genius and his fellow men."[15] Though difficult to attain, genius becomes readily available to those lucky enough to "engage in work that is also a pleasure" (9), and with the will to subordinate "everything else" to a "definitely chosen" goal. Cobb's genius, it appears, is not the industrial worker but the professional or the manager, loving his job but "avoid[ing] all detail work that can be delegated to others" (19).

Enter the North State Fitting School for Boys, a small private school founded in 1912, when Thomas Wolfe was in still in grade school; after some cajoling, his mother agreed to pay the tuition for her youngest son. Typical of many private schools founded in this period, the Fitting School was a hybrid institution, hedging its bets by offering a traditional Classical curriculum strongly inflected with what a youthful Wolfe proudly called "new and novel" educational ideas, such as allowing students to devise their own assignments. On the one hand, that is, Wolfe was supplied in this school with the traditional equipment of the gentleman, a Classical education, a course of study pursued by means of what *Look Homeward* would criticize as the "hard rut of method and memory" (180). "'What's the good of all this stuff?'" asks a student, hitting the progressive note, in Wolfe's evocation of a debate that springs up one day in Eugene's Greek class. "'What good's it going to do [a fellow] when he goes to work?'" asks another. "'It teaches a man to appreciate the Finer Things. . . . It trains his mind'" (183) is the teacher's traditionalist response. On the other hand were Wolfe's English classes, where he was encouraged in the early stirrings of his own genius.

Here, under the tutelage of a teacher he would later describe as his "spiritual mother," Margaret Roberts, Wolfe sat beneath the "magnificent trees" in the schoolyard and began to invest his imagination in romantic poetry, conforming to the wishes of his beloved teacher by strongly identifying himself with the rebellious individuality of the artist. This is why, even as his Classical studies were certifying him as possessing the traditional mental discipline of the educated gentleman, Wolfe could say of himself, as he says of his character Eugene, that he actually "learned little of discipline" in this school that seemed so much like a home, that he "came even to have a romantic contempt for" discipline (254) as a quality pertaining to the herd. Preparing for college, Thomas Wolfe imbibed a heady cocktail of cultural capital, one comprised of equal parts of *traditional* cultural capital—that is, a body of admirably useless knowledge earned in and as mind-training—and of *counter-cultural* capital, which is to say, a fund of personal "coolness" (as it would later be called) associated with romantic-bohemian resistance to puritanical regimes of moderation, self-discipline, and obedience.[16]

When Wolfe arrived at the University of North Carolina in 1916 he found himself in an undergraduate social milieu designed to serve him this cocktail all day long. A self-consciously modernizing Southern institution, UNC brought Wolfe into contact with two of the great, opposing higher educational polemicists of the era: the unapologetically scientific literary scholar Edwin Greenlaw, from whom Wolfe took several classes, and, more glancingly, the neo-humanist critic Norman Foerster, who would leave UNC to become a key figure in the founding of the Iowa Writers' Workshop.[17] Another consequential influence was Frederick Koch, a former student of George Baker's whose classes in playwriting were part of UNC's efforts to modernize its curriculum by actively seeding the present-day cultural life of the state. Koch's classes were centered on the production of what he called "folk-drama": since the rural background of most of the materials at hand in North Carolina could be assumed, this was articulated as the idea that plays should emerge not in imitation of the dramatic tradition but from people and places of the student-writer's own experience. Perhaps fatefully for his student Thomas Wolfe, Koch's pedagogy stressed the complementary idea that, "writ[ing] from our hearts," we "don't need any rules" for writing plays.[18]

On the ambiguously autobiographical evidence of *Look Homeward, Angel* it would appear that Wolfe, seizing the existential benefits of the conformist nonconformity available in his educational milieu, sustained himself in the belief that while the success of his undergraduate peers at UNC was evidence of their obedience, his own was a product of his daring originality:

> The yokels, of course, were in the saddle—they composed nine-tenths of the student body . . . and they took good care that their world should be kept safe for yokelry and the homespun virtues. Usually, these dignities—the presidencies of student bodies [etc.]—were given to some honest serf who had established his greatness behind a plough before working in the college commons, or to some industrious hack who had shown a satisfactory mediocrity in all directions. Such an industrious hack was called an "all-round man." He was safe, sound, and reliable. He would never get notions. He was the fine flower of university training. . . .
>
> In this strange place Eugene flourished amazingly. He was outside the pale of popular jealousies: it was quite obvious that he was not safe, that he was not sound, that decidedly he was an irregular person. He could never be an all-round man. . . . Well, thought they benevolently, we need some such. We are not all made for weighty business. (406–407)

This written by a young man who, editorializing in the *Tar Heel,* had piously warned his peers not to drink at college dances, and to desist from "rowdyism" at public meetings.[19] I say this passage counts as "ambiguously autobiographical" evidence because, of course, it is true that Eugene Gant is a fictional character, and that Pulpit Hill is not quite Chapel Hill. And yet, again—owing to an education concerned as much with putting stu-

dents "on the pulpit," as it were, as self-expressive individuals as with so-
cializing them to the enclosing discipline of "the chapel"—this prophylaxis
against critical naïveté is of only limited value. In *Look Homeward's* prefatory note, "To the Reader"—written at the behest of Max Perkins when
the editor realized that the novel was "almost literally autobiographical"
(x)—Wolfe admits that he has "written of experience . . . which was once
part of the fabric of his life," and that if "any reader, therefore, should say
that the book is 'autobiographical' the writer has no answer for him."
Nonetheless, if only by authorial fiat—claiming, consistent with the doctrine of creativity, a sovereign freedom even from the facts of personal
experience that ground his writing—"he would insist that this book is a
fiction"; and indeed Wolfe professed to be mortified when many of his
family, friends, and neighbors were deeply offended by their often savagely
unflattering portrayal in the book. His "shock" at this reaction would be
recorded in the fourth, posthumously published novel, *You Can't Go Home
Again* (1940), which centers on the return of a novelist to his hometown
after publishing a novel much like *Look Homeward, Angel.*[20]

The intensely—but in my account predictably—ambiguous ontological status of this text as an "autobiographical fiction" is reinforced by
the particular quality of its third person narration, a mode that might have
heightened the distance between the narrator and the central focalizing
character, Eugene. This distance is minimized, however, in *Look Homeward,* and insofar as it is maintained, it becomes the space not so much for
an ironic accounting of mistakes made, signs missed, or lessons learned,
but for narcissism: writing in the third person, that is, Wolfe can more effectively take "himself" as an object of narrative desire. "In this strange
place Eugene flourished amazingly"; "he was an irregular person": note
how the narrative cannot decide whether it is the place that is "strange" or
Eugene that is "irregular"; whether his "flourishing" is amazing in the
sense of having been improbable, or rather his flourishing is the sign of an
amazingly good fit between young man and institution (which would suggest that he, too, is a "fine flower" of sorts). "Well, thought they benevo-
lently, we need some such": here the narrator apparently breaks with the

perspective of Eugene, momentarily channeling the collective conscious-ness of the institution that affectionately patronizes Eugene's arty uncon-ventionality—a jagged shift in focalization that gives voice to the conven-tionality so tightly braided with that unconventionality.

SELF-EXPRESSION AND SCENIC METHOD

It was "unconventionality" that progressive educators in the 1920s were trying somewhat paradoxically to conventionalize as the rule of the mod-ern school, the rule of non-rule that Harold Rugg would proudly call the "doctrine of self-expression." Indeed, in centering education on quali-ties—curiosity, originality, creativity—which the child was understood al-ready to possess when she arrived in the classroom, the externalities repre-sented by *teacher* and *school* loom large in progressive educational theory as potential sources of *obstruction* to education.[21] But the paradox of con-ventional unconventionality is only intensified when it is narrowed to the specific issue of formal instruction in literary creativity, where the essence of the thing taught is understood to be originality. How can the teacher give instruction in this area without falsifying it from the beginning? One answer would be to try to separate the question of talent and originality, which cannot be taught, from the question of technique, which can. No one has trouble making this distinction in the training of, say, painters. The need for such an adjustment in progressive creativity doctrine became pressing when, as creative writing entered the professional-vocational do-main of graduate education, its sponsors and practitioners began to care more for the quality of the works created than for the quality of the edu-cational experience of which they are the occasion.[22]

In this way the whole enterprise began to run afoul of a long tradi-tion in aesthetic philosophy which says that the "genius" of the fine artist is *essentially* unteachable; indeed it is defined in Kant's *Critique of Judgment* by an "exemplary originality" for "which no definite rule can be given."[23] Insofar as the example of the genius "gives rise to a school, that is to say, methodical instruction according to rules," Kant continues—prefiguring so many latter-day critiques of the creative writing program—fine art practice becomes the occasion for a "soulless" art of "imitation," "aping," and "copying." From the very beginning, in George Baker's modest conception of what his graduate classes could actually do for his students at Harvard, to the strikingly cautious mission statement of the Iowa Writers' Workshop of the present day quoted in my Introduction, the practice of creative writing has been haunted by the question, "Can it be taught?"[24] This is true even as it has been widely insisted that, if only on the evidence of insatiable student demand—that simultaneously progressive and consumerist value—it certainly *should* be taught.

In Baker's time, as in our own, the bureaucratic rationale of graduate creative writing instruction combined liberal and professional-vocational elements. It's clear that the establishment of the Drama 47 Workshop was possible only in the context of the revolution in undergraduate education initiated by Charles W. Eliot, the Harvard president who in the 1870s controversially abolished compulsory courses of study in favor of a system of what he called electives. His thinking, stressing both the importance of the student's interest in his studies and the diversity of those interests (and abilities) from student to student, was "progressive" in everything but name, and an elderly Eliot would lend his name as honorary president of the Progressive Education Association when it was founded in 1919.[25] In the classes of some of Baker's colleagues at Harvard, including LeBaron Russell Briggs and Charles Copeland, the spirit of Eliot's "elective idea" was pushing composition instruction away from the regime of error-correction toward what would later be called "creative self-expression."

In Barrett Wendell's advanced composition classes—where, since he occasionally accepted verse and fiction for credit, D. G. Myers locates "the true beginnings of creative writing" on the collegiate level—students were assigned short daily themes whose only "requisites," as Wendell put it, "are that the subject shall be a matter of [the student's own] observation during the day when it was written . . . and that the style shall be fluent and agreeable."[26] Thus was the injunction to "write what you know" woven deep into the fabric of creative writing instruction from the outset. Tilted toward a crudely empiricist conception of knowledge as that which the author has directly observed, this injunction was nonetheless served up with the subjectivist proviso that it should be the observer-experiencer himself who, interacting with his object, is the true subject and end of the composition. Ultimately, this experiential-observational emphasis would contribute both to the dominant position of realism (whether regionalist, ethnic, or domestic) in the postwar creative writing establishment *and*—as "observation" turns inward to that feature of authorial experience which is the act of writing itself—to the strong presence there of a metafictional aesthetic. The latter would be founded on practical-fictional analyses of the narrative conventions of realism and their associated philosophical difficulties, beginning with the one built into that near-contradiction in terms, "realist fiction."

Classes like George Baker's Drama 47 were thus of a piece with large-scale transformations in the higher educational system, in particular changes in composition instruction, which were gearing it toward the pleasurable cultivation of the self. And yet, for Baker, the larger part of the motive for the establishment of the 47 Workshop had been to aid the development of an artistically and commercially viable indigenous American theatrical tradition. This was something that, until Baker's students Eugene O'Neill, Edward Sheldon, and Philip Barry broke onto the scene, the United States had always seemed to lack, and it was something he would attempt on an even larger scale when he was recruited from Harvard to found the Yale School of Drama. Baker hoped to ignite a genuine American theater by treating his students as pre-professionals, envisioning their time in the classroom as continuous with hands-on experience in mounting theatrical productions in Cambridge, and from there feeding them into the professional theater of New York and elsewhere.[27] Hence the notably utilitarian term "workshop," literal versions of which the Gary schools had provided for the training of their future manual laborers, and which Baker appropriated for use as a description of a writing class.[28]

As it is portrayed in Wolfe's second novel, *Of Time and the River*

(1935), in the character of "Professor Hatcher," Baker "prudently forebore from making extravagant claims concerning the benefits to be derived from his course. He did not say that he could make a dramatist out of any man" if he did not have "genuine dramatic and theatric talent to begin with."[29] He did however feel that the "artist would benefit . . . by the comment and criticism of the various members of the class" (167–168). This practice seems to have been inspired by Baker's appreciation of Renaissance theater as a highly disciplined, interactive group endeavor. Reversing the long-standing scholarly tradition of treating Shakespeare's plays as autonomous works of literature, Baker had taken the practicalities of group endeavor and staging techniques in Renaissance theater as among his central scholarly concerns.

Here, then, is at least one point of origin of what would become the dominant model of creative writing instruction in the postwar period, the *workshop*. While its immediate inspiration came (no doubt) from the hands-on practicality valued so highly in early progressive educational discourse, its more distant precursor was the theatrical troupe like the one that had surrounded and enabled the prototype individual literary genius himself, whose members could say to Shakespeare (as has been said to innumerable postwar workshop participants), "that line doesn't work for me." Folding the act of individual authorship into the socio-dynamics of a small community, the workshop would ever after be subject to two competing, if complementary, descriptions. On the one hand, as the first head of the Iowa Writers' Workshop, Wilbur Schramm, would argue in his 1941 brief for the legitimacy of creative writing as an academic pursuit, the university through the agency of the workshop "offers the [students the] opportunity to associate intimately with other young writers." Here the workshop becomes a medium for mutually instructive camaraderie, the basis or generator of an institutionally produced writer's "scene"—a campus variant of the mutually supportive urban bohemian collectivities typically centered in cafés or private homes. But the same sociality that cures the writer's loneliness also makes the classroom a small-scale "pathological public sphere," an occasion for violence done to the youthful writer whose presentation of (typically) autobiographical fiction has "opened" him or her to outside view. In Francine Prose's campus novel *Blue Angel* (2000), the creative writing teacher protagonist wonders, as the group discussion of a student story begins, "What maniac invented this torture, this punishment for young writers? . . . It's not an academic discipline, it's fraternity hazing. And the most appalling part is that it's supposed to be helpful."[30]

Wolfe was allowed to bypass the normal admission requirements to the 47 Workshop because he had studied playwriting with Baker's former student Koch, but he seems to have found his peers at Harvard a more intimidating lot than the "yokels" he had dominated at UNC. His defensively ungenerous opinion (expressed as "fiction") was that his pretentious "*ass*-ociates" around the seminar table "belonged to that unnumbered horde who think that somehow, by some magic and miraculous scheme or rule or formula," they can be told how to write. Few of the 47 Workshop plays, Wolfe thought, "had any intrinsic reality, for most of these people were lacking in the first, the last, the foremost quality of the artist, without which he is lost: the ability to get out of his own life the power to live and work by, to derive *from his own experience*—as a fruit of all his seeing, feeling, living, joy and bitter anguish—the palpable and living substance of his art" (*Of Time,* 169–170; emphasis added). Wolfe's own failure as a playwright was not, he believed, because he, too, was disconnected "from his own experience," but, if anything, because of his excessively passionate attachment to it.[31]

"Whatever other talents I had for playwriting," he explained in an invited lecture shortly before he died, "the specific requirements of the theatre for condensation, limited characterization, and selected focus were really not especially for me." Instead "something in me, very strong and powerful, was groping toward a more full, expansive, and abundant expression of the theatre of life than the stage itself could physically compass: it was something that had to come out sooner or later, as a pent flood bursts a dam—and in 1926"—as he began to work on *Look Homeward*—"I found it."[32] Dropping his plans to become a playwright, Wolfe now began to write down, mostly as narrative, but sometimes simply in long lists, everyone and everything he had ever seen, felt, or believed, filling "enormous ledgers, filling book after book in [a] furious attempt to define the physical limits" of his "experience."[33] The enormous crates of manuscript he left behind as a result of this "torrent" of self-expression would provide the material not only for the two massive tomes published in his lifetime, *Look Homeward, Angel* and *Of Time and the River,* but also for the very long, posthumously published third and fourth novels, *The Web and the Rock* (1939) and *You Can't Go Home Again* (1940), which introduce a new novelist-protagonist, George Webber.[34] Designed to prove to his critics that he could write about someone other than himself, these novels nonetheless essentially take up the story of Wolfe's life where it left off as the story of Eugene Gant, telling it now as the story of George Webber. One can almost imagine Wolfe, spared the tuberculosis that killed him, living to complete the circle, as it were, of his autobiographical-fictional project, arriving at last at the Borgesian day when he must admit that what his novelist-protagonist has just done is write the sentence just written by Thomas Wolfe.

One way to diagnose Wolfe's relation to the 47 Workshop would be to say that while he responded fervently to the general aura of theatricality that hovered around it, staging his career as a performance of the role of literary artist, he took nothing of the disciplining "scenic method" that Henry James, some twenty years earlier, had claimed as the hard-won fruit, for his practice as a novelist, of his own bitterly frustrating foray into playwriting. Minimizing the intrusions of the narrator, the scenic method seeks to emulate the focused intensity of the drama by arranging the fiction in discrete scenes of action and dialogue.[35] Interestingly, as we have it from George Baker's treatise on the scenic method of the theater itself, *Dramatic Technique* (1919), the qualities of "greater concreteness" and "greater vividness" evinced in the "illustrative action" of live theater are what should rightly differentiate it from the novel. Writing in a time when the novel seemed to have achieved a disturbing omnipresence in cultural life, Baker lamented the "widespread and deeply-rooted belief that any novelist or writer of short stories could write plays if he wishes" because they too rely on "story, characters and dialogue."[36]

The installation of this ideal—whether known as the Jamesian "scenic method" or in the homelier form of the dictum "show don't tell" (which we might rephrase as "dramatize don't generalize")—represents a deep penetration of narrative poetics by the techniques of dramatic writing. Taken up by Fitzgerald, Hemingway, and subsequently by a great many of the writers who would be associated with writing programs after the Second World War, the poetics of "show don't tell" would gradually evolve into a more general understanding of good fiction as founded on discipline, restraint, and the impersonal exercise of hard-won technique. Thus we find Fitzgerald, in an avuncular letter to his fellow Max Perkins protégé, encouraging Wolfe to cultivate "a more conscious artist" in himself, and to consider the aesthetic benefits of subtraction, as in the example of Flaubert, whose greatness is measured as much by what he left out as by what he put in. Wolfe's response to Fitzgerald was both churlish and impressively learned; he invoked a parallel tradition in the novel, including works like *Don Quixote* and *Tristram Shandy*, produced not by "taker-outers" like Flaubert but by "putter-inners" like himself. All he could take from Fitzgerald's advice, he wrote, circling back as always to the primacy of authorial selfhood, was that "you think I'd be a good writer if I were an altogether different writer than I am."[37]

For Wolfe, whatever discipline would be applied to his writing would have to come from the editing process, and the labors of Max Perkins in this regard were notoriously large—to the extent that they became the inspiration for Bernard DeVoto's recognizably Jamesian critique of Wolfe's first two novels in the essay "Genius is Not Enough" (1936), where he complains of Wolfe's "long, whirling discharges of words, unabsorbed in the novel, unrelated to the proper business of fiction, badly if not altogether unacceptably written, raw gobs of emotion, aimless and quite meaningless jabber, claptrap, belches, grunts."[38] Laying out the terms by which—as Fitzgerald had presciently warned him—Wolfe would indeed begin to be driven out of the modernist canon, DeVoto accused Wolfe of having "mastered neither the psychic material out of which a novel is made nor the technique of writing fiction."

Invited to address the recently established Colorado Writer's Conference in 1935, Wolfe had in fact been quick to abjure any attempt to speak in general terms about the art of fiction, preferring instead to discourse on something that "has a pertinence and a direct relation to my own experience which topics of a critical or academic sort do not have."[39] He would simply tell the story of the writing of his own novels, subjecting even the form of the lecture to the law of reported experience. And indeed, if it were just recast from first into third person, one could easily imagine large portions of this lecture-text being offered as the experiences of Eugene Gant.[40] Unable to generalize from his experiences as a writer in order to discuss broadly applicable questions of narrative form, as Henry James had so influentially done in the prefaces to the New York Edition of his novels, Wolfe felt compelled to state to this audience of literary craftsmen that he was "not really a professional writer" at all, but a man who happened to have had the experience of writing a few novels. But as DeVoto sensed, this was not so much an expression of Wolfe's humility in the face of Jamesian literary professionalism as it was his sense of himself as a genius, a figure who, speaking from the heart, need not abide by any rules of literary form.

Wolfe's dedication to the idea of his own literary genius had been represented, in *Look Homeward,* in young Eugene Gant's self-interested fascination with Shakespeare, about whom he writes a prize-winning essay (as Wolfe himself had done) during the general hubbub surrounding the tercentenary: "My Shakespeare, rise! He rose. The bard rose throughout the length and breadth of his brave new world [as] his tercentenary . . . was observed piously from Maryland to Oregon. . . . Eugene tore the Chandos portrait from the pages of the *Independent* and nailed it to the calcimined wall of the back-room. Then, still full of the great echoing paean of Ben Jonson's, he scrawled below it in large trembling letters: 'My Shakespeare, rise!' . . . [and] plunged back into the essay littered across his table" (307). Eugene converts Jonson's paean to the Bard into a personal exhortation to an internal Shakespeare, the genius inside himself who must rise to the occasion of essaying the genius of Shakespeare. In doing so, Eugene converts admiration into self-admiration, Bardolatry into Autobardolatry, in much the same way suggested by contemporaneous progressive treatises like Cobb's *Finding the Genius Within You*. A useful contrast to this process is the complex interaction of the poet-protagonist with the classical traditions of Chinese and Korean poetry in Younghill Kang's *The Grass Roof*. Kang's novel is similarly concerned to represent the production of Chung-pa's "originality" in this dynamic, and it too offers continuous evidence of young Chung-pa's extraordinary successes as a student. At one point, before the Japanese invasion has destroyed his childhood idyll, he tells his boyhood friends "one of the stories I had made up. It was a talk on the creation of the earth. I told them that *I* had been the creator, and that I had moved that big rock from a certain spot in the pine grove, and planted the big tree in front of that village. The details of the creation all came out of my own head" (25). Here, although it is recounted with a sense of retrospective irony largely absent from Wolfe, the "genius" of Chung-pa's creativity is raised even above Shakespeare's, to the level of the uncreated creator Himself.

A crucial difference between the two writers, of course, is the historical contingency that put Wolfe's NYU colleague in a radically less authoritative position with respect to the American reading public than Wolfe, who could entertain the possibility of "speaking for everyone," absorbing the national body into his own Bardic self like a Whitman from hell. An authority on Korean culture, Kang could only aspire to (and lobby Congress for) legitimate "American" authorship, and this put limits on the scope of his identification with, let alone mastery of, his audience. Documenting the "dragon surge[s]" of ego that prompted him to be "too original" as an upper-class Korean boy, Chung-pa's story pointedly represents him working as a *translator* of English literature into Korean—translation representing something like the negation of self-expressive creative writing. Kang would in turn thoroughly suffuse the autobiographical narrative of *The Grass Roof* with English translations of classical Asian poetry, and would pitch the novel in a more general sense as an act of "translation" of Korean culture for the benefit of American readers. In this sense, although the United States barely figures in the story, it is present everywhere at the ground of its utterance. However "free" these acts of translation might now seem, it is important to see how this structure disciplines Kang's self-expressive narrative in ways that seem mostly absent from Wolfe.[41]

Self-expression could be a problem, then, but it would persist as a crucial element of the enterprise that took not Wolfe but Ernest Hemingway, the paragon of "discipline," "craft," and "technique," as its model author. The complexity of the situation can be glimpsed in the fact that Hemingway's early novels, not unlike Wolfe's and Kang's, were notoriously autobiographical fictions, willing and able to cruelly jab the "real life" models of characters, including the Jewish pariah-figure Robert Cohn in *The Sun Also Rises* (1926), transparently modeled on the editor and novelist Harold Loeb. Furthermore, countering the aura of highly crafted journalistic "objectivity" that we find in works like *Sun Also* and *A Farewell to Arms* (1929) is the fact that these novels are written as the *first person* narratives of (the unmistakably Hemingway-like) Jake Barnes and Frederick Henry, respectively. Henry James, by contrast, had explicitly eschewed first person narration as being too personal.

The combination, in Hemingway, of first person narration with a more or less rigorous application of the rule of "show don't tell" makes it clear that what is being restrained in the craft of his fiction is, precisely, self-expression, enough of which must remain to produce the aesthetic pleasure of its active restraint. By contrast to popular genre fiction—telling of outlaws, detectives, vampires, moon men, and other things the writer has probably never seen—autobiographical self-expressivity would remain an essential element of the late modernist writing program aesthetic, providing a dialectical counter to the professional impersonality of craft.[42] Whatever else this does, it has the effect of managing an uncomfortable proximity between the high-art fetishization of craft (or "tech-

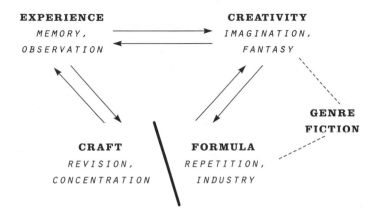

Formula in the unconscious of craft: only in the most highly mediated way can the science fiction writer be said to deploy the faculties
of memory or observation in her work, and this violation of the law
of "write what you know" would become part of the modernist
brief against the shoddy inauthenticity of genre fiction of all kinds.
Meanwhile, the dangerous proximity of technique (good) and formula (bad) facilitates the romantic critique of the creative writing
program as damaging to originality.

nique") and the shamefully (from the modernist perspective) "formulaic"
nature of non-autobiographical genre fiction, which is as "impersonal," in
some ways, as Henry James could have wished.

At the same time, as James was always at pains to point out, to court
the charge of being "too personal" would have its own risks in a mass culture increasingly and, from his perspective, tackily obsessed with celebrity,
personality, and publicity at the expense of art.[43] Such are the vicissitudes
of a system whose conception of individuality poses it at one and the same
time as a form of heroic resistance to the conventionalities of mass culture
and as the finest flower, the proudest product, of that culture. It would fall
to the institution of the family—and to the schools that understood themselves on the model of the family—to attempt to stabilize this paradox.

SCHOOLING THE FAMILY ROMANCE

Since its republication in the 1980s, Nella Larsen's semi-autobiographical novel *Quicksand* (1928) has been the object of a number of astute and theoretically intense rereadings, as the unsettling psychological complexity of its peripatetic mixed-race protagonist, Helga Crane, has become an occasion to consider the broader complexities—sexual, racial, geographic, and aesthetic—of the cultural politics of the Harlem Renaissance. Given these matters of major cultural historical and theoretical interest, it is no wonder that critics have paused so briefly on the novel's strong engagement, in its early chapters, with contemporaneous debates on education. But when we meet her, Helga is an unhappy college English teacher at a Southern Negro educational institution called Naxos, modeled apparently on the Tuskegee Institute founded by Booker T. Washington, where Larsen herself worked for an unhappy year before moving to New York. And this unhappiness has more than a little to do, we are told, with the "method, the general idea behind the system" of the "so-called education" meted out there in the form of militaristic "discipline": "This great community, she thought, was no longer a school. It had grown into a machine. It was now a show place in the black belt, exemplification of the white man's magnanimity, refutation of the black man's inefficiency. Life had died out of it. It was, Helga decided, now only a big knife with cruelly sharp edges ruthlessly cutting all to a pattern, the white man's pattern. Teachers as well as students were subjected to the paring process, for it tolerated no innovations, no individualisms."[44]

While many of the notes struck in Helga's critique of Naxos seem recognizably "progressive" ones, it would be more accurate to say that Larsen's novel represents a transitional moment *within* the discourse of progressive education, when the movement's initial thrust toward the efficient assimilation and vocational training of the immigrant (here African-American) working class began to turn, in the later 1920s, toward the fostering of the child's "originality" and capacities for self-expression. Naxos is "progressive," that is, when seen against a long tradition of restricting higher education to a tiny percentage of the population of mostly white upper-class men, but regressive compared to later progressive educational enterprises in its "intolerant dislike of difference" (5).

The more important point is that at this moment in the 1920s, Helga's/Larsen's critique of the Naxos "machine" must be made from a position distinctly *outside* the educational system, in an urban-bohemian milieu, Harlem, where creative self-expression and cultural difference are celebrated. This is why *Quicksand*'s progressive critique of Naxos-style education can also be seen as a modernist one, and why this novel prefigures, in some surprising ways, the convergence of literary modernism and progressive education in the postwar writing program. Alain Locke's preface to the "bible" of the Harlem Renaissance, *The New Negro* (1925), conveniently marks the distance between the assimilative "uplift" of Naxos and the pluralist aesthetic ideology that not only "tolerates" but celebrates difference in Harlem. Locke establishes the book's intent to focus mostly on "self-expression and the forces and motives of self-determination" in "the culture of the Negro," even to the disadvantage of discussions of "important interactions between the national and the race life."[45]

And yet, transitional moment that this is, it comes as no surprise to find that *The New Negro* contains, along with fiction and poetry, a celebration of the apparent model of Naxos, Tuskegee, whose terms are unmistakably Deweyan: "The one subject which [Booker T. Washington] taught was life. Arithmetic, reading, geography, history, were all interpreted in terms of the life surroundings of his students. He talked of the life they lived. Every day he put them to work creating life for themselves."[46] So too had John Dewey promoted a "hands on" conception of learning that would (conceptually at least) permeate the wall separating "school" from "life," and so had his model of education argued for a shift from liberal (useless) toward vocational (useful) pursuits. Later, after the progressive school had seized upon creative self-expression as its primary value, it could become—especially at the university level—an institutional pa-

tron of the arts, providing occasions for the kind of original cultural productions patronized by wealthy individuals in Harlem in the twenties and
thirties.[47]

In this way the progressive school becomes hospitable not only to
the "innovations and individualisms" to which Naxos seems so hostile but
also, more specifically, to the personification of these values, the modern
artist. For isn't Helga Crane some sort of artist—an artist manqué? That
has been one of the implications of feminist readings of the novel, such as
Ann E. Hostetler's, that have drawn our attention to Helga's attempts to
"use her attractiveness as power."[48] One of the more interesting autobiographical displacements in *Quicksand* is the one that transforms the
almost-autobiographer Larsen, in some ways strikingly like her protagonist, into the "passive" individualist Helga, who is not an aspiring writer
as Larsen was when she wrote the novel but by turns a teacher, editor,
secretary, woman of leisure and, finally, unhappy wife and mother. Sitting
alone, when she is introduced, in a room "furnished with rare and intensely personal taste" (1), Helga is nonetheless consistently recognizable
as a type. Surrounded by "oriental silk" and nasturtiums, and obsessed
with the beauty (or painful ugliness) of her surroundings, she is a belated
fin-de-siècle aesthete—which is to say, a person whose relation to beauty
as a beholder is pursued at a maximum of intensity without yet crossing
over into the domain of the producer.[49] It is tempting to read the sequence
of her sub-literary jobs as *proximate negations* of the career of artist or
writer, that artistry having been displaced onto her person in the form of
her beautiful, colorful clothing; tempting indeed to think of Helga as a
sort of "performance artist" manqué, using not the pen or the brush but
her person as a medium of self-expression.

Perhaps the most interesting in Helga's series of jobs, in this regard,
is her work as editor of the speeches of the lecturer Mrs. Hayes-Rore,
which prove to be "merely patchworks of others' speeches and opinions.
. . . Ideas, phrases, and even whole sentences and paragraphs were lifted
bodily from previous orations and published works of Wendell Phillips,
Frederick Douglass, Booker T. Washington, and other doctors of the race's

ills" (38). As the editor of someone else's plagiarized speeches, Helga is even farther removed from the exercise of self-expressive originality than Chung-pa was as translator. The same problem will arise, in a different form, when Helga sits passively as an artist's model in Copenhagen and sees her self-presentation subsumed by the primitivizing artistic vision of another. The *almost-ness* of Helga's artistry might then be decoded as Larsen's recording of the sheer difficulty for a woman in her position to lay claim to a socially inscribed identity as an artist, which is associated rather with the pompous high society painter, Axel Olson. Larsen's own commitment to the value of originality, though perhaps not to her right to claim it, would become apparent when, accused of plagiarizing a new short story, she abruptly ended her nascent writing career. It was as though to continue as an "artist" with the taint of "unoriginality" upon her was unthinkable.

And so, pursuing this line of thinking, it is not only as a sort of "performance artist" but as an "artist-in-residence" manqué that Helga dwells at Naxos. Certainly the reasoning behind the pleas to Helga to stay on at hateful Naxos bear some resemblance to the rationale for inviting artists to spend their days on campus amidst sober-minded scholars. "'It's nice having you here, Helga,'" says her colleague in the English department, Margaret. "'We all think so. Even the dead ones. We need a few decorations to brighten our sad lives'" (14). But the new principal blows the pitch when, telling Helga that Naxos needs "'more people like you, people with a sense of values, and proportion, an appreciation of the rarer things in life,'" he then clumsily exposes the class fantasy, the "family romance," underpinning her aesthete persona: "'Perhaps I can best explain it by the use of that trite phrase, "You're a lady." You have dignity and breeding.'" While the Wolfean modernist artist eagerly claims his quasi-aristocratic superiority to the "gross peasant beef," Helga's painfully orphaned relation to her mixed-race paternity will not allow her to do so openly:

> "If you're speaking of family, Dr. Anderson, why, I haven't any.
> I was born in a Chicago slum."

The man chose his words, carefully he thought. "That doesn't at all matter, Miss Crane. Financial, economic circumstances can't destroy tendencies inherited from good stock. You yourself prove that!"

. . .

"The joke is on you, Dr. Anderson. My father was a gambler who deserted my mother, a white immigrant [who subsequently married the white man, Helga's stepfather, who paid for her education]. It is even uncertain that they were married. As I said at first, I don't belong here. I shall be leaving at once." (21)

The usual version of the family romance has the child, raised by ordinary parents, fantasizing that he or she is the lost progeny of royalty. This is the structure of Kang's *Grass Roof,* where an upper-class boy, descended from a line of great poet-scholars, sees these family ties severed in a suddenly (after the Japanese invasion) post-traditional Korean society that redefines him as a refugee and immigrant. Seen from the perspective of this new existence, the childhood self described in the first half of the novel is something like a prince in a fairy tale. By contrast, Helga's good taste is taken by her peers as evidence that she is indeed extraordinary, a "lady" if not quite a princess, even as she knows herself "in truth" to be the lost progeny of a lowly black gambler and a white immigrant. "No family. That was the crux of the matter" (8): as Helga sets out from Naxos on the journey that will take her to Chicago, Harlem, Copenhagen, and finally back to the deep South, the lack of upper-class "family connections" that makes her an outsider at Naxos will linger in its significance. Indeed— since "figuring out" Helga has become something of sport for critics—it may be the best explanation for her notable inability, as she travels around, to find a functional resolution of the kind of radical individuality she experiences in Denmark, where she feels special but ultimately lonely, and the racial community she experiences in "teeming" Harlem, where she feels related but ultimately obliterated: "She didn't, in spite of her racial markings, belong to these dark segregated people. She was different. . . . It was something broader, deeper that made folk kin" (55).[50]

The suggestion is that the "good family" that Helga lacks would have had not only a socially certifying but a developmental function: situated at the "crux" of individuation and socialization, it would mediate these two forces, simultaneously nurturing the individuality of the highly valued child and, since the family is itself a social grouping, beginning the process of socialization to external norms. In the absence of this mediation, Larsen suggests, Helga swings back and forth between ontological extremes. Naxos, meanwhile, although it snobbishly respects upper-class family connections, is in its violently machine-like "patterning" of individuality the functional negation of the "nurturing" family. In this respect, even though it opposes urban-bohemian Harlem in most other ways, Naxos already poses a version of the problem that Helga will encounter again in the North: obliteration by the social group. Progressive education was, among other things, an attempt to solve this problem.

For progressive educators, as we have seen, it was important that the "educational experience" be meaningfully tied to "life experience." What this really meant—"how difficult it is of expression and description!" said Stanwood Cobb in his account of progressive education, *The New Leaven* (1928)—was not always easy to say, but in practice, since most students are children, at least one thing it meant was that the progressive school would seek to emulate the nurturing family life to which, or so it was optimistically assumed, the student would return at the end of the day.[51] Progressivism, in this sense, would "dissolve" the walls of the school in two opposing directions—one leading outward to the publicity of modern urban life and the labor market, the other leading inward to the privacy of the family. In liberal education, by contrast, the school is understood as being profoundly separate from the family and the labor market alike.[52]

Describing an admirable parent of his acquaintance who, reluctant to submit his boys to the "drill and routine of the ordinary school," has chosen instead to educate them amongst the "lawns, gardens," and stables of their own "charming home" in Brookline, Cobb applauds the way "the

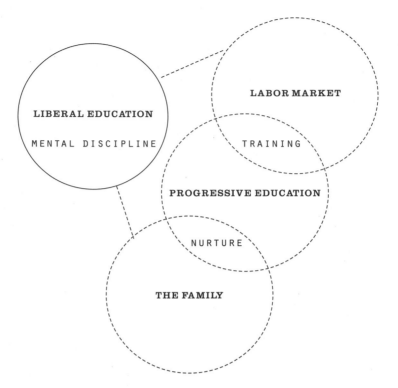

Progressive versus liberal education: while liberal education (especially as founded on the Classics) is understood to stand apart from the practicalities of everyday life, progressive education aspires to be an enterprise "without walls" and thus intimate on the one hand with the institution of the family, and on the other with the needs of the labor market.

modern parent is becoming an interested and intelligent partner with the professional educator in the training of her child." The "modern educator," meanwhile, "welcomes this partnership, so pregnant with possibilities for the further perfectioning of education."[53] Second only, perhaps, to the social institution of the family in the depth of its formative designs on the child, the institution of the school has always been intimately coupled with the institution of the family, in loco parentis, though conceptions of its role in that coupling might hold for the school's necessary negation (as appears to be the case at Naxos) of family intimacy in favor of more public forms of sociability. The progressive school of the 1920s and 30s, by contrast, would adore children as the little individuals their mothers and fathers knew them to be, and not try to cut them to a pattern. No less than the ideal family, that is, the ideal progressive school would be knit together by bonds of love, and once conceived in this way, could even begin to show up the actuality of its model, the nuclear family, as the gothic freak-show that it is.

This, in any case, is what seems to happen to Eugene Gant in *Look Homeward, Angel,* when he begins to attend the private school located in "an old pre-war house, set on a hill wooded by magnificent trees" (176). This school becomes "the centre of his heart and life" for the next four years, a negation of the "bleak horror" of his chaotic home, an antidote to "all the loneliness and imprisonment of his own life which had gnawed him like hunger." Eugene is convinced, and tells them so, that his large family "hates" him and knows "nothing whatever about" him: "I have lived here with you for seventeen years and I'm a stranger" (419–420). The school community thus becomes an alternative family; his "spiritual mother," Margaret Leonard, an alternative parent. The relation between these two spaces, home and school, begins to produce the strange effects of mirror reversal.[54] As traditionally conceived, home would be the primary site of natural, the school of sociocultural, reproduction, but here each begins to seem, at various moments, like versions of the other. This confusion is already evident in the term "nurture," which in debates about heredity is the social-constructionist opposite of "nature," but which in the context of educational progressivism is a "natural" maternal alternative to cold institutional "training," the breast to traditionalism's bottle.

This theme appears in the novel when Eugene's biological mother realizes "that in her dark and sorrowful womb a stranger had come to life, fed by the lost communications of eternity, his own ghost, haunter of his own house, lonely to himself and to the world. O lost" (66). Discovering a "stranger" where no stranger could possibly be, Eliza Gant's womb is imagined here as a haunted public space. Similarly, and even more explicitly, she envisions her womb as a kind of schoolroom: Eugene's talents as a student having become evident, she proudly claims credit for having "read every moment I could get the chance the summer before he was born" (67). Reversing the traditional sense of the school as the site of socialization to collective norms, the novel instead associates the educational domain with opportunities for individualism, in contrast to the biological family, which offers Eugene ample genetic resources of greatness but also a cloying set of emotional and other de-individuating demands. Thus Eugene associates the "loneliness" of family life with its crowdedness (he is the youngest of many siblings), and even at school his favorite time is "in the afternoons when the crowd of boys had gone, and when he was free to wander about the old house, under the singing majesty of great trees, exultant in the proud solitude of that fine hill"(192). For young Eugene, reversing the original impulses of Deweyan progressivism entirely, the ideal school would have only one student. It might seem that this model is reversed again, back in the direction of democratic sociability, when Eugene experiences the "flowering of the joining spirit" in his "golden years" at Pulpit Hill. But not really, since in this case—as though living the dream of dictators—what he finally sees is not the obdurate otherness of the other but his own "genius" reflected back at him at almost every point. As Wolfe could do when he opened his senior yearbook, the *Yackety-Yack*, which he edited, and read the text beneath his photo (which he most likely wrote): "Editing the *Tar Heel*, winning Horace's philosophy prize when only a junior . . . it is no wonder" this "young Shakespeare" is "classed as a genius."[55]

Any irritating remainder of otherness that persists in that strikingly homogeneous institution is put to the psychic work of justifying Eugene's sense, against all evidence to the contrary, of his stark, individualistic opposition to the aggregate of yokels who make up the campus community as such. In this mission, Eugene partly reverses his flight from family to school, turning back to reclaim the eugenic genius that is the "terrible destiny of his blood." In the town of Altamont, based on the Asheville of Wolfe's upbringing, the Gant family's "status was singular—if they could have been distinguished by caste, they would probably have been called middle-class," but this would do injustice to the "strange rich color of their lives" which "twisted the design of all orderly life" with a "mad, original, disturbing quality" (52). Near the end of the novel, significantly, the same Eugene who had earlier claimed himself a stranger to his own family "felt again the nightmare horror of destiny: he was of them—there was no escape" from these people "smelling of the earth and Parnassus" (479).

The Gants, in other words, are crypto-bohemian geniuses, and his affiliation with their mad originality protects Eugene from being entirely unmarked, merely "ordinary." As Gertrude Stein put it in her capacious family novel, The Making of Americans (1925): "Middle-class, middle-class, I know no one of my friends who will admit it, one can find no one among you all to belong to it, I know that here we are to be democratic and aristocratic and not have it, for middle class is sordid material unillusioned unaspiring and always monotonous."[56] Warding off this "monotony," Eugene's earthy Parnassian blood becomes, in this sense, the structural equivalent of the racial marking that makes Helga Crane "prominent" in hyper-white Denmark. Ironically, it is Eugene's problem—an oppressive over-muchness of family which nonetheless becomes the source of his personal distinction as an artist—that most closely prefigures the oppressive-but-enabling topos of "family" in the work of later, ethnically marked writers from Philip Roth to Maxine Hong Kingston to Arturo Islas. (Having "no family," that is, Helga is at least spared a few guilt trips.)

More specifically, though, Wolfe's oeuvre is father-obsessed from first to last, and George Webber of the later novels no less than Eugene Gant of the early ones constructs his identity in a lavishly passionate patriarchal imaginary. In Look Homeward, significantly, Eugene's father W. O. Gant, himself a great haranguer and pontificator, is the only other character in the novel to whose psychic interior the narrator claims significant access, as though the paternal biological bond can produce contiguous psychic spaces in the narrative. Shifting the affiliation of his protagonist from the patriarchal family to the nurturing school, as necessary, Wolfe traces the dialectical construction of Eugene's triumphantly phallic singularity as an artist. Helga Crane, by contrast, abandoned by her biological father, disavowed by her white stepfather, and worrying over the "lack somewhere" (7) at the crux of her being, circles irritably in the lonely psychic space of Larsen's free indirect discourse, awaiting her fate as the depressed wife of the Reverend Mr. Pleasant Green.

THE RACE OF ARTISTS

In 1924 New York University was undergoing an enormous expansion, swelling with large numbers of first- and second-generation immigrant students from the Lower East Side; and some of the school's administrators, watching this happen, were themselves feeling unusually expansive. This is why Homer Watt, the otherwise unapologetic taskmaster of the human teaching machines of the large, composition-oriented English Department housed at Washington Square, thought it proper to write the following in a letter to young Thomas Wolfe of North Carolina, author at this point of not much, but recently graduated with a Master's degree from George Baker's famed Drama 47 Workshop at Harvard: "I believe there is room in a department, especially in New York City, not only for excellent teachers and good scholars, but for men who have the creative impulse. Indeed, I have a feeling that the department can absorb with profit a reasonable number of temperamental gentlemen like yourself who have color and imagination to inspire students as well as to teach them."[57]

Here, several decades before the fact, Watt supplies some of the rationale that would drive the expanding U.S. universities of the postwar period to hire practitioners to teach creative writing. There, as here, a sense of the comfortably absorptive largeness of a suddenly swollen faculty body would encourage the admission of a different and riskier sort of individual, representing a substantially different relation to literary knowledge, into the usual mix of teacher-scholars. There, as here, the welcoming of the literary artist into the faculty lounge would not indicate an entire revamping of the procedures of college literary study. (As has often been observed, universities almost never revamp anything entirely—they add things on.) While his presence would indeed be symptomatic of large-scale shifts in the guiding premises of U.S. higher education, the role of the "temperamental gentleman" would in a more local, departmental sense be supplemental: it would be his job to *personify* the "creativity" that students would more frequently continue to analyze, with the help of the usual professors, in the relatively inert form of the literary text.

The creative writing teacher or writer-in-residence can thus be understood as an embodiment of the principle of individual creativity, a higher-dimensional apparition, as though the "author function" has emerged from the flatness of the page and begun to speak out loud. For students, the charismatic presence of the artist in the quadrangle or classroom is "inspiring," an occasion for emulative desire. In this process the body of the artist is crucial, since it will serve as a desirable vehicle of beauty whether it is physically appealing in its own right or not: in this sense all artists on campus, whatever their medium or genre, are, like Helga, performance artists manqué. At least in its initial theorizations, the question of the measurable success or failure of the instruction offered by this artist-presence was conceived of as secondary. In his contribution to *Creative Expression* (1932), a volume of reprints from the official journal of the Progressive Education Association, Matthew Black notes some recent attempts to "induce poets of repute to lend their presence to this or the other campus, to be there, merely, and communicate themselves through informal and invisible channels," and he professes to find the "lack of tangible results" in the form of great new works of literature "in no sense discouraging." What matters is that "in all of these experiments there has been a stimulus and an outlet for the creative spirit in writing; something, in fact, of the freedom, the companionship, and the inspiration of the atelier of a master."[58]

For George Baker, we recall, the relevant precursor social form of the creative writing workshop had been the Renaissance theatrical troupe;

here in Black we are instead introduced to the metaphor of the "atelier," where students become "companions" not so much of each other as of an individual master *practitioner* (which Baker, a scholar and critic, was not). This individual might be thought of as a kind of professional upgrade of the "kindly and intelligent teacher-workmen" hired from the community to teach practical skills in the Gary schools.[59] Having introduced the metaphor of the atelier, however, Black then admits that circumstances at most universities, such as his own University of Pennsylvania, require that creative writing classes be staffed by mere "professors, since the supply of artistic luminaries, even supposing all of them stout-hearted enough to attempt such work, is readily exhausted. In our own department the bulk of the creative writing courses are conducted by the younger men, since it has been our experience that the students will talk more readily to them of their lives, and of what there is in their lives to write about. In truth it is not necessary that the 'master' be a great master, but merely that he be a little more mature than his students in the ways of life" (246). The charismatic power of the body of the artist is partially transferred to the priest-figure, the young male professor, who converts that blinding luminosity into a more ordinary, if still quite energetic, social intimacy between student and teacher: "There must be talk, eager, impassioned, time-forgetting talk." And the topic of that talk is clear: "finding what in [the student's] own experience is worth artistic expression" (247).

Standing at a husky, blustery six-foot-six, Thomas Wolfe brought a lot of artist into every classroom he entered. At UNC he had taken the lead in the production of a play he had authored, and here at NYU his histrionic urges were channeled into loud renditions of texts from the English poetic tradition, performances that apparently took up a great deal of class time.[60] But if Wolfe personified the genius of the syllabus, he did so officially as a composition instructor, a relatively low-status job he was not prepared to appreciate. Later teacher-practitioners in the discipline of creative writing would crucially *not* be understood or treated as temperamental composition instructors, as they were at NYU during these years. Writing in 1984, the famed writer-teacher John Gardner would aver that "learning to write fiction is too serious a business to be mixed in with left-overs from freshman composition. The teacher, if he knows what he's do-ing, is too valuable to be wasted in this way."[61] Wolfe, by contrast, now at-tached to a coeducational institution nearly thirty times larger than the socially homogeneous "little university" of boys he had swallowed whole at Chapel Hill, typically had over one hundred students in his classes at any given time, all of them writing weekly themes; grading more than a thou-sand papers per term left little time for work on his own writing.[62] He con-sidered it the artist's job "to wreak the vision of his life, the rude and pain-ful substance of his own experience" into "an everlasting form" that will "enslave and conquer" mankind (*Of Time*, 550); the authority of the com-position teacher seemed by contrast a conspicuously servile one, where the teacher is put at constant risk of the "frightful insubordination and re-bellion" of the immigrant student mob.

At first Wolfe could (almost) be speaking for legions of brain-addled paper graders, then and since, when he describes Eugene's having "lost ir-revocably into the sponge-like and withdrawing maws of their dark, oily and insatiate hunger . . . all of the rare and priceless energies of creation," and thinking with "weary and impotent fury of great plans and soaring ecstasies of hope and ambition—of poems, stories, books which once had swarmed exultantly their cries of glory, joy and triumph through his brain" (478). The potential for this conflict is of course endemic to research uni-versities and colleges where the duties of faculty are bifurcated between teaching and research, the latter functioning both as a "luxury" for the re-searcher and as a path to higher status within the profession. With the rise of the academic creative writer in the postwar period, the category of re-search would be expanded to include the writing of fiction and poetry, understood now as a kind of practical research into the possibilities of self-expression. In his lecture in Colorado, Wolfe—who at UNC, we recall, had been the devoted student of perhaps the most forceful proponent of liter-ary study conceived as scientific historical research, Edwin Greenlaw—would describe the labor of novel-writing in just these terms: "What I was really doing . . . was really to explore day by day and month by month with a fanatical intensity, a devoted thoroughness that would make the most patient and minute researches of German scholarship seem superficial by comparison, the whole material domain of my resources as a man and as a writer."[63] Working as a composition instructor at NYU, alas, Wolfe's "researches" as a novelist were not given significant institutional support.

And yet, as it traces Eugene's painful career as a college teacher, the novel's tirade against the demands of students gradually evolves into something more disturbing than the usual self-pity of the overworked and underpaid college instructor. If the idea of the writer-in-residence is to bring the luminous body of the artist into the classroom, there to stimulate the creativity of students, Eugene soon enough feels this student desire as a burden and, what's worse, as a provocation to his own desire, as "the potent young Jewesses, thick, hot and heavy with a female odor, swarmed around him in a sensual tide . . . pressing deliberately the crisp nozzles of their melon-heavy breasts against his shoulder," looking "at him with moist red lips through which their wet red tongues lolled wickedly" (*Of Time,* 478–479). The eroticized body of the artist in the classroom becomes, in the overheated interplay of desire and disgust, a vehicle for the emergence in *Of Time and the River* of the problem of race:

> The successive stages of his journey from his room . . . to the brawling and ugly corridors of the university, which drowned one, body and soul, with their swarming, shrieking, shouting tides of dark amber Jewish flesh, and thence into . . . the class room with its smaller horde of thirty or forty Jews and Jewesses, all laughing, shouting, screaming, thick with their hot and swarthy body-smells, their strong female odors of rut and crotch and arm-pit and cheap perfume, and their hard male smells that were rancid, stale, and sour—the successive stages of this journey were filled with such dazed numbness, horror, fear and nauseous stupefaction as a man might feel in the successive stages of a journey to the gallows. (419–420)

Here the body of the individual artist meets the racialized student body, an encounter that produces a run-on stream of prose strikingly convergent with contemporaneous 1930s Nazi propaganda.[64] Converting what was by all accounts an ethnically diverse, if predominantly first- or second-generation immigrant, group of students at NYU into a mass of repulsive Jews, Wolfe's novelistic hate-speech attests to a problematic, if evidently pleasurable, permeability of the individual (male) body's boundaries. Yes, Eugene is wounded and disgusted, but what a joy to express this disgust and fill these wounds with what Wolfe no doubt thought was some pretty powerful writing on his part. Back in the North Carolina of his youth, where racial divisions and hierarchies had been much clearer, Eugene could feel a "need for the negroes" grown "acute" (*Look Homeward,* 250), and could regularly satisfy his sexual desires with the prostitutes of "Niggertown" without much worry. Here in New York the sheer numerousness and categorical ambiguity of the immigrant Jew—a race apart but, owing to the assimilative force of educational institutions like NYU, "whitening" every day—poses the more intricate ontological threat of the artist's fragmentation and absorption by a grotesquely embodied other.[65]

If it is ironic, it is also in a sense predictable that Wolfe should have found himself in these years so near the origins of the pluralist ethos that another graduate of Baker's Drama 47 Workshop, the philosopher Horace Kallen, and many others, including Randolph Bourne, Ruth Benedict, and Alain Locke, were theorizing all around him as a response to the period's unapologetic xenophobia. Kallen's conception of what he was the first to call "Cultural Pluralism" extended the philosophical pluralism he had learned from his teacher at Harvard, William James, into the domain of cultural politics, where it became the century's most influential brief on behalf of the value of maintaining cultural diversity against the assimilative neutralization of difference in the "melting pot." Summing up a position developed over the course of several essays, Kallen argued that "in manyness, variety, differentiation, lies the vitality of such oneness" that American culture as a whole might manifest; maintaining this "vitality," he asserted, will require social institutions that "encourage individuality in groups, in persons, in temperaments, whose program liberates these individualities and guides them into a fellowship of freedom and cooperation."[66]

For Kallen the appropriate figure for the national body was not the Wolfean genius, enslaving the nation to his artistic vision, but the disciplined interaction of a multicultural "orchestra" where each ethnic group is imagined as playing a certain kind of musical instrument in the symphony of American culture. As Sollors and others have noted, this metaphor raises as many questions as it answers (who is the conductor here? who wrote the score? what if I get sick of playing trombone?), and it seems to naturalize ethnic cultures as unitary and static. As Kallen infamously put it, "Men may change their clothes, their politics, their wives, their religions," but "they cannot change their grandfathers" (122). Defending cultural difference from the racism of aggressive Americanization policies, Kallen thus exposes his anti-racist project to charges of its own "racism," much as the Harlem Renaissance would do with its replacement of negative racial stereotypes with positive ones. Symmetrically, of course, anti-racist pluralism criticizes (false) universalisms like the "melting pot"— which disavow the importance of ethnic and racial particularity, but tacitly assume a white Anglo-Saxon norm—as "racist." Since racism and anti-racism are systemically codetermined, each unthinkable without the other, they are perpetually subject to "scandalous" conceptual interpenetrations of this sort.

The more immediate problem for proponents of cultural pluralism, however, was how to make arguments against the melting of the ethnically specific individual into what Bourne called the "grey mass" of American mass culture without simply establishing that ethnic culture as a new source of coercive homogenization. At one end of a spectrum of responses to this dilemma was Kallen himself, with his use of the term "individuality" to describe the particularity of an ethnic *group*. For Kallen, indeed, "the very conception of the individual himself has changed. He is seen no longer as an absolute distinct and autonomous entity, but as a link in an endless historic chain which is heredity" (59). A more enduring approach to the issue is evident in Harold Loeb's novel *The Professors Like Vodka* (1927), written about experiences Loeb had soon after the trip to Pamplona portrayed in *The Sun Also Rises.* This novel understands the ethnic group on the same model of the family discussed earlier in relation to Larsen and Wolfe—that is, as an intermediary construction between pure individuality on the one hand, and an obliterating social "ordinariness" on the other. Of course, as the very model of consanguineous human relations and the engine of biological reproduction, the family has always been nested deeply in larger constructions of cultural nationalism, and progressive education's alliance with the first supplies the logic of its eventual alliance with the second.[67]

Loeb's novel recounts the travels of two fussy American college professors, one of them a Jew utterly "lacking in race consciousness," in the excitingly diverse café-culture of Paris of the 1920s.[68] Freed from the monotonously pastoral campus of a college called Greensborough, Professor Mercado soon falls for a mysterious young woman, the daughter of a czarist general and a refugee from the recent Bolshevik revolution. Days into their courtship (Mercado never having mentioned his Jewishness), they are found romantically ensconced at a Left Bank nightclub, a place whose most obvious characteristic, from Mercado's provincial perspective, is its diversity: "'I've never seen such a heterogeneous collection of weird human specimens before,'" he tells his companion, watching two black women dance together in the swirling smoke. It is here, amidst the diversity of Parisian café culture, that Mercado at last encounters the racial prejudice that has been (somewhat surprisingly) absent in all his years at WASPy Greensborough. Misunderstanding his comment as racist (in fact he means it as heterosexist), Cleopatra speaks up:

> "You Americans," she said, "why do you hate the negroes? . . . They can't help being black."
>
> Mercado was piqued at the reflection on his lack of tolerance. He particularly prided himself on having no prejudices

of that kind. Smiling quizzically, to conceal his resentment, he replied:

"I have often heard that you Russians hate the Jews."

"Jews!" she said, and looked dreamily at the polished thumb-nail on her left hand. "But they're not people.

"I've killed many Jews," she added agreeably. (131)

Confronted with the racism of a woman for whom pogroms were a youthful pastime, some fun to be had with her dad, Mercado now feels "the fibers of his racial consciousness vibrat[ing]" (139). Indeed, he is reborn as a Jew: "He had always thought of himself as a teacher of literature, drowsing through uneventful days in an American college town. All at once he was the last of a mighty race, courting a murderess who had tortured his brethren" (139–140).

This is interesting enough for the way Cleopatra's anti-Semitism is invoked in the context of her liberal tolerance for "negroes," though her construction "they can't help being black"—as though it were a fault that needs to be excused—already suggests the potential proximity of that tolerance to racism. More interesting is the way the novel sees "race consciousness" as a product of racism itself, which functions as a form of social ascription of the individual to a racial identity. This in fact would take over from Kallen's problematically positive hereditary model of ethnic identity as perhaps the strongest and most enduring account of how race matters necessarily in the life of the ethnically or racially marked subject: it is American society that insists upon reading this marking as (for the most part negatively) significant, which the socialized subject has no choice but to feed back into the system as her own racial identification—only converting it, if possible, into a mark of pride, a badge of distinction, cultural capital.[69]

While Eugene Gant wards off the threat of "ordinariness" by (re-) claiming blood ties with his mad Parnassian family, and Helga Crane experiences her racial markings in Denmark, at least for a time, as a pleasurable form of individual "prominence," Mercado constructs his own individual/racial distinction by contrasting it with the disappointing ordinariness of the Russian anti-Semite herself, whom he had mistaken for a daringly original femme fatale. As he explains it to his traveling companion, Professor Halsey:

> She was essentially ordinary. . . . An ordinary person, he defined, is one whose reactions to life are governed by various external codes, and never by the exercise of their personal and peculiar mind. . . .
>
> Religions, patriotisms, ethical systems and standardized novels provide a large selection from which they are free to choose their feelings and ideas. . . . Society may be likened to an endless chain depending for its progress on a few real people, sports in the biological sense, who unless very careful, are outlawed. In the old days the "sports" normally rebelled against the current mythologies and were branded as heretics; nowadays . . . they become artists or revolutionists. (145–146)

Following the narrative logic that moves quickly from Mercado's fantasy of fighting as the "last of a mighty race" of Hebrew warrior kings to this articulation of an evolutionary elitism, the implication is that, confronted with murderous Russian racism, Mercado has been brought into consciousness not only of his Jewishness but also *simultaneously* of his artistic "individuality" as what he calls a "sport" (which Merriam-Webster's dictionary defines as "an individual exhibiting a sudden deviation from type beyond the normal limits of individual variation usually as a result of mutation especially of somatic tissue").

An impressive freak of nature, the sport is strongly reminiscent of the "genius" as defined by Kant, who is likewise one of "nature's elect," though the sport adds a sexy element of embodied outlawry to the mix. What is left out of this double construction, we notice, or rather is passed over in silence, is the category of the *ordinary Jewish person*—the Jew who passively accepts the religion and perhaps even reads "standardized novels." It would be wrong to say that this construction solves or even simply

		COLLECTIVITY	
THE INDIVIDUAL	THE FAMILY	ETHNIC CULTURE	MASS CULTURE
	DIFFERENCE		

Collectivity and difference: in postwar American fiction the family and the ethnos become the ground of the symbolic negotiation of the competing values of collectivity (or community) and difference, the ultimate redoubt of the latter being "individuality" defined as difference from everybody else.

dismisses the dilemma of ethnic homogeneity, by-product of the need for solidarity in the face of threats from without, that Kallen solves by folding personal individuality into hereditary group "individuality." Rather, much as "the family" does on a smaller social scale, this construction of ethnic individuality manages the problem by *not* resolving it, that is, by continually relaying the emphasis from term to term along a continuum of increasing social scale.

After the Second World War, cultural pluralism would gradually assert itself as an ideological dominant of the American campus, where talk of "diversity" is now everywhere in the air, and the complex dynamics of the ethnic family would prove to be one of the most productive of postwar literary themes. At this earlier historical moment, by contrast, the American college professor, grown tired of "inculcat[ing] overgrown schoolboys with embalmed classics" (21), must leave the pastoral milieu of the college in order to "expand [his] experience" (13) of difference: "'Our minds,'" Mercado tells his friend, "'are being stultified by monotony. Fifteen years on a university campus would turn a dragonfly into an oyster'" (15). Greensborough, it appears, has neither been influenced by progressive educational values nor ethnically diversified in the manner of NYU, whose expansion from its original suburban campus into the heart of downtown New York during this period was motivated in part by a desire to combine formal education with the stimulating experience of modern urban life. In the postwar period, as the following chapters will recount, the geographic trajectory of Loeb's ex-campus novel would routinely be reversed, and it would be urban-bohemian novelists like himself who would be invited out to the suburbs, out even to the cornfields of Iowa, to enliven the pastoral American campus.

Thomas Wolfe, meanwhile, upon the publication and fabulous success of *Look Homeward, Angel,* was freed at last from his enslavement to the university, and could turn his attention to expressing himself full time.

2

Understanding Iowa:
The Religion of Institutionalization

> "It's a curious machine," said the officer to the explorer,
> and despite the fact that he was well acquainted with the
> apparatus, he nevertheless looked at it with a certain
> admiration, as it were.
>
> FRANZ KAFKA, "In the Penal Colony"

> A WARNING TO THE READER: Do not read this book if you
> believe that writing is fun, fun, fun.
>
> PAUL ENGLE, *On Creative Writing*

FOUCAULT ON THE FARM

In a letter dated April 2, 1960, Flannery O'Connor took a moment to back-stab her friend Robie Macauley, who had been with her at the Iowa Writers' Workshop in the late 1940s when both were getting their Master of Fine Arts degrees there, and whose opinions she normally respected. Although he would soon coauthor a textbook called *Technique in Fiction* (1964), Macauley must at some point have expressed approval of a writer from the previous generation whose disregard for technique had become notorious—an object lesson in the badness that can result from uncontrolled "self-expression": "As for R.M.," she wrote to another friend, "he is a great admirer of Thomas Wolfe & in my opinion anybody that admires Thomas Wolfe can be expected to like good fiction only by accident."[1]

As we have seen, the combined effect of Wolfe's experiences at an innovative private day school in Asheville, and later at the University of North Carolina, and finally as a helplessly undisciplined student play-wright in George Pierce Baker's Drama 47 Workshop at Harvard had been to convince him that the central task of the literary artist must be to defend the sovereignty of his genius against any forces that might pre-sume to diminish or contain it. Coming of age in the 1920s and spraying himself across the pages of American literary history through the thirties, Wolfe produced novels that can be taken as emblematic exaggerations of the self-centered literary practices institutionalized in the new progressive educational activity called "creative writing," which, as codified in works like Stanwood Cobb's *Discovering the Genius Within You* (1932), sought to counter a "mob mind" that "does not wish us to devote ourselves to great achievements."[2]

The stories of Flannery O'Connor can be seen as the correction of those pages of American literary history in red pen. If Wolfe's fiction is best read by analogy to the cybernetic concept of positive feedback, whose dysfunctional form is the piercing shriek of the microphone, then O'Connor is a case study in modulation by way of negative feedback, in which the output of a system is to some degree reversed before re-entering it as input. This is the model of homeostasis, as when a thermom-eter registers the heat it has triggered as too high and temporarily shuts the heater down, and its literary version is a "classical" style that is neither maximalist nor minimalist, neither over- nor under-written: along with O'Connor, one might think of the lovely, not-too-challenging sentences of F. Scott Fitzgerald or of the consummately controlled-but-lively "good writing" of John Updike. The dysfunctional form of negative feedback, then, would be that of simple *silencing* by intimidation. This is what hap-pened to Nella Larsen when she was accused of plagiarism, and it is the threat against which the post-1960s "claiming voice" paradigm of minority and feminist fiction understands itself to struggle.

Although she, too, was a product of progressive education, having attended an experimental high school attached to her subsequent alma mater, Georgia State College for Women, O'Connor deeply regretted being coddled there as what she called a "self-expressive adolescent," feeling that she had lost out on the real education in the classics that even Wolfe had managed to acquire.[3] And while we can reasonably insist, nonetheless, that the systematic incorporation of creative writing in the curriculum of this progressive school may have had something to do with the writer she became, O'Connor's fiction was more overtly shaped by the institutionalization of painstaking craft in graduate creative writing programs in the postwar period. From her time at Iowa until her death in 1964 at the age of thirty-nine, O'Connor never once wavered from a disciplinary aesthetic regime as extreme, in its way, as Wolfe's blathering had been. Reminiscent instead of Wolfe's fellow Max Perkins protégé, Ernest Hemingway, who served as the model literary craftsman in the first several decades of the Program Era, she labored obsessively over each line of her prose, revising again and again. Unlike Hemingway, whose forms of narration varied over the course of his career, O'Connor employed the same precisely calibrated mode of narration—the "third person limited" form favored by Henry James and promoted by her mentors as the surest path to "impersonality"—in every one of her stories without exception.

The rise of the creative writing program in the postwar period presents a case study in dialectical conjoining of opposites: while the existence of degree-granting entities like the Iowa Writers' Workshop was the result, in part, of a new hospitality to self-expressive creativity on the part of progressive-minded universities willing to expand the boundaries of what could count as legitimate academic work, the founders and promoters of these programs more than met the institution halfway, rationalizing their presence in a scholarly environment by asserting their own disciplinary rigor. In Norman Foerster's contribution to the volume *Literary Scholar-*

22222

ship: Its Aims and Methods (1941), he argues for the propriety of "imaginative writing" to the scholarly domain on several grounds, including its utility for the student's understanding literature "from the inside," and the beneficial counter-example it might set to the "massive pedantry" of turgidly Germanic scholarly prose. Hired away from Wolfe's alma mater, the University of North Carolina, to head the newly constituted School of Letters at the University of Iowa, Foerster found himself in a position to act on his conviction of the "vitalizing interrelation between creation and scholarship," and his support was crucial to the establishment of the Program in Creative Writing, more familiarly known as the Iowa Writers' Workshop, at that institution.[4] In the same volume the Workshop's first director, Wilbur Schramm, insisted that the process of "long and arduous selection, emphasis, organization" which the creative writer must endure in completing his work "is comparable both in quality and in severity with the discipline of any other advanced literary study" (190). Creative writing should therefore be considered an "honorable discipline" which can "deepen and sharpen the minds of those students who pursue it seriously" (191).

Soon enough, the same arguments that had served Schramm in legitimating Creative Writing as a sufficiently arduous discipline had been fully converted into an entity that served, at Iowa and elsewhere, simultaneously as a pedagogical and a compositional method. Beginning in "self" but ending in disciplined "impersonality," this process was strongly reminiscent of the one described in James Joyce's *Portrait of the Artist as a Young Man* (1916), where the "personality of the artist, at first a cry or a cadence or a mood and then a fluid and lambent narrative, finally refines itself out of existence."[5] In 1961, in the preface to a large volume of stories and poems written exclusively by Iowa Workshop graduates, Schramm's more famous and long-standing successor as director of the program, Paul Engle, explained how students there, hearing their work discussed in class while they sat silent, were persuaded not to look "at writing as the spontaneous outpouring of immediate feeling."[6] Correcting the "excess of self-commitment" this betrays, the workshop provided an environment where "every word and every attitude is subject to constant scrutiny" (xxiv) under the communal gaze, forcing the student, if necessary by "terrifying" him, to assert the "control necessary to achieve form, without which the moving cry becomes only screaming" (xxv). Thus the "screaming" narcissist, internalizing the punitive authority of the peer group, becomes a "moving" masochist whose pain has become an occasion for refined aesthetic pleasure.

Whereas educational progressivism had assumed the inborn presence of an artist in every individual, who needed only to be set free from external constraints to flourish—and thus had had to do some fancy footwork to rationalize the role of externalities like the school in this process—the postwar creative writing program was founded on the assumption that artists are forged in the imposition of these institutional constraints upon unfettered creativity; its fancy footwork, reciprocally, would be put to the task of explaining the continuing import of inborn talent, the human "raw materials" with which the workshop works. Engle's colorful way of putting it was to say that "we do not pretend to grow blonde curls on an autumn pumpkin," admitting that "good poets, like good hybrid corn, are both born and made." Hitting upon a ready analogy for the pseudo-eugenic procedures of this negative making, Engle points to "Maxwell Perkins editing the massive manuscripts of Thomas Wolfe into presentable shape" as "the sort of teaching we believe can be done" (xxiv), and this indeed was the sort of teaching that Flannery O'Connor got. With its vision of teaching as akin to editing, the early rhetoric of the workshop was remarkably light on progressive-style paeans to the "nurturing" quality of the "community," and relatively vague about the positive knowledge it could impart to the budding artist. As O'Connor would put it, "I believe the teacher's work should be largely negative. . . . We can learn how *not* to write."[7]

If there was a positive element to workshop training—beyond the perennial call to "write what you know"—it was in the offering of examples: for creative writing pedagogues as well as for writers, the overriding approach was "show don't tell." Supplementing the charismatic presence of the writer at the head of the table were the published stories that students were encouraged to study, frequently gathered in textbooks edited by the instructors themselves. Indeed, in order to understand the institution of creative writing in the immediate postwar period, we need to see how this "institution" extends beyond its most literal definition as a community of common purpose housed in brick and mortar to encompass other, more obviously "virtual" institutional forms like those textbooks, which stabilized a set of literary values even as it put them in circulation throughout the U.S. educational system.

Of course, in a sense, all institutions are to some degree virtual entities, even ones with impressive physical plants to house them. The institution as such is a personating abstraction, a "corporation" in the philosophical-theological, and often also in the legal, sense. This is why, as Jeffrey Williams has noted, the meaning of "institution" ranges so easily in our usage from social organizations housed in buildings and supplied with proper names, such as the University of Iowa; to individuals like Henry James or James Joyce, who become "institutions" of a kind; to a more diffuse sense of institutions as "established practices," as in the institution of the family, or literature, or slavery.[8] It is an observable characteristic of institutions that they are understood relationally and analogically, with habitual disrespect for the distinction between public and private spheres, or between "repressive state apparatuses" (the army, the police) and "ideological state apparatuses" (the school, the media), as canonically defined by Louis Althusser. The adolescent tells himself that his high school is a "prison"; the corporation tells its employees that they are part of a "family": these sorts of analogies would prove crucial to the self-understanding of the creative writing program. If a social entity is vast enough—for example, society as such—we tend to cross over to terms like "system" or "economy" or "nation," and to analyze it not as an institution but as a collectivity of institutions.

Falling somewhere on the spectrum between the institution proper and the institution as established practice was the circulating aesthetic institution established by the textbook-anthology. This genre, typically taking the form of a collection of modern short stories lightly larded with editorial commentary and "questions for further study," would flourish after the passage of the G.I. Bill, when undergraduate enrollments in American colleges began their manifold increase, and the basic tenets of sophisticated formal literary analysis were disseminated to an unprecedented number of persons. Textbook-anthologies embodied much the same conception of literary value as the workshop, and they circulated throughout the system of higher education, introducing the elitist discourse of literary modernism to the self-same social masses it typically held in such contempt. There were many of these textbooks, including Wilbur Schramm's early entry into the field, *The Story Workshop* (1938), which makes the relay between the concrete and the virtual-textual institution quite clear in its title, and Caroline Gordon and Allen Tate's *The House of Fiction* (1950), which, quoting a famous phrase of Henry James's in its own title, would perform an institutionalization or "housing" of Jamesian narrative poetics in postwar pedagogical practice. But undoubtedly the most important of the postwar fiction textbooks, familiar to generations of students, was Cleanth Brooks and Robert Penn Warren's *Understanding Fiction* (1943 / 1959; a companion to their earlier poetry volume), which O'Connor used at Iowa and resonantly called her "bible," recommending it for years afterward to aspiring writers.

Although this textbook's central agenda was to encourage "close analytical and interpretive reading of concrete examples" of fiction—the famed New Critical practice of close reading—it understands that the "student reader of fiction" may also be a "student writer of fiction" and includes an appendix specifically directed at her. Excluding the historical and philological concerns that had dominated academic literary studies since the late nineteenth century, this textbook confirms how much the discipline of creative writing as we know it owes to the large-scale intrusion of practitioner-critics like Warren himself into the domain of literary scholars, beginning in the late 1930s.[9] The New Criticism put the point of view of the artist at the very center of postwar literary studies, where the New Critical textbook served as an aid to understanding, and potentially emulating, his "creative process." This idea—shielded from our hindsight by the notoriety of Wimsatt and Beardsley's "Intentional Fallacy" essay (1946/1954), but dominant until the Theory insurgency of the 1970s systematically reasserted the independence of the reader's interpretation from the author's intentions—was put most explicitly in novelist Caroline Gordon's treatise *How to Read a Novel* (1957).[10] Here O'Connor's longtime mentor argued that if "we are to become good readers of fiction" we must understand reading both as a "self-abasement" before the authority of the author and as a humble "kind of collaboration" with that author. "By putting ourselves, as best we can, in his place, we share to some extent in the sacrifice he made in order to write his book and are therefore in a position to reap our share of the rewards."[11] The potentially formative effect of the New Critical textbook institution, and its capacity to reproduce itself over time, are powerfully exemplified in O'Connor's case: obediently studying the stories and commentary in the 1943 edition of *Understanding Fiction* in her Iowa City boarding house, she saw one of her own stories, "A Good Man is Hard to Find," included in the revised edition of the textbook published in 1959.

But the stories of Flannery O'Connor were more than simply a product of a multivalent institutionalization of the value of painstaking craft at mid-century. Even as she was doggedly faithful—outside of her bracingly opinionated lectures and essays—to the dictum "show don't tell," her stories can also be read as passionate allegorical arguments for the necessary pleasures of the "discipline" they so famously manifest. Indeed, in O'Connor's thinking, the significance of this term and its cognate, "limitation," extended far beyond the domain of the literary. If one of the central projects of educational progressivism had been to make room for Eros in education, conceiving it as the provocation of the student's built-in desire to learn, she instead saw it as the task of the school to *instill* appropriate forms of desire in the student, if necessary through the infliction of pain. "For the reading of literature ever to become a habit and a pleasure," she wrote, "it must first be a discipline." And "if the student finds that this is not to his taste? Well, that is regrettable. Most regrettable.

His taste should not be consulted; it is being formed."[12] For O'Connor, a devout Catholic who made something of a show of her obedience to the institutional authority of the Church, not only was religion understood as a kind of discipline, a willed acceptance of human "limitation" before an Almighty God; but so was discipline itself a kind of religion, an article of faith arguably as basic to her thinking and writing as her specifically theological commitments. Discipline meant obedience to rules, and rules were established and maintained by institutions; and to submit to the authority of these institutions, while painful, was also a source of great potential pleasure, aesthetic and otherwise. Not that O'Connor's sense of institutions was either monolithic or simplistic. Seen in the light of her devotion to the Church, the authority of worldly liberal institutions like universities was certainly questionable, and subject to her usual humorous derision. And yet the habit of obedience to the one was obviously transposable, under the right conditions, to the other, where what Sarah Gordon has called her "obedient imagination" could be cultivated as a specifically literary resource.[13]

Thus, in O'Connor, the discipline of narrative form can be seen as a masochistic aesthetics of institutionalization. The model of institutional authority here, as everywhere in the modern Europeanized West, is the transcendental authority of the Church (the model of executive authority being the king), but as it unfolds in her work the aesthetics of institutionalization becomes applicable to various secular entities including the school, the family, the community, and the state. This project is powerfully alert to the threats that institutionalization might seem to pose to the romantic conceptions of artistic individuality reinforced in and by educational progressivism, but more concerned to make a case for the many possibilities that emerge from limitation and obedience. In this, although she speaks from the opposite side of the political spectrum and with a different affective investment in its truth, O'Connor prefigures Michel Foucault's insistence, in *Discipline and Punish* (translated in 1977), that "we must cease once and for all to describe the effects of power in negative terms: it 'excludes', it 'represses', it 'censors'. . . . In fact, power produces."[14] From this perspective, while "power" should be understood to be in force even in such things as the "freeing" progressive educational regime of "self-expression"—which could, after all, be redescribed as subtly coerced testimony—so must the apparent negativity of discipline be understood as productive. O'Connor's more succinct formulation simply insisted that "possibility and limitation mean about the same thing."[15] She is thus not only one of the first major figures of what I am calling the Program Era, when American writers in large numbers made their first awkward professional embrace of institutions like the Iowa Writers' Workshop, but also one of the prime rhetoricians of the transformation of literary modernism into a discourse of institutional being.

PROCESSING IMPERSONALITY

We don't tend to think of Flannery O'Connor as a producer of self-referential metafiction, or as a writer of "postmodern" sensibilities, however they might be defined; she is rather known as a regionalist, a literary mode whose commitment to the observable specificities of place might seem also to commit it to realism—or, at most, to the highly self-conscious yokelism of a work like Wilbur Schramm's *Windwagon Smith and Other Yarns* (1941), with its tall tales of flying tractors and prairie schooners that literally sail across the empty landscape of the Midwest. To the extent that O'Connor's stories obviously stray from a realist mode of representation, they do so, famously enough, in the direction of an aesthetic of the "grotesque" whose excesses O'Connor nonetheless defended as "a kind of realism" which "lean[s] away from typical social patterns toward mystery and the unexpected."[16] O'Connor's narratives do contain oddballs who do unexpected things for mysterious reasons, but the stories don't often, for all that, take a metafictional turn, drawing attention to the mystery of narrative itself. Rarely in her fiction does one even encounter an enthusiastic storyteller—to represent the *raconteur* in action is perhaps inevitably to invite a heightened reflexivity into one's text—although O'Connor claimed that a fervor for storytelling was one of the things that distinguished her region from others, especially the North. As she put it in a panel discussion held at Wesleyan College in Macon, Georgia, "I have Boston cousins and when they come South they discuss problems, they don't tell stories. We tell stories."[17] And yet she did not often write stories about storytelling.

Be that as it may, it's hard to know what other than "metafiction" to call her story "The Crop" (1947), which she wrote when she was a student at Iowa and included in the collection of six stories that made up a master's thesis dedicated to the Workshop director, Paul Engle. The events of this story about storytelling begin just as the tedious daily ritual of a family breakfast, held at a "regular hour" so as to encourage "other regular habits," concludes.[18] Miss Willerton, free at last from the tedium of this "system in their eating," is left alone to crumb the table and ponder the story she is about to write: "First, she had to think of a subject to write a story about. There were so many subjects to write stories about that Miss Willerton never could think of one. That was always the hardest part of writing a story she always said" (732). Representing Miss Willerton's individual authorship as an inauthentically mechanical enterprise, this announces what will prove to be a mercilessly satirical metafiction, a catalogue of amateur literary mistakes.

And indeed, turning to the first pages of Schramm's *The Story Workshop*, one finds a chapter titled "What Shall I Write About?" Here at the outset of this textbook, as at the outset of Miss Willerton's day, the question posed is one of subject, and it seems uncannily like a prospective rebuke to the would-be Southern lady writer when Schramm warns that great stories "are written not because someone says, 'Go to! I shall write a short story. Now—ho hum—let me see. What shall I write about?' They are written because someone has a story aching to be told."[19] Nevertheless, continuing to ponder her options in just this manner, Miss Willerton considers writing a story about foreign bakers, who are "very picturesque," or about schoolteachers, who are, on second thought, not "timely" enough, not "even a social problem": "Social problem. Social problem. Hmmm. Sharecroppers! Miss Willerton had never been intimately connected with sharecroppers but, she reflected, they would make as arty a subject as any, and they would give her that air of social concern which was so valuable to have in the circles she was hoping to travel!" Momentarily representing her thoughts directly, then dropping back into a more conventional, if equally damning, third person limited narration, O'Connor shows Miss Willerton to be ignoring Schramm's advice to writers to "look into your own heart" for literary material, to write "about things near and dear to you, things you feel and know."[20]

Not only is Miss Willerton neglecting to write what she knows, but she is doing so as a cynical ploy for advancement in an "arty" liberal crowd. These are some of the many people whose view of fiction, as O'Connor would often complain, has had a "dreary blight" cast over it by "social science."[21] Indeed for her, as for many other conservative Southern intellectuals whom she read, respected, and knew personally, this adoption of the perspective of "Northern" social science was tantamount to treason. Associated with the progressive urban intellectualism of places like Chicago and New York, "social science" and "sociology" were shorthand among this group for the condescension to and pathologization of the South that had begun with H. L. Mencken's infamously mocking "Sahara of the Bozarts" essay, which facetiously called for a systematic study of the "cranial indices" of the region's many morons. This attitude had been exacerbated by the hugely embarrassing mega-bestsellers of the traitorous Georgian novelist Erskine Caldwell, *Tobacco Road* (1932) and *God's Little Acre* (1933), which, like Miss Willerton's story, focus on the lives of ignorant, violent, and wildly libidinous white Southern sharecroppers. Presuming to remedy these pathologies, the progressive social sciences were of a piece with the project of Southern "modernization" that O'Connor's teachers, including her adviser at Iowa, the former Fugitive-Agrarian Andrew Lytle, had tried to resist. Given the contempt with which sociology is treated here and elsewhere in her writings, one is surprised to find that only a few years earlier, in college, O'Connor had majored not in English but in Social Studies, taking classes such as "Current Social Problems" and "Current Economic Problems" to fulfill the requirements for her degree. She had furthermore showed up at Iowa to study journalism—another domain strongly associated with the investigation of "social problems"—and only appealed to Paul Engle for admission to the fiction workshop a year later.[22]

But that, as several critics have noted, is the rule of O'Connor's satire: it is frequently shot through with strong biographical connections between the satirist and her targets. It is not surprising, then, if one frequently sees the traces, in "The Crop," of the complex psychodynamics of its autopoetic construction. Not only this would-be writer, but the several irritated young intellectuals and artists O'Connor would go on to invent— Hulga in "Good Country People" (1955), Asbury in "The Enduring Chill" (1958), Julian in "Everything That Rises Must Converge" (1961), all of them living with their mothers, as O'Connor was forced to do when she fell ill with lupus—and many other characters besides, produce the same effect. Here in "The Crop," as Frederick Asals has suggested, the satirical autobiographical projection is put to a specific purpose: it is the risk the story must take so that it can work as a kind of auto-exorcism, on O'Connor's part, of the spirit of the amateur "penwoman."[23] Although she is a writer of sorts, Miss Willerton is precisely the kind of writer whom O'Connor herself—impressively credentialed by the Iowa Writers' Workshop partly in recognition of *this very story*—will soon, thank God, have avoided becoming. "The woods are full of regional writers," she shuddered in one of her lectures, "and it is the great horror of every serious Southern writer that he will become one of them."[24]

The metafictional exorcism conducted in "The Crop" would work, as the religious practice of exorcism always has, by casting out the evil spirit with words. But in this case the words remain on the page, objectified in and as the construction of a fictional character. And who can fail to see how this structure allows the exorcised figure to linger in the composition, waiting to trouble a too-neat separation of author and "author"? From our perspective, that is, this is bound to look like a failed exorcism, or at least an incomplete one. For instance, are we supposed to see the following sequence as merely laughable?

"Lot Motun," the typewriter registered, "called his dog."
"Dog" was followed by an abrupt pause. Miss Willerton always did her best work on the first sentence. "First sentences,"
she always said, "came to her—like a flash! Just like a flash!"
she would say and snap her fingers, "like a flash!" And she built
her story up from them. "Lot Motun called his dog" had been
automatic with Miss Willerton, and reading the sentence over,
she decided that not only was "Lot Motun" a good name for
a sharecropper, but also that having him call his dog was an
excellent thing to have a sharecropper do. "The dog pricked
up its ears and slunk over to Lot." Miss Willerton had the sentence down before she realized her error—two "Lots" in one
paragraph. That was displeasing to the ear. The typewriter
grated back and Miss Willerton applied three x's to "Lot."
Over it she wrote in pencil, "him." (734)

Here the narrator's mockery of Miss Willerton's facile enthusiasm for first
sentences sits awkwardly with the woman's obvious concern for revision
and the careful crafting of sentences. So too the verb "slunk," not a little
evocative of the movement of yard dogs, is pure Flannery O'Connor, who
would unironically avail herself of it in the stories "The Comforts of
Home" and "Parker's Back." Similarly, we might then compare Miss Willerton's "[building] her story up" from the first sentence to O'Connor's description, in later years, of how she began to write "Good Country People": "I merely found myself one morning writing a description of two
women that I knew something about, and before I realized it, I had
equipped one of them with a daughter with a wooden leg."[25] The difference here is that while O'Connor presumably writes what she knows—in
fact her class-conscious mother was adamant in denying that her daughter
ever consorted with the lowly folk who so often appear in her stories—
Miss Willerton knows about sharecroppers only from the best-selling fiction she has read.

But if Miss Willerton does not write what she knows, she certainly cannot be accused of not knowing what she writes: apparently she is an obsessive stylist, just as O'Connor was learning to be at Iowa. And if she cannot be fully exorcised, then perhaps a better strategy is one that will attempt, not to eliminate, but to discipline her. O'Connor does this by literalizing Miss Willerton's excessive "involvement" in the story she is writing as her conversion from its impersonal author into a participant character. This occurs after her imagination, dissatisfied with realism, gives the "shaggy" sharecropper straight teeth and the romantic "nonchalance" of a natural gentleman, and then provides him with a dubiously appealing female companion: "The woman would be more or less pretty—yellow hair, fat ankles, muddy-colored eyes." When soon enough the sharecroppers she is inventing fall into the kind of hateful, lunging knife fight that she imagines sharecropper couples frequently have, Miss Willerton can "stand it no longer. She struck the woman a terrific blow on the head from behind. The knife dropped out of her hands and a mist swept her from the room. Miss Willerton turned to Lot. 'Let me get you some hot grits,' she said" (736).

Thus Miss Willerton, as author, is shown to have an affliction traditionally associated in the modernist tradition with female *readers* like Flaubert's Madame Bovary, who cannot distinguish fact from fantasy.[26] Closer at hand was Eudora Welty's "A Piece of News" (1942), included in *Understanding Fiction,* which portrays the confused panic of a simple backwoods woman who happens upon an old newspaper article about someone with her (very common) name being shot in the leg by her husband, and now frantically fears her own husband's return. In this case, somewhat as though Welty herself were shoved into her own condescending story, Miss Willerton enters the lower-class fictional world she is in the midst of creating to become a sharecropper's wife. This violates *thematically* what, in the Jamesian narrative poetics favored and codified in the New Criticism, is considered the cardinal *formal* sin of pre-modernist narration: authorial intrusion. As O'Connor summarized it in one of her many talks to college creative writing classes, "The novel as we usually find it today is [characterized by] the disappearance from it of the author" who had been so apt to draw attention to himself in earlier times. Effacing this pontifica-tory presence, that is, the modern writer works "by showing, not by say-ing,"[27] leaving the reader to figure out the larger significance of the story on her own.

And yet it seems significant that Miss Willerton's authorial intru-sion is not represented here as a function of her narrative method: we do not see her indulge in the narratorial act of "saying" instead of "show-ing," or see her lapse into first person narration, or any other violation of the Jamesian "dramatic method." Indeed, precisely as James would have wished, the scenically represented action is limited to the intimately re-corded perspective of one character at a time, a mode which Gordon and Tate called the "Technique of the Central Intelligence," and which more recently has come to be called "third person limited" narration. Here a dis-embodied narrator is understood to hover above the focalizing character in a dimension whose impersonal separateness from the space-time repre-sented in the novel is built into its grammatical structure. The more recent term for that technique, though somewhat drab, is felicitous in at least one respect: it suggests not only the nature but one of the perceived appeals of this narrative mode. In staging a *limitation* of knowledge—a substantial eclipse of the omniscience whose display, by logical implication, is always an option for the godlike author—it purports to *gain* something. What is gained is, among other things, "experiential intensity." This intensity is shared by diegetically-embodied first person narrators who speak "from experience" but is in theory improved by the removal of this speaking in favor of an ironically more direct, because disinterested, narration-from-without. (In third person limited narration, that is, we see what the char-acter *really* feels, not what he *says* he feels.) Furthermore, in retaining, if only as a spectral effect of grammar, a disembodied "higher" presence in the text, third person limited narration could be said to continually rein-force the limitedness of the central character's point of view—to ironize it in a way that only the most flagrantly "unreliable" first person narrators do for themselves.

It was Thomas Wolfe's achievement, in *Look Homeward, Angel* and elsewhere, to have all but eradicated this ironic distance, putting the authority of his third person narrator to work attesting to the genius of the novel's autobiographical central character. For Wolfe, that is, the "third person" was a special effect of what was essentially first person narration. It was Flannery O'Connor's achievement, beginning in "The Crop," to maximize the ironic distance between her central focalizing characters and her disembodied narrators, and to attest thereby to the cognitive limits of any embodied human life, including certainly the author's fragilely embodied own. In her fiction all human beings are always ridiculous imbeciles, which suggests that the point of view from which they are being observed is a perfect place indeed. One could say that her third person narration aspires to the unimaginable condition of "fourth person" narration —narration from a higher dimension.

Leaving this form intact even as Miss Willerton fantasizes herself into her own story, "Willie's" acts of writing are now taken up and absorbed into "The Crop's" own narration, which continues to tell her tragic tale of love amidst crop failure with her as a character in it, as though without her help. In other words, while its content grows increasingly ridiculous, its narrative form remains rigorously impersonal. If the description of Miss Willerton's relationship with Lot Motun is to be understood, as on one level it must, as an emanation of her narcissistic imagination, she proves herself dangerously indistinguishable from O'Connor herself: "Willie woke in the night [in Lot Motun's bed] conscious of a pain. It was a soft green pain with purple lights running through it. She wondered if she were awake. Her head rolled from side to side and there were droning shapes grinding boulders in it" (738). Perched ambiguously between wakefulness and dream, reality and fiction, this O'Connoresque rendering of pain is an accurate representation of the story's own thoroughly ambiguous status, as the dialectical relation of author-as-character and author-as-narrator continues to oscillate across narrative levels. In effect, then, the story becomes an allegory *simultaneously* of authorial intrusion

(Miss Willerton/O'Connor enters her own story) *and* of narrative impersonalization (Miss Willerton/O'Connor is effaced from the narration of
that story).

If this metafiction attempts to exorcise the spirit of the literary amateur from O'Connor's career, it also announces another project on
O'Connor's part: the disciplining of the egoistic authorial self with the
whip of impersonal narrative form. In the ironically amateurish heavy-
handedness of its satire, "The Crop" allows us to see this project at its
point of first assemblage. Later versions would be more subtle, and would
be put to other thematic ends, but the structure would be essentially the
same: the author simultaneously commits a "sin" of individual pride (as
autobiographical projection, as character) and punishes herself for it (as
impersonal narrator). Enabled by the amalgam of intimacy-and-distance
embedded in third person limited narration, this auto-punitive enterprise
could be described as the narrative equivalent of self-flagellation.

Although this structure can be seen to be at work in O'Connor's two
novels, it is more essentially attuned—as indeed were both the workshop
setting and the textbook anthology—to the short story form. Because the
shortness of the short story enables the student to study a sequence of
aesthetic "unities" (a crucial term for New Criticism) rather than mere ex-
cerpts of larger forms, it enables the writing student to engage in the corrective repetitions we call "training"—or, in O'Connor's case, to approximate the staccato action of spanking. As Alfred Kazin put it in a review of
her *Complete Stories* (1971), where the sheer sameness of her output became easier to perceive, "Each story was complete, sentence by sentence.
And each sentence was a hard, straight, altogether complete version of
her subject: human deficiency, sin, error."[28] Thus, while the repetitiveness
of Thomas Wolfe *within* his monstrously discursive novels was one of the
signs of his sloppiness as a writer, O'Connor could be said to have written
the same perfectly crafted short story again and again. No wonder, then,
that they sometimes seem pre-packaged for close reading in the classroom:
they are, in essence, a systematic production of that institutional space,
and of its virtual supplement, the New Critical textbook. And indeed,

A 1941 promotional photo showing the dedicatee of O'Connor's Iowa Master's thesis, program director Paul Engle, at his desk with a whip. Whether he intends to use it on himself or someone else is not clear. Photograph from the *Des Moines Register.*

O'Connor's was only an unusually extreme execution of the writing program aesthetic that understood the writer's process, on the Joycean model, as a disciplining of the individual authorial voice. Any one of her fellow students, teachers, colleagues, and friends, even the godless ones—even the ones who spent most of their time in Iowa City stinking drunk—might have agreed with her when she told Betty Hester that "all writing is painful and . . . if it is not painful then it is not worth doing" (*Habit,* 242).

This way of reading O'Connor rather flagrantly puts her person back into her "impersonal" narration. Not only must we rely on our knowledge of the author's biography in doing so, but we more or less dismiss the relevance of a potential distinction between O'Connor as author and her impersonal narrators, merely insisting that we see that narrator as only a partial manifestation of a larger autopoetic process that also involves the construction of her characters. Thus we might seem to flout O'Connor's own New Critical understanding of how literature should be read. But in R. V. Cassill's first entry into the textbook genre, *Writing Fiction* (1962)—his name would become familiar to later generations of students as the editor of the 1978 *Norton Anthology of Short Fiction*—this prominent Iowa (later Brown University) creative writing teacher prescribed the autopoetic compositional process thusly: "The writer of an original story begins to shape his material by accepting an emotional commitment to it—very much as if he himself were the first character to appear in the story to be." This "scaffolding" is then "totally replaced by structural elements of the story itself before the story is done."[29]

From this perspective, even a project like O'Connor's, formulated in strict opposition to the idea of "self-expression," can be seen as the expression of a self, however heavy the scare quotes we might wish to put around the relevant terms. In fact, upon closer inspection, the New Criticism was not as rigorous in removing the biographical identity of the author from consideration in the close reading of the literary text as it is sometimes assumed, and as figures like T. S. Eliot would no doubt have preferred. For instance, the edition of *Understanding Fiction* that contained O'Connor's "A Good Man is Hard to Find" also contained several essays in which a given author—including Katherine Anne Porter, John Cheever, Eudora Welty, and Robert Penn Warren himself—"undertakes to give the genesis of a story and its relation to his personal life," thus demonstrating to the student that "formal considerations spring from deep personal urgencies."[30]

Thus the literary historian doesn't commit too large an offense against the church of "impersonality" when he attempts, in a sense, to reverse-engineer the "urgent" process of formal impersonalization in O'Connor. This task is complementary to the one conducted in the previous chapter, where the solipsistic-seeming self-expression of a writer like Thomas Wolfe was traced back to the conventions, literary and educational, that occasioned and structured it. In doing this, we can take seriously the concessions even O'Connor must make to the idea that something like "self-expression" is fundamental to literary production. Feeding literary production from the trough of "personal experience," the idea of "self-expression" is not obliterated in the postwar formation but is rotated to the minor position in relation to the more widely touted cluster of values that includes impersonality, technique, and self-discipline. In other words, the dictum "write what you know" (from personal experience) is not negated by the dictum "show don't tell," but is folded into a larger entity that includes both positive and prohibitive imperatives (something like "show, don't tell, what you know"). As a minor term in a dialectical binary, "self-expression" lies in wait, ready to reassert itself not as a contributory feature of the literary work but as the end-point of it all. It was already doing so in the Beat movement in the 1950s and would soon do so on an even larger scale in the progressive educational revival of the 1960s, which saw the emergence of the now ubiquitous pedagogical imperative to "find your voice."

When her friend Betty Hester noticed the uncanny similarities between O'Connor and her character Hulga in "Good Country People," O'Connor responded at length:

> Your comments on how much of oneself one reveals in the work are a little too sweeping for me. Now I understand that something of oneself gets through and often something that one is not conscious of. Also to have sympathy for any character, you have to put a good deal of yourself in him. But to say that any complete denudation of the writer occurs in the successful work is, according to me, a romantic exaggeration. A great part of the art of it is precisely in seeing that this does not happen. . . . Those elements of the personality that don't bear on the subject at hand are excluded. Stories don't lie when left to themselves. Everything has to be subordinated to a whole which is not you. Any story I reveal myself completely in will be a bad story. (*Habit,* 105)

Of course, O'Connor's main purpose here is to deflect her friend's attention away from the denuding "biographical" to the "impersonal" reading

of her story, and to reject the romantic notion that the literary work succeeds to the degree that it fully manifests the selfhood of the author. But
one can see, even here, how she builds concessions to that authorial self
back into the story, at least as a function of *process*. What survives this disciplinary process in "Good Country People" is a character, Hulga, who is a
single Southern woman in her thirties with a Ph.D. in philosophy, who
lives, because of her compromised physical mobility, at the family farm
with her widowed mother, and who has a congenital illness she knows
she's likely to die from in middle age. The differences between her and
O'Connor are unimportant but for two of them: while Hulga is a philosophical nihilist, O'Connor is an orthodox Catholic; and while Hulga has a
Ph.D., O'Connor has only an M.F.A. Outranking her author, Hulga is predictably punished for her godless intellectual pride through the agency of
the "simple" bible salesman who sexually humiliates her and steals her
wooden leg. So much for the process of impersonalization in "Good
Country People." When, as in "The Crop," the writing process *itself* becomes part of the representational "whole" toward which a story aims,
these acts of *exclusion* are paradoxically *included,* and you get the hall of
mirrors of metafiction, where you write what you know by showing how
you tell. But in either case—and in this O'Connor speaks to the condition
of so many postwar writers—you will be showing what you've learned in
school.

LIMITATION THEOLOGY: REGIONALIST INSTITUTIONS

It would be wrong to say that the Iowa Writers' Workshop was an epiphe-
nomenon of literary regionalism, but not entirely wrong. As detailed by
Stephen Wilbers in his quasi-official history of the program, it did emerge
amidst a thriving, self-consciously Midwestern cultural scene, and it was
infused with further regionalist consciousness by the several prominently
southern Southerners who traveled north to teach and study there in the
early years of its existence.[31] Opposed equally to a dislocated mass culture
and to a deracinated cosmopolitan high culture, regionalism's celebration

of the particularities of place was fundamental to the aesthetic sensibilities imparted at Iowa, and to the continuing power of the injunction to the individual writer, raised among those particularities, to "write what you know." The very term "workshop," which may have seemed a little odd when it was used to describe George Pierce Baker's playwriting classes at pompous old Harvard, would seem well fitted to a writing class conducted in Iowa City, hard by the seasonal practicalities of a farm economy.

It would be more accurate, though, to say that the Iowa Writers' Workshop was a product of the moment when regionalist literary institutions, which had always been peeking over their shoulders at New York City in any case, turned to face the imperial capital of U.S. cultural production head on. Coming of age in the early 1920s, Thomas Wolfe had hightailed it out of North Carolina, first to Cambridge, then to New York City and Europe. This was the natural trajectory for an American writer, like him, of unlimited ambitions, the only significant geographical boundary to his expansive "genius" being, in the tradition of Whitman, the vastness of the U.S. nation-space. Beginning in the 1930s, however, regional literary institutions began to see themselves as competing with those centered in the Northeast and, because of their proximity to the rural American "heartland," as having a potentially more significant claim to a nationally representative status. John Frederick's changing the title of *Midland: A Magazine of the Middle West,* which he edited for many years in Iowa City, to *Midland: A National Literary Magazine* might be taken as emblematic of this heady regionalist/nationalist moment, which was also, necessarily, a moment of crisis for regionalism, since the very sense of cultural difference from the national, New York-centered mainstream which had been its inspiration was here confronted with the possibility of its dissolution by expansion. How could regionalist institutions go national and also, as we say, keep it real? This was also the time when the journals edited by former Fugitive-Agrarians at small Southern schools—the *Kenyon Review, Sewanee Review,* and *Southern Review*—became among the most prestigious literary journals in the United States, venues where any serious writer or critic, from whatever part of the country, might fervently wish to publish his or her work.

The establishment of the Iowa Writers' Workshop, however, provides an even better emblem of regionalism's increasingly outward orientation than the nationalizing of the piddling *Midland,* which soon went out of business in any case. Though it was constructed from the outset with an eye to acquiring national prestige for a regional institution, the Workshop eventually lunged, as it were, clear over the border of the nation and established itself—in its own mind at least—as a prestigious *international* center for writers. This aspect of the Iowa phenomenon was owed mainly to the efforts of the regionalist-poet-turned-liberal-internationalist, Paul Engle, and is likely to surprise those who think of Iowa only as the engine of high literary American whiteness—which, make no mistake, it also was. But not only did the Workshop early on begin to recruit American minority writers to the program—for example Margaret Walker, who took a Master's degree in poetry writing in 1940 and returned to write the novel *Jubilee* (1966) as a doctoral dissertation in the early 1960s—but since the 1950s, Wilbers notes, "Engle had been bringing to Iowa City writers from Ireland, Japan, Taiwan, South Korea, the Philippines, Iran, Canada, England, and Sweden."[32] Engle's formation, in 1963, of the International Writing Program, co-directed by his wife, the transplanted Chinese novelist Hauling Nieh, marked the outermost reach of the regionalist, nationalist, and internationalist ideologies in play in Iowa City in these years, and the publication of anthologies like *The World Comes to Iowa* (1980) was meant, reciprocally, to project the reputation of Iowa farther out into the world. It was a complex palimpsest of cultural geographies, none of them succeeding in fully canceling out the others; the common polestar of this regionalist/nationalist/internationalist tangle was the pursuit of institutional and individual prestige. As Engle put it, explaining his take on the matter, "I have the warmest feelings about the Midwest and have written much about it, but the Workshop had to strive for excellence, not localism."[33] In other words, "localism" was no longer the path to "excellence" it had only recently seemed.

Not everyone agreed. We can make at least one very broad distinction between the two regionalisms, Midwestern and Southern, that crossed paths at the Iowa Writers' Workshop during and after the Second World War. While both were caught up in larger historical trends toward institutional growth that tested their definitional borders, the explicit ideological trajectory of the two moved in opposing directions. Put simply, while Midwestern regionalism, as exemplified in Engle, looked outward and sought prestige through expansion, the Southern regionalists insisted that the regionalist project must turn inward and achieve literary excellence through exclusion, through the willed imposition of limits.

Embedded in these positions are two different conceptions of what, in essence, an institution is. For figures like Engle the institution was a social *technology,* a way of mobilizing human and other resources to achieve external ends. For figures like O'Connor, however, the institution was an embodiment of *tradition,* a place where the authority of past practices is contained and conserved.[34] This accords with what David Holman has noted are the two substantially different mythical personae underlying the two regionalisms: the Midwestern pioneer, on the one hand, who is a seeker, a traveler with his eye on the next horizon; and, on the other, the aristocratic Southern planter who lives happily within the bounds of his organic traditional society.[35] Given these opposing emphases, it is perhaps predictable that the "Midwestern" soon weakened as a meaningful contemporary regionalism in American culture.

Meanwhile a distinctly and self-consciously Southern tradition in American writing, especially fiction, continues unbroken to this day.[36] This was accomplished even as these self-same spiritually separatist ideologues of Southern regionalism were largely responsible for establishing New Critical pedagogy as a feature of U.S. education on a national scale. And that *this* could be true alerts us to the, in a sense, *merely* ideological nature of the split I am describing: as both sides met at Iowa, so both never ceased to inhabit the same higher educational system, a system capable, for instance, of removing figures like Robert Penn Warren and Cleanth Brooks from their lovely Southern habitats and installing them at stone-cold Yale.

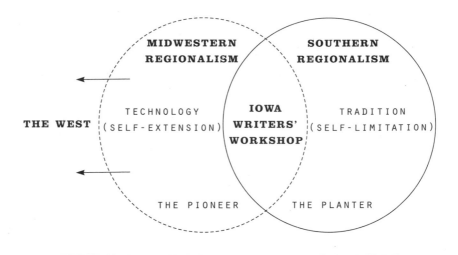

The Iowa Writers' Workshop is born in the conjunction of two regionalisms, Midwestern and Southern, with two competing emphases and two distinct characteristic historical figures.

Like the textbooks that made them famous, these figures circulated nationally. In order to understand Iowa as an institution, then, these two opposing impulses of regionalism, the expansive and the limiting, the technological and the traditional, should be seen as two elements of one dialectical configuration, subject to all of the interpenetration and ironic mirroring that this implies. In fact, this dynamic is thoroughly characteristic of the postwar higher educational system as a whole, which has grown ever larger even as the diversity of its activities has increased, which has assimilated ever-greater numbers of students and made ever-greater numbers of distinctions between them. No doubt this is common to all modern institutions, a formal principle of their systemic development. Modern institutions, that is, tend to grow simultaneously larger and more internally differentiated, or complex.

Nowhere is the Southern regionalist impulse to impose limits more evident than in Allen Tate's essay "The New Provincialism" (1945), which asked some very basic questions of regional, national, and international cultural geography as the Second World War began to wind down: "Will the new literature of the South, or of the United States as a whole, be different from anything that we knew before the war? Will American literature be more alike all over the country? And more like the literature of the world?"[37] Without explicitly prophesying answers to any of these questions, Tate makes his own preferences abundantly clear: he would have Southern literature retain its distinction both from American literature and from World literature, neither of which can hope to share in the South's "local continuity in tradition and belief." Indeed, for him, "mere regionalism, as we have heard it talked about in recent years, is not enough. For this picturesque regionalism of local color is a byproduct of nationalism" (536). Dissatisfied with theorizations of the sort proposed by New South progressives like UNC's Howard Odum, for whom regionalism was indeed the very form of a healthily pluralist American nationalism, and satisfied still less with regional stereotypes, like Erskine Caldwell's, concocted for national mass consumption, Tate wanted a more severe form of intra-national cultural difference.

Equally problematic for Tate, and the central target of the essay, is what he calls the "New Provincialism." This was his term for a literary internationalism that wishes, as he put it, to overcome the "limitations of the mere regional interest," trading them "for a 'universal' point of view, a political or social doctrine which would 'relate' or 'integrate' the local community with the world." This in effect is to envision the world as "one vast region." But this "is the trouble with our world schemes today: they contemplate a large extension of the political and philosophical limitations of the regional principle. 'Let's get closer to the Chinese.' 'Know your fellow men, and you will like them better, and cease to fight them'" (537). For Tate, while there are no limits to the claims of the Southern past upon the Southern present, there are absolute spatial-geographical limits to the scale upon which the felicitous "limitations" of "regional principle" can operate. To exceed them is merely to produce an inflated "provincialism" unmoored from the authenticity guaranteed by shared experience. Although this was not written as a cruel rebuke to Paul Engle, with its dig at "getting close to the Chinese," it might as well have been. Engle's regionalism was what nowadays we might call a "post-regionalism"—regionalism unbound, unlimited. Tate, by contrast, wished to reestablish limits.

And so, for that matter, did Flannery O'Connor; and so did O'Connor's adviser at the Iowa Workshop, Andrew Lytle, a novelist and lifelong creative writing instructor (he founded the program at the University of Florida) who supervised her as she was drafting *Wise Blood* during her third year in Iowa City. And so did the Southern novelist Caroline Gordon, who soon thereafter took over from Lytle as O'Connor's lifelong mentor and first reader. Gordon was married to her co-editor of the *House of Fiction*, the former Fugitive-Agrarian Allen Tate, who was himself a lifelong friend of Lytle's (and Warren's and Brooks's et al.). The attraction of this close-knit group of conservative Southern intellectuals to the idea—indeed to the very term, which peppers their writings—of "limitation" is striking. It could in fact be said that their interest in limitation far exceeded the limits of their concern for regionalism, and that the appeal of regionalism itself may have stemmed from a broader commitment to the idea—more precisely, the ethos—of limitation *as such*.

For instance, Gordon and Tate's case for "limited" forms of narration—either embodied first persons or, preferably, Jamesian third person limited—as against profligate displays of free-ranging narrative "omniscience" seems easy enough to map to a system of belief concerned to stress the limits of merely human knowledge and experience, as represented by fictional characters, in the face of ultimate Mysteries; and this in turn can be mapped to the Southern regionalism that claimed cataclysmic defeat in the Civil War as a hard-won lesson in human limitation. But so too did "limitations" enter into O'Connor's conception of the proper attitude of any serious writer, who must "first of all be aware of his limitations as an artist—for art transcends its limitations only by staying within them."[38] Later she adds a specifically modernist dimension to the idea of limitation, echoing Clement Greenberg's arguments for the aesthetic virtues of medium-specificity: "It has been my experience that in the process of making a novel, the serious novelist faces, in the most extreme way, his own limitations and those of his medium." In sum, "We are limited human beings, and the novel is a product of our best limitations."[39] If I call this congeries of limitations a "limitation theology," it is only as a way of giving body to what, above all—even more basically than it is a commitment to literary impersonality, or to social order, perhaps even more than it is a commitment to God—is a faith in *formality* in its most abstract sense.

O'Connor's last suggestion—that limitation is not only limiting, but *productive*—is what ties the Southern limitation theology to the postwar institutionalization of literary production, and makes these figures such powerful advocates for the latter. The arguments they make are precursors, in many respects, to those underlying contemporary systems theory, whose foundational constructivist claim that "everything said is said by [from the limited perspective of] an observer" is already built into the unapologetic regionalist embrace of the cognitive limitations of the "regional perspective." The same would be true, come the later 1960s, of the "ethnic perspective." For systems theory, and for limitation theology too, knowledge as such only begins when an observer makes a distinction, imposing form on an otherwise amorphous environment, but also necessarily limiting the range of what the observer can see by its means. The obvious political conservatism attached to the Southern advocacy of self-limiting formality—a conservatism with which systems theory, with its skepticism about our ability to work "outside the system," has often been charged as well—draws attention to a technical "conservatism" that is in fact essential to all definitions of the "institution," even those that see it as a progressive technology. There may be politically conservative institutions, that is, or liberal ones, or even radical-revolutionary ones, but all of them are "conservative" in the sense that their function is to establish continuities of practice in advance of individual action. Although it would be hard to imagine any society without social institutions, the fact that they can't help asserting the authority of norms is bound to lend the very term "institution" an ominous aura when seen from the romantic perspective of an idealized freedom or pure potentiality. This of course contributes to what, to this day, is a discomfort in some quarters with the very idea of the creative writing program, which stands accused of "limiting," by institutionalizing, creativity.

In the well-known essay "Criticism Inc." (1937), John Crowe Ransom, the dean of the Fugitive-Agrarians and the New Criticism, had simply stated outright that, as a practical matter, literary criticism of the kind he hoped for, which must be the "collective and sustained effort of learned persons," must therefore be "incorporated" in the university as one of its institutional functions.[40] The same argument, tweaked slightly, justifies the presence of artists on campus. O'Connor's contribution was more abstract—an argument not for universities or even for creative writing programs per se, but for what we might, after one of her own phrases, call the habit of institutional being. This is what motivates her critique of the "particularly pernicious and untruthful . . . myth of the 'lonely writer,' the myth that writing is a lonely occupation, involving much suffering because, supposedly, the writer exists in a state of sensitivity which cuts him off, or raises him above, or casts him below the community around him" (52–53). She thought this was especially untrue of the Southern writer, since, if he is defined and thus limited by his interactions with a specific community, he is also fundamentally enabled by the South's respect for traditional manners—that is, its social formality: "To call yourself a Georgia writer is certainly to declare a limitation," she admitted, "but one which, like all limitations, is a gateway to reality." Similarly, the case for creative writing programs, gathering writers in institutional communities, had to be made against what she called the "common cliché" of writing as a lonely occupation, which she believed was "a hangover probably from the romantic period and the idea of the artist as Sufferer and Rebel."[41] The same argument that saw the Southern writer comfortably situated in his

local community, that is, could conduct him comfortably into the professional arena of the classroom or faculty lounge.

While one can certainly speak of the institutionalization of "the
South" in American literature, it would of course sound odd to describe
the South itself as an institution. The South was not an institution but
something larger—a region or even, in some accounts, a region of regions,
a "section." Committed to the limitations of the regional principle, but
faced with this obvious problem of scale, conservative Southern regionalists would have to search for ways to define the limits of their region by
way of the particular institutions it contained. One of these, of course,
was the "peculiar institution," the institution of slavery, which along with
the prison and the mental hospital would serve as the very figure, from
the liberal standpoint, of *bad institutionality*, institutionalization as entrapment. Nonetheless, its aftereffects were claimed by Ransom as one of the
"tragically" defining characteristics of Southern cultural difference: "The
darkey is one of the bonds that make a South out of all the Southern regions."[42] Other Southern intellectuals, loath to admit the "darkey" so inti-
matcly into the ontology of the South, found different ways of scaling the
region down, of delimiting it. From their positions at universities, several
drew attention to the traditional partner-institution of the school, the one
with which it shared responsibilities for the character formation of individuals: the family.

Andrew Lytle, for instance, argued that "of the South, . . . too much
is made of ethnic complications as its distinguishing feature, although of
course this can in no way be ignored. But it is the family which best describes the nature of this society. And by the family I mean the total sense
of it, the large 'connections of kin' amplifying the individual unit. There
are the geographical limits which allowed the family in this larger meaning (it was the community) to spread itself in a mild climate and over allu-
vial soils to give to the institution a predominance as not just one but *the*
institution of southern life."[43] Note how in Lytle's paradoxical formulation
it is a "limit" that allows the family to "spread" and acquire its larger mean-

ing as "the community." Note also how the loaded question of whether the Southern "family" includes black people is invoked but not quite addressed. For Lytle, predictably, the family is first and foremost a *disciplinary* social relation, though it is also a warmly emotional one. In the family he describes, "each member is called upon to deny much of his individual nature in the service of the whole, and this service sustains the common love and life. But the service must rest upon domestic laws, the principal one of disciplining children and servants, if there be servants."[44]

Thus New Southern modernity arrives in and as the collapse of family discipline, something represented in O'Connor's stories again and again, most often in the form of a struggle for authority and/or autonomy between individuals of different generations in a typically fatherless modern Southern household. Allen Tate's novel *The Fathers* (1938) traces the precipitous collapse of traditional authority back to the Civil War: "As in all highly developed societies," notes Tate's aged narrator of the Old Southern ways, "the line marking off the domestic from the public life was indistinct. Our domestic manners and satisfactions were as impersonal as the United States Navy," and the patriarch could take for granted the family's unity under his rule.[45] Come the war, this "impersonal" family institution is assaulted by a grasping individualism. Speaking of the Northerners who visit his father early in the novel, the narrator notes how, though they "spoke briskly, without warmth," there was "yet something personal in their demeanors."[46] The North, in this formulation, is the worst of all worlds, with all the "coldness" we associate with bad institutionality (think linoleum hallways and plastic chairs) combined with the obnoxiousness of individual self-assertion. What is lost in modernity's cruel advance through the countryside is the Old South's example of impersonal fellow-feeling, that is, of warm institutionality.

What takes the place of the Civil War in O'Connor's fiction is the contemporary Civil Rights Movement, whose rapidly transformative effect on Southern traditions undermines the authority of the older generations in much the same way as Tate's war does. A complex treatment of this theme is performed in "The Artificial Nigger" (1955),[47] in which the time-defying kinship of Mr. Head and his surly grandson, Nelson—who look "enough alike to be brothers and brothers not too far apart in age" (CW, 212)—is brutally severed by Mr. Head's cowardly denial of "his own image and likeness" (CW, 226) when the boy gets in trouble on the streets of Atlanta. Although this story, whose title even Ransom found offensive and entreated O'Connor to change, has been read as demonstrating that racism is "learned" behavior, in fact the story's climactic encounter with the artifice of race suggests the opposite.[48] Mercy for Mr. Head comes in the debased aesthetic form of the eponymous "plaster figure of a Negro sitting bent over on a low yellow brick fence . . . pitched forward at an unsteady angle" (CW, 229). This figure, at once a black double of little Nelson and a kind of inverted Jesus, has an inexplicably powerful effect on the two, who are making Nelson's first trip to the city from the (apparently) all-white county in Georgia where they make their home:

> Then as the two of them stood there, Mr. Head breathed, "An artificial nigger!"
>
> . . .
>
> "An artificial nigger!" Nelson repeated in Mr. Head's exact tone. . . .
>
> They stood gazing at the artificial Negro as if they were faced with some great mystery, some monument to another's victory that brought them together in their common defeat. They could both feel it dissolving their differences like an action of mercy. . . .
>
> Mr. Head opened his lips to make a lofty statement and heard himself say, "They ain't got enough real ones here. They got to have an artificial one."
>
> After a second, the boy nodded with a strange shivering about his mouth, and said, "Let's go home before we get ourselves lost again." (CW, 229–230)

The stereotyped figure of a form of black servitude is converted here by the overdetermined language of "common defeat" into a figure of the oppression of the rural white South. The shared horror that Mr. Head and Nelson feel for this figure is instantaneous and instinctive, binding them together in the construction of a racial boundary. If that horror seems strangely under-motivated, perhaps that is the point. In this story, that is, when Lytle's white Southern family proves insufficient to hold Southern regional identity together against the disintegrating forces of modernity, the figure of Ransom's "darkey" appears in the cityscape to reestablish the family bond. Miraculously dissolving differences between alienated white family members, reunifying the Southern family in dialectical opposition to an aesthetic excess of urban blackness, racism is represented by O'Connor as a gift from God.

LIBERATION TECHNOLOGY: POST-REGIONALIST SYMPATHIES

"Possibility and limitation mean about the same thing": no less than the Southerners, the Midwestern regionalists at Iowa, the ones with the home field advantage, lived the truth of O'Connor's paradox every day. Schoolteachers one and all, it was a primary fact of their institutional being, and if they sometimes stood alone on two-hearted rivers, fishing for deeply personal truths, they always returned to campus, to the rule-bound space of the institution, to get things done. And yet their orientation toward this truth was the opposite of O'Connor's. For her its import was deflationary, a way of releasing gas from the delusions of unfettered romantic individualism and socially-minded progressive optimism alike. To put it more simply, she was really making a case for limitation, not possibility. For figures like O'Connor's Iowa Workshop classmate R. V. Cassill—Iowa native, Iowa graduate, famed Iowa Workshop and Brown University instructor, Norton Anthology editor, founder of the Associated Writing Programs, and author of twenty-two novels—institutional limitations were the flip side of a technology of possibilities: the talented student submits to the discipline of the program and is enabled, launched on a literary career that can go anywhere. The tenured literary artist submits to the demands of the dean—they are relatively modest—and finds himself freed, when class lets out, from his enslavement to the mass market, free to pursue his researches into the possibilities of literary creativity wherever they may lead. The institution is viewed as a practical technology of social advancement, but a theological element nonetheless re-enters the enterprise from an unknown but surely "limitless" future. Enamored of human possibility, liberal Midwestern regionalists were arguably more enthusiastic in the task of institution *building* than their conservative Southern counterparts, whose more basic commitment was to the authority of the *already* instituted. But the Midwesterners were also more likely to be troubled by the limits necessarily imposed upon individuals by institutions—both the ones they participated in building and the ones, like the family, that seemed to have been around forever. For them, the term *institutionalization* always had a potentially ominous ring. As much as they loved them, institutions could imprison. They could enslave.

The latter becomes obvious in Cassill's first novel, *The Eagle on the Coin* (1950), which examines the plight of young Andrew Cameron, a white liberal academic historian newly arrived with his wife and small child and subscription to the *Nation* at an obscure college in the small Ohio town of Riverton.[49] In order to advance his career and get the hell out of this narrow-minded, racially segregated backwater, he will write a Ph.D. thesis on the town's one illustrious historical figure, an abolitionist named Mountwood who was hanged by the townspeople in the antebellum period. In the course of his research Cameron befriends the town's one political radical, the grizzled saloonkeeper Kettle, whose grotesque (and, as it turns out, homosexual) body "contained the evidences of dissension that all the people who ever lived had made against the institutions that again and again hobbled them short of the freedom they sought, the kind of life they had to lead" (333). Drawing Cameron into his effort to elect a black man, Jackson, to the all-white school board, Kettle sets the stage for a struggle between Cameron's commitment to what the novel understands as inherently conservative "institutional" commitments of family and school—to scholarly research, to his job at the college that salaries him, to the family he must support with that salary—and the heroic political practice that becomes the novel's symbol of individual agency as such. When the campaign fails miserably, and Kettle is run out of town in a sex scandal, Cameron returns to teaching and reconciles himself to writing the history of a political activist rather than being one, dedicating himself to the modest possibilities for liberation that remain within institutional limits: "All right, he thought, I am whipped down enough to . . . believe that the writing, the knowledge, would have to be worth the impotence" (344). Inhabiting the past and the future of heroic agency but not its present, the white liberal academic can only tell himself, in the novel's final words: "Do nothing yet. Remember. Believe. Wait" (346).

A decade later Cassill's Ph.D. thesis advisee at Iowa, Margaret Walker, was pondering many of the same issues in her Civil War epic, *Jubilee* (1966), which, as though reversing the angle of racial vision of *The Fathers* or *Gone with the Wind* (1936), sees that period from the point of view of the slaves. Set in contrast to the unambiguously "hobbling" institution of slavery, however, her take on the family and school, two institutions explicitly forbidden to slaves in the South, is substantially different from Cassill's. For him, family and school are soft slaveries that neutralize individual agency: they "whip" his character down, "hobble" him; for Walker they are the opposite of slavery, the indispensable ground of individual possibility and the source of this novel's very existence. If they are necessarily limiting in their own right, the logic of O'Connor's paradox enables the significance of this limitation to be turned inside out: if the family, as Lytle had it, requires the person to "deny much of his individual nature in the service of the whole," that limiting "whole," internalized, becomes the very engine of individual self-transcendence and expansion toward "something larger." Pursuing this paradoxical logic, even the institution of slavery will appear, in the unfolding of the dialectic, as the negation of "slavery"—a possibility most famously raised by Hegel's dialectic of master and slave.

Jubilee is dedicated to the novelist's family, not only the members who lived with her during the many years of its composition but also the unbroken lineage of grandmothers which supplied her with the cultural capital of a narrative legacy. Based on the life of Margaret Walker's great-grandmother and namesake, Margaret Brown, who was born into slavery as a Georgia house servant, the novel's more immediate source was the stories told to Walker by her grandmother, Elvira Dozier, from whom the novel's protagonist, Vyry, takes her name. Following Vyry through the astonishing historical upheavals of the time, the novel finds continuity along the axis of biological reproduction, as the compulsory breeding practices of the antebellum period are finally transformed into true motherhood. In the first chapter Vyry's mother Hetta is dying, her body laid waste by the fifteen children she has had by her master. By the novel's conclusion Vyry has survived the manifold terrors of the war and Reconstruction to become "the best true example of the motherhood of her race, an ever present assurance that nothing could destroy a people whose sons had come from her loins."[50] With her emancipation into legal motherhood, a family—the one that transmits her story, if not her material property—is established on her matriarchal line. Unlike *Quicksand*'s Helga Crane, whose lack of family, as we saw in the previous chapter, is the "crux of the matter" of her maladjustment at Naxos, Vyry's/Margaret's heirs will feel they belong in school.

But while Walker's novel is dedicated to the family whose story it is, she also takes pains to acknowledge debts of another kind. Moving from "dedication" to "acknowledgment," she thanks the many "people of different races, colors, and creeds" who "have given me material assistance in the creation of this story," including all her "teachers at Iowa," most importantly her "instructor, R. Verlin Cassill." *Jubilee* is indeed a conspicuously "educated" text, a product of the merging of narrated experience and archival scholarship, of family and school—institutions that in Walker's case, with a family full of teachers, might well have blurred together. In the novel, the unlettered Vyry is obsessed with seeing her children educated, and the novel itself is, at long remove, the issue of the same obsession. Narrating the emergence of agency from slavery, the novel understands itself (much like the nonfictional slave narratives it recalls) as a rhetorical-performative re-liberation—an auto-liberation—from that hobbling institution. The novel's own model for this act is the character Brother Zeke, who sneaks among the various plantations and holds secret prayer meetings, heavy in their emphasis on Moses, which "served a double purpose," religious and political. Ezekiel can move with impunity across the heavily policed landscape because he "could write his own pass: *This nigger preacher belongs to me. He has my consent to go to town*" (56). Not only is Ezekiel's practice of liberation theology enabled by the technology of letters, but his literate practice serves as a model of self-ownership performed in and by writing.

As Walker described it in the essay "How I Wrote *Jubilee*" (1972), the novel grew "out of a welter of raw experiences and careful research. . . . Most of my life I have been involved with writing this story about my great-grandmother."[51] In fact she began writing the novel as early as 1934, in an advanced composition class at Northwestern University which, on the model of Barrett Wendell's classes at Harvard, accepted creative writing for credit. Putting it aside in frustration, she worked on her poetry, and the M.F.A. thesis she wrote at Iowa with Paul Engle, *For My People* (1942), won the prestigious Yale Younger Poets prize. Researching the novel sporadically for the next two decades while she taught college and raised a family, she returned to Iowa to finish it as a Ph.D. thesis, and it was here that she worked with Cassill:

> He spent painful hours explaining how I was "telling" and not "showing." . . . Meanwhile he had taught me how to read the masters of fiction, such as Chekhov, in order to learn how they put their material together. Cassill had not only put his finger on the problem, but he showed me how to dramatize my material and make it come alive. I had never had any trouble with dialogue, but now under his tutelage I was learning how to do close critical reading, and how to make character charts, establish relationships, and control the language more powerfully and effectively. (58)
>
> . . .

For the technique of the novel, I found studies made by James Warren Beach in his *Twentieth Century Novel* quite relevant, and I was also forced to read Henry James. I bought, of course, Cassill's book *Writing Fiction* and read it from cover to cover, but then who is the greater teacher, the book or the man? (58/64)

If the text of *Jubilee* was nurtured in the family, it was disciplined at the Iowa Writers' Workshop: Walker's narrator, too much a teacher, had initially been an intrusive one, offering her own judgments of the actions taking place; her plot, whose kernels had come to her in the form of discrete anecdotes told over the course of her childhood and had then been supplemented by her reading of period documents, had been disorganized. As a personal presence and a purveyor of textbooks, Cassill inspired Walker to *control,* to *dramatize,* to *revise,* to *impersonalize*—in short, to assert a mastery over her material on the example of the Master, Henry James, whom she was "forced" to read. Thus if the novel, as the end-product of a family's increasingly higher education, performs a rhetorical auto-liberation from slavery, it does so by means of its submission to the no doubt infinitely less painful, if nonetheless very difficult, compositional demands of Jamesian literary form. More precisely, it performs the transformation of the peculiar institution of slavery into the enabling institution of creative writing.

There are of course many features that tie this historical novel to the unusually extended present of its own composition, which stretched across the entire first phase of the postwar civil rights era. Perhaps most notable is the way the universalist ethos of that period can be seen to pressure the novel's definition of the "family" as a genealogically and racially exclusive unit. No doubt the matriarchal family founded in *Jubilee* functions as a symbol, most importantly, of the enduring unity of a race in the ethnically restricted sense; to this degree *Jubilee* appears to be a belated Harlem/Chicago Renaissance work (Walker came of age in the 1930s in Chicago, where she knew Richard Wright and was attached to the WPA), working in the idiom of the folk and folk culture which has attracted the attention of most of her critics.[52] However, a universalist understanding of the family sits on the novel's margins, exerting its gravity. In this it echoes the expanded understanding of "family" underlying the period's most idealistic vision of liberal internationalism, the photo exhibition entitled *The Family of Man* (book version, 1955), organized by Edward Steichen to include 503 images from 68 countries arranged along the continuum of the human life cycle.

Like Robert Penn Warren's *Band of Angels* (1955)—the melodramatic tale of the pampered daughter of a planter who learns that she is "really" black when he suddenly dies in debt and she is sold off into slavery—*Jubilee* pays careful attention to the "ethnic complications" of the Southern family, the ones warded off by the intervention of a Segregating God in O'Connor's "Artificial Nigger." Indeed, Vyry herself, the founder of her family, is the offspring of her white master, and the novel pays considerable attention to how, as a child, she seems uncannily to belong in the big house with the white daughter, Lillian: "'My but those children look so much alike, are they twins?'" (21). Even beyond the blood relation, simply growing up in that pious Christian household is understood to have had a profound, and she believes positive, effect on her. One character observes that the "prim and prissy" lady who was Vyry's mistress "left her mark on everybody around her, including Vyry" (482).

Founded on this "complication," the novel ends up exquisitely poised between a strong pluralist assertion of racial difference and the universalist assertion of human sameness. When Marse John dies, Vyry reflects that she "was as much his child as Miss Lillian and she looked as much like him. But she was also his slave as her mother had been before her, and now her children were slaves. When she saw Miss Lillian weeping in grief over the death of her father, Vyry felt no sympathetic emotion" (197). Here the affective politics of slavery trumps the biological consequences of slavery. Later in the novel, however, having established her own homestead, it is Vyry who resists the separatist militancy of the father of her children, Randall Ware, in favor of trans-racial human sympathy, voicing the liberal aspiration of "mutual understanding" pervasive in the immediate postwar period: "'I don't believe the world is full of peoples what hates everybody. I just don't believe it. I know lots of times folks doesn't know other folks and then they gits to thinking crazy things, but when you gits up to peoples and gits to know them, you finds out they's got kind hearts and tender feelings just like everybody else'" (474). Also evident in Southern liberal integrationist fictions such as Carson McCullers's *The Heart is a Lonely Hunter* (1940), structured around an ideal of communication that might cure the titular loneliness, the liberal ideology of "mutual understanding" was not far from the sentiment an irritated Allen Tate had called New Provincialism.[53]

Asked in 1960 why "Negroes [don't] figure more prominently" in her stories, Flannery O'Connor's reply had taken a notably narratological cast: "I don't understand them the way I do white people. I don't feel capable of entering the mind of a Negro. In my stories they are seen from the outside. The Negro in the South is quite isolated; he has to exist by himself. In the South segregation is segregation."[54] Although her description of her stories is not entirely accurate—one of her thesis stories, "Wildcat," had been focalized through a black man—her way of answering the question suggests that we might add another to the long list of "limitations" to which she was committed. Hardly a passionate critic of racial segregation, O'Connor sees that fact of Southern life as being doubled, internally, by a segregated cognition. Thus while she, even burdened by a graduate degree, can "enter the mind" of abjectly ignorant poor whites like Nelson and Mr. Head with little trouble, racial difference produces an impenetrable barrier to "understanding" which in turn conditions the form of her fiction.

Margaret Walker, more attuned to the self-transcendent possibilities of literature than to limitation, took the opposite approach. Encouraged by Cassill to "show" her characters rather than "tell" about them as a narrator, she includes in the first part of the novel long swatches of action focalized through Marse John and his Legree-like plantation manager, Grimes. Thus, even as they are condemned by their own thoughts, the technical "sympathy" built into the narrative form is always threatening to condition this harsh judgment. For instance, we are given access to Grimes's unspoken admiration for Marse John's wife, a "high quality lady who knows and acts the difference between niggers and white people. She ain't no nigger-loving namby-pamby like that s.o.b. pretty boy she's married to." In this moment the *form* of interracial sympathy (between a black author and a white character) frames even the thoughts of a champion of racial division. But we are also, more simply, shown his plight as a poor white man with dreams: "Most folks would never guess how he longed some day to have a farm of his own. He knew darn well how to run a farm" (27)—a sentiment endorsed by Vyry herself when she thinks how, in some ways, the poor whites of the region "suffered more than the black slaves for there was no one to provide them the rations of corn meal and salt pork which was the daily lot of the slaves" (59).

A few years after *Jubilee* was published, by which time *segregation* had been met with its double in late-1960s *separatism*, this sort of interracial sympathy would prove most unwelcome among black nationalist intellectuals, especially if it moved in the reverse direction, from white to black. This, ironically, would rotate Flannery O'Connor's segregated narratology into a position of relative political correctness in the emergent regime of cultural pluralism. In a black-authored work like Richard Wright's *Savage Holiday* (1954), third-person focalization through a white protagonist might serve a political purpose even now, in this case that of exposing the spiritual desolation beneath the moralizing of the sexually repressed white corporate tool. But the reverse form of interracial sympathy would run the risk of being redescribed as—some would say *revealed* as—an aggressive, even emasculating, appropriation of the cultural capital of "black experience." This was the fate of William Styron's Pulitzer-winning *Confessions of Nat Turner* (1967), in which the white Southern author converts the brief historical text by that name, dictated to Thomas Gray in 1831 while Turner awaited execution for leading a slave rebellion, into a 500-page first person narrative told from Turner's point of view.

The "surprising point of view" trick, most famously evident in the

Benjy section of *The Sound and the Fury* (1929), had by this point been institutionalized as a minor modernist mode. Enabled by the general post-Jamesian fascination with the technicalities of point of view, it turns the perspectival restriction of narrative focalization, valued by Gordon and Tate for the limits it imposes, into a demonstration of the author's unlimited virtuosity, her ability to range across human and sometimes non-human experience and inhabit it convincingly. An interesting example from the period is John Gardner's novel *Grendel* (1971), where the famed creative writing teacher and novelist (and Ph.D. medievalist) rewrites Week One of the English literature survey from the monster's point of view. In Styron's case, refusing the perspectival limitations imposed by his own whiteness, his novel aspired to be a massive—and daringly modernist—project of racial self-transcendence. His account, in a 1992 Afterword, of the genesis of his novel bears some striking resemblances to Margaret Walker's description of hers, but with a difference. Like her, Styron credits his reading of Georg Lukács's *The Historical Novel* (translated in 1962) with supplying him with the correct epistemological orientation toward the genre—the author "should have a thorough . . . command of the period with which he is dealing, but he should not permit his work to be governed by particular historical facts"—and credits himself with being "an amateur historian [who] had absorbed a vast amount of reading on slavery in general . . . and much recent scholarship in the exploding field of the historiography of the slave period."[55]

But while Walker's inherited relation to her story worked to guarantee that, even beyond her hard labor in the library stacks, she was writing what she knew, Styron's experiential claims were of a different order:

> Like some young boys who are troubled by their "unnatural" sexual longings, I felt a similar anxiety about my secret passion for blackness; in my closet I was fearful lest any of my conventionally racist young friends discover that I was an unabashed enthusiast of the despised Negro. . . . I wanted to confront and understand blackness.

Then there was the incomparable example of my grandmother. In a direct linkage I still sometimes find remarkable, I
am able to say that I remain separated from slavery by only
two generations, and that I was related to and was familiar
with and spoke to someone who owned slaves. (436–437)

Recall Cassill's assertion in *Writing Fiction* that the writer "begins to
shape his material by accepting an emotional commitment to it—very
much as if he himself were the first character to appear in the story to be."
In this case, while the conscious emotional commitment on Styron's part
was to the cause of civil rights, the novel's origins in his own childhood,
with its "unnatural" passion for Negroes and proudly filial relation to the
slave *owner*, suggests a more complex set of emotions at work. It is perhaps no wonder, then, that the autopoetic process of impersonalization
in Styron's *Confessions* was found, by his critics, to be woefully incomplete, an inadvertent "confession" of what one of the authors of *William
Styron's Nat Turner: Ten Black Writers Respond* (1968) called his "demented
fantas[ies]" about black people.[56]

Offended by Styron's invention of what seemed to them a stereo-
typical lust, on Turner's part, for the young girl who was the only one of
the fifty-five white victims of the revolt to die by his hand, these writers
rotate the entire structure of interracial lust 180 degrees: thus the narrative technique of sympathetic entry into Turner's "skin" is reinterpreted
as a rhetorical rape of the slave by the master. This formal intrusion is furthermore doubled, in the novel's plot, by a scene in which Turner's religious passion effervesces into homosexuality, thus making him symbolically available for Styron's penetration. Taking "magisterial command"
not only of the period about which he writes, but also of the period's most
violently rebellious slave, Styron in verbal blackface is accused of inappro-
priate mastery: "Nat Turner, the literary creation, suffers the same fate as
his real-life namesake: he is enslaved" (67). As one contributor, John Oliver
Killens, rather mercilessly put it, "Marse Willie . . . has not been able to
transcend his southern-peckerwood background. . . . [Pretending] to tell
the story from the point of view of Turner . . . was a colossal error" (36).

An even profounder problem for Styron's critics, however, was what they took to be the novel's faulty understanding of the institution of slavery as, ironically, *wholly* limiting of its victims. One of Styron's admitted departures from the historical record was to have Turner grow up, like Vyry, in the big house of a prosperous plantation, where an indulgently liberal master notices his instinctive love for books and allows him to be educated. It is only after his promised liberation from slavery is revoked (when, in the familiar melodramatic trope, the "good" master dies) that Turner vengefully turns his powers of literacy and eloquence, like Walker's Brother Zeke, to the ends of black liberation. Without that broken promise, Styron suggests, Turner might have remained entirely socialized to the institution of which he was here imagined to have been a distinctly privileged inmate, content to live out his days in the plantation workshop where, somewhat like a writer-in-residence, he could perform the "deeply satisfying" labor of carpentry with the "smooth professionalism" of a man dedicated to "craft" (344–345). In Killens's rebuke of this notion, he quotes Margaret Walker's novel from the previous year: "Every black American, then and now, was and is, a potential Nat Turner. As Margaret Walker writes in her powerful novel about slavery, *Jubilee:* 'No matter what a white planter said, every slave craved his freedom'" (37).

Asserting the freedom of the literary artist from the "governance" of mere historical fact, Styron projects the object of his representation into bondage so strong that his craving for freedom must be inspired by the divine intervention of the author's liberal imagination. Flannery O'Connor would no doubt have recognized that craving from the outset; she just wouldn't have sympathized with it.

IOWA UNLIMITED: THE COLD WAR CONCENTRATION CAMP

The poet W. D. Snodgrass tells an interesting story about Paul Engle, who did not found the Iowa Writers' Workshop but who did more than anyone else to make it what it became and no doubt remains to this day: the most influential linking of an educational institution with literary production ever. Engle had grown up in Iowa; he left for New York and then England on a Rhodes Scholarship, returning home to become the golden boy poet of the early 1930s. Writing in a Midwestern regionalist idiom, paying sentimental homage to the land, he won the Yale Younger Poets Prize in 1932 for a collection called *Worn Earth,* followed it up with one called *Corn,* and seemed to have a bright future ahead of him. Which he did, but not in the way it first appeared. His later works failed to make the splash of the early ones, and slowly but surely his ambitions seemed, in a sense, to turn themselves inside out. Appointed as an instructor in the newly formed Iowa Workshop in 1937, he was made its director in 1941, a job he held for nearly twenty-five years. As head of the Workshop he may well have been, as Kurt Vonnegut claimed, the single most helpful writer to other writers in human history—at least in the practical, material sense.[57] Testimony abounds of his indefatigable search for exciting new students and teachers, of the tenacity with which he sought out the fellowship money to sustain them, of the enthusiasm with which he promoted their later careers and, even more so, the reputation of the Iowa Writers' Workshop as a whole. Stranded in the fields like a rusty farm implement, his own poetic project was increasingly ignored, and the modern institution became his true medium. Artist turned administrator, he was also the administrator as artist, and in this role Engle became lastingly famous, a legend, much written about though all but entirely unread.

That there may have been a complex psychological dimension to this inside-out literary success story is suggested by Snodgrass's account of a party given for—who else?—visiting luminary Robert Penn Warren:

> Paul shocked everyone by telling his recurrent nightmare. He was a prisoner, he said, in a concentration camp where he'd been singled out for a specially degrading punishment. Along the camp's outer rock wall, about six feet off the ground, was a series of holes or depressions. Brought out naked before the massed prisoners, he had to bend over and grasp his ankles, then hoisted by the guards, put his feet in two of those depressions. The guards and prisoners jeering at him, he must then

draw out one foot at a time, moving it on to the next hole and so proceeding around the wall like a fly. But, he said, after a while he found he could do this surprisingly well—better, in fact, than anyone had ever done it. In time, he was simply whizzing around the wall while guards and prisoners, no longer jeering, looked on with amazement and admiration.

We were astonished not only by the horrors of this dream but also that he would recount it at a party where many (Warren not least) would understand.[58]

Of course any institution, including a university, can from a certain perspective seem like a "concentration camp," and Snodgrass encourages us to understand Engle's nightmare in this allegorical light.

The many repetitive rituals of the educational institution—the cycles through which it daily, weekly, semesterly turns—can seem to be, for its inhabitants, a form of circular movement around prison walls, a laborious frenzy of going nowhere, like the proverbial gerbil on his wheel. And for Engle this nightmare of repetition is, appropriately enough, a *recurrent* nightmare, repetitive in its own right. This way of viewing the school is perhaps especially open to the teachers and administrators who work there, since what is for students a transcendental ceremony of departure toward a "limitless" future—graduation—is for the more permanent inmates just another appointment on the calendar.

Seen favorably, as occasions for enabling intimacy, the bounded social spaces of the institution tend to be called "communities," as when Engle, in the dedication to a textbook-anthology entitled *On Creative Writing* (1964), thanks the corporate and other donors who in "recent years . . . have given funds to the Program in Creative Writing at the University of Iowa, so that young writers from all regions of the USA and many areas of the earth could come here and make an international community of the imagination."[59] But the dark side of this public intimacy is the public humiliation of the individual by the group, which in Engle's dream becomes a kind of collective specular sodomy—which is one way of describing the humiliation any workshop participant might feel as his story is discussed in class. Somewhat like the punitive apparatus in Kafka's "The Penal Colony"—a story made available to students for close reading in Warren's own *Understanding Fiction*—that procedure inscribes whichever of the laws has been broken directly upon the body of the student writer, in this case the laws of literary inscription itself.

But of course what is most fascinating about Engle's dream, and most telling, I would argue, about postwar American literary production as a whole, is the way it turns suddenly from a nightmare of public humiliation into a fantasy of individual triumph. The concentration camp is not converted into a nurturing community, exactly, but the same persons who jeered at him, guards and prisoners, teachers and students, have now become the captive audience of Engle's magnificently skillful performance, the best that has ever been seen.

This is a "transcendent" performance, to be sure, but rather than visibly taking him *over* the wall to freedom, as we might expect, his performance *reiterates* the wall, identifies him with it, as though in perfect embodiment of the formal principles of its operation. Ceasing to exhibit the excellence of unfettered, extramural originality, he now exemplifies an excellence of institutional being. In this dreamwork, at least, limitation and possibility mean exactly the same thing. Is it so large a step, really, from this commanding performance to the position of commanding officer of the camp? One can well imagine the guards and other inmates beginning to report to the dream-Engle, as Iowa Workshop students were required to report to the real Engle every fall, lining up outside his office door. Entering one by one to make their plea for fellowship money, they would talk about their needs, their goals, and Engle, unhampered by codifications or committees, would announce the figure that seemed to him just. The dominant literary values at Iowa may have been strictly formalist, but in its bureaucratic operations, as a former student observed, "informality reigned" (*Community*, 99). This meant, of course, that they were especially subject to the force of individual personality and whim.[60]

The other side of Engle's "selflessness," that is, was his dictatorship, a quality that made him enemies as well as fawningly grateful friends. As he put it, "You do not create new programs without driving hard and if you drive hard you're going to irritate people"; he described his ideal managerial style as one of "delicate and imaginative aggression."[61] This aligns him with the bedridden Iowa patriarch in his only novel, *Always the Land* (1941), which he completed just before taking over the program. This patriarch sits in a throne-like bed in a house perched high above his vast acreage, surrounded by his collection of "whips of every kind," including "racing whips," "stiff buggy whips," "cattle whips," "riding crops," and one "endless bullwhip" which "bordered the wall, tip finally meeting handle, like a snake with [its tail] in its mouth. Even hanging limp from hooks it had aliveness, as if it could at any time lash out, the long supple length leap from the wall, break through the door, to coil around a man's throat."[62] Rather than signifying his feeble powerlessness, here the immobility of the patriarch makes him the symbol of an abstract principle of authority: too lofty to walk among men, he is able, nonetheless, to control and punish them, containing them in the self-consuming, self-referential circularity represented by the "endless" circular whip. *L'État, c'est moi.* What I assume, you shall assume. As analysts of sympathetic, self-dissolving Whitmanian poetic subjectivity have pointed out, the potential return of the imperial self is built into the dialectic of absorption *by* the other as, circling back to its origin, it becomes an imperial absorption *of* the other by the voice of the poet.[63] Muting his own poetic voice, Engle gathers talent for the institution whose glory is his own.

For all of its luridness, Engle's concentration camp dream is borrowed from the common stock of postwar imagery, when the Cold War was getting under way, and the real concentration camps of World War II were still fresh enough in everyone's mind not to need Kafka's story as a reminder. Squatting on the prairie, the Iowa Workshop remained connected to a larger world of normalized death and destruction, enlisting the literary imagination in the larger cause of the Free World. To this degree it was functioning literally as an Ideological State Apparatus in Althusser's sense. Many of the students who were arriving in Iowa City in the early years of Engle's tenure were returning soldiers supported by the G.I. Bill, and for more than two decades, until 1966, the Workshop classes were held in military-style Quonset huts set up along the Iowa River.[64] The grizzled student-veterans through whose testosterone haze Flannery O'Connor cautiously moved had recently been set free from an institution, the United States Military, dedicated to the systematic diminishment of individuality in favor of disciplined uniformity. Like the protagonist of her story "Parker's Back" (1965), a Navy veteran whose sense of his own distinction is inscribed in the colorful tattoos covering most of his body, these veterans were now converting that uniformity back into expressive individuality. And yet—again somewhat like Parker, who desperately tattoos his entire back with a glaring Jesus, thereby to attract his God-fearing wife to the authority inscribed on his body—they were doing so by submitting to the authority of impersonal craft.

The two extremes of this structure are exemplified by Richard E. Kim and Kurt Vonnegut, who were, respectively, a student and a teacher in the Iowa Workshop in the early sixties. Kim was a South Korean veteran of the Korean War who, in *The Martyred* (1964), would produce a novel so coldly disciplined that it seems to have been riveted, not written. Taking place in wartime Korea, the novel is to all appearances utterly uninterested in the cultural specificities of Korean-ness or the idiosyncrasies of the individual voice, absorbed instead by the self-sacrifice of the religious martyr who disregards his own well-being for that of his Church. Vonnegut's *Slaughterhouse Five* (1968), by contrast, while it records the traumatic wartime experiences of its author during the horrific firebombing of Dresden, massively reintroduces the quirky first person authorial persona into the fiction, as though this comical assertion of Fieldingesque telling and not showing can compensate for the trauma that his protagonist experiences as becoming "unstuck in time."

Referencing the famous *Partisan Review* symposium of 1952, "Our Country and Our Culture," whose editors had announced the end of the alienation of the American writer from his country under the threat of communism, Engle pointed to the corporate support of the Workshop as proof that "in an open society such as ours, writer, businessman, and university can join to make an environment which is useful to the writer, friendly for the businessman, and healthy for the university" (vii).[65] Flannery O'Connor could never have written such a treacly, toadying sentence, worthy of a Chamber of Commerce pamphlet. But for Engle, the postwar U.S. corporate liberal consensus was like a large inflating balloon. Attaching the Workshop to it through the medium of business sponsorship would guarantee the continual expansion of the program's cultural presence and prestige. And it has to be said, however nostalgic one might feel for good old-fashioned modernist "oppositionality" as exemplified (from the right) by O'Connor, that rarely does one encounter an institution as thoroughly dominant in its discipline as the Iowa Writers' Workshop. Not only was it the first full-fledged program of its kind, it has never been other than the most prestigious example thereof, even as some 300-odd competitors have arisen in its midst.

Other programs—often at equally unlikely locations like Houston, Irvine, and Buffalo—have attained considerable cachet at various points, but none of them has held on to this status long enough to produce the kind of narcissistic collective self-appreciation and memorialization that attaches to Iowa, whose graduates have been amply willing to announce and remember and discuss their affiliation with the program and its participants. While critics of the program, as we have seen, sometimes assert that it produces a "corporate" or de-individualized "Iowa style," the singular eminence of Iowa is such that it counts, in a field dedicated even now to the image of the writer as heroic loner, as a kind of collective-individuality. The many volumes of reminiscences, histories, and anthologies that continue to appear partake of the self-fulfilling, self-reproducing public relations project set in motion by Paul Engle. Appropriately enough, given the heroic horizontality of the landscape it has so self-consciously inhabited, Iowa has dominated its field not so much through direct competition with other programs as through a "viral" process of self-reproduction across the system of higher education, as innumerable Iowa graduates have gone on to found similar programs elsewhere. Thus, even

as at one level it stands conspicuously alone in its collective-individual eminence, Iowa is in a sense everywhere. Its wider "importance to American
letters" is accurately described by Daniel Marder as lying "in its connections. It tends to create a kind of literary establishment not with a strong
core as in New York but as a network of fibers with sense endings everywhere."[66] This network aids the careers of writers as writers, of course,
since they are enabled by its means to place their work nearer the top of
the five-foot-high submission piles that crowd the offices of most literary
magazines. And yet increasingly, as the number of programs grows, this
network has become a network of *teachers* whose primary function is to
distribute teaching jobs. The term for this sort of dominance is "hegemony," and, as in the late lamented best-case-scenarios of the New World
Order, the rule of Iowa in the field of creative writing has been a peaceful
and prosperous one for all concerned.

Indeed, if Paul Engle had had his way, the same would have been the
case for the entire globe. Convinced of the power of institutions like his
own to do good for humankind, he dedicated himself to the cause of
world peace, which he imagined could come about through the "mutual
understanding" produced uniquely in and through the medium of literature. Having (ironically) come into irresolvable conflict with the Iowa English Department, which still held nominal administrative supremacy over
the Workshop, he resigned as director in 1966 to devote all of his energies
to the International Writing Program. This was a project dreamed up
by his wife, Hualing Nieh Engle, who co-directed it, but it was funded in
large part by the United States Information Agency as one of its many
Cold War propaganda initiatives. In the two decades and more of the Program's existence under Engle's watch, the USIA enabled hundreds of writers from seventy different countries and six continents to come to Iowa
City to work on their writing.

Arranging a collision of nationalities that typically only occurs in
large cities, the directors of the Program hoped to lead these writers to the
realization that the "unintelligible sounds made by a person from another
side of the world are really expressing the same ideas and emotions as

their own language."[67] The related Translation Workshop arranged for the publication of many of their works, frequently pairing the foreign writer with a younger American translator who did not speak the original language. Together, hashing it out with dictionaries, they would produce a "joint translation" meant to stand as evidence of the potential for the trans-linguistic harmony of all humankind. "Translation is part of the world's survival," the directors claimed. "People translating each other are not killing each other, unless"—and it is a significant, if joking, exception—"the person whose text is being translated is unbearably outraged at the result and draws a handgun on the translator. But surely this is justifiable homicide."[68]

None of their translators having been shot, and having taken the institution of creative writing about as far as it could go, Paul Engle and Hauling Nieh were nominated for a Nobel Peace Prize in 1976. Engle died in 1991 at O'Hare International Airport. He was en route to Poland to accept an award.

PART TWO

"Find Your Voice"
(1960–1975)

3

The Social Construction of Unreality:
Creative Writing in the Open System

> The empirical fact remains that institutions do tend to
> "hang together." If this phenomenon is not to be
> taken for granted, it must be explained.
>
> BERGER AND LUCKMANN, *The Social Construction of Reality*

OPENING UP

Wallace Stegner liked to say that he had been inspired to found the graduate creative writing program at Stanford University when the very first student story submitted in the first creative writing class he taught there amazed him. The year was 1945, and a fortuitously timed dinner with the wealthy brother of his department chair soon matched the inspiration with some serious funding. As recalled by his wife Mary, Stegner sold oilman Edward Jones on the idea that the recently repatriated veterans in his classes, like the marvelous young writer he had just discovered, "had lots to write, but they were married and some had children. . . . He said they needed a place where they could write and talk, like a coffee house in Europe."[1] It was typical of Stegner that, inspired by an example of individual excellence, his next thought was of camaraderie, and the next after that of an academic program in which it might be embodied. This, along with his considerable achievements as a novelist, is what makes him a pivotal figure in postwar American literary history.

Stegner was as familiar as anyone at the time with the ways and means and rationale for this strange new medium of literary camaraderie. He had graduated from Iowa a few years before the official founding of the Writers' Workshop, and once observed of himself, "If I was not the first creative M.A. in the country I was one of the first two or three."[2] In fact, he was on the scene of virtually every hotspot in the emergence of the program as we know it, and his daughter-in-law Lynn Stegner had ample reason to claim that "with less than a handful of others" he had "essentially invented creative writing as a field of study within the Academy."[3] Rooming at Iowa with the man who would become the Workshop's first director, Wilbur Schramm, Stegner went on from there to become a Briggs-Copeland lecturer in writing at Harvard, and while there became a fixture at the Bread Loaf Writers' Conference, held at an adjunct campus of Middlebury College in Vermont. Founded in 1926 at the urging of perhaps the first true "writer in residence" in American literary history, Robert Frost, Bread Loaf brought together students with their professional elders for a few weeks every summer and was an obvious precursor to the writing programs that would assert themselves as the proper business, not of summer vacation, but of the regular school year. Finally, in 1945, Stegner was wooed back west by a job offer from Stanford, and a year later, impressed with that student story and armed with funds from Edward Jones, he founded the well-known graduate program there.

"Rest Camp on Maui" (1946) was by Eugene Burdick, a recently repatriated Navy veteran who would go on to coauthor *The Ugly American* (1958) and *Fail Safe* (1962), and the short story he wrote for Stegner is notable for the way its handling of point of view studiously reinforces its theme. A small group of soldiers on leave, gathered together by a fatuous news correspondent looking for the "personal angle" on the war, are invited to contribute to the wartime public relations machine. Claiming third-person access to the memories of the individual soldiers in succession, Burdick is able to set the true horror of vividly described combat in counterpoint to the superficial tripe the correspondent scrawls in his notebook: "'Marines like Aussie girls, but first love still clean-cut American girls.'"[4] On one level, then, the story could be read as an allegory of the superiority of technically proficient literary fiction to the newspaper, which as a clichéd mass cultural medium cannot plumb the intimate depths of consciousness that fiction can (though in the 1960s the New Journalism would attempt to rectify this deficiency). But in exploring the traumatized interiorities of the soldiers in succession, the effect is also one of the creation, in the medium of narrative, of a small group consciousness—a platoon consciousness—grounded in shared experience and the maintenance of social boundaries. Only within these boundaries, it seems, can the authenticity of the community of soldiers, the truths that they alone know, be preserved from the ambient unreality of the organs of wartime propaganda. We are reminded of the veteran Krebs from Ernest Hemingway's story "Soldier's Home" (1923), who grows painfully self-conscious about the "lies" he feels he must tell about war to those who weren't there. Here, however, the soldiers are not alone with their pain. They have company.

We mark an even greater distance from the alienation of 1923 to the camaraderie of 1946, however, when Burdick's story crosses the theme of "platoon identity" with the question of cultural identity and prejudice that loomed so large in the popular culture of the immediate postwar period, as exemplified by Elia Kazan's Academy Award–winning *Gentleman's Agreement* (1947, from the novel by Laura Hobson). In Burdick's story the news correspondent asks the soldier Selfensky about the experience of Jews in the army—"I'd like to give them a good write-up" (12)—and while Selfensky withholds the story he wants to tell from the correspondent, who is not worthy to hear it, the narrator gives it to the reader straight from Selfenksy's brain, where we "remember" the horrific, heroic death of his friend Lieutenant Cohen, proudly Jewish but an American soldier, too.[5] The community of Jews on the one hand, and of soldiers on the other, are here ontologically opened one to the other, but narrative form steps forth to ensure that they each maintain their integrity. Having, in any case, already allowed the reader to intrude upon these intimacies, narrative form becomes here a technology of cultural pluralism, facilitating its paradoxical embrace of identity and difference, unity and multiplicity, openness and closure—and communicating more or less the same message that the correspondent would have.

Stegner was impressed with the unusual authority and maturity with which the veterans packed into his classroom in the late 1940s could respond to the call to "write what you know," and they became the measure by which subsequent generations of creative writing students at Stanford seemed to him to pale in comparison. His attachment to this group, or rather to the values they embodied, is what lent a certain pathos to his tenure at Stanford, where it would be his fate, come the 1960s, to personify the indignant past. He is a "pivotal" figure of postwar literary history not simply in helping it pivot into the Program Era, but also because the Program Era pivoted off of him into a future he could not endorse. But this would be of only limited interest if it didn't index something much larger, a widespread transformation in the understanding of the university and of fiction writing alike. We can put it crudely by saying that whereas for Stegner, as for his New Critical contemporaries, the first task of a formal social grouping was to find its principle of definition—which is to say, its principle of closure and thus of integrity—for writers who came of age in the late 1950s and 1960s the problem was rather one of liberation: how can people come together in an intimate grouping and still be free? The answer (again put crudely) was to conceive all institutional relations on the model of an "open market"; and this merely confirms that the politics of the sixties were, in retrospect, more complex than a simple rejection of the capitalist status quo: it was after all the regulatory bureaucracies of the still-hegemonic liberal welfare state that were often identified as the problem for sixties radicals, and it was Goldwater Republicanism that, for Ken Kesey, Joan Didion, and others, might provide an antidote. Our interest here will focus instead on the surprising way this apotheosis of openness was associated, in the literary imagination of the generation, with a softening of the boundaries between "standard" versions of reality and the "fictional" realm of utopian-consumerist desire.

Although Stegner was not himself a combat veteran, the idea of men working in small groups at a common task was keenly appealing to him, as one can see in his story "Saw Gang" (1945), published the same year he had Burdick in class. Told from the point of view of an adolescent boy, the story explores the camaraderie of a group of men who come together to help their neighbor cut a two-year supply of firewood in a single day. Since none of these men likes to talk while working, the story becomes a Hemingwayesque study in the way extreme linguistic parsimony can go hand and hand with the deep mutual understanding and sympathy between men. Giving their labor to each other as a gift, they mark the boundaries of their community in their bemused contempt for some shoddy work done by a dude from the city which they see along the way to their worksite.[6] In what proves to be one of the story's only instances of gratuitous self-expression, the men walk "along together, not talking. Ernie, matching his behaviour to theirs, walked steadily, watching the woods. Only when Donald Swain breathed his lungs full of air, shifted his axe to the other shoulder, and said, 'Good workin' weather,' the boy looked at him and they grinned. It was what he had wanted to say himself."[7] In fact one could say that Stegner, who grew up in a tiny settlement on the desolate northern plains, was obsessed by small- to medium-sized associational groups, whether in the form of work gangs, or small village democracies, or consumer cooperatives, or the groups that come together around a seminar table to talk about writing. One of the ongoing projects of his Western regionalist fiction, of a piece with its passionate environmentalism, is to correct the fiction that the relative "emptiness" of the region encouraged an unfettered individualism in its inhabitants.

Stegner's interest in human group interaction seems an adjunct to his more comprehensive interest in the integrity of ecological systems of all kinds, and, although he was a political liberal, he was every bit as comfortable with the idea of socially imposed limits on the individual as Flannery O'Connor was. His rebuke to myths of individualism is of course most powerfully embodied in the institution he built, where apprentice artists gather in groups, and it is also amusingly symbolized in the experience of the protagonist of a story called "Genesis," included in the innovative amalgam of history, memoir, and fiction, *Wolf Willow* (1962). This novella tells the story of a young gentleman who has come to the American West to experience the romance of it all, but who is soon caught in a deadly blizzard with other men. Far from further individualizing him, the man's exposure to the elements on the vast blankness of the Western landscape throws into relief his radical dependence on others: "Given his way," the story concludes, "he did not think that he would ever want to do anything alone again, not in this country. Even a trip to the privy was something a man might want to take in company."[8]

Even as he was writing *Wolf Willow* in the early sixties, Stegner was becoming increasingly distressed by the many transformations going on around him on campus and in the Bay Area at large, which made everything seem a little bit unreal. This surreal ruckus was exemplified in the behavior of countercultural figures like his student Ken Kesey, who acted like he was on drugs, and often was. For Stegner, Kesey's behavior was the quintessence of individualism run amok. And it makes obvious sense that Wallace Stegner became in turn, for Kesey, the living representative of institutional staidness. As the founder of the writing program at Stanford, and the namesake of the "Stegner Fellowships" awarded to students like Kesey even while Stegner was still around, he was a walking and talking institution. Brought together in the small seminar meetings in the Jones Room, neither Stegner nor Kesey was at first able to perceive the large area of overlap in their interests. For his part, Stegner misunderstood, or at least grossly simplified, the social historical phenomenon for which his obstreperous student became for him a symbol—or rather, the inspiration for a symbol: graduate student guru Jim Peck in Stegner's novel *All the Lit-*

tle Live Things (1967). Here, matching his narrative technique to a personal need to vent, Stegner's stridently opinionated first person narrator lays bare the selfish cynicism at the core of "Peck's" smelly beatnik charisma.[9] "Allston's" ideas exactly reflect Stegner's nonfictional screeds against the general phenomenon of "the sixties," which he criticized for its "pretense that it is breaking entirely with the Establishment and the past," insisting that it would one day "have to acknowledge the absurdity of its cult of total individual freedom."[10]

But "total individual freedom" is at best a weak description of the general object of desire in youth movements, circa 1967, and an even weaker description of the aims of Kesey and the group—the troupe—that gathered around him in the environs of Stanford and went by the anachronistic name of the Merry Pranksters. Say what you will about their libertarian ideological bent, they were conducting what it is fair to describe as a series of experiments in small group membership. According to Tom Wolfe, the oft-repeated, Manichean mantra of the famous trip the Merry Pranksters made across the U.S. in a crazily-painted schoolbus was "You're either on the bus . . . or off the bus," which, however vague in some ways, is perfectly clear in posing the question of group membership to the individual in the starkest terms.[11]

Indeed, it seems quite strict by comparison to the representation of the open campus we find in Thomas Pynchon's *The Crying of Lot 49* (1966), where Oedipa Maas, recently named executrix of the estate of Pierce Inverarity, pauses to take in the sight of Sproul Plaza on the campus of the University of California at Berkeley across the bay: "It was summer, a weekday, and midafternoon; no time for any campus Oedipa knew of to be jumping, yet this one was. She came downslope from Wheeler Hall, through Sather Gate into a plaza teeming with corduroy, denim, bare legs, blonde hair, hornrims, bicycle spokes in the sun, bookbags, swaying card tables, long paper petitions dangling to earth, posters for undecipherable FSM's, YAF's, VDC's, suds in the fountain, students in nose-to-nose dialogue."[12] Oedipa's trip to the Berkeley campus is in one sense fruitless. It turns out that the professor who was supposed to help her puzzle through the textual variants of an obscure Jacobean revenge play, *The Courier's Tragedy*, decamped some time ago to a job at San Narciso College, outside Los Angeles, from whence she has just driven and to which, sure enough, she will soon yo-yo on back.[13]

However brief Oedipa's pause may be at ground zero of the sixties—for Barrett Watten, Sproul Plaza is the very scene of the "formation of the subject-position of the student radical"—her visit provides her with something she gets nowhere else in the novel: a solid sense of her own identity.[14] But identity comes to Oedipa on campus as the ironic effect of her feeling of generational alienation from everything she sees around her. FSM? YAF? These acronymic icons of student politics, both left-wing and (notably) right, make her realize just how much a product of the quietist 1950s she is.[15] But not only this—also how much of an old-fashioned *English major* she is: the patriarchy of the fifties "had managed to turn the young Oedipa into a rare creature indeed, unfit perhaps for marches and sit-ins, but just a whiz at pursuing strange words in Jacobean texts" (83). It would be worth meditating on this moment if only for the slight hesitation it demands before the claim that Pynchon's antic sensibility is a quintessential product of the culture of the 1960s. Perhaps it is after all, but it seems important to register how its author, who like his character Oedipa was a 28-year-old Cornell graduate when *Lot 49* was published, communicates through her a sense of his own distance from campus youth culture circa 1964, just as it is about to erupt into protest. But unlike Wallace Stegner's, Pynchon's attitude toward this culture was a positive one.

Having turned down a job teaching creative writing at his alma mater, Pynchon might not have been, like his contemporary John Barth, an instructor of student youth in the classroom, but for him as for Barth the student body was a dramatically expanding market to which his work might sell.[16] Indeed, with its ever-swelling canon of youthful anti-hero protagonists, from J. D. Salinger's Holden Caufield to Philip Roth's Neil Klugman to Sylvia Plath's Esther Greenwood, one can see the entire literary field of this period beginning to bend heliotropically toward the "value" of youth in several senses. Candidly explaining his uncharacteristic swerve into short fiction in *Lost in the Funhouse,* Barth would note that he "wanted to be in those anthologies" which he himself, as a teacher, frequently used in the classroom.[17] Something of the same motive can perhaps be attributed to Pynchon (or his publishers), who, pausing to produce the brief *Lot 49* amidst the long haul of the monumental *Gravity's Rainbow* (1973), made himself conveniently teachable to undergraduates happily ever after. (With the publication of his early stories in the volume *Slow Learner* [1984], which Pynchon hoped would be "illustrative of the typical problems of entry-level fiction," he would make a contribution to writing pedagogy in particular.)[18] In a sense that will become completely clear only in the third part of this book, we could say that *Lot 49 miniaturizes* his more typical sprawling maximalism, with its roots in the spontaneous expressivity of the Beat aesthetic of the 1950s and its embrace of subject matter of unruly "historical scope."

But whatever Pynchon's motive may have been for producing a short novel, its frequent use as a college textbook produces the novel's most powerful form of reflexivity. Strictly regulating the commerce between the reader and the third person narrator who might (in theory) have solved the mystery of the Tristero rather than letting it ride, Pynchon aligned the experience of untold thousands of college students who have tried to understand *The Crying of Lot 49* with an English major protagonist who is doing much the same thing.[19] Indeed, the absented, impersonal and thus, as Brian McHale describes him, "classically modernist" narrator of *Lot 49* seems the formal equivalent on the one hand to the character Pierce Inverarity, whose death sets the story in motion and whose absence keeps its mysteries mysterious, and on the other to Pynchon himself, whose famously deliberate absence from the postwar economy of authorial celebrity has inspired an obsessive curiosity on the part of many of his fans about the real author behind the implied one they encounter in the work.[20]

Unlike Stegner, with his gaze trained fondly on a more dignified past, Pynchon's Oedipa is clearly impressed by what she sees in the present at Berkeley: a place "jumping" with youthful communication. As well she might be, champions of the "dialogic" might say, since not only is the campus delightfully lively with self-expression, but the "individual voices" there, resisting the narcissistic pleasures of monologue, are clearly engaged in a group thing. This is what Stegner could not see, and this in turn blinded him to the "conservative" element in all the unkempt creativity in his midst. Theirs is a dialogue that, as J. Peter Euben has noted, pointedly includes the political right (the Young Americans for Freedom) as one of its participants, and it is apparently to be appreciated beyond the bounds of any particular political commitment. The situation is similar with the Tristero, the long-running historical conspiracy that sometimes seems politically subversive and thus a model for the stealthy action of the "disinherited" of the present day: in fact if we look closely we see that the Tristero has as frequently been associated with right-wing causes as with left-wing ones. Not that, God forbid, the confessed "young Republican" Oedipa is simply to be confused with her author. But we would be bad and disloyal scholars not to take the historical conjecture about the Tristero finally offered to Oedipa by Professor Emory Bortz quite seriously: "He held . . . to a mirror-image theory, by which any period of instability for Thurn and Taxis must have its reflection in Tristero's shadowstate" (134).

The conspicuous complementarity of official and unofficial postal services that Bortz conjectures—suggesting that, like Coke and Pepsi, or Microsoft and Apple, they are not in mortal but loyal opposition as major and minor terms in a familiar sort of commercial rivalry—troubles the idea that there could be radical transformation through the agency of the Tristero. It is hard to deny the authority of Bortz's account, at least as measured by everything else that happens in the novel (in the real world, as we know, society as we know it could come down in flames at any moment). Everything we are told about the Tristero suggests that it represents a purely formal sociological principle of oppositionality. It appears, then, that *Lot 49* is not pitting the utopia of "anti-system" against the system, but one *kind* of system, "open," against another, "closed."

As any serious reader in the fifties or sixties could have told you, closed systems are bad because they are subject to what the economist Kenneth Boulding, observing the world from his perch at the Center for

Advanced Study in Behavioral Sciences in the hills above Stanford, called the "Entropy Trap." Here, reversing the historical association of chaos and nonconformity, the second law of thermodynamics guarantees the closed system's gradual decline into chaotic conformism. Without the exertion of new energy from without, that is, systems become "lukewarm" in a literal and metaphorical sense, and then grow cold.[21] To apply this analysis of physical systems to social and economic systems proved irresistible: as against Tocqueville's famous attribution of this quality to the citizens of the United States, "conformism" would have to become a negative value associated with the "closed" societies and economies of the Eastern Bloc. But for Norbert Wiener, the great theoretician of cybernetics from whom Pynchon gleaned his understanding of one of his signature themes, there is no remedy for the well-nigh un-American truth that everything we know is "running downhill" into entropy. Our efforts to create and maintain "pockets" of energetic order—open systems—wherein we experience something like "progress" may at best, in their heroic helplessness against fate, inspire the "purging terror of Greek tragedy."[22] This, in itself, explains a lot about the overall tone of *Lot 49,* where the minor successes of Oedipa are set against a general backdrop of enervated and hysterical, if not quite tragic, dread.

But it also explains the novel's total commitment to the open system as the best we can hope for, even if that entails creating systems open to the incursions of commercial or ideological competitors. An open system is one that, as defined by Stanford systems theorist W. Richard Scott, is "capable of self-maintenance on the basis of a throughput of resources from the environment," and this means that the open system must have an outside to relate to in the first place.[23] The universe is one system that might not have an outside, and if so it must decline over time (if not anytime soon) and grow cold. Another is pictured, famously, in the *mise-en-abyme* of the Remedios Varo painting that Oedipa remembers seeing in Mexico when she was there with Inverarity, where some damsels appear as "prisoners in the top room of a circular tower, embroidering a kind of tapestry which spilled out the slit windows and into a void, seeking hopelessly to fill the void: for all the other buildings and creatures, all the waves, ships and forests of the earth were contained in this tapestry, and the tapestry was the world" (11). One obvious way to interpret this painting is as a vision of narcissistic subjectivism: what appears to be outside you, the environment, is in fact projected from within you. But we might also pause to take the medieval imagery of the circular tower at face value, that is, as an image of the entropic enclosure not of selves but of a certain kind of institution—namely, the Ivory Tower.

This is not to say that the circular tower in *Lot 49* is literally a representation of the architecture of the self-contained university, the alter ego of the "open" institution in Berkeley. That would negate its obvious relevance to the theme of suburban entrapment of women also broached in works like Betty Friedan's *The Feminine Mystique* (1963). But this image does take part in the period's general preoccupation with the sources of pathological decline in institutions of all kinds. An alternative vision of this decline saw it as the result not of system closure but as a drama surrounding the system's inevitable porousness. This is what is envisioned in Albert O. Hirschman's *Exit, Voice, and Loyalty: Responses to Decline in Firms, Organizations, and States* (1970), which the economist (inevitably) conceived and wrote as a fellow at the Center for Advanced Study in Behavioral Sciences at Stanford. Here Hirschman proposed the patently dramatistic terms "exit" and "voice" as two competing responses to the inevitability of decline in any social organization. The first, which he conceived as proper to his own discipline of economics, describes a simple act of departure from group membership, as when the customer goes elsewhere when no longer satisfied, or when the employee of the failing firm "jumps ship" for another place of employment. In classical economics this loss becomes, in itself, a competitive motivation for change in the firm. By contrast, "voice," a concept proper to political science, describes how the group member might instead stay and complain about the firm, changing it politically "from within."

While exit and voice have coequal conceptual status in Hirschman's model of membership, voice, as the heretofore "neglected" option in economic theory, is the one he wants to speak up for, since it holds the promise of the firm's retaining the *enlivening energy* of its most alert members rather than letting it dissipate into its environment (or, worse, find its way into another firm). Hirschman understands himself to be working between the disciplines of economics and political science, but it should come as no surprise to us, having witnessed the concept of "voice" acquire a near-hegemony in academic thinking about authorship, when his account bends explicitly toward concepts proper to the humanities: "While exit requires nothing other than a clearcut either-or decision [to stay or to go], voice is essentially an *art* constantly evolving in new directions." Its unpredictability means that it must be nurtured against the easier option of exit lest it *"atrophy the development of the art of voice."*[24]

While Hirschman was interested in theorizing how organizations can avoid "heat death" by retaining the human energy they already have, the alternative was to consider ways of recruiting new energy into the organization. Commercial advertising is no doubt the most familiar of these ways, inspiring a desire for the firm (or its products) that yields a throughput of consumer capital and new employees. Similarly, educational institutions began in this period to orient themselves "outward" to the domain of new external resources—financial, human, and otherwise—on a scale never before seen in the history of higher education. In practice, this meant orienting the university to the needs of the military-industrial complex, to the industrial and post-industrial economy more broadly, and to "society" most broadly of all—all of the constituencies brought together in Clark Kerr's multiversity. One of the energetic "resources" waiting to be captured by the university was the student body, that collective, corporeal vehicle of the future. Indeed, since millions of new students were suddenly able, as a result of the G.I. Bill and the Education Act of 1965, to secure grants and loans from the federal government for college—and, even more crucially, since federal and state aid to higher educational institutions was most often keyed to their enrollment numbers—colleges had a strong self-interest in wooing these young customers and keeping them happy. If they could not be kept from exiting four years later upon graduation, the sentiment of institutional loyalty that Hirschman theorized as a helpful disincentive to exit could at least be put to the purpose of generating alumni contributions.

Among the many beneficiaries of the intensified institutional desire for the student body in the 1960s were the small-time operators known as creative writers, who, building on the example set by Iowa, Stanford, Johns Hopkins, Denver, and a handful of other early movers, began to be hired in great numbers to staff a tenfold multiplication of creative writing programs across the land. Consecrated to the unpredictable value of "creativity" and the "art of voice" in a literal sense (we will see just how literal in the next chapter), these programs embodied an institutional aspiration to be open to "outside influences" that would keep them alive and lively and new. They were also, more simply, a way of giving students what they intensely wanted: a chance to express themselves. Installing a respect for creativity in the system of higher education would, in theory, counteract what was becoming a boilerplate neo-progressive critique of the school in the 1960s on the grounds of its similarity to a prison. It may have "no prison bars, or locked doors like an insane asylum," observed Charles Reich in *The Greening of America*, "but the student is no more free to leave it than a prisoner is free to leave the penitentiary."[25] This called, in Ivan Illich's phrase, for a general "deschooling" of society.[26] Stegner's irritation and befuddlement with these heady times was not simply a testament to the limits of his imagination, but also a symptom of an objective sociohistorical contradiction that called forth responses of various kinds. Turning inside out and back, the writhing multiversity of the sixties was experiencing a profound crisis of definition in a literal sense, struggling to negotiate and maintain the boundary between itself and the wider social environments into which it extended itself and from which it drew resources. As noted by Scott, this is a feature of all open systems: "Because of [their] openness . . . determining their boundaries is always difficult and sometimes appears to be a quite arbitrary decision."[27]

In this, the university of the sixties found itself at the center of a more general phenomenon of American culture that we can describe, somewhat abstractly, as the vertiginously dialectical mobilization of the

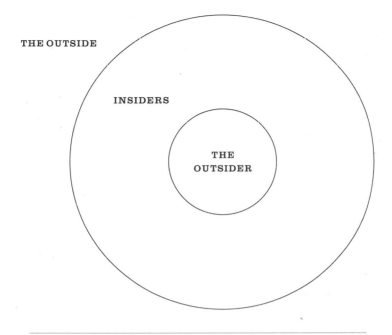

THE OUTSIDE

INSIDERS

THE
OUTSIDER

The system of the 1960s: "Externalism has become established or-
thodoxy. At an increasing number of levels, being 'way out' has replaced being 'in' as the most trenchant expression of 'belonging,' of
social acceptance" (Walter Ong).

distinction between "inside" and "outside." Cast in terms of institutional
subjectivity, this became a confused dialectic of "insiders" and "outsiders."
Noticing the cultural paradoxes in play in this period, Walter Ong described a strange world where "externalism has become established or-
thodoxy. At an increasing number of levels, being 'way out' has replaced
being 'in' as the most trenchant expression of 'belonging,' of social acceptance."[28] Hence the period's intensification, in the domain of fiction, of
something long evident in U.S. culture, especially in the genre of the Western: the ironic centrality of the figure of the outsider, both as a threat
to social order and as a source of spiritual purity and violent renewal of
that order.[29]

Another, more canonical image of the outsider is found in John

Gardner's *Grendel* (1971), which gives voice to a narrator-monster which the original *Beowulf* can only glimpse from the institutional enclosure, as it were, of the mead hall. But note that Gardner's treatment of the outsider is essentially conservative: this monster is no existential hero, but a young fellow (of sorts) who seems to have read too much in existentialism. Wisdom in the novel instead resides with the dragon, who could be speaking for any number of theorists of the open system when he notes that the "'essence of life is to be found in the frustrations of established order. The universe refuses the deadening influence of complete conformity. And yet in its refusal, it passes toward novel order as a primary requisite for important experience.'"[30]

Perhaps the most powerful participant theorization of the "inside-out" culture of the sixties is found in the work of the symbolic anthropologist Victor Turner, whose concepts of "liminality" and "communitas" in ritual practices seemed easy to transpose from the African tribal examples from which they were derived to the contemporary American scene, where beatniks and Blacks were, as Hirschman described it, performing acts of "*demonstrative* 'otherness'"[31] paradoxically at once "un-American" and profoundly American. The state of "liminality," for Turner, is one in which the person exits temporarily from the status hierarchies of everyday social structure into an ecstatic, inversive experience of community. Here, for a time, the lowly "outsider" becomes the ultimate "insider" or bearer of spiritual authenticity and authority. This, writ large, was what Stegner's student N. Scott Momaday was noticing when he spoke of how "to be an Indian on the Berkeley campus now, is to be *somebody*. Everybody listens to you. They are curious about you, and they look at you with a great deal of respect."[32] If Native Americans and African Americans could be understood as "liminal" figures in American culture, then the white primitives of the counterculture could at least become "liminoid."

What tended to be left out of the enthusiastic countercultural embrace of ritual liminality as superior to the squareness of structure was Turner's clear indication of the *functionality* of these rituals within the larger structure of the everyday.[33] Religions might, in the foundation of monasteries, attempt an "institutionalization of liminality"—a suggestive description of the college as well—but society more typically demands a return from the ritual state back to the usual hierarchical order: "There is a dialectic here, for the immediacy of communitas gives way to the mediacy of structure, while, in *rites de passage*, men are released from structure into communitas only to return to structure revitalized by their experience of communitas. What is certain is that no society can function adequately without this dialectic."[34] If something similar can be said of the experience of college, it can also be said of the liminal experience of literary art, at least as it was understood in the sixties, where the novelist creates spaces much like those that Foucault in 1967 called "heterotopias."[35] To wit: fiction as a trip. Here too, though, as we can see by examining the case of Ken Kesey, these alternative visions are bound everywhere by their attachment to the institutional settings from which they emerge, and in which they have real and consequential roles, however small, to play.

SMALL GROUP MEETINGS

Take an old yellow school bus and paint it crazy colors. Now stock it with thirteen or fourteen friends, three movie cameras, recording equipment, and a bucket of hallucinogens and head out on the open road. The vehicle at the center of Ken Kesey's recipe for his third significant work of art—the first two were the novels *One Flew Over the Cuckoo's Nest* (1962) and *Sometimes a Great Notion* (1964)—made a vivid mark on the popular culture of its time and has remained, mainly thanks to Tom Wolfe's best-selling account of its travels, *The Electric Kool-Aid Acid Test* (1968), an icon of freewheeling countercultural endeavor. With its lurid swirls and reconfigured seating arrangements, its souped-up sound system and retrofitted topside observation deck, the chugging behemoth that came to be known by its announced destination, "Further," seemed aptly designed to declare a transcendence of the squareness of American life as it emerged from the 1950s and lurched toward the Summer of Love.[36] Much imitated, the original "magic bus" was of course only the most recent entry in a long tradition of vehicle symbolism running through American culture, from the sailing ship to the covered wagon to the locomotive and beyond. Most important to Kesey, no doubt, was the precedent of the car in Jack Kerouac's transcontinental Beat narrative, *On the Road* (1957).

But Kesey's bus, acquired at least in part as a result of his growing impatience with the loneliness of novel writing, attempted a more complete vehicular literalization of the idea of *social movement* than was possible with the suspiciously individualistic automobile. In this it hearkened back to the extended-family-sized vehicle of *The Grapes of Wrath* (1939) and to Steinbeck's *Wayward Bus* (1947), and to the more recent significance, as recalled in Flannery O'Connor's "Everything That Rises Must Converge" (1961), of the bus as a resonant setting of Civil Rights conflicts. Underlining the genealogical link between Kerouac's and Kesey's vehicles, it was none other than Neal Cassady, real-life inspiration for Kerouac's protagonist, who maintained and drove Further as it made its way in the summer of 1964 from California to New Orleans to New York City and back, stopping along the way to allow for unscripted, blurrily filmed encounters between the Merry Pranksters and whatever or whomever they found beside the road. "You could regard the multicoloured bus as Kesey's third novel," observes Tony Tanner, pointing us down a path of interpretation we will eventually want to follow a few more steps, "only this time he was inside it and at the wheel."[37] Amidst all of the hoopla, it has been too easy to lose sight of the simple fact that Further was a *school* bus, for this turns out to be highly suggestive both of the nature of Kesey's larger aesthetic enterprise, of which the performance art of a self-documenting bus trip was a part, and of the bourgeoning university discipline of creative writing that counted him, when the Pranksters set off on their journey, one of its proudest recent products.

Ken Kesey was a writing program graduate? He was—and also, eventually, having earned an M.A. at Stanford, he became a creative writing instructor at the University of Oregon. The fact that Kesey, of all people, was a creative writing graduate student tells us a lot, however indi-

The retrofitted school bus called "Further," a.k.a. "Furthur," in 1964: the inscription along the top of the bus reads "A VOTE FOR BARRY IS A VOTE FOR FUN," suggesting at least one conjunction of the counterculture with Republican politics in an attack on the New Deal liberal status quo. Photograph by Allen Ginsberg / Corbis.

rectly, about the role of the writing program as an institution among institutions, the way it was designed to make space in the larger context of the university for the values and practices of creativity. If doing so opened the technocratic university of the Cold War to some of the wild unrealities of art, it was also a way of incorporating some of that liminality and putting it to work. A bus trip meant to symbolize an escape from institutionality to the freedom of the open road can, with a minimal squint of the eyes, start to look like a reestablishment of institutionality on different, more progressive—literally—terms. In this it looked forward to the founding of unusual institutions like the Buddhist-inspired Naropa University in Boulder, Colorado in 1974, devoting itself to what it calls "contemplative education." It was here that Allen Ginsberg, Diane DiPrima, and other figures of the Beat movement who one might have thought of as obvious exceptions to the rule of the Program established what they called the Jack Kerouac School of Disembodied Poetics, which has been offering an M.F.A. degree in creative writing since 1976. The Merry Pranksters spoofed the school bus, yes, but in some obvious ways they remained school kids at heart; they were "performance artists" before that term came into use, but these performances bore more than a passing similarity to the venerable fraternity prank. And in this they can be said, not to have transcended the school, but to have radicalized the institutional logic of creative writing instruction, with its roots in a progressive educational movement that was all about making the classroom more responsive to the creativity, if not necessarily the "disembodiment," of the student.

This gives us a new way of reading what would appear to be one of the classic anti-institutional texts of all time, Kesey's *One Flew Over the Cuckoo's Nest,* which was one of a number of literal or figurative "prison narratives" produced in the period, including Stanley Elkin's *A Bad Man* (1967) and, a little later, John Cheever's *Falconer* (1977).[38] Pitting the rowdy cowboy-figure, Randall Patrick McMurphy, against the emasculating rule of Big Nurse on a mental hospital ward, Kesey's novel would seem to strike a devastating symbolic blow against the cloying "momism" of the liberal welfare state. As seen by the novel's schizophrenic Native American narrator, Chief "Broom" Bromden, McMurphy's role is to inspire his fellow inmates to reclaim their manhood from the devious congeries of feminizing social institutions he calls the "Combine," of which the mental hospital is only, we take it, the example nearest to hand: "Under her rule," Bromden observes, "the ward Inside is almost completely adjusted to surroundings, [but] she works with an eye to adjusting the Outside world too."[39] The depth of this novel's anti-institutionality has made it a favorite choice for high school and college syllabi, where it has helped reel untold thousands of unsuspecting "disaffected youth" back into the educational groove. Stephen Tanner speaks more tellingly than he knows when he notes that it is "not surprising that the novel has been used as a text for courses in a variety of subjects and disciplines."[40]

Fascinatingly—and from the literary historical perspective, crucially —McMurphy's flagrant individualism and loudness on the ward find a partial analogue at the source of the narrative utterance. Bromden, inhabiting the stereotype of the silent Indian, has played for years at being deaf and dumb. But now, as he begins to tell the story of McMurphy, he declares his intention to shatter this silence in the telling of the story we are about to read: "It's gonna burn me . . . telling about all this, about the hospital, and her, and the guys—and about McMurphy. I been silent so long now it's gonna roar out of me like floodwaters and you think the guy telling this is ranting and raving my *God;* you think this is too horrible to have really happened, this is too awful to be the truth! But, please. It's still hard for me to have a clear mind thinking on it. But it's the truth even if it didn't happen" (7–8). The ambiguities of this intention to roar are many, since they only reverse the prior ambiguity of his silence: was the latter a self-defensive radicalization of the general societal "silencing" of marginal voices like his? As in: you won't really hear me anyway, so why waste energy moving my lips? Or was it rather a more pointed form of resistance to the doctors' "incitement to discourse," in which the mental patient, far from being repressed in his speech, is forced to speak so as to implicate himself in the policing of his own insanity: "Talk, he says, discuss, confess" (47).

Under no obligation to be consistent, it probably carries both of these significances. And yet the proto-Foucauldian insight that Bromden's silence might be understood to embody—silence as resistance—would, as the decade unfolded, gradually fade from the cultural scene (only to re-emerge, as we shall see in Chapter 5, as one of the central components of the deliberately "uncommunicative" literary minimalism of the 1970s and 80s). A floodwater of *ex-pression:* we want to attend to the root meaning of this term as a *pressing out,* for as such it becomes visible as the linguistic analogue of a widespread obsession not only with *liberation,* but even more essentially with *externalization.* No sooner did American institutions (in many cases begrudgingly) open their doors to outsiders of various kinds than these newly minted insiders often wanted to get back out, if only in a spiritual sense. This is already evident in the fabled bus trip, which enacted the outward flight of the Pranksters from the confinements of a settled life and released Kesey himself from the lonely confinement of novel writing, freeing his art from the flatness of textuality into the full bloom of an extra-dimensional, "intermedial" presence. So situated, the writing component of this enterprise could be delegated to an outside observer, Wolfe, a New Journalist looking for an "inside view" of the counterculture.

Technologically equipped to blare amplified words at the surrounding world, the bus called "Further" was a *vehicle of expression* in many senses. Seen in this context, Bromden's narration in *One Flew Over the Cuckoo's Nest* is interesting for the way it can announce but not quite, not yet, actually embody a condition of pure expressivity. Instead it presents us with an unusual fusion or palimpsest of silence and speech: Bromden's wordlessness amidst the events he describes in the present tense remains palpable even as it is being systematically negated in the (extradiegetic) telling. No wonder that the narrative, as it unfolds, is really nothing like the onrushing rant Bromden tells us to expect. Rather, it reads like what we would expect from someone Gordon Lish would defend as a "writer of impeccable discipline," a writer schooled in modernist narrative techniques by the apostles of craft who taught at the Stanford University creative writing program.[41] These included not only Wallace Stegner but also Malcolm Cowley, the intimate of Hemingway and Faulkner who was teaching in the program in the late 1950s, when Kesey first arrived there, and the Irish writer Frank O'Connor, author of a well-known study of the short story, *The Lonely Voice* (1962), a book whose very title could be said to predict Kesey's impatience with the medium of writing. Working with these teachers, Kesey would learn to pitch his narratives at a precisely calibrated spot on the continuum between silence, on the one hand, and ranting and raving, on the other.

While he was a fellowship student at Stanford Kesey famously offered himself as a paid subject in the government-funded experiments with LSD being conducted nearby, and eventually took a job as an overnight orderly in the mental health ward of the local Veterans Administration hospital. In different ways, all three sources of income entailed what we might call an institutionalization of unreality. The writing program enlisted the university in the production of fiction, while the LSD studies were exploring the practical uses of hallucination for the military. Only the VA mental hospital, dedicated to containing and curing insanity, understood its relation to unreality in simply negative terms. As Bromden summarizes it, the "theory of the Therapeutic Community" practiced on the ward amounts to the idea that "society is what decides who's sane and who isn't, so you got to measure up" (47). And this meant that it must run afoul of the period's increasing commitment (even within the avant-garde of psychotherapy) to the idea that each person should be the creator of the autonomous "fiction" of his or her own life.

Be that as it may, working on the ward introduced Kesey to the mental patients he would transform into fictional characters, and left him ample time to work on the novel he would set in their sadly confined milieu. Superimposing the popular genre of the Western on this bleak institutional space, Kesey's idea was to represent the inmate-patients as a modern version of the "terrorized townsmen" one sees in works like Oakley Hall's *Warlock,* with the difference that here it is the "sheriff," in the form of Nurse Ratched, who is doing the terrorizing. By his own account, Kesey saw McMurphy as a kind of "Shane that rides into town, shoots the bad guys, and gets killed in the course of the movie," an "almost two-dimensional" character who "gains dimension from being viewed through the lens of Chief Bromden's Indian consciousness."[42] Thus the act of writing fiction on the ward enacted an imaginary transcendence of the institutional scene of the novel's making, where "Indian consciousness" is understood above all as an *out-of-doors* consciousness—a consciousness, even in an empirical condition of confinement, of an original freedom from institutionality.

But the situation is more complicated than that. What, for instance, are we to make of the fact that as the novel's chapters were drafted, they were submitted for credit to the creative writing workshop classes Kesey was attending while he worked at the hospital? James Baker Hall remembers being at Kesey's "elbow as he read *One Flew Over the Cuckoo's Nest,* a chapter at a time, to the advanced fiction workshop at Stanford in the school year 1960–61, a group of twelve or so gathered to an oval around a big modern Danish table." "Hardly Big Nurse, the spirit surrounding the Jones Room at Stanford," he notes, but "hardly City Lights Bookstore up the freeway" either.[43] In the Jones Room, on any given day, Kesey might look across the table at his fellow students and see Robert Stone, Larry McMurtry, Wendell Berry, Ernest Gaines, Tillie Olsen, and several other now well-known writers—a busload of future literary glory that even Iowa would have been hard pressed to match. Rather than a pure transcendence of institutionality, this presents us with a vision of a novel produced in the shuttling from one kind of institutional space to another.

Knowing this, it is difficult to read the scenes in the novel where patients gather in a circle for Group Meeting without seeing an afterimage of the Stanford seminar room hovering behind them. They are all of them—the writing workshop, the group therapy session, the psychedelic bus trip—strikingly similar in their intermediate social scale, and it makes sense that these forms of small group association would achieve, in experience, a level of analogical inter-substitutability. It is hard to read about the bad behavior of McMurphy in the Group Meeting, his all-too-evident disrespect for Nurse Ratched, without connecting it to Kesey's well-documented antagonism toward his teacher Wallace Stegner, whom, as John Daniel reports, Kesey saw as the "epitome of academic staidness and convention" even as Stegner found Kesey irritatingly "half-baked."[44] Explicitly linking the ward to a classroom, Bromden notes how the acute patients "look spooked and uneasy" when McMurphy laughs, "the way kids look in a schoolroom when one ornery kid is raising too much hell with the teacher" (17).

But Daniel adds that the "trouble between them, I think now, may have stemmed as much from their likeness" as self-consciously uncouth Westerners in the world of literary culture "as it did from their differences."[45] And in fact, a letter from Kesey to fellow Prankster Ken Babbs written during the period of the novel's initial composition indicates the direct influence of Stegner on its structure:

> I'll discuss point of view for a time now. I am beginning to agree with Stegner, that it truely is the most important problem in writing. The book I have been doing . . . is a third person work, but something was lacking; I was not free to impose my perception and bizarre eye on the god-author who is supposed to be viewing the scene, so I tried something that will be extremely difficult to pull off, and, to my knowledge, has never been tried before—the narrator is going to be a character. He will not take part in the action or ever speak as I, but he will be a character to be influenced by the events that take place, he will have a position and a personallity . . . Think of this: I, me ken kesey, is stepped back another step and am writing about a third person auther writing about something. Fair makes the mind real, don't it?[46]

What is most interesting about this planning, for our immediate purposes, is simply how it shows a young writer conscientiously puzzling through the classically Jamesian question of point of view bequeathed to him by his teacher, and discovering for himself how the discipline of perspectival limitation might intensify the story he wants to tell. As Stegner had advised in a 1942 article in *The Writer*, if the author, sacrificing the easy privileges of omniscience, "approaches the material as if he were one of the characters, if he lives the story before he writes," he "has imposed upon himself a limitation which is likely to pay dividends in credibility."[47] Communicating these New Critical values to his students, Stegner enabled the production at Stanford of a great number of technically dazzling works of fiction, including Tillie Olsen's free indirect fugue of despair and decline in an immigrant grandmother, "Tell Me a Riddle" (1961), and Ernest Gaines's hypnotic inhabitation of a child's consciousness in "A Long Day in November" (1964).

Stegner's own novels and stories often took the form of reflexive

studies of the question of point of view. This is evident in his most celebrated works, *Angle of Repose* (1971) and *The Spectator Bird* (1976), but even
more remarkably so in a lesser-known early novel, *The Potter's House*
(1938), which activates the modernist program of perspectival limitation
by telling the story of a deaf family from their radically imagistic point of
view, rigorously excluding any aural metaphors from the text.[48] Establishing at the outset that the ample dialogue included in the novel is being
generated by the silent physicality of sign language, Stegner launches us
into a narrative that continually asks us to imagine that we are *seeing* language, as the deaf person must do, rather than hearing it. In this sense, *The
Potter's House* seems an uncanny allegory of the aspiration to "show" not
"tell" a story in print—or, if you prefer, the inability to do anything *but*
show a story as visible print upon the page.

As it happened, Kesey was not quite able to "pull off" the somewhat
blurry conception of a third person narrator-cum-character that he described to Babbs. Instead, in the invention of his schizophrenic Native
American war veteran, Bromden, Kesey reached back to synthesize two
classic modernist models of narration, both of them variations on the in-
tradiegetic first person: somewhat as if *The Great Gatsby* had been narrated
not by Nick Carraway but by a smarter Benjy from *The Sound and the Fury,*
Kesey splits the jobs of narrator and protagonist between Bromden and
McMurphy and openly allows Bromden's insanity to color his account of
McMurphy's antics. In this way Bromden's "unreliability" becomes the vehicle of a "deeper," if admittedly "fabular" and paranoid, revelation of the
truth of life in the Combine. Unlike either of those schoolroom classics,
however, Bromden's narrative is told entirely in the present tense, as
though what he is describing is occurring before our eyes on a stage.[49] As
Terry Sherwood first noted, this complicates our sense of the narrative as
issuing from outside the ward, and as evidencing Bromden's self-expressive
liberation from the confinements of the Combine. Is that liberation, too,
merely imaginary?[50] In donning the shackles of the Jamesian and New
Critical model of narration, we could say, Kesey is driven to the *formal* re-
institutionalization of the narrator who has set himself free.

So Kesey seems to have learned a lot from Stegner, who seems to have misunderstood his student. But to deny that the charge of "total individualism" is rightly directed at the youth culture of the 1960s is not to claim that the problem of individuality in the group was thereby eliminated, or the importance of individuality entirely negated; rather, it was constantly taken up as an object of practical inquiry and referred to the related-but-different problem that looms so large in Sigmund Freud's account of group psychology: leadership. Lee Quarnstrom remembers a favorite Prankster activity called the Power Game, which combined the arbitrary erotic democracy of Spin the Bottle with its opposite: "We had this spinner that would be spun around and whoever it pointed to would get all the power for the next half hour. They could use it or abuse it. They could say 'We're all gonna clean my car,' or they could just walk around and have everyone follow them. It was a particular high to have twenty people staring into your eyes for thirty minutes. It was Kesey's way of being psychedelic without drugs."[51] Crucial here is the time limit on this power trip: except for the unfortunately irrevocable nuclear option, a future in which everyone is dictator for thirty minutes might not actually be so bad, especially if, as seems to be the case here, dictatorship becomes all but interchangeable with *attention-getting*. In that case it would be a Poli Sci version of Andy Warhol's famous dictum about the democratization of celebrity. As with celebrity culture, the jacked-up narcissism of the Power Game seems to produce an effect of unreality; or rather it produces the hyper-reality of the drug high, in which the act of perception is enriched to the point of seeming to author the world it perceives—or, more accurately, to the point of realizing the neurological truism that, in a limited sense, it *does* author that world. And yet these mini-dictatorships were only a respite from the more or less constant call to socialize in a more positive and submissive sense. As Wolfe reported, "it was like it had been ordained, by Kesey himself" that "no one was to rise up negative about anything, one was to go positive with everything," one was to *"go with the flow"* (88).

What Stegner perceived as a desire for "total individual freedom" in the youth of the sixties was, I think, something somewhat different: the contradiction between its desire on the one hand for liberation from official authority figures—preeminently parents and schoolteachers—and its desire to submit to unofficial forms of authority on the other. As Ruth Sullivan puts it in her mercilessly derisive reading of *Cuckoo's Nest:* "To permission for indulgence in self-pity and attacks on loved and hated authority figures, the novel adds permission to gratify dependency wishes," telling the reader: "allow yourself to depend on the good, omnipotent father [McMurphy]; he will help you conquer the wicked stepmother [Nurse Ratched]."[52] This was, after all, the ultimate age of the guru, an alternative pedagogical authority figure whose cultural otherness makes submission to a higher power more existentially palatable than is possible with the usual white schoolmarm or lawman. Hence the hilarious amounts of abuse taken by Carlos Castaneda at the hands of the Yaqui Indian sorcerer, Don Juan, as recorded in the book series that began with the UCLA Anthropology Ph.D.-thesis-turned-best-seller, *The Teachings of Don Juan* (1969). Here access to a "separate reality" goes hand in hand with obedience to a teacher. And then there were the decidedly less hilarious things demanded of the followers of Charles Manson. Kesey was, relative to this context, a rather benign guru—remarkably generous with his money, which funded the entire "Further" adventure, and a person whom innumerable people seem glad to have known even after the effects of the Kool-Aid had worn off. He was at least conflicted, if not entirely candid, about his role as "Chief" of the Pranksters, and for the group this issue became what Wolfe calls "The Unspoken Thing": "Kesey's role and the whole direction the Pranksters were taking . . . Kesey took great pains not to make [it] explicit. He wasn't the authority, somebody else was: 'Babbs says . . .' 'Page says . . .' He wasn't the leader, he was the 'non-navigator.' He was also the non-teacher. 'Do you realize that you're a teacher here?' Kesey says, 'Too much, too much,' and walks away. Kesey's explicit teachings were all cryptic, metaphorical; parables, aphorisms: 'You're either on the bus or off the bus'" (131). In the presence of *this* contradiction—the contradiction between equality of individuality and the group's apparent need for the special individuality of leadership—a very loud group of people falls silent.

Stegner and Kesey shared an interest in the theory and practice of the small group meeting, and both of them were leaders of a sort. The differences between them were, in many senses of the term, formal. Kesey's "I took LSD, and he stayed with Jack Daniels; the line between us was drawn" is one way of putting it.[53] Another would be to say that Stegner the environmentalist was mainly interested in the question of the *scale* of institutions—what size of human grouping is neither too large (a bureaucracy, a Combine) nor too small (a nuclear family, lonely individuality)? For Stegner, once one has found the right scale of institutional life, one is more or less allowed to be staid, and the institution can be closed against further development. In this, his Western conservationist mind-set is easily linked to the Southern regionalism of a figure like Allen Tate. Kesey, by contrast, was more interested in the essential *temporality* of institutions, their need to keep moving so as to stay open to the unpredictable. This in turn can be linked to the Midwestern regionalist mind-set of individuals like Paul Engle, a cold warrior for whom open markets and system-expansion were an inherent good.

The bus, of course, made Kesey's investment in the movement of institutions quite literal—it was Fluxus on wheels. It put the school in motion—or, more precisely, made the journey to and from school an endless one. But beyond this, it was a challenge directed at the institution Stegner loved most of all—the institution of the well-crafted novel. Explaining the genesis of "Further," Ken Babbs remembers that "before the bus trip we were talking about 'rapping' novels out instead of typing—because typing is so slow. We were going to take acid and stay up all night and rap out novels and tape record them. Then . . . we started talking about getting the movie cameras and filming it. So we were very swiftly going from a novel on a page to novels on audio-tape to novels on film."[54] And when, during the "writing" of the "novel" that took the innovative form of a bus trip, some iffy reviews of the actual novel *Sometimes a Great Notion* started to come in, the Prankster reaction, according to Wolfe, was "the hell with it. Kesey was already talking about how writing was an old-fashioned and artificial form and pointing out, for all who cared to look . . . the bus" (107).

And sure enough, once having lost faith in and abandoned the form of the novel, Kesey never wrote another important one, though eventually, having exhausted the materials in the so-called Prankster Archive, he tried.[55] He did however become a creative writing teacher, and a passionately innovative one. His idea for his first class as an instructor at Oregon was that he and a group of thirteen students would write a novel together. Here was yet another solution to the problem identified by his friend Robert Stone: "He was not, I think, enough of an individualist by nature to want to become a novelist. . . . He disliked the loneliness and the isolation of the writer's life."[56] The result of months of group creation and negotiation—but with Kesey himself at the head of the table, in the driver's seat—was a novel called *Caverns* (1990). It tells the story of (what else) the adventure of fourteen characters, one of them a notoriously eccentric outlaw, in a large vehicle out on the open road. Published by a major press under the pseudonym O. U. Levon (i.e., "University of Oregon Novel"— though with "Introduction by Ken Kesey" splashed prominently on the cover), it stands as one of the most literal instances of "program fiction" ever to have appeared in print. There's no telling what Stegner thought of it, if anything, but it did inspire some new thoughts on Kesey's part about Stegner: "I began to appreciate Wally much more after I had been a teacher."[57]

AMBIENT UNREALITY

Let us consider, briefly, the balloon—or rather, "The Balloon," one of the best-known stories in what has come to seem a quintessentially "sixties" collection of short fiction, Donald Barthelme's *Unspeakable Practices, Unnatural Acts* (1968). The balloon in "The Balloon" is about as clear a symbol of art as a *public presence* as one could imagine, beginning as it does on

Fourteenth Street and expanding "all one night, while people were sleeping, until it reached the Park," finally covering "forty-five blocks north-south and an irregular area east-west, as many as six crosstown blocks on either side of the Avenue in some places."[58] Hardly trapped in some Ivory Tower, or even on the flatness of the page, this balloon is the work of the first person narrator of the story, and he takes considerable pride in his artistic achievement: "Now we have had a flood of original ideas in all media, works of singular beauty as well as significant milestones in the history of inflation, but at that moment there was only *this balloon*, concrete particular, hanging there" (54).

The balloon may be, as he later confesses, a "spontaneous autobiographical disclosure" (58), but as an impersonal-seeming work of public art it also quite literally intrudes into the daily lives of the residents of the New York City, who make of it what they will. Living amidst and underneath this artwork, they engage in "a certain amount of initial argumentation about the 'meaning' of the balloon," some finding its "apparent purposelessness . . . vexing," while others, "especially . . . persons to whom change, although desired, was not available," find pleasure in the possibility it offers for "mislocation of the self" (54; 55; 57). And while we are assured that "since the meaning of the balloon could never be known absolutely, extended discussion was pointless" (54), a few important questions continue to assert themselves even after it has been deflated, if not about the balloon then about "The Balloon."

For instance, if the balloon is a symbol of the artwork-in-public—Barthelme's connections to the world of visual art were quite extensive—does that mean that it also functions as a symbol for the work of literature, even a tiny one like "The Balloon"? This story barely stretches over five short pages of print, let alone whole city blocks. Granted, when it was published, as many of Barthelme's stories were, in the *New Yorker*, it became one of the more widely exposed works of experimental fiction ever, and the debates about the meaning of the balloon on the streets of the publishing industry Imperium bear a suspicious resemblance to the ones provoked by Barthelme's playfully inscrutable texts. Stories like "The Balloon" are something like the balloon itself in their lack of fully developed characters and plots, in the way they assemble or elaborate (inflate) a more or less static idea, then stop. Still, the concrete particularity of the balloon's presence on the street is something that a work of literature, with its comparatively modest if numerous physicalities, would have trouble matching. Words among words, they are part of the hum of publicity but relatively ignorable, easily lost in the clutter in a way the intrusive balloon is not.

Thus, even if we might take it as an allegorical figure for Barthelme's own fiction, the balloon might also be a dream of its remediation to a higher power, a fantasy of escape from the 2-D prison of the page. In fact, the entire story collection, if not the entire Barthelme oeuvre, seems to embody this aspiration to escape from the institution of textuality, as story after story is set not in private but in overtly public spaces, whether that be the street, or a television studio, or the White House. We can see how the balloon might be taken as a symptom of the omnipresence not of art, exactly, but of its proximate other, mass culture. Barthelme's intimacy with and appreciation for the ways and means of mass culture is, for Jerome Klinkowitz, one of the keys to understanding stories that might otherwise seem to emanate from the haughty margins of the culture, and Kathleen Fitzpatrick has written of a broader "anxiety of obsolescence" on the part of postwar novelists in relation to television.[59] From this perspective the balloon would stand for everything with which literature was increasingly forced to compete for public attention in the increasingly loud and colorful 1960s. Because of the relatively recent insinuation of the broadcast media into the very air of daily life, mass culture had recently attained what seemed to many observers an aggressively ambient, enclosing presence, as though the nation-space had become a virtual prison-house of fictionality. If, once upon a time, the growing omnipresence of novels in an increasingly literate world could produce this effect—for Leslie Fiedler, perhaps the most notorious prognosticator of the imminent "death of the novel" in the early 1960s, the genre had represented "the beginnings of popular culture, of that machine-made, mass-produced, mass-distributed *ersatz* which, unlike either traditional high art or folk art, *does not know its place"*—now it seemed comparatively unambitious in its assault on the real.[60] Bright images and amplified sounds were everywhere.

This, no doubt, is part of what underlay the period's many critical iterations of the paradoxical theme of the encroaching "unreality" of contemporary American reality, to which condition the response could be a call either to "get real" or—the more sophisticated postmodern response—to replace the official fictions with better, more creative political alternatives. Perhaps the best known of these, and very much in the "get real" camp, was Daniel Boorstin's *The Image* (1961), a systematic analysis of the bad reflexivity of life in the time of what he called the "pseudo-event"—the event staged only for the media coverage it will get. For Boorstin, making a first pass through the territory of later media-analytical concepts like "simulacra," "hyperreality," and the "media apriori," the pseudo-events of the modern day beget other pseudo-events in "geometric progression" until "illusions . . . flood our experience." The genius of this book, whose perpetually renewed disappointment in contemporary culture from topic to topic otherwise gets a little tiring, is in its prescient perception of the powerlessness of media criticism like itself, whose exposure of the pseudo-event as inauthentic only increases the pseudo-event's presence and power: the "story of the making of our illusions—'the news behind the news'—has become the most appealing news in the world."[61] The weakness of the book is in its understanding of the encroachments of unreality as a symptom merely of a generalized failure of personal character in times of widespread economic plenty. A better approach would have been to analyze the pseudo-event as a fundamental feature of an emergent information economy—or, better, "creative economy"—that still (as the Watts riots in Los Angeles soon enough revealed) kept many people in a condition of desperate want.

A similarly alarmist tone had been struck in the young Philip Roth's famous address delivered at the Esquire Magazine Symposium held at Stanford University in 1960, "Writing in America Today," and here it was understood as a problem for novelists in particular. Roth spoke to the Bay Area audience of a world in which the phantasmagoria of everyday reality outdoes the "meager imagination" of American novelists, driving some of them to embarrassing extremes to garner attention. Roth took this as a symptom of a loss of faith in the efficacy and relevance of the medium of writing and the book.[62] Even within the fiction of the period, according to Roth, one can detect how the literary effect of "reality"—the impersonal realism of the Jamesian tradition—is "taking a back seat to personality," which is not even "the personality of the imagined character, but of the writer who is doing the imagining," who seems to say, "Look at me, I'm writing."[63] This was before the amazingly antic performance of his own *Portnoy's Complaint* (1969), and before the invention of Roth's fictional alter ego, Nathan Zuckerman, who would become the vehicle of his own long-running, self-centered analysis of the personality of a writer.

The substitution of attention-getting "telling" for impersonal "showing" is one way of describing fiction's struggle for a place in the general economy of cultural attention, where competition for the leisure time of readers was beginning to heat up and the novel's aura of deep cultural relevance and authority was, according to some observers, beginning to dim. Another was the retreat from the open market to the economic refuge of the university. In this context, even failure as a commodity, for a literary work, might count as (existential) success-in-the-market as long as that failure earned sufficient cultural or spiritual capital for its producer to seem "worth it," and especially if that capital could be converted into credentials for an academic job that could act as a permanent hedge against the low odds of high sales. Barthelme himself would eventually set up shop at the University of Houston, founding a creative writing program that, as they will tell you on their website, has always been near the top of the heap in institutional prestige, at least as measured by entities like *U.S. News and World Report*.

Even in retreat from the market, however, the academic writer of the sixties often glanced nostalgically back across his shoulder. One sees this in the period's many instances of what must be called meta-genre fiction, where a popular genre—romance, western, science fiction, fantasy and detective fiction—is both instantiated and ironized to the point of becoming dysfunctional in the production of its conventional pleasures. Genre forms still commanded huge numbers of loyal paying customers even if they never appeared on the syllabus, the integrity of the latter having been defined in opposition to easily consumable mass cultural forms. By the same token, genre fiction was not tainted by the institutional respectability that had put a glaze upon the great experimental works of the interwar modernist era. To some degree, valuing genre fiction meant reversing the ideological valence given to mass culture by T. W. Adorno, Dwight Macdonald, Mary McCarthy, and other intellectuals of the 1950s: no longer the domain of a regressive, proto-fascist mass mind, popular culture would now be understood as a force of liberation from the straitjacket proprieties of "official" high culture. Just as important, it entailed a revaluation of the bad conventionality associated with genre fiction, the "formulaic" quality that can make individual titles seem the literary equivalent of widgets coming off a conveyor belt. Instead, the charge of "conventionality" would be aimed at the formerly insurgent, but now wholly respectable, modernist literary tradition itself, sitting there fat and happy on the college syllabus.

The latter position was staked out most eloquently by Ishmael Reed, in the introduction to his anthology of experimental writing by men of color, *19 Necromancers from Now* (1970), where it is presented as a meta-lesson about the exclusions enacted in the canon:

> I was to learn that White authors, as well as Afro-American authors, are neglected by the American university. Before I arrived at Berkeley, there was no room in the curriculum for detective novels or Western fiction, even though some of the best contributions to American literature occur in these genres. At another major university, the library did not carry

books by William Burroughs, who at least manages to get it up beyond the common, simple, routine narratives that critics become so thrilled about. . . .

I had [my students] translate these works with the same enthusiasm encouraged by the English faculty for explicating a later poem of Yeats. I suspect that the inability of some students to "understand" works written by Afro-American authors is traceable to an inability to understand the American experience as rooted in slang, dialect, vernacular, argot, and all of the other putdown terms the faculty uses for those who have the gall to deviate from the true and proper way of English.[64]

As we can see from Reed's paean to vernacular orality, the academic embrace of genre was allied with the valorization of folk culture and the oral storytelling tradition that will concern us in the next chapter. Denying its reduction to the status of mere commodity, genre fiction, he insisted, was the contemporary American version of folk culture, the culture of the people. That the money behind it was very much continuous with the money behind "official" high culture didn't for the moment matter.

Defining himself as a culturally advanced and to some degree oppositional figure, a writer like Reed could not however embrace popularity in its own terms. This is why he sets genre fiction and avant-garde postmodern fiction *alike* over and against official modernism, where the exuberant implausibility of the one and the gnarly experimentalism of the other are brought into creative alignment against an enslavement to official versions of the real. This was a fragile alliance, to say the least, requiring a strategic denial of the obvious continuity of modernist and postmodernist experimental impulses like Reed's, as well as a partial repression of the bid for academic respectability built into the very task of packaging experimental writing in a student anthology.

These tensions suffused Reed's famously fractious relations with the university that eventually tenured him, the University of California at Berkeley, and they are visible in his "Hoodoo Western," *Yellow Back Radio*

Broke-Down (1968), which was only the most surreal of the period's many high-literary engagements with the Western genre. Here the link to the popular oral storytelling tradition, in this case to the tall tale, is announced immediately:

> Folks. This here is the story of the Loop Garoo Kid. A cowboy so bad he made a working posse of spells phone in sick. A bull-whacker so unfeeling he left the print of winged mice on hides of crawling women. A desperado so onery he made the Pope cry and the most powerful of cattlemen shed his head to the Executioner's swine.
>
> A terrible cuss of a thousand shivs he was who wasted whole herds, made the fruit black and wormy, dried up the water holes and caused people's eyes to grow from tiny black dots into slapjacks wherever his feet fell.[65]

Staging the presence of the storytelling voice, the novel falls from here back to a more conventional deployment of the dramatic method, with minimal description, even less narrative summary, and long stretches of dialogue between characters engaged in an epic struggle for the future of Western Civilization. Reed would have been happy to see it topple in favor of a genuinely "multicultural"—he was one of the first to use the term—"techno-anarchist" paradise. As Reed described it: "I based the book on old radio scripts in which the listener constructed the sets from his imagination—that's why 'radio'; also because it's an oral book, a talking book. People say they read it out loud."[66] The popular medium of radio was in turn connected in his mind to pulp fiction. He called the novel "Yellow Back," he said, "because that's what they used to call Old West books about cowboy heroes: they were [quoting from a reference work] 'yellow covered books and were usually lurid and sensational,' so the lurid scenes are in the book because that is what the form calls for."[67]

Without denying for a minute the great good time that can be had reading this novel, one cannot help noticing Reed's tall tale beginning to bend from the emplotted pleasures of genre fiction toward the loftier demands of poetic prose even in the novel's opening lines quoted above, which, exercising the reader's skills at sense-making, seem ominously unsubservient to the story they are beginning to tell. This effect is reiterated formally by the text's unusual organization into bursts of left-justified text that look a lot like poetic stanzas. Fusing genre "popularity" with the paratactic, allusive difficulty of the literary avant-garde, this version of postmodernism posed no real threat to the hold of Louis L'Amour and Zane Grey on the hearts of the reading masses. And this, by Reed's own account, is part of why he teaches creative writing classes at Berkeley. Not only do you "learn a lot about craft from teaching it," but "writing the kind of fiction I'm writing, you have to earn a living from different sources. You have to hustle."[68] Perhaps, then, we can be forgiven for thinking that the remarkably inventive energy of the book owes as much to the late modernist "literariness" of which the university had become the primary institutional custodian as to its faithful instantiation of a popular generic form.

The book's commitment to fictionality as a path to liberated consciousness is dramatized in the novel when Loop Garoo and his band of fellow circus entertainers, traveling through the desert on Further-like "wagons that was painted real weird" (20), are suddenly "surrounded by children dressed in the attire of the Plains Indians" (15). Explaining why they have run their parents out of town, the children describe a life not only of violent exploitation, but of bad, boring education: "For three hours a day we went to school to hear teachers praise the old. Made us learn facts by rote. Lies really bent on making us behave. We decided to create our own fiction" (16). And so, with the help of the university, they did.

PRISON EXPERIMENTS

In a 1987 lecture delivered at San Francisco State University, where she had taught creative writing for several eventful years in the late 1960s and early 1970s, Kay Boyle expressed the opinion that creative writing workshops "should absolutely be abolished."[69] To her friend James T. Farrell, meanwhile, she had jokingly asked for "a spirited lament for the plight of those who once rocked Paris and who now, with spectacles on their noses, try to teach" (*Author of Herself,* 401).

Boyle was not the first—she may have been the five hundredth—creative writing instructor to express this opinion. Such are the apparent contradictions between inherited notions of the unprogrammable nature of creativity on the one hand, and institutionality on the other, that even a figure like Wallace Stegner, a Program Man if ever there was one, was known to have had moments of skepticism about the worth of the enterprise. But the force of the confluence of interests that come together in creative writing instruction—the student's desire to be a writer, the writer's desire for a steady paycheck, the institution's desire to be responsive to the desires of its inmates—is so strong that it marches on and expands even despite an occasional bad-mouthing from its bystanders, victims, and beneficiaries. While Kay Boyle, as a creative writing teacher, may have seen it as her duty to "save the creative writer from academia," her own case is arguably one of a creative writer saved *by* academia: come the 1960s, when she was herself in her sixties, this living link to the heroic oppositionality of expatriate Paris had very few readers and almost no income. The high-paying *New Yorker,* where her stories were a staple in the 1930s and 40s, was no longer interested in her work, and novels about Europeans caught up in the currents of European history—her specialty—were no longer in vogue. However poorly paid, the tenured position at SF State was a godsend for her.

As we have seen, it is precisely an unresolved tension between the "confinement" of institutionality and the "freedom" of creativity that gives creative writing instruction its raison d'être as an *institutionalization of anti-institutionality.* Viewed from this perspective, Kay Boyle, no less than Stegner or his nemesis Ken Kesey, might seem a quintessential figure of the Program Era, if only in the intensity of her drive to speak for and from the "outside"—wherever that seemed to her, at any given moment, to be. For it was the paradoxical role of creative writing in the university to bring the outside in; that is, to represent the outside on the inside. The most obvious way that Boyle did this was by representing, in her person, a living link back to a more glorious period in American literary history, when giants like Hemingway and Faulkner had been in their prime and when Paris, not Iowa City, was where every young American writer wanted to be. Although readers have thus far judged her creations inferior to the great works of the interwar era, we can point to at least one feature of her writing that connects it vividly to that of Hemingway, whom she always professed to loathe: like his, her fiction is obsessively autobiographical. The subtitle of Joan Mellen's biography of Boyle, "Author of Herself," is more technically accurate than one at first realizes.

The more apt comparison is perhaps to Thomas Wolfe, another writer whose reputation has not aged well: for Boyle as for Wolfe there is only the thinnest pane of refraction separating "the life" from "the work," so much so that it can seem that experience and the literary representation of that experience, truth and fiction, have become too tightly intermeshed ever to be pulled apart. In the work of both authors, the use of third person narration tends not to impersonalize the writing, as the Jamesian tradition would have it, but to facilitate the aggrandizement of whatever character is a stand-in for the author. One difference, however, is that while Wolfe was highly educated, Boyle had had only minimal schooling, instead adopting the "haughty, defensive scorn of formal education" that she continued to cling to even as a college professor (*Author of Herself*, 203). This ironically put her in sync with the neo-progressive educational insurgency of the sixties, which likewise was at war with educational formality. Another important difference between Boyle and Wolfe is that while the paranoid Wolfe would, if he could, have made the world submit to a sovereign artistic subjectivity that stood above mere politics, Boyle was wont to fling herself into the political currents of her time, counting on them to produce the exciting sense of malleability in the world—the sense that "anything can happen"—that authors like Reed produce by the strenuous use of the imagination. In brief, she was a woman of many causes, great and small. And this meant that she was only tenuously committed to the cause of literature as an end in itself, and thought the New Criticism "a complete hoax" (*Author of Herself,* 402).

Critics would revile Boyle's weakness, no less than they did with Wolfe, for the late romantic "cult of experience" that made her pay too little heed, not only to the imagination, but to the other side of the Hemingway model of artistic practice, which balanced the pursuit of extreme experiences with a meticulous attention to literary craft. Increasingly she was convicted of adhering to the fallacy that interesting experiences in highly charged political situations could of themselves give birth to good writing. This tendency, combined with the constant imperative to make as much money as quickly as possible from her writing (Boyle continued to have children with various impecunious men), led to her gradual branding as a pretentious hack whose "heavy, yearning seriousness" of manner (*Author of Herself,* 189) could not make up for her general shoddiness. Thus, while she embodied the romantic-experiential principle of "creative" anti-institutionality at the core of creative writing, from another perspective Kay Boyle's teachings couldn't have been more of an affront to its equally passionate attachment to the ideal of craft. If she was the bearer of the sputtering torch of interwar modernism, this modernism was what we might describe as a primarily *existential,* rather than a formal, one. She lived most of her life outside the native country she considered drab and narrow-minded, and well outside the conventions of bourgeois morality. She had nary a kind word for Enlightenment rationality or for schools. If something was "official," she was likely to be opposed to it. Her goal in her classes at SF State was to make of her students not so much writers as revolutionaries. As one of her favorites, Shawn Wong, remembered: "Everything we wrote had to be relevant" to the cause (*Author of Herself,* 464–465). Say what you will about the validity of this pedagogy, having people like this on the teaching staff can make a school very lively.

Even Boyle's great nemesis, S. I. Hayakawa, the linguist-turned-bureaucratic-strongman hired to quell the uprising at SF State, might have granted as much. The text in which she settles accounts with Hayakawa, "Long Walk at San Francisco State" (1970), explains itself in terms that remind us of Kesey's impatience with the slowness of novel-writing, though here the sense of hurry is explicitly politicized: "In other years, I might have done a fiction piece" about subtle aspects of the unrest, but "now I can only mention these things quickly in passing because of the other things that cannot wait to be said. . . . A novel takes at least two years to write, and the young can't wait that long to have the story of their lives and deaths dredged out of the ruins."[70] Describing herself on a march up Nineteenth Avenue, she asks herself "what I was doing feeling committed to a college. I had lived on mountain tops, carried my babies in a rucksack on my back when I skied, believed in poets more than any other men, honored French Resistance fighters and Italian partisans. . . . And now, through force of circumstance, I was, of all unlikely and unsuitable things, a college professor. I was a professor, moreover, who spoke of her institution as if it were a possession of the heart. 'That's because of the students,' I said to myself. That's because they're the great and vital thing."[71]If one is looking for a teacher willing and able to identify unironically with youth, the antithesis of Wallace Stegner, then Kay Boyle is your woman. No mere sympathizer-from-a-distance, as Pynchon's Oedipa was, Boyle was an official member in good standing of the Black Panthers; she was arrested and sent to jail for her political activities on more than one occasion.

But even she, when she got around in quieter times to writing her novel about her role in the sixties uprisings, *The Underground Woman* (1975), could not help expressing disquiet about certain features of the youth culture. To be sure, "Athena's" short-term imprisonment in the novel is understood and celebrated as the negative image of the peaceful liberation toward which she, as mother to the revolution, and her students understand themselves to be striving. "Everybody inside jail trying to get out, and you working your . . . you working yourself into a lather trying to get in" says her exasperated friend, and her self-satisfied glee as she sets out for jail with "fifteen people seated in the patrol wagon" is a perfect, politicized inversion of the journey of Further.[72] And yet the tendency of youth to submit to the "bondage of idolatry" of gurus like Kesey remains a lasting worry to a woman whose secret shame is her outré (in this con-

224

text) individualism; this, combined with a love of literature she can't help wanting to defend from the charge of "irrelevance," confuses the issue of what side of history, ultimately, she is really on. Just as Boyle did, the professor-protagonist of this novel has a daughter who has fallen under the influence of a guru and now lives in a cult, which, while it may be a critique of modern bureaucratic institutionality, is from another perspective the reestablishment of institutionality (as with Kesey's Pranksters) on new grounds. It thus becomes subject to the same pathologies explored by sociologist Philip Zimbardo in the famous Stanford Prison Experiment of 1971, where undergraduates were hired to be "imprisoned" or to work as guards in a make-believe jail, and soon became so coweringly or sadistically invested in their roles that the experiment had to be shut down.[73] This experiment has been interpreted as evidence of the power of environment to determine behavior. Less discussed, but in some ways more disturbing, was the students' related capacity to forget what they knew very well going into the experiment: that it was *not a real prison* but a make-believe one. When one of the novel's cult members steals some things from her home, they leave behind a copy of *One Flew Over the Cuckoo's Nest,* as though to tempt Athena to read it and readopt the proper attitude—Chief Bromden's attitude—of resistance to standard definitions of the real. Is the college which has become a "possession of the heart" perhaps to be protected from, as well as simply opened up to, those who would wrench it to their own ends?

One of the contemporary works of fiction that Boyle introduced to students at San Francisco State was Barthelme's *Unspeakable Practices, Unnatural Acts.* The companion piece to "The Balloon" in that volume, "The Indian Uprising," might have spoken eloquently, if obscurely, to her dilemma. It begins: "We defended the city as best we could. The arrows of the Comanches came in clouds. The war clubs of the Comanches clattered on the soft, yellow pavements. There were earthworks along the Boulevard Mark Clark and the hedges had been laced with sparkling wire. People were trying to understand. I spoke to Sylvia. 'Do you think this is a good life?' The table held apples, books, long-playing records. She looked up. 'No'" (108). Even in their absurd, cinematic conventionality, it's not hard to see these whooping wild Indians of the Wild West as an evocation of the two social groups who became the collective protagonists of a violent historical transformation: student youth and the racial other. Whether through the big boom of generational bio-power or the suddenly amplified moral force of decolonized subjectivity, these "demographics" were on the streets and in the airwaves, and their voices were being heard far beyond the boundaries of San Francisco State.

But what exactly were they saying? What, ultimately, does this Indian uprising mean? The question lingers even as Barthelme's story begins to fragment into semi-arbitrary surrealistic bits: "'Vertical organization is also possible,' Miss R. said, as in

> pewter
> snake
> tea
> Fad #6 sherry
> serviette
> fenestration
> crown
> blue.'" (112)

"People were trying to understand": and we too, the people who read "The Indian Uprising" itself—there are many of us, it is widely anthologized for use in the classroom—might find ourselves "trying to understand." Students will attest to what a struggle it is to bring interpretive order to a "postmodern" story like this one, which comes at the reader like Comanches on acid, attacking everything you thought you knew about fiction. So much so that you could easily forget that the narrator of the story is defending the city *from* the Indians, not the reverse.

4

Our Phonocentrism: Finding the Voice of the (Minority) Storyteller

> The aesthetic revolution drastically disrupts things:
> testimony and fiction come under the same regime of meaning.
>
> JACQUES RANCIÈRE, "The Distribution of the Sensible"

TELL ME AGAIN

How different from the carefully measured, coldly humorous stories of Flannery O'Connor are works like Philip Roth's *Portnoy's Complaint* (1969), with its final ascent from hyperactively neurotic narration into this soaring spasm of exclamation: "Aaaaaaaaaaaaaaaaaaaaaaaaaaaaaaaaaaaaaaaaaaaaa aaaaaaaaaaaaaaaaaaaaaaaaaaaaaaaaaaaaaaaaaaaaaaaaaaaaaaaaaaaaaaaaaaaaa aaaaaaaaaaaaaaaaaaaaaaaaaaaaaaaaaaaaaaaaaaaaaaaaaaaaaaaaaaaaaaaaaaaaa aaaaaaaaaaaaaaaaaaaaaaaaaaaaaaaaaaaaaaaaaaaaaaaaaaaaaaaaaahhhh!!!!!"[1] Portnoy's parting howl would seem to declare defiant allegiance to one side only in the ongoing struggle in American fiction between the compositional values of self-expression and self-discipline, departing about as loudly as one could from the Jamesian tradition of narrative decorum aligned with the latter. The truth is somewhat more complicated than that.

Within the confines of that tradition as it was institutionalized in writing programs in the 1940s and 50s, authors like O'Connor had been taught to show not tell. They had been schooled in the belief that they should recede into the background of the stories they wrote, and had been taught that the best way to achieve this desirable effect of impersonality was in the third person narration of a succession of dramatically presented fictional scenes. Eschewing the convenience of narrative summary and resisting the urge to opine, narration by way of what James called the "dramatic method" would typically include a lot of dialogue, and at times might even look on the page like the text of a play. Dwelling as much as possible in the narrative present, it could venture into the psychic interiors of characters or not—in O'Connor, as in James, it almost always does —but if so the third person point of view would help assure that even these interiors would be analyzed "objectively," that is, from the outside of the inside. And if it must be first person? Then let it at least be a "cool" first person like Hemingway's Jake Barnes, one far enough removed (temporally, emotionally, or otherwise) from the experiences he describes to achieve an effect of impersonality nonetheless.

At first glance Roth's novel would appear to commit the most vulgar conceivable violation of the law of impersonality understood along these lines, speaking with what he intriguingly called a "fourth voice, a less page-bound voice" than the discipline of dramatic method could possibly permit. In the tradition of the great first persons of the previous two decades, such as Ralph Ellison's diverted collegian and all-purpose orator, the eponymous Invisible Man, or Saul Bellow's brainy book thief, Augie March, or the silver-tongued Humbert, Portnoy is not simply a narrator but a person who narrates, a storyteller with a fictional body. But as if a conventional first person narrator has sprung himself loose from the flat world of words, the effect of Portnoy's phallomaniacal "fourth voice" on the reader is akin at times to percussion, with a dense forest of exclamation points and occasional bursts of all-cap enthusiasm—"LET'S PUT THE ID BACK IN YID!" (124)—working as typographical analogues to loudness. This is part of what makes the concluding lines of *Portnoy's Complaint,* where the reader learns that he has not in fact been the primary addressee of the narrative, so strangely effective. A last-second "punch line," as it is labeled, containing an italicized, bracketed tagline—"So [*said the doctor*]. Now vee may perhaps to begin. Yes?" (274)—rewrites the novel as a third person narrative that has only been feigning for 273½ pages to be the first-person ravings of Portnoy. Instead, in what must have been the longest appointment of all time, it has been a story told by a patient to his psychoanalyst. Supplied with a source of analytical authority external to the analysand, the "talking cure" can now, we take it, even as the novel comes to a defiant close, properly get under way.

Thinking through the serious implications of this final comic flourish, we see how in this novel a devotee of Jamesian literary professionalism no less ardent than O'Connor has exploited a fundamental ambiguity in the dramatic method and, in doing so, has turned the Master's dignified procedures on their head. As exemplified by starkly dialogue-driven stories like Hemingway's anthology favorites, "The Killers" and "Hills Like White Elephants," or by the more complex, free indirect narrative staging of the effect of orality in works like Zora Neale Hurston's *Their Eyes Were Watching God* (1937), the properly impersonal narrator must try, however quixotically, to relinquish her speaking role, distributing as much of it as possible to characters in the story and retreating to the back of the imaginary theater of fiction to pare her fingernails. But what if one of the characters on stage, having been allowed to speak, refuses to shut up? Soon enough he might begin to function as a mouthy narrator in his own right, entertaining us by telling us more than we should really want to know. A predictable consequence of this way of proceeding, for Roth, was that some of his readers became convinced that the fictional character Portnoy was speaking for—or perhaps simply *was*—his author. A "less page-bound voice" is, after all, a voice on its way to inhabiting the same ontological domain as its living and breathing author and his readers, who could be understood to exist in a higher, or at least thicker, dimension than the strangely compelling flatlanders we know as fictional characters. At the very least, narrative in the "fourth voice" might seem to share the constitutive uncanniness of theater, where fictional characters are supplied with real human bodies.

The appearance on the scene of American fiction of a voice like Portnoy's—miming the emotional, improvisational rhythms of a *spoken* voice, which is also necessarily an *embodied* voice and in this case a distinctly *Jewish-American* voice—in the work of a self-consciously Jamesian craftsman like Roth announces a new turn in the dialectic of program era fiction as dramatically as we could wish. This, in narratological terms at least, is the true import of Portnoy: he is a symptom of a profoundly (let us dust off the term) *phonocentric* literary historical moment, when the New Critical ideal of narrative impersonality was rotated into a minor position in relation to a dominant ideal of vocal presence, but persisted in the assumption that this presence should not speak directly to the reader but should be *staged*.[2] The "staginess" of voice is therefore the trace of the institutional space of its emergence, and of the artifice—indeed, of the technology—that enables a textual performance of vocal authenticity. The merger of a metaphysics of voice with technology in writing of the 1960s occasions what can only be called the period's technoromanticism—and indeed, insofar as the discipline of creative writing conjoins the project of authentic self-expression with the "machinery" of the program, I'm not sure that the term isn't applicable to postwar fiction as a whole. It's just that, in the aesthetic formation I call high cultural pluralism, whose origins I will trace in this chapter, the investment in experiential authenticity is strong enough that the agency of this machinery is generally repressed.

As with the institutionalization of New Critical doctrine in American schools in the 1940s and 50s, the increasingly widespread concern with the voice of the storyteller in the sixties and seventies was both a scholarly-pedagogical and an artistic preoccupation. If there was a single scholarly text hovering behind the reflexive return to orality, it was surely Albert Lord's *The Singer of Tales* (1960), which promulgated a series of profoundly influential claims about the origins of the Homeric epics as oral compositions. Lord's thesis was based on fieldwork begun in the 1930s with his teacher at Harvard, Milman Parry, with whom he traipsed about the Yugoslavian countryside recording the living vestiges of its ancient, illiterate storytelling tradition on audiotape. The central motivation for doing this was to be able to reverse-engineer from this contemporary survival an understanding of the (oral) making of the foundational texts of Western (print) culture, but a secondary consequence was a powerful positive revaluation of orality in its own right.

Walter J. Ong, who with Marshall McLuhan would come to symbolize the period's fascination with the relation of print and other media technologies to the human voice, described these findings as "revolutionary in literary circles," and was sympathetic to what amounted to a critique, on Lord's part, of the ignorant snobberies of print culture.[3] Trapped in a print mind-set, this culture cannot see that traditional storytelling formulas are not the "ossified clichés they have a reputation for being" but rather the mnemonic tools of an organic epic tradition that is only ever instantiated in distinctively "original" individual performances.[4] Indeed, Lord asserted, a traditional "oral poem is not composed *for* but *in* performance" (13); the stock phrases and patterns of the tale should be understood by analogy to grammar, the relative rigidity of which does not impede the language speaker's ability to improvise new sentences. It is instead print culture that has produced its own problem of "unoriginality," since our habits of mechanical reproduction-of-the-same have left us unaccustomed "to thinking in terms of fluidity. We find it difficult to grasp something that is multiform. It seems to us necessary to construct an ideal text or to seek an original, and we remain dissatisfied with an ever-changing phenomenon" (100).

Reading this defense of multiform fluidity, one begins to see a line connecting the Yugoslavian countryside of the 1930s, via Harvard, to college campuses of the 1960s—on any one of which McLuhan, professor of English, either in person or in paperback, might have been seen announcing the collapse of the Gutenberg Galaxy and the dawn of a technoprimitive "electronic age" that would reestablish the primacy of voice in Western culture. McLuhan introduced *The Gutenberg Galaxy* (1962) as an explicit companion or sequel volume to Lord's *Singer of Tales* that would extend the latter's insights from the "*forms* of oral and written poetry . . . to the *forms* of thought and the organization of experience in society and politics."[5] Put simply, his theory was that the rise of electronic media, with their capacity for the abolishment of space and time, was reversing the now centuries-long trend toward rationalistic disenchantment and objectification embodied in print consciousness in favor of the re-sacralized holism of the so-called "global village."

Closer to the immediate compositional concerns of contemporary novelists was Wayne C. Booth's *Rhetoric of Fiction* (1961), which overturned several decades of New Critical narrative doctrine by exposing what it called the "radical inadequacy of the telling-showing distinction."[6] For Booth, as summarized by Dorothy Hale, this distinction should be replaced by the more comprehensive concept of "voice," which designated the "authentic self-expression of identity that is integral to and inevitable in any act of novelistic communication."[7] In turn, the "voice" that we cannot help but "hear" in even the most impersonal modern narratives should be understood as issuing from what Booth called an "Implied Author" who unifies the text as the product of a coherent intention and/or moral sensibility. This famously helpful formulation was meant to split the difference between the admitted absence of the actual author from the scene of reading, and our seemingly ineradicable sense that novels are among other things *personal statements,* however artfully ambiguous, and for that matter fictional, these statements might be. As Ong put it: "The morass of personality which surrounds the work of art . . . establishes the personalist aberration as a permanent threat. As contemplation enters upon a more serious stage, the human being is driven by the whole economy of what it is to be a man to find opposite himself, in that which he contemplates, a person capable of reacting in turn. This drive is primordial and will not be denied."[8] Booth's arguments for the artistic respectability of novelistic "telling" and the inevitability of authorial self-implication were thus part of a widespread return to the idea that a human being might remain present, in some way, in the dead print the reader holds in her hands.[9] For him—and for Hale, James Phelan, and other inheritors of this line of thought—this presence is what grounds the novel as an ethical utterance even in cases where the narration is highly fractured or unreliable. But it also made an aesthetic appeal. In this context, a reflexive narrative staging or quotation of the act of storytelling, even as it might in fact mask the identity of the actual author, or induce readers to confuse him with his narrator, was one way of folding some of the higher-dimensional vivacity of oral performance back into the very medium thought to have killed off oral traditions.

A few years later, these ideas had found expression in the domain of writing pedagogy, where, owing to the discipline's structural commitment to the construction—as opposed to deconstruction—of student subjectivity, their staying power would prove extraordinary. The Derridean critique of phonocentrism disseminated in the U.S. had in any case been absurdly one sided. In the extremity of his efforts to save writing from the long-standing Socratic charge of being merely supplementary to a more authentic speaking, this otherwise most dialectical of thinkers could not fully register the extent to which, as Lord and Ong and McLuhan had been pointing out, writing had already asserted itself as the locus of supreme authority in modernity, whether in the inscription of constitutional documents or in the printed pages of the Bible. (One can think of the law-inscribing torture machine in Kafka's "In the Penal Colony" as the most lurid depiction of this scriptural authority.) For them, as we have seen, it was rather orality that needed to be saved from the charge of being inferior to writing, which in the form of *literacy* becomes visible, not as an abject supplement to speaking, but as valuable and unequally distributed cultural capital. It was left to Henry Louis Gates, in *The Signifying Monkey* (1988), to combine the emphases of Ong and Derrida in what amounted to a valorization of the African American trickster voice, and the African American vernacular more broadly, as sophisticatedly *self-deconstructive* (that is, already a form of "writing" in Derrida's expanded sense).[10]

But the staying power of "voice" is not simply owed to a pragmatic disciplinary resistance to some less-than-useful truths of Derridean deconstruction. It is also attributable to its useful vagueness, which allows quite distinct and even contradictory ideas to match and mingle as necessary in the various educational practices that it helps to authorize in the name of student subjectivity. For Walker Gibson, writing in the early 1960s, the concept of voice was valuable as a teaching tool because it raises the student's awareness of narration as the essentially mobile adoption of variable "roles" for different communicative purposes.[11] This was a pedagogical reflection of literary modernism's fascination with the artifice and mobility of personae, and was easily assimilable to later postmodern accounts of fractured and multitudinous subjectivity. As we saw in the discussion of William Styron's controversial *Confessions of Nat Turner* in Chapter 3, "voice" understood in this way conceives authorship as a kind of ventriloquism and raises the specter of offensive appropriation, which is an offense against the rule of writing what you know. Another energetic early advocate for the pedagogical utility of voice was Albert Guerard, whose understanding of the concept reflects rather the persistence of a self-expressivist romanticism even within the broader context of a modernist aesthetics of impersonality. Guerard's critical readings of figures such as Dostoyevsky, Conrad, and Faulkner set about exploring how these writers, overcoming various internal and external impediments, found the "true voice" that speaks from their major works. In the preface to an anthology of student readings called *The Personal Voice* (1964), he and his fellow editors told students that while "bad prose often gives the impression of having been ground out by a machine . . . all good writing (even the most objectively scientific and descriptive and even the most ornate or poetic) is related to the speaking voice."[12]

Note the rapport the pedagogical rhetoric of voice sought to sustain between fiction and nonfiction, creative writing and composition, and the authority it sought as a literary concept relevant even to scientists. This was a wise course of action in an institutional climate where hard scientific research was, post-Sputnik, looming ever larger in the Cold War university's sense of mission.[13] Note also how Guerard's insistence on the importance of voice in writing condenses Parry and Lord's macro-historical account of the origins of Western literature in oral tradition into the developmental situation of the individual composition student. Before he is a writer, the student is naturally a speaker, and his original speaking voice remains a resource for his writing voice. The pedagogical narrative of the search for voice faults the student's failures of originality but sanctions them as part of a learning process, as in, "I think you're still finding your voice here." Jauntily reversing the traditional formula, Guerard's motto as a creative writing teacher, according to the novelist Alice Hoffman, was "Tell, don't show."[14] The more positive version of this admonition was "find your voice," and in that form it has become one of the controlling imperatives of writing instruction of all kinds, more pervasive even than "write what you know" and "show don't tell" because of its applicability to fiction and nonfiction writing alike.

For all that it might seem philosophically naïve, the romantic understanding of personal voice, no less than the modernist one, would in practice prove to be compatible with a poststructuralist or postmodern sensibility. This compatibility was facilitated by a shared subjectivism: the imperative to "find your voice" reverses the epistemological directionality of the imperative to write what you know (about the outside world from personal experience), shifting attention explicitly (it had always been there implicitly) to the writing subject herself as the original and ultimate source of existential authority. So seen, this could serve as an existentially celebratory form (I make my own truth) of an otherwise melodramatically bleak postmodern skepticism (there is no truth). In the domain of fiction writing, this meant that a realist fidelity to the probabilities of empirical or objective experience would be traded for an appreciation of the writer's sovereign ability to constitute flagrantly imaginary realities or "fabulations," as Robert Scholes called them.[15] One thinks immediately of prominent

figures in sixties fiction like Robert Coover, Donald Barthelme, and especially John Barth, whose post-realist metafiction is in fact more accurately
described as *meta-storytelling* in that it almost always begins and ends with
the predicament—for Sharazad in *Chimera* (1971) it is a matter of life and
death—of the teller. For white male postmodernists like these, flagrantly
reflexive displays of the power of fabulation were first and foremost an
assertion of professional potency amidst the bright blare and clang of an
ever more amplified mediasphere. (Think here again of Barthelme's assertive balloon in "The Balloon.")

For writers of color, however, the vocal power of fabulation tended
to take on a further meaning. Here the subjectivism of the imperative to
find your voice was an even more conspicuously corporeal one, circling
back again and again to the housing of the storytelling imagination not
only in a human body, but in a racialized and gendered body with "blood-
lines" or "roots" in an organic community or culture with its own reposi-
tory of storytelling tradition. For the ethnically-marked or woman writer
especially, it might not be good enough to simply search so as to find one's
voice; that voice, it was understood, might have to be "claimed" in defiance of the silencing forces of social oppression and cultural standardiza-
tion. This converts Portnoy's howl into a more explicitly political form of
expression—a demand to be heard in the public square. This line of
thought would eventually lead to Carol Gilligan's classic of feminist educational psychology, *In a Different Voice* (1983), with its insistence that
"without voice, there is no possibility for resistance, for creativity, or for a
change whose wellsprings are psychological," and to assertions of the importance of voice in the African American tradition from Robert Stepto's
From Behind the Veil (1979) to Gates's *Signifying Monkey* to Gayl Jones's *Lib-
erating Voices* (1991).[16]

Thus if the call to "find your voice" in the sixties must be said, on
one level, to have occasioned a return to the preening act of self-expression
so loathed by Flannery O'Connor and her New Critical mentors, it was
nonetheless a return with an important difference in that it incorporated a
great deal of the *volkish* and conventionalist ethos of the Southern Agrar-

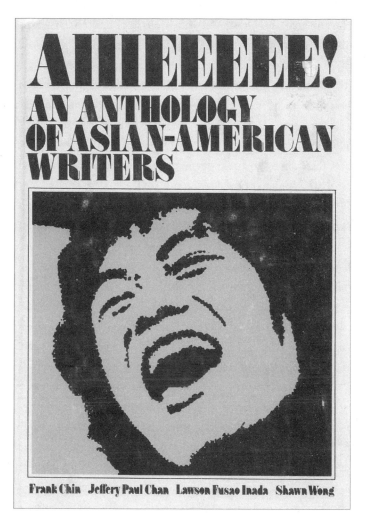

Finding the voice of the Asian-American writer, 1974. Jacket design by Bob Onodera, photograph by Ken Gaetjen, reproduced by permission of Howard University Press.

ian substratum of the New Criticism itself. It is true that the resurgent teller of sixties fiction draws attention to himself. As N. Scott Momaday asserted, "To the extent that [the storyteller] re-creates his vision in words, he recreates himself. . . . He declares in effect: *Behold, I give you my vision in these terms, and in the process I give you myself.* . . . The storyteller and the story told are one."[17] But the voice of this storyteller, in this case the Native American storyteller, was typically understood as a synecdoche for the voice of the (variably defined) social collectivity from which it emerged and into which it feeds back. Hence the reflexive "Jewishness" of Roth's Portnoy, whose verbal individuality is not only at war with, but also patently a product of, the talkative immigrant culture of his upbringing.

This model of storytelling is what has been termed an "autoethnographic" one, in which the autopoetic reflexivity of modernist and postmodernist narrative in general, as discussed in the Introduction to this book, is inflected by an anthropological understanding of cultural collectivity. Occasioning the act of self-expression, the cultural formation I have been calling "high cultural pluralism" reflected nonetheless Franz Boas's assertion that "the group, not the individual, is always the primary concern of the anthropologist," an idea amplified in McLuhan's account of the obsolescence of individualism in the interconnected global village.[18] Our task will be to trace the autoethnographic project of "finding" or "claiming" one's voice as a storyteller back to its origins in the system of higher education. Not that the period's fascination with the visceral power of the human voice was in itself new. Voice is arguably—and, more important to me, was in the sixties frequently argued to be—essential to all literature, wittingly or not, and various overt forms of what Gates calls the "speakerly text" have been around for centuries.[19] My focus here is on the way that long history intersected with the "machinery"—both social institutional and overtly technological—that produced the increasingly paramount value of "cultural difference" in postwar American fiction.

The implications of performing such a contextualization are expressed with admirable economy in John Barth's short story "Autobiography," from the collection *Lost in the Funhouse: Fiction for Print, Tape, Live Voice* (1968). In this story it soon becomes clear that the first person narrator of the story is the story "Autobiography" itself, as though an instance of this narrative form could be freed from its supplementary relation to a human life and personified as an autonomously self-expressive being. Barth's ambiguously serious indication, in the preface to this collection, that the story would ideally be heard emanating from a tape recorder while the author (presumably Barth himself) stands silently by, adds another layer of significance to the story. This one allows us to see how narrative forms—in this case the genre of autobiography and its associated conventions—can themselves be understood as recording technologies of a kind. And while we should not be induced to believe that either a narrative form or a recording apparatus could actually speak for itself like a person—that would be taking a science fiction trope too literally—we can at least see, thanks to the ironically "silent" Barth, how persons necessarily *give voice to forms* even when they speak for themselves.

INDIANS MADE OF WORDS

Can there be such a thing as an authentically Native American novel? For Karl Kroeber, apparently not. That at least is the implication of his rather stringent reading of N. Scott Momaday's *House Made of Dawn*, the work Momaday began as a graduate student at Stanford in the early sixties and published to considerable acclaim, including the Pulitzer Prize for fiction, in 1968. No matter that it opened the way for James Welch, Leslie Silko, Louise Erdrich, and many other Native American novelists who seem to have found the genre congenial to their ends. For Kroeber, Momaday's novel is a hopeless attempt to "evoke an 'Indianness' for his readers (the majority of whom presumably will not be Indians) through an Anglo-American literary structure that must prohibit any authentically Indian imaginative form." The "inappropriateness of the genre for the expression of . . . Indianness" becomes obvious to Kroeber in the novel's "jarringly obtrusive" debts to Hemingway and other white modernists, and in a "schematic symbolizing" false to the Native American traditions from which it feebly, through the medium of the ethnographic archive, attempts to borrow.[20] As an antidote to such a pale rendering of Native American culture, Kroeber recommends translations of oral narratives such as *The Golden Woman,* which was spoken onto audiotape by Colville storyteller Peter Seymour the same year Momaday's novel was first published. Thus, very much in the spirit of Albert Lord, and of his own renowned anthropologist father, Kroeber reverses the charge of "unoriginality" so often directed at illiterate oral tradition, finding it instead in the sophisticated textual practices of Native American literary modernism.

With its heavy reliance on his own aesthetic judgments to make what is at base an ontological, and not aesthetic, argument about genre and culture, Kroeber's is only one of several recent readings of Momaday's novel that, as summarized by Larry Landrum, "view the text as participating in the dissolution of cultural integrity through its eclectic borrowings, many of which are contaminated by ethnographic assumptions."[21] Consenting to the idea that "Indian art is not necessarily identical to art produced by Indians" (777), Landrum's own way of resisting the dismissal of Momaday's novel as derivatively un-Indian is to attribute to it a profoundly critical force: far from passive in its relation to modernism, *House Made of Dawn* "shatter[s] the exclusionary and oppressive practices of modernism" (781), opening them up to the realities of Native American life as they are made manifest in indigenous traditions.

Another, more direct way of resisting readings like Kroeber's, however, might simply be to back up a step and deny that Indian art could or should be anything other than "art produced by Indians." Indian art, in this view, is no more static and unchanging than non-Indian art, and should be no more vulnerable to the essentialist charge of cultural "contamination" than voraciously assimilative modernism is. In other words, rather than being contaminated by modernism, Indian art now *includes* modernism as one of its elements, much as the buffalo hunting culture of the Plains Indians included horses (a European import) at its core and is rarely considered less than authentic for having done so. But to insist that Momaday's modernist novel, having been written by an Indian, is therefore also real Indian art solves one problem only to create another: who counts as a real Indian?

Surely not Momaday's Stanford classmate, Ken Kesey. What real claim could a white frat boy wrestler from Oregon have on the "Indian consciousness" represented in *One Flew Over the Cuckoo's Nest?* For Kesey, as described by Tom Wolfe, the advent of his narrator Chief Broom was the miraculous product of peyote, as if that drug's effects must express the culture with which it is associated: "Kesey starts getting eyelid movies of faces, whole galleries of weird faces, churning up behind the eyelids, faces from out of nowhere. He knows nothing about Indians and has never met an Indian, but suddenly here is a full-blown Indian . . . the solution, the whole mothering key, to the novel."[22] Kesey's own account, decades later, was somewhat different, having more to do with his occasional interaction with Native Americans in the Oregon of his youth, if not on the Stanford campus. But even this claim for an experiential link to Native America leads to conclusions bound to seem dubious, at least to most contemporary literary academics: "So this Indian consciousness has been very important in all of the stuff that I write," he told *The Paris Review,* "it is the dispossessed Indian spirit that's trying to reconnect with the white male spirit."[23] Rather, we might retort, it looks like the "white male spirit" trying to connect to the "Indian spirit," hoping in that way to ground itself as both authentically American and authentically, but relatively painlessly, oppositional. Kesey's appropriation of Indian consciousness may not have been as egregious as Forrest "Asa" Carter's simulation of an Indian identity in the "memoir" *The Education of Little Tree* (1976), in which a white supremacist terrorist represents himself as a Native American orphan.[24] Nor did it amount to a serious enough intervention into Native American history on Kesey's part to have inspired the loathing felt by some for Styron's entry into the consciousness of the black slave-rebel in the *Confessions of Nat Turner.* And yet the image of Kesey, in his later years, dressed in full Indian costume as he read his faux–Native American folktales *Little Tricker the Squirrel* (1990) and the *Sea Lion* (1991) to schoolchildren around the country can only give one pause.

Against these flagrant acts of "Going Native" or "Playing Indian"—

the titles of two recent books on the long history of white appropriation of Native American identities—Momaday's claims to possession of a legitimate Indian consciousness would seem to be fairly strong.[25] Indeed, in the essay "On Indian-White Relations" he claimed that his "genetic constitution" as an Indian allows him access to an "Indian way of looking at the world" (*Man Made of Words*, 51) that no white writer could possibly have. And yet it makes sense to interpret the strenuousness of this genetic claim to racial consciousness as a symptom of Momaday's anxiety about who he is exactly—or at least about the artifice that being who he is entails. As the object, in turn, of exterminationist and assimilationist federal violence, traditional Native American cultural practices became conspicuously dependent on the ethnographic archive for their persistence and availability for "reactivation." For someone like Momaday in particular, to found a Native American identity on Native American traditions was necessarily as much a matter of hard study as of passive inheritance. In this he followed in the footsteps of his part-Cherokee mother, who Momaday tells us began her life as a "Southern belle" in Kentucky and only later "began to see herself as Indian. That dim native heritage became a fascination and a cause for her, inasmuch, perhaps, as it enabled her to assume an attitude of defiance."[26] Cementing her identification with Native America, she left home to attend the famous Haskell Institute, an Indian school in Kansas, and went on to marry Momaday's Kiowa father. Arriving at the end of a childhood in which he was, by his own account, just as happy to play the Cowboy as the Indian, Momaday emulated the "act of imagination" on his mother's part that led her forward from Southern whiteness back to Indianness.[27] In laying claim to a Native American identity, however, Momaday still confronted a problem:

> From the time I was born my parents spoke to me in English, for that was my mother's native tongue, and she could speak no other. My father, however, was Kiowa, and . . . the house and the arbor of the homestead on Rainy Mountain Creek in Oklahoma crackled and rang with Kiowa words, exclama-

tions, and songs that even now I keep in my ear. But I would only learn a part of the whole, and I would never learn to converse easily in Kiowa. . . . My Kiowa family spoke to me in broken English, or their Kiowa words were translated into English for me by my father. (*Man Made of Words*, 7)

Insofar as Momaday would add his own voice to the collective "Native voice" in American literature, he would have to do so in the tongue of the invader. But so strong was the habit, in the pluralist thinking of the sixties, of accounting for deep cultural differences by tying them to linguistic difference that Momaday thereby risked seeming stranded in a cultural no-man's-land. As Sam Deloria put it at the first Convocation of American Indian Scholars held at Princeton University in 1970, echoing the influential theories of Benjamin Whorf, "I would like to point out the difficulty in expressing many of the ideas that we want to express, by virtue of the fact that we are using the English language. I suspect . . . that there are certain patterns in the English language tending to focus communication" in certain ways, making it difficult to "bring an Indian world view into . . . a conscious, systematic philosophy."[28] Thus the assertion of a genetic claim to Indian consciousness, on Momaday's part, is a way to stake a claim to Native identity on grounds deeper than language. At the same time, *pace* Kroeber, it authorizes the existence of an authentically Native American novel in English, since if blood is thicker than language, it is no doubt thicker than genre, too.[29]

For all the extremity of its genre essentialism, Kroeber's analysis of *House Made of Dawn* is valuable for the way it draws attention to the agonistic laboriousness of the novel's making. Momaday did not simply emit the work from the well of his romantic Indian soul but, to his credit as a craftsman, slowly forged it over the course of seven long years of close study, writing, and revision while he was first a Stanford graduate student, then a professor at UC Santa Barbara, Berkeley, and other institutions where he was involved in the formation of the emergent discipline of Native American Studies. For Momaday, "finding his voice" as a writer was a process facilitated at every point by educational institutions that not only *removed him from* but also, on another level, *returned him to* Native American traditions. If the aesthetic formation I have called high cultural pluralism entails the joining of the elevated aesthetic values of literary modernism with autoethnographic cultural specificity, then the novel *House Made of Dawn* is a textbook case.

The textual inheritance of modernism came to Momaday, as to so many fiction writers of the fifties and sixties—and perhaps especially to those able to take classes with Malcolm Cowley—in the puzzlingly contradictory, but nonetheless powerfully motivating form of what we can summarize as the Hemingway/Faulkner dialectic, which is perhaps only to add proper names to a more basic struggle between literary minimalism and maximalism. In any case, the prestige of these recent recipients of the Nobel Prize in the 1960s, both of them exhibiting an important Native American presence in their writings, would be hard to overstate. It would also be difficult to overstate their interest to Momaday in particular, whose first published poem, "The Bear," was directly inspired by Faulkner's famous coming-of-age story of the same title.[30] Engaging with these two writers as a student, Momaday was by stages returned to the oral tradition to which he was exposed (in translation) in his youth, and eventually claimed it as an indigenous resource for his own textual practice.

I have already spoken, and will speak further, of the long shadow thrown by Hemingway across the Program Era, which extends into the present day as the bearer of an interconnected cluster of values attached to the authorship of fiction, including, most centrally, the value of craft as represented by the practice of multiple revision. Almost as important was the value of (preferably extreme or unordinary) "personal experience," as revealed in the constant bending of modernist fiction, including Hemingway's, toward the autobiographical. This economy or ecology of experience and writing—which, as we have seen, swallowed the quite different literary projects of Thomas Wolfe and Kay Boyle whole—underlay Hemingway's redefinition of the novelist as (potentially) a "man of action," which provided the model for a number of aggressively male celebrity

writers in the sixties. But just as importantly, as a poet of brooding masculinity, Hemingway came to represent the noble pathos of understatement. The extreme of this position was sketched out near the beginning
of Hemingway's career, notably in the context of a stereotype of the silent
Indian. No one who has read the story "Indian Camp" (1923) could forget
how the Native American father of a child just delivered with great difficulty by Nick Adams's father ("I don't hear [the mother's screams] because
they are not important") is discovered to have silently slit his own throat
sometime in the night because, the doctor feebly speculates, he "couldn't
stand things, I guess."[31] Here already, in this screaming mother/silently
suffering father pairing, is a version of the gendered binary that structures
so much of Hemingway's work, as well as that of his literary heirs, including Momaday.

House Made of Dawn distributes the competing values of silence and
expression to two different characters who dominate different sections of
the novel. First is the troubled young Native American man, Abel, who
like Hemingway's Nick Adams, Jake Barnes, and Frederick Henry—and
O'Connor's Hazel Motes and Kesey's Bromden and so many of the protagonists of Tim O'Brien—is a war veteran. But in Abel's case, war trauma
is merely the latest, most dramatic and geographically literal form of
alienation he has suffered. His spiritual injuries began, we gather, with the
death of his father and mother and brother in close succession when he
was a child. Earlier still was the massive cultural trauma that began with
the "bad dream of invasion and change" (52) that was the arrival of Europeans.[32] Like Bromden's, Abel's maladjustment to his environment expresses itself as a general unwillingness to self-express, but unlike Bromden, Abel never becomes the narrator of his own story: "Had he been
able to say it, anything of his own language . . . would once again have
shown him whole to himself; but he was dumb. Not dumb—silence was
the older and better part of custom still—but *inarticulate*" (53). For Kroeber, "Abel's inarticulateness reflects Momaday's generic deprivation" (21);
but this is only half true, as we can already begin to observe in the distance
from Abel built into the narration, which communicates not a little pity

and even contempt for the novel's "troubled youth" protagonist. This distance makes Abel available to the reader as an object of desire—including certainly the *interpretive* desire generated by his inarticulacy. When we are told that Abel's white patron Angela, standing in an upper floor of her rented hacienda, "smiled and looked down from an upstairs window as he chopped the wood" (28), we see this desire projected into the fictive world as a literalized socio-spatial relation of higher- to lower-class persons. And when, later, Angela imagines what *his* eyes can see—"some vision out of range, something away in the end of distance, some reality that she did not know . . . What was it that they saw?" (33)—Abel becomes for her, as Native Americans would become for so many Americans (including of course Native Americans themselves), a "liminal" figure, a human link to transcendent authenticity.

That said, Kroeber is of course right to detect currents of identification running between narrator and character. They are not simply distant from each other but *variably* or even *unstably* so, as though Momaday is conducting a literary practicum in the lively debate in postwar anthropological theory surrounding the relative validity of "emic" (that is, internal, or intellectually indigenous) vs. "etic" (external, or professional-analytical) descriptions of cultures; or, more simply, negotiating the terms of his own identity as a Native American intellectual.[33] In the Prologue to the novel, Abel is running on the mountainous road near his hometown, and "he could see the horses in the fields and the crooked line of the river below." A few sentences later, however, we find that "against the winter sky and the long, light landscape of the valley at dawn, he seemed almost to be standing still, very little and alone" (2). In the first instance, the narrator shares the character's superior view of the world below him; in the second, Abel has become the puny object of the narrator's (and hence the reader's) higher vision. Thus when Abel is shown again and again in the novel to seek a higher topographical perspective on his world—for instance, "he was high above the town and he could see the whole of the valley growing light" (10)—we can read this either as a projection of the narrator's alienated intellectual superiority into his character, or as Abel's attempt to leave his world to share the transcendent perspective of the narrator, or both at once. In this way, the classically modernist question of point of view is sewn deep into the fabric of the narrative as an existentially flexible autopoetic technology, a way of making the name, *Momaday,* of a Native American writer by re-imagining a homophonic house *Made of Dawn.*

Abel, then, is the "Hemingway" character in this novel, but his structural complement is the preacher Tosamah, a conspicuously articulate figure of Kiowa background whom Abel meets in Los Angeles after he has been released from jail and left the pueblo. If Abel's silence reflects Momaday's "generic deprivation," Tosamah's eloquence would seem, dialectically, to reflect Momaday's sense of his generic resources in the Native American oral tradition. As such, it makes sense to call him the "Faulkner" character in the book. Faulkner, as we know, made his name as a writer with the pyrotechnic formal achievements of works like *The Sound and the Fury* and *As I Lay Dying* and "A Rose for Emily," and Momaday's novel, with its richly heterogeneous combination of narrative perspectives and time schemes, shows more than a little influence from Faulkner in this respect. But just as important, ultimately, was the model of fiction as oratory that Faulkner increasingly provided, moving into the structural position vacated by the now-too-embarrassing Thomas Wolfe. In the incantatory, quasi-preacherly mode of narration he increasingly favored, the principle of prose elevation is accessed directly rather than, as in the plain speech of literary minimalism, indirectly. Faulkner, in other words, came to symbolize the value not of *craft* but of sublime *genius,* licensing the students of the Program Era to—linguistically speaking—*let it fly.* Comparing Faulkner favorably to his other favorite writer, Hemingway, Ken Kesey described how in "The Bear" the "prose just tumbles out like water out of a spring."[34]

As Tosamah stands at the podium in a seedy basement in Los Angeles, speech tumbles out of him like water out of a spring. With this character, Momaday shifts gears from the creation of a moody object of interpretive desire to the narrative staging of a voice. And what this voice says is, reflexively enough, something about language itself, about how a text-based culture wastes words while an oral culture cherishes them:

> "'In the beginning was the Word.' I have taken as my text this evening the almighty Word itself. Now get this: 'There was a man sent from God, whose name was John' . . . and he said, 'In the Beginning was the Word . . .' And, man, right then and there he should have stopped. There was nothing more to say but he went on. [. . .]
>
> Now, brothers and sisters, old John was a white man, and the white man has his ways. Oh gracious me, he has his ways. He talks about the Word. He talks through it and around it. He builds upon it with syllables, with prefixes and suffixes and hyphens and accents. He adds and divides and multiplies the Word. And in all of this he subtracts the truth. [. . .]
>
> On every side of him there are words by the million, an unending succession of pamphlets and papers, letters and books, bills and bulletins, commentaries and conversations. He has diluted and multiplied the Word, and words have begun to close in upon him." (82–84)

While the partiality of the narrator's identification with Abel is negotiated in the instability of focalization, here that partiality registers as tonal complexity: falling into recognizably Baptist cadences, Tosamah's preaching voice is (to my ear at least) both racialized and ironically "de-Indianized" as African American (or African American / Faulknerian). Then again, there is the obvious internal contradiction in what Tosamah is saying: the fervency of his verbosity and the repetitiousness of his sermon on the white man's waste of words would seem to contradict his own message, suggesting more than a little affinity on the part of the *writer* of this voice, Momaday, for the print culture mind-set that Tosamah critiques. Not that Tosamah accepts his own verbosity as a contradiction; for him, as for Parry and Lord, the meaning of repetition in oral culture is fundamentally different from the profligate excesses of a text culture, having more to do with mnemonic continuity through time than with the multiplications and divisions of text culture. Contrasting the Word of the Bible to the Native American oral tradition passed on to him by his illiterate grandmother, Tosamah claims that, for her, "words were medicine; they were magic and invisible. They came from nothing into sound and meaning. They were beyond price; they could neither be bought nor sold. And she never threw words away" (85). Set off against an overpowering surrounding silence in nature, even the wordiest oral expressivity retains a privileged relation to a "silence" which is not simply inarticulacy but "the older and better part of custom still." Which it may well be; but from the literary historical perspective we must understand it as a continuing recognition, even amidst the task of finding the voice of the Native American writer, of the importance of knowing what not to say.

THE PRIDE MACHINE

The theatricality of the Merry Pranksters' journey aboard the colorful school bus called Further had been self-evident, and the datedness of the whole Ken Kesey enterprise—seen now at forty years' distance—only slightly less so. Designed to draw attention to itself as an expression of the "now," it was perhaps fated no less than the grayest daily newspaper to convert rapidly into a thing of purely historical interest, though, to be sure, one with a long-lasting, small-scale aftermarket in nostalgic reconsumption.

Less obvious than its theatricality, but no less important for understanding its symptomatic relation to creative writing in the 1960s, is the related fact of the trip's multiply redundant self-reflexivity. Perhaps because so little actually came of the hundreds of hours of film and audiotape the Pranksters burned through—leaving it to the outsider-journalist Tom Wolfe to imagine his way inside the minds of Pranksters in the old-fashioned medium of writing—we could easily forget the extent to which human interactions on-board and off were accompanied everywhere with the operation of sound and video recording equipment. While the presence of the audio recorder and camera no doubt contributed to the engaging aura of theatricality hovering about the trip, it is also a testament to the project's equal and opposing impulse toward the anti-theatricality of aesthetic autonomy. As a self-documenting venture, that is, the gap between actors and observers on the bus—since they are one and the same—would in theory be closed, and the gawking "audience" along the road reduced to the status of props. The evidence suggests that the Pranksters were at best secondarily interested in the American places they passed through, and even less so in the people inhabiting those places. For all of the openness-to-the-unpredictable it was meant symbolize, the bus was in several senses a self-confirming enclosure. "It was assumed," as Tom Wolfe puts it in *The Electric Kool-Aid Acid Test,* making clear the existential directionality of the enterprise, that "more and more of what was already inside a person would come out and expand, gloriously or otherwise" (91). Covering thousands of miles, the bus trip was after all circular, ending up right where it began, in the Bay Area, and not a bit less "Bay Area" than when it started.

But at least at one moment during the trip, Further's gleeful parrying of the scenery through which it traveled found some "otherness" poking through. This was in New Orleans, when the Pranksters decided they would escape the summer heat by taking an acid-enhanced dip at Lake Pontchartrain. "What they don't know is," recounts Wolfe, "it is a segregated beach, for Negroes only. The spades all sitting there on benches sit there staring at these white crazies coming out of a weird bus and heading for New Or-leans 30th-parallel Deep South segregated water." The Pranksters have, as it were, stumbled down a rabbit hole and found themselves in a bit of social space where segregation shores up black privilege, not white. When a few of the legal users of the beach become mockingly hostile to the interlopers, the trip, in several senses of the term, starts to go bad. Adopting the techniques of fiction, Wolfe tells us how in the mind of one of the Pranksters, the world

> is orange and then he looks at the writhing mass of Negroes,
> out every window, nothing but writhing Negroes mashed in

around the bus and writhing, and it all starts turning from orange to brown. Zonker starts getting the feeling he is inside
an enormous intestine and it is going into peristaltic contrac-
tions. He can feel the whole trip turning into a horrible bum-
mer. . . . Luckily for Zonker, maybe for everybody, the white
cops turn up at that point and break up the crowd, and tell
the white crazies to drive on, this is a segregated beach, and
for once they don't pile out and try to break up the Cop
Movie. They go with the Cop Movie and get their movie out
of there. (95)

By the shores of Lake Pontchartrain, we could say, fear heats the Prankster spirit until the watermark of its racial specificity becomes visible. This
at least is how it seemed to Tom Wolfe, whose "fictionalizing" here, set
against the constant return to the American comedy of race in his later
novels, makes us wary of simply taking this scene as reliable reportage.

　　But whether this moment of racial paranoia took place in the mind
of a Prankster or the mind of Wolfe, this was not the first time a project of
transcendental American self-inflation had the air taken out of it by the
contradictions of race. And it does point out for us a (evidently functional)
confusion in the social meanings attached to technology, summed up by
Fredric Jameson as that "familiar and ancient philosophical antinomy: does
it relate or does it separate and disperse? Is it the sign of identity or multiplicity?"[35] If technology is, as McLuhan famously called it, an "extension"
of humankind into the world, does this extension *abolish* difference or *discover* it, or perhaps even *produce* differences as it goes? McLuhan himself
was somewhat shifty on this point. One can be forgiven for thinking that
the idea of a "global village" prophesies global cultural homogeneity: one
expects a village to have one culture, however internally complex, not
many, and nothing in McLuhan's work of the early sixties dissuades us
from this assumption.

　　But by 1969 this conceptual model, now heavily dented by the recent explosion of nationalist and decolonization movements in North
America and abroad, obviously needed to be revised. Thus in an interview

we find McLuhan claiming that "the instant nature of electric information movement is decentralizing—rather than enlarging—the family of man into a new state of multitudinous tribal existences."[36] But doesn't this formulation dissolve the global village at least part of the way back into the same old plurality of villages? The trajectory of McLuhan's shifting account of the global village is similar to the one that landed the Pranksters in hot water at Lake Pontchartrain: what at first seems to promise a transcendence of difference for a condition of self-sameness becomes, instead, the discovery of difference. The recurrence of this phenomenon here and elsewhere suggests, at the broadest theoretical level, that the social processes we describe as "homogenization" and "differentiation" are dialectically interrelated phenomena, and that to bemoan one or the other is always to miss something important. In fact the trajectory from homogeneity to difference can easily be reversed, the "scandalous" discovery of difference becoming, instead, the scandalous discovery of the threat of "machine made" homogeneity. That, I would argue, is what is happening when the birth of the modern Native American novel in Momaday is redescribed as yet another instance of coercive assimilation to white (in this case modernist) norms.

The implications of this "familiar and ancient philosophical antinomy" for an educational system that was telling some students to find your voice as ethnic or racially-marked subjects become clear when we examine one of the more literal installations of the value of voice in postwar pedagogy, something called the "Voice Project: An Experiment in Teaching Writing to College Freshmen." This was an initiative conceived in a 1965 meeting of the Panel on Educational Research and Development of the U.S. Department of Health, Education, and Welfare and carried out at Stanford in 1966 and 1967. The panel was chaired by Walter Ong and included both Albert Guerard of Stanford, who was the project's most important cheerleader, and his former student John Hawkes, the experimental novelist and Brown University professor who took a year's leave to serve as its director. Run by a quintessential "writers' writer"—a notably populous category in the Program Era—the Voice Project brought together in Hawkes the severest imaginable avant-garde literary sensibility with an earnest-seeming progressive educational concern for the "personal growth" of students. In this it hearkens back to the progressive educational insurgency of the 1920s, which at least in the mind of educators like Harold Rugg was aligned with the renovating energies of literary modernism.[37] What would make the Voice Project distinctive was its use of recording technology to aid the student in finding her unique voice as a writer.

Hawkes's motive for participating in the Voice Project came, by his account, from his experiences working with the Actor's Workshop in San Francisco in 1964, where this "entirely new and intense involvement in theater life" after fifteen years of solitary novel-writing convinced him "that it was essential to approach the teaching of writing in terms of visible behavior as well as in terms of already written words."

> During rehearsals I was constantly moved by a single observation. That is, the progressive and externally evident effort of the actor working in the rehearsal area corresponded to a creative process which previously I had thought existed only as a psychological process within the individual man or artist. In other words, I was able to see something very like the writing process being acted out unintentionally by people who, as actors in a community situation, were nonetheless closely related to the "silent" writer. I became increasingly aware that acting, which reveals the almost immediately perceivable relationship between gesture and word, could be a very real means for bridging the various distances that exist in writing courses and for making concrete the problems and realities of voice.[38]

Several things are notable here: for starters, the weakness of his claim for a link between the actor, working at vocalizing a text written by someone else (in this case Hawkes), and the writer staring at the blank page. To me the analogy speaks less to the actual similarity of the situation of the actor and the freshman composition writer, such as it is, than to the aura surrounding the idea of live oral performance in this period.[39]

Of course the link becomes more plausible if, as frequently happens in the earliest theatrical productions of a play, the playwright rewrites his lines on the spot as he hears them rehearsed by actors. This would begin to look something like an externalized performance of the mental process of writing fiction. Even before the act of revision per se, the "writing process" usually contains a certain amount of looping back through words the writer has already written as well as the addition of new words, and the back-and-forth of author and actor in the rehearsal space could be understood to dramatize this.[40] Hawkes's theatrical inspiration for bodily composition pedagogy reminds us of the beginnings of creative writing instruction in and around the composition, rhetoric, and especially drama classes offered at Harvard at the turn of the previous century. Hawkes's own alma mater was Harvard, and the class that he (and John Updike and many others) took there with Albert Guerard was the institutional descendant of those offered by the likes of LeBaron Russell Briggs, Barrett Wendell, and George Pierce Baker fifty years earlier (and by Wallace Stegner ten years earlier). The art of playwriting taught in Baker's Drama 47 workshop may have been pushed to the margins of a discipline dominated since the 1930s along the parallel tracks of fiction and poetry; but an element of "performance" freed from any particular generic associations has never been less than central to an enterprise that occasions the physical presence of the literary artist in the classroom. Even more basically, by exposing it to the alternately savage and supportive sociability of that classroom, the creative writing workshop theatricalizes the writing process, just as, in a different way, the enduring promotional-communal ritual of the public reading does.

In essence, the Voice Project took the idea of voice "in a community situation" as Hawkes experienced it in the theater and *technologized* it with the use of tape recorders. For instance, on the model of Parry and Lord, students were sent out with tape recorders to collect and listen to "original folklore from their parents, from other students in dormitories, from unlikely places in the community—such as a junkyard in East Palo Alto."[41] Listening to these tapes, students would in theory learn to appreciate the vivacity of everyday storytelling and, set free from the "rationalistic approaches to writing" usually foisted upon freshmen (*Writers as Teachers*, 91), would try to emulate it in their own assignments. This sheds light retrospectively on the crucial role of technology in the various folkloric projects that arose in the 1930s, including Parry and Lord's, which preserved an art form defined as much by its evanescence as by its vibratory human presence.[42] But the recording technology used in the Voice Project's Palo Alto folkloric activity was more consistently put to the purposes of generating self-reflexive feedback in the classroom, thus to make the student as writer coincide with the student as speaker. Sitting amongst her peers, the student would listen to her recorded speaking voice, comparing its inflections and emphases with the words she puts on the page and asking herself how her text might better embody her voice; or the class might listen to recordings of another person or persons reading that student's writing, comparing the distortions wrought by their vocalization on her own, "truer" voice.

This was the order of business at Stanford on February 8, 1967, when readings of a poem by student Helen Williams called "Hey, Bruce Hopkins" (reminiscent of Jimi Hendrix's "Hey Joe" in being an apostrophe to a killer) were recorded by several faculty members in succession. These included Kay Boyle's colleague Leo Litvak from the creative writing program at San Francisco State, and a visiting John Barth, who had been hired as an official consultant to the Voice Project and was engaged at the time in writing *Lost in the Funhouse*. First, as we know from the log kept by a teaching assistant, the poem was read out loud by Hawkes in what he thought of as a "voiceless" monotone. Students were then asked to speculate on the social "type" of the writer (who was assumed to be the same person as the poem's speaker). They were then asked to make up a very short story about this speaker, filling in the elements of her world based on what they could hear in Hawkes's "voiceless" reading. Next they listened to the faculty recordings, discussing the importance of intonation to the variable meanings assignable to such lines as "Don't kill *me*—I feel for you Bruce." Finally they heard from the "poetess herself," listening to the "characteristics of her voice" and "getting nearer to the realities of the poem by hearing the seriousness of her reading."[43] Thus, by a series of steps, the "true voice" at the center of the poem was rediscovered, and everyone could ponder its relation to the inert, silent words on the page.

Of course, the student is already made an auditor of his own voice simply by reading his writing out loud, as often happens in writing classes. Removing the distraction of having also to be the speaker of one's words, the application of recording technology to composition instruction can be seen as only supplementing the externalization of intellectual activity intrinsic to all classroom teaching, where the "technology" is the institutional form itself. This is particularly true in the formal study of literature, which takes what has become in modern times a primarily solitary and silent experience—reading—and re-mediates it in the audible, paraphrasal form of the lecture or classroom discussion. In a way, all literature when it enters the classroom is rewritten in Roth's "fourth voice" in that it is made physically (if fragmentarily) present as vocalized sound. Creative writing classes do the same thing to literary texts, but with the added pathos that the authors of these texts are on hand to be mortified by their self-exposure. But in the Voice Project, as in 1960s literary culture in general, the urge to *extend* and *amplify* and *externalize* reached new heights of intensity, ensuring that the Stanford freshmen would be forced to confront some of the same contradictions discovered by the Pranksters in New Orleans.

As an organizational entity, for instance, the Voice Project was remarkable for the populist energy with which it attempted, like a robot arm, to extend the reach of an increasingly elite institution into the putative "real world" of its regional surroundings. The 100 freshmen participants were matched with "working writers" from the Stanford creative writing program and various other institutions, who were assisted, in turn, by Stanford graduate teaching assistants.[44] Segments of these classes would then spread out throughout the Peninsula school system, conducting the same writing exercises with children of various ages as had been tried on campus. This impressive advance outward toward the goal of social "relevance" was then carried on through the summer of 1967 as part of a Readiness Program at the College of San Mateo, focusing on black students who, as Hawkes put it, "had experienced so much failure in school and had been told so often that they should not take difficult courses that most of them had little or no self-confidence" (*Writers as Teachers*, 97). Voice, in this context, would come to be understood as a vehicle not only of a vivacious human *presence* but also of its affective analogue, *pride*.

Hawkes regarded this last phase of the Voice Project as one of its "particularly important" achievements. And it's worth remembering what was going on at Bay Area educational institutions around the time of the Voice Project, less than a year in advance of the tumult that would begin at San Francisco State with the Black Student Union's call to strike. As Litwak would put it in his memoir, *College Days in Earthquake Country* (1970), the "theater" that black students "were to perform with the police would involve us more powerfully than had the white radicals [of the earlier sixties]. The blacks would compel us to acknowledge truths about the way we lived. . . . It was farewell to our dreams of a campus sanctuary."[45] The Voice Project took Stanford students out of their own campus sanctuary and, exposing them to the Wild West of contemporary race relations, enlisted them in the cause of bringing the Negro voice into official public presence.

Here in San Mateo, as in the countryside of Yugoslavia, recording equipment would be used to capture and appreciate oral forms unjustly thought of as inferior to the literate standard. One of these students, Lee Cohens, recorded the story of an imaginary high school graduation trip to Rome—a real one was far beyond the means of a young man who worked nights at the Ampex factory in Redwood City, which, ironically, produced the portable recording technologies that made the Voice Project feasible. At the next class he was asked to compare the "beautiful . . . rhythms and inflections" of his recording both with the awkwardness of the written transcript and with the blandness of the story as re-recorded by a white Stanford student. Thus the original voice on the tape was doubly authenticated and valued as *oral* and as *Negro*.

But not knowing how exactly to get the admirable energy of the black oral performance into writing (the mere transcription had proved insufficient), the class, which was after all a composition class, seems to have reached an impasse. Some of the students apparently thought the Stanford teachers "were romanticizing their spontaneity of thought and speech" in ways that would make it difficult for them to get good jobs. And yet, Cohens is quoted as saying, "'I wanna get that job, but not so bad that I wanna lose my voice'" (*Writers as Teachers,* 115). "Perhaps," reflected one of the graduate teaching assistants, "I should have urged the transformation of these spoken strengths into their writing, but I felt it was more important for the students to see the value in something they already possessed—their own speaking voices" (113). Of course, the effective use of Standard English is to this day professionally enabling, if undeniably "homogenizing" to some degree, and the competing imperatives of the correction and affirmation of dialect remain a vexed issue for liberal composition theory. Unable to solve this dilemma within the confines of Freshman Comp, the Voice Project found itself under attack from other important figures at Stanford, including Wallace Stegner, for its lowering of standards. But even for Stegner, when the dilemma is referred to a specifically aesthetic or literary milieu, the affirmation of the "different" voice became acceptable. In the domain of literary production, by contrast, the question is whether the Standard English of the corporate workplace is *aesthetically* disabling because it is "voiceless" and "machine made," issuing with the hollow regularity of a player piano. If this is so, then one will certainly want to sound "different."

The novelist Al Young, on campus as a Stegner Fellow in 1966–67, reports that when he handed in a story written entirely in black vernacular Stegner loved it, telling him he had finally "tapped into a voice . . . that was wonderful"[46] and that—while it would presumably have been useless for merely "getting a job"—it could make his career as a writer of fiction. Absent the utilitarian imperatives of the workplace, that is, the writer of fiction is given free reign to do what is necessary to make racially marked orality work on the page. In practice this usually entailed the deployment of a hybrid of dialect and Standard English, the "organic" voice and the "machine-made" voice. In the novel he published a few years later, *Snakes* (1970), Young thematized the values of the Voice Project in the character nicknamed "Shakes" for his prodigious ability to quote Shakespeare from memory. Possessed of his own version of Thomas Wolfean autobardolatry, he is a brilliantly verbal young man who (note the progressive educational theme) does not get good grades in school because he can't stay "innerested long enough."

> "I just wanna knock out chicks and show these other dudes they aint hittin on doodleysquat when it come to talkin trash. I got it down, jim! You hip to Cyrano de Bergerac? I musta seen that flick fifteen-twenty times. Talk about a joker could talk some trash! . . . Taught me you can get away with anything if you talk up on it right. I got it down cold!" . . . Shakes sighed. "Ahhh such is the simplicity of man to hearken after the flesh, if you can dig it. That I were more modest a lad than I appear to be."[47]

The virtuosic collision of vernacular and high literary accents in Shakes's voice embodies a desire to connect African American orality with artistic genius in such a way that they might transcend the machinic standardizations of the classroom altogether. But, no less than the lesson taught to the Pranksters by the shores of Lake Pontchartrain, the lesson Shakes is taught by Cyrano is an ambiguous one, since the rightness, or not, of one's talk is bound to be judged differently in different contexts.

FIRST PEOPLE

If the figure of the Native American has been made to personify the aesthetic value of silence in U.S. literary history, then the African American has been the patron saint of voice, and first person has been his preferred narrative mode.

The case for first person narration as the natural vehicle for this voice comes into focus when one considers the slave narrative. First person may have been suspect in the eyes of Henry James and the New Critics for its seemingly inherent lack of impersonality—or, rather, its difficulty in producing the literary effect of impersonality—but the appeal of *speaking for oneself,* or of *having one's voice heard,* is obvious when it is considered as an act primarily of political self-representation.[48] Whatever other functions it may have assumed—specifically literary ones, for instance—the slave narrative was most definitely a bid for the recognition of the rights and interests of black people by the United States government and the good Christian citizens who, in theory, authorized its actions. As Henry Louis Gates, among others, has pointed out, it was only by finding, or perhaps stealing, his voice as a writer that the slave could effectively "have a voice" in antebellum debates about the peculiar institution that imprisoned him, although the live public speaking engagement remained crucial, too. But not only this—the very process of writing a slave narrative was understood to have a powerfully autopoetic function. As Charles T. Davis and Henry Louis Gates put it in their introduction to *The Slave's Narrative,* the "slave narrative represents the attempts of blacks to *write themselves into being.* What a curious idea: through the mastery of formal Western languages, the presupposition went, a black person could become a human being by an act of self-creation through the mastery of language. Accused of having no collective history by Hegel in 1813, blacks responded by publishing hundreds of individual histories."[49]

In the 1960s, even as the last living survivors of the peculiar institution were passing away, the historical dilemma of the slave arose as the paradigm and clinching case of the obvious social value of self-expression in American culture, and so it remains. Works like Claude Brown's *Manchild in the Promised Land* (1965), John Williams's *The Man Who Cried I Am* (1967) and—these titles speak volumes—Maya Angelou's *I Know Why the Caged Bird Sings* (1969) were easily recognizable as "neo-slave narratives," meant to continue the incomplete project of African American self-liberation the originals had begun, although now in the register of cultural expression rather than political expression per se. Moreover, through the medium of progressive education, this model of self-expressive liberation —and frequently these very texts—would be distributed throughout the American educational system, where it would be made available to other racial and ethnic groups and suburban white kids alike. The centrality to the genre of the "scene of instruction," where the slave more or less heroically learns to read and write, meant that works like Frederick Douglass's *Narrative* (1845) and its generic heirs would, as textbooks, enable a powerfully reflexive concatenation of content, form, and pedagogical context.

Recall that the earliest phases of the progressive educational project, with their Deweyan emphasis on learning by doing, had been pointedly assimilationist in intent, a way of preparing immigrants and Southern blacks for their roles as worker-citizens in modern America; and how in the 1920s and 30s it had moved to the suburbs, to the country day schools, where it was dedicated to freeing the student's proto-professional creativity from the deadening discipline of learning by rote. In the nascently multiculturalist schools of the 1960s the latter project continues, while the former—at least on the surface—is reversed: the problem of "conformity" to which "creativity" is the response is now seen in its racial dimension, as a capitulation to "white" norms. Thus progressivism allies itself with "difference" against "assimilation." Even for the white student, the progressive educationalists argued, learning something about difference might prove salutary—enlivening and liberalizing at once.[50]

Of course, no less than in the contentious domain of representative democracy, where it is possible to feel utterly unrepresented by one's representative, the efficient reduction of "communal" to "individual" voices in the sixties and seventies came with considerable anxieties and inspired much debate. A good example is Ishmael Reed, who in the introduction to the anthology *19 Necromancers from Now* (1970) draws attention to a problematic naïveté in authors of recent "neo-slave narratives" who, as he sees it, "somehow confuse their experience with that of 30 million other people."[51] But so, too, could the collective authority of those 30 million people produce discomfort from the opposite direction: the continuing power of the ideology of individualism even amidst group movements meant that the necessary limits they set upon individual difference, the conformity they demanded to one or another set of conventions, would become a point of contention at the very heart of the project of first person self-expression.[52] Maxine Hong Kingston's *The Woman Warrior* (1976) is a classic—perhaps *the* classic—in the genre of postmodern ethnic autobiography, being all about the assemblage, from misogynist Chinese storytelling traditions, of a viable voice for the modern Chinese American woman. And this almost perfectly reflexive autopoetic construction—since the "voice" so assembled is presumably the very one that has "spoken" the text we are reading—was famously given hell upon its publication by activists like Frank Chin, who (in a rather spectacular case of male hysteria) read its feminism simply as a sellout to anti-Chinese racism. Similar charges, as we know, would be lodged against Alice Walker and Toni Morrison as women writers critical of the behavior of black men, exemplified in the literary sphere by the embarrassingly unconscious sexism (for all of his talk, therein, of "exclusions" from the canon) of all-male anthologies like Reed's. Especially in the seventies, the crucial fault line in the autoethnographic project proved to be the ontological divisions of gender, which make any one voice seem drastically less than representative. But really any conceivable social division or difference—including certainly differences of class—can become a source of the problem.

These "worries" were strong enough to issue in the meta-fictional "intermissions" that trip up the episodic flow of Charles Johnson's neo-slave narrative *Oxherding Tale* (1982), which Johnson began to write in the late sixties and returned to, as though finally to solve the conundrum of the formal conventions of the genre, a decade later. Unlike *The Man Who Cried I Am,* Johnson's novel is actually set in the nineteenth century, and is perhaps better described, despite Ashraf Rushdy's cogent analysis of the novel under this rubric, not as a neo-slave narrative but as a meta-slave narrative. The crucial distinguishing feature of the latter genre, which we could perceive as one part of the larger tradition of black meta-fiction theorized by Madelyn Jablon, is its obvious fictionality.[53] Like Barth's metafictional "Autobiography" in *Lost in the Funhouse,* the narrative convention that Johnson's novel reflects upon at greatest length is the first person narrator. However offensive to Jamesian and New Critical sensibilities, which forbade the preacherly tonalities endemic to the slave narrative form, the first person narrator was at least well equipped to adhere to the aesthetics of cognitive limitation, since this narrator would in theory not know everything about the world he inhabited, only what he had seen and felt. Sounding less like a slave than like someone schooled in creative writing (as Charles Johnson in fact was when he studied with John Gardner at the University of Southern Illinois), the narrator of *Oxherding Tale* claims that "what we value most highly in this viewpoint are precisely the *limitations* imposed upon the narrator-perceiver, who cannot, for example, know what transpires in another mind; . . . what we lack in authority, we gain in immediacy."[54]

Which is to say, in this context, that the immediacy of the relation of writing self to experiencing self in the slave narrative becomes a form of *aesthetic* as well as moral authority. But lest we think that the authority produced in and by this intensifying limitation is therefore circumscribed and trivialized, Johnson's narrator later insists that the strength of first person slave narrative is that it really speaks for all others, indeed for *everything* other: "The Subject of the Slave Narrative, like all Subjects, is forever outside itself in others, objects; he is parasitic, if you like, drawing his life from everything he is not." Thus to "think the Slave Narrative properly is to see nowhere a narrator who falteringly interprets the world, but a narrator who *is* that world: who is less a reporter than an opening through which the world is delivered: first person (if you wish) universal" (152–153). In *Middle Passage* (1990), the National Book Award-winner influenced by Gardner's novella *King's Indian* (in which, uncannily enough, Johnson himself had appeared as a minor character), this comes full circle to the mystical insight, interestingly hedged by a parenthetical, that "the (black) self is the greatest of all fictions."[55]

It is a point perhaps too obvious for Rushdy to have made in his account of the "neo-slave narrative": it is a kind of *novel*. It is in other words part of what Kenneth Warren has cogently analyzed as the cultural turn in black politics since Reconstruction, when properly political forms of representation became unavailable to black populations who instead were forced to pursue self-determination in the form of a now fully "literary" voice.[56] The fundamental difference between this genre, which I am proposing instead to call the meta-slave narrative, and its generic progenitors is that it announces and embraces its own fictionality as a sign of the author's creativity. For the authors of nineteenth-century slave narratives, as we know, writing had been an occasion for the demonstration of black rationality, and "fiction" had hovered over their narratives as a potential term of abuse and rhetorical disqualification; as testimony, that is, the slave narrative is only valid if it is the whole truth and nothing but the truth. This, speculates Richard Yarborough, is why so few African American novels used first person narration in the nineteenth century: to "openly fabricate" a first person voice as fiction would do damage to the larger project of African American self-representation as testimony.[57] Not so for the writer of the postwar meta-slave narrative, who asserts the same right to fictionalize that Harriet Beecher Stowe did when she converted the life of Josiah Henson into one of the more politically consequential novels of all time. In the postmodern context, the wild meta-fictional fabulations and disjunctions of works like Johnson's *Oxherding Tale* or Ishmael Reed's *Flight to Canada* (1976) testify to the unbound power of the African American imagination to reorder reality at will. Indeed, for Reed and other aggressively experimental writers who came of age in the sixties, the very idea of realism implies a submission, if not "enslavement," to the actual as officially defined. Against this threat, the fictive "trip" offered to readers of avant-garde fiction presents some of the same potential for liberated consciousness as LSD, though in this case it is inflected by the question of race.

The core utterance of the first person fiction—"I am"—may be an unoriginal phrase, even as spoken by a fictional character, but to the degree that it is understood as a performative utterance—an utterance that does not so much describe as *create* a state of affairs—it can be understood as original in an even deeper metaphysical sense. Here, to be able to say "I am" is to be able to create a useful, perhaps even a happy, fiction of autonomous selfhood. Transposed into the progressive educational domain, the "fictionality" of student creative writing functions something like the transitional object as conceptualized in W. D. Winnicott's *Playing and Reality*, where the child's toy mediates the relation between the illusory omnipotence of his imagination and his subjection to the laws of external reality. So, too, does finding one's voice as a creative writer produce, as Winnicott put it, an "intermediate area of *experiencing,* to which inner reality and external life both contribute." Safe from the heavy shackles of fact, this special area "is not challenged, because no claim is made on its behalf except that it shall exist as a resting-place for the individual engaged in the perpetual human task of keeping inner and outer reality separate yet interrelated."[58]

In the broader context of the Cold War university, meanwhile, the linked values of fictionality and creativity were ascending to new heights of academic respectability. The multiplication of creative writing programs as shrines to vivacious American individualism was one manifestation of this phenomenon, but there were many others. In the discipline of philosophy, for instance, Nelson Goodman and others were beginning to make a case for the respectability of "fiction" as an object of analytical philosophical inquiry, while even the hypotheses of the "hard" scientist were increasingly understood as "fictions" of a kind (though, to be sure, ones that aspire to a condition of nonfictionality). Certainly the *creativity* (or not) of the scientist was a matter of great concern, worth a great deal of institutional investment in conferences, panels, and research projects that would cumulatively aid in keeping "Free World" scientists ahead of their competitors behind the "Iron Curtain." In anthropology, Clifford Geertz and others were describing the yield of ethnographic research and writing as a kind of "fiction," less objective in nature than the discipline might once have hoped but no less valuable as a foray into "otherness."

This explains odd occurrences like UCLA's granting of a Ph.D. in anthropology to Carlos Castaneda for the patently fictional *Teachings of Don Juan* (1969) and, less embarrassingly, the tongue-in-cheek granting of an honorary master's degree in anthropology to Kurt Vonnegut by the University of Chicago for his fictional "thesis" on religious practices, *Cat's Cradle* (1963).[59]

Still, the embrace of its own fictionality introduces a potential problem for the meta-slave narrative, in some ways the inverse of the problem for the slave narrative proper. Put simply, if the meta-slave narrative is under no obligation to be truthful, does that mean that it sacrifices some of its legitimacy and effectiveness as a political utterance? The example of *Uncle Tom's Cabin* suggests that it needn't do so, and novelists who want to believe that their fictions can effect large-scale political change will always have this example to guide them (even if it was a work of sentimental realism, whose form was anathema to modernist sensibilities). Whereas the slave narrative attempts to fuse author and narrator in a voice of sincerity, the meta-slave narrative separates the narrator from her implied author, adding a narrative level that makes room for the cognitive freedom embodied in that old friend of literary criticism, *irony*. This irony is the harbinger, perhaps, of more positive states of freedom, but it means that the literary work lives under threat of being perceived as politically trivial because it is merely literary. It's not clear, in other words, that a novel, especially an avant-garde novel, could have the same impact on political debate that *Uncle Tom's Cabin* did in the mid-nineteenth century, before the social sciences and "objective" journalism claimed pride of place as the forms of discourse most relevant to political debate, and television and movies claimed the lion's share of the capacity for mass-address. Could meta-slave narratives be as tightly integrated with the civil rights movement as slave narratives had been with abolitionism? The autonomy of fictionality, in other words, may come at a price.

This is the question lingering in the background of what was arguably the first meta-slave narrative, Ernest Gaines's *Autobiography of Miss Jane Pittman* (1970), which is among other things a study in the potential polyphony at the heart of the "simple" first person voice, which can be made to contain the kind of complex autopoetic transactions between narrative selves and others that we saw in the more obviously modernist *House Made of Dawn*. While Gaines's work is not in fact an autobiography, or even a particularly "autobiographical" novel in the usual sense of the term, it is not hard to find figures of the author within its pages. No narrative voice can be expected to fully escape an implied identification with the person whose name is conventionally put on the book's cover, even one as flagrantly far removed from the experience of an illiterate 110-year-old Louisiana woman as an ambitious young male Stanford M.F.A. living in San Francisco. He and she, the invisible authorial fact and the first person fiction, are of course fused in every word we read, including the word Gaines typed out again and again as he wrote: "I". As a literary historian, one only wants a believable principle of transformation from one state of being to another.

In this case, over and above the purely technical or grammatical coincidence of he and "I", is the minority culture that the young man author and the elderly woman character were assumed to share. Long before Gaines, having first graduated from San Francisco State, became a Stegner Fellow at Stanford, he had determined that his true voice as a writer could only emanate from the Louisiana he had left behind as a young boy: "that Louisiana dialect—the combination of English, Creole, Cajun, Black. For me there's no more beautiful sound anywhere—unless, of course, you take exceptional pride in 'proper' French or 'proper' English."[60] But in American literature of the 1960s and 70s, as we have seen, very few people were taking exceptional pride in proper English, and hybrid vernacular projects like this one were all the rage. Braiding the dialect that surrounded him as a child with the Standard English acquired through his long years of schooling, Gaines's narrative could be said to reinforce an existential link between the adult author and a younger version of himself in the unlikely medium of the voice of ancient "Jane Pittman," who in turn refers both man and boy back to the even longer collective history of which they are the offspring.

But the novel is bookended by two figures who seem more obvious projections of Ernest Gaines than she, and who together sum up the promise and problems of the meta-slave narrative as a form. First is a nameless young man, a history teacher who speaks in a fictional introduction to the novel, only to disappear. He purports to have collected and edited the words we are about to read, deriving them from tape recordings he has made on successive visits to a Louisiana plantation to hear Jane Pittman's story. Here again is the technological supplement to orality that, making the human voice durable, gives it a fighting chance against the tyranny of print (even as it becomes a natural resource to be exploited by print). Speaking into a microphone, Jane Pittman has given an account of a life that has, remarkably, bridged the entire period between the last days of slavery and the civil rights movement of the narrative present, the late 1950s. Accurately predicting the widespread use of *Jane Pittman* in the classroom, the fictional teacher-editor tells Jane that the value of her first person narrative will be in its use for students: hearing her voice, he tells her, will help him "explain things" to them in a way that the dry facts laid out in textbooks cannot. The truths of history, in this view, cannot be understood except as registered in the voice of the first-person eyewitness, speaking for herself. As B. A. Botkin put it in the introduction to an anthology of Federal Writers' Project oral slave narratives, *Lay My Burden Down* (1945), which Gaines read in preparation for writing his novel, "From the memories and the lips of slaves have come the answers which only they can give to questions which Americans still ask: What does it mean to be a slave? What does it mean to be free? And, even more, how does it *feel?*"[61]

Even as Jane Pittman's life story is an individual one, the teacher-editor takes pains to invite us to read it as a collective narrative, too: and this, true to the novel's time, is facilitated by its orality, which reconnects the individual voice, as embodied, to the communal racial body of which it is a part. "I should mention here," says the history teacher, "that even though I have used only Miss Jane's voice throughout the narrative, there were times when others carried the story for her. When she was tired, or when she just did not feel like talking anymore, or when she had forgotten certain things, someone else would always pick up the narration" for her (vi–vii).[62] Thus, although the fictional editor has tried his "best to retain Miss Jane's language," her "selection of words" and "rhythm of speech," her story is in a deeper sense "all of their stories."

At the other end of the novel, this time within Jane's first person narrative, is young Jimmy, who emerges from the plantation community to become a civil rights activist and martyr whose death is announced just as the novel comes to a close. His partial likeness to Gaines becomes clear in the service he provides as a child to the mostly illiterate plantation community: "Side reading the newspapers, he used to read the Bible for us, too; and he used to read and write our letters. Knowed how to say just what you wanted to say. All you had to do was get him started and he could write the best two-page letter you ever read. He would write about your garden, about the church, the people, the weather. And he would get it down just like you felt it inside. I used to sit there and look at him sitting on my steps writing and water would come in my eyes. You see, we had already made him the One, and I was already scared something was go'n happen to him or he would be taken from us" (216–217). While the history teacher's job is to look backward, finding historical truth in personal experience as recounted to his tape recorder, Jimmy's role as community amanuensis (Gaines had done the same thing as a child) is to intervene in the scripting of the present. And if his letter writing "fictionalizes" the experiences of the community? So be it. It may not be accurate description, but it is an authentic expression of the spirit of the community and thus "true" in a performative sense. The commitment of the community to fictitious versions of itself becomes clear when a more literal-minded letter writer replaces Jimmy and, simply telling it like it is, is immediately and harshly judged to be "not the One." Jimmy's role as a political leader, meanwhile, orients his actions not to the past but toward the future, the Promised Land.

Taken as a pair, the history teacher/editor and the amanuensis/activist are fascinating as much for how they don't quite converge in Gaines's novel as for how they almost do: although the reader meets him first, the history teacher is in fact legible as a slightly belated double of the recently martyred Jimmy. As partial projections of Gaines himself, they suggest both his aspiration to "speak for his people" and his modest sense of the gap between the autoethnographic novelist, producing historical fictions of racial community, and the political leader on the barricades with his eyes on the prize. As the scene of a turn from politics to culture, that gap writ large has provided space for the emergence of a specifically literary form of African American autonomy, but it is shadowed by the implication that, even as one voice has been found, another, more forceful voice might have been lost.

PART THREE

Creative Writing at Large
(1975–2008)

5

The Hidden Injuries of Craft:
Mass Higher Education and
Lower-Middle-Class Modernism

> *Love of work. The blood singing*
> *in that. The fine high rise*
> *of it into the work. A man says,*
> *I'm working. Or, I worked today.*
> *Or, I'm trying to make it work.*

> RAYMOND CARVER, "Work"

LOCATING CARVER COUNTRY

The unnamed narrator of Raymond Carver's short story "Night School" sits alone at a neighborhood bar drinking beer. Out of work, sleeping on a cot in his parents' hallway, he is the kind of figure John W. Aldridge would seem to have in mind when he describes the typical Carver character as "wholly without talents, ambitions, or prospects," someone who fails "to put up any resistance of will" to his lowly fate, "float[ing] in listlessness" through his desperately monotonous days.[1] But something about this one suggests an elevation, however slight, above the slough of total hopeless-ness. Two women sitting further along the bar strike up a conversation:

> "What do you do?" the first woman asked me.
>
> "Right now, nothing," I said. "Sometimes, when I can, I go to school."
>
> "He goes to school," she said to the other woman. "He's a student. Where do you go to school?"
>
> "Around," I said.
>
> "I told you," the woman said. "Doesn't he look like a student?"
>
> "What are they teaching you?" the second woman said.
>
> "Everything," I said.
>
> "I mean," she said, "what do you plan to do? What's your big goal in life? Everybody has a big goal in life."[2]

Pressed further, he coughs up the name of the school he sometimes at-tends, "State College," and, ordering another beer, even consents to iden-tify that big goal: "Teach. Teach school" (95).

To be sure, an air of evasion and vagueness attaches to the narrator's identity as a sometime student and would-be teacher—the "everything" they are teaching him sounds a lot like "nothing in particular"—and his distance from the classroom, as he sits in this bar, is very much to the point. And yet when it turns out that the women, although they are "about forty, maybe older" (94), are students, too, we gather that the theme of schooling invoked by the story's title will not be put to rest just yet. "'We take a night class,'" one of them tells him. "'We take this reading class on Monday nights . . . We're learning to read . . . Can you believe it?'" (95–96). "'I'd like to read Hemingway and things like that,'" the other one says, "'but Patterson has us reading stories like in *Reader's Digest*'" (95–97).

Everybody is getting some education, it seems, if not as much as they could use. It's hardly a dazzling display of talent, ambition, or pros-pects, Aldridge might protest, but it does suggest a slight inaccuracy in his account of Carver's characters, whose ambitions may simply be too small-scale or down-market for him to discern in the stream of understatement. There is actually a tremendous "resistance of will" shown in these stories, but it is a resistance to the language of self-assertion itself, to the forward-looking, affirmative language in which "big goals" are made visible and exposed to public judgments of failure or success. In this view, the usual disposition of Carver's characters, as of his narrators, is not one of hopelessness, exactly, but rather of wariness and waiting and protective self-concealment. And that, I would like to argue, is to say something important about the *form* of these stories, too, which have become some of the touchstones of postwar American creative writing.

Waiting is what the young man seems to be doing in the story "What Do You Do in San Francisco?" narrated by his postman, Henry Robinson, who builds his speculations upon the man's curiously static, homebound existence from the glimpses he gets when he delivers the mail. And so, on a different level, the reader must do the same. The man's wife seems to be a painter, and the man himself does "something along the same line," but Henry disapproves. Things along that line don't count as work, and he believes above all "in the value of work—the harder the better" (112;111). When the young man begins to meet him at the mailbox every day, obviously desperate for a letter, Henry sympathetically assumes that it has something to do with his woman, who has recently moved away. Finally one day it comes:

> He took it from me without a word and went absolutely pale. He tottered a minute and then started back for the house, holding the letter up to the light.
> I called out, "She's no good, boy. . . . Why don't you go to work and forget her? What have you got against work? It was work, day and night, work that gave me oblivion when I was in your shoes." (120)

But perhaps the point is that the young man *has* been working, and the drama of acceptance and rejection that Henry is witnessing is somewhat more complicated than he can surmise. For Robert Rebein, Carver's "true and lasting legacy" was in teaching writers of his generation "how to be a serious artist without taking art as his subject," and there is something obviously persuasive in this claim.[3] A story like this one could hardly be further from John Barth's "Autobiography" or Donald Barthelme's "The Balloon." At the same time, the application of slight interpretive pressure reveals a reflexive theme of art underlying the surface of Carver's stories— or, rather, the theme of the writing life as an occupation, a form of labor. Carver's first wife would remember, years later, the day her husband's first story acceptance arrived in the mail, the way it put them "on top of the world."[4] These are indeed the kinds of letters we hold up to the light— these and the ones that may or may not contain money.

Since Henry cannot know for sure, and since this is a Raymond Carver story, none of this will be made entirely clear. We can see, though, how the leisure imposed by the narrator's unemployment in "Night School" might foreshadow the particular form of working life encoded in the act of narration itself: writing. This, in any case, is the explicit situation of the husband in "Put Yourself in My Shoes," who has quit his job as a textbook editor to work full time as a writer, supported by his wife. Both his work ethic and the abject domesticity of the struggling writer's life are established at the outset, where he is seen vacuuming the house, and when he drives to meet his wife at a bar it seems that life itself—more precisely, the act of observation—must be converted into literary labor if he is to maintain his self-esteem: "He tried to see everything, save it for later. He was between stories, and he felt despicable" (134).

Carver found himself in a similar position when he was laid off from his job as a scientific textbook editor in Palo Alto—the first white-collar job he had ever held. Maryann Carver supported him then, as she had often done during the years since they were married and became teenage parents: "His career, his writing, he and I put it on such a pedestal, we'd sacrifice anything for that, first, last and always."[5] Some of her misery in this role is recorded in his story "The Student's Wife," in which a man dreamily asks his spouse what she wishes were different about their low-rent life, and gets a humiliatingly long list. And yet Carver's subsidized

Brooding on a Big Two-Hearted River. From Bob Adelman, *Carver Country: The World of Raymond Carver* (New York: Scribner's, 1990). Photograph by Bob Adelman.

unemployment, a sort of unofficial, highly gendered fellowship he held in advance of the real one he got at Stanford University a few years later, is what gave him the time he needed to revise "The Student's Wife" itself. During this period, when he was also collecting unemployment insurance, he worked on "Night School," "What Do You Do in San Francisco?" and many of the other stories contained in his first collection, *Will You Please Be Quiet, Please?* (1976), which paid a lot of bills after it was nominated for the National Book Award.

Bankruptcy in Sacramento. Photograph by Bob Adelman.

Does the same fate await the seemingly immobilized narrator of "Night School," sitting on his barstool, drinking beer with his fellow students, halted in his progress toward a college degree? They want to read Hemingway, the iconically laconic author to whom Raymond Carver himself, interestingly enough, would most often be compared. Perhaps, no less than Carver—famous for the amount of drinking he did and the number of shit jobs he lost, but still more famous as one of the most influential American writers of the postwar period—he might look up one day and find himself in Carver Country. This was the region of polluted rivers, little ranch houses, overflowing ashtrays, bars, old cars, and other artifacts of unglamorous life pictured in a handsomely bound coffeetable book of photographs by that title.[6]

Supplied with relevant extracts from Carver's writings, *Carver Country* (1990) was published as a posthumous homage to the writer, dead of

An aesthetics of shame? Photograph by Bob Adelman.

lung cancer at age 50, in recognition of the unlikely beauty he tried to lend to such things—things that reflect neither the spiff of upper-class existence nor even what Arno J. Meyer calls the "romance of utter wretchedness," but something floating uncomfortably in between.[7] Carver Country was known to be located in the Pacific Northwest of the United States, where the writer originally came from and where he set many of his stories, but its borders were shifting, stretching to encompass almost any overtly ordinary, obscurely hurtful American place.

Thus one could say that the citizens of Carver Country included not only the downbeat people who populate Carver's own stories but the large group of short story writers—Tobias Wolff, Ann Beattie, Jayne Anne Phillips, Frederick Barthelme, Amy Hempel, Mary Robison, and others—who rose to collective and individual prominence in the late 1970s and 1980s under the banner of the ordinary, the modest, the minimal, and the

Raymond Carver at Syracuse. Photograph by Bob Adelman.

real. Strongly associated with the influence of Carver, and with the editorship and tutelage of Gordon Lish, this was the kind of fiction to which
was affixed the tellingly contemptuous label "Kmart Realism," separating
it from the relative neutrality of "minimalism" and associating it instead
with low-end retail. Bill Buford called it "Dirty Realism," and published
two special issues of the British literary magazine *Granta* in the 1980s ex-

ploring the phenomenon. The ambiguous placement of Carver Country suggests that it may have been, more than anything else, a region of the mind, a domain of professional activity and camaraderie in which the desperate tackiness and dailiness of American lower-middle-class life is meant to be retained but somehow, against all odds, dignified, aestheticized.

And in this sense, as critics like Aldridge are wont to point out as though it were something to be ashamed of, Carver Country was less a geographical place than a "school" in an almost literal sense, an institution barely included in the purview of the stories themselves but arguably underlying them all. As Rebein has aptly noted, Carver's "entire career was informed and shaped by the world of the university," and writers like Carver and Richard Ford were, in Ford's words, "'seeking improvement in the standard postwar American way: through some sort of pedagogy.'"[8] As the book *Carver Country* subtly makes clear, Carver Country was located as much on the campus of Syracuse University—only the last of a long succession of institutions where he first studied and then taught creative writing—as anywhere else you could point to on a map.

"Teach. Teach school." As Carver's student Jay McInerney put it, "I think he believed it a peculiar fate that led him to be a teacher. He thought it strange that so many American writers supported themselves by teaching. On the other hand, he thought it was better than sweeping floors or pumping gas, which he had done in the past."[9]

THE SHAME OF LARGE NUMBERS

The rise and spread of the creative writing program over the course of the postwar period has transformed the conditions under which American literature is produced. It has fashioned a world where artists are systematically installed in the university as teachers, and where, having conceived a desire to become that mythical thing, a *writer,* a young person proceeds as a matter of course to request *application materials.* It has in other words converted the Pound Era into the Program Era. But that transformation has itself been part of a more comprehensive shift in U.S. higher education, one so fundamental that Clark Kerr, who as president of the University of California would become one of its most controversial apologists, saw fit to call it the "Great Transformation in Higher Education," likening the scale of its importance to the first appearance of religious colleges in the colonial wilderness and to the emergence, after the Civil War, of the sprawling, science-oriented research universities and land-grant institutions.[10] One can only be impressed with the pace of growth that has seen the single creative writing program of the late 1930s multiply and become hundreds of such programs spread out across the land, in a kind of flattening of the steep slopes of Parnassus. But that multiplication seems modest, in absolute terms at least, when compared with the numbers attached to the rise of mass higher education over the same period.

In the 1940s, fewer than 10 percent of traditional college-age Americans were attending college of some kind; by the 1980s more than half of them were doing so, and the very concept of the delimited college age, with the rise of continuing education, job retraining, and other part-time extension initiatives, was beginning to weaken somewhat. During this period universal access to higher education became a widely shared, if only partially realized, national ideal embodied in educational grant and guaranteed loan programs offered to individual students on an unprecedented scale. Beginning with the Servicemen's Readjustment Act, better known as the G.I. Bill, which offered college funding to hundreds of thousands of veterans of World War II and subsequent military conflicts, this initiative was extended further in the epochal Higher Education Act of 1965, which authorized massive federal tuition assistance to students of exceptional financial need. But these were only the most important of a great many federal and state legislative initiatives that fundamentally altered the demographics of higher education.

The number of colleges and universities in the U.S. doubled in this period, the vast majority of them now public, and so did the average enrollment at individual institutions, which scrambled to build new physical plants and academic programs to accommodate the mass of new students bearing hopes and dreams and tuition subsidies. Even after 1980, when the great bulge of the postwar boom had passed through the system and the growth rate in higher education slowed, enrollments in U.S. colleges held steady, and the percentage of Americans attending college continued to creep upward. The university, responsive not only to an ideology of educational populism but also to large-scale shifts in the U.S. economy that called for increases in the number of persons with scientific, technical, and managerial training, would be described by Daniel Bell as the "axial institution of postindustrial society," the center around which the postwar economy moved.[11]

We have barely begun to register the full significance of the great transformation in higher education for postwar American literature. This is not to say that the dominant contexts and themes that have been delineated by its critics and historians up to now are unimportant; as the earlier chapters of this book amply attest, the multiplying ways and means of high technology and mass mediation, usually analyzed under the rubric of "postmodernism," must feature centrally in any comprehensive account of the field. So, too, the systematic incorporation and reproduction of cultural difference in that field, represented preeminently, though not exclusively, by the rise to prominence of the ethnically or racially marked writer, is of obviously fundamental importance to postwar literature. The interacting aesthetic formations associated with these socio-historical phenomena, which I am calling "technomodernism" and "high cultural pluralism," sit at the peak of prestigious postwar literary production. The advent of television; the Cold War; the civil rights movement; grassroots and academic feminism; the sexual revolution; the faltering economy of the 1970s; the conservative retrenchment of the 1980s and gradual dismantling of the liberal welfare state; the ubiquitization of computers and the Internet; globalization and resurgent religious fundamentalism—all of these phenomena, and many more besides, can and should assert their rightful claims on the attention of the literary historian.

But the fact is that, at least insofar as we remain interested in literature per se, the rise of mass higher education in the postwar period might well claim an objective priority over all these other elements of socio-

historical and political context, if only in the literal sense that it is something we should account for first if we are to understand postwar American literature in genuinely historical materialist terms. This is so not
because it is either inherently or ultimately more important than the rest,
but because the university has been the indispensable and all but omnipresent institutional mediator of the relation between postwar text and
postwar context. In league with the lower levels of the school system, it
has been the engine of the production and reproduction of the very literary practices that would engage with the wider socio-historical world as
such, the "liberal" part of a widely distributed package of language and
writing skills that also includes grammar, punctuation, and, at the college
level, composition. Cumulatively, then, we must begin to speak of postwar American literature as a product of what Langdon Hammer has called
the "culture of the school."[12] More specifically, I would like in this chapter to explore how postwar American literature is driven by a dialectic of
shame and pride, self-hatred and self-esteem—a dialectic that is also, and
not at all coincidentally, at the heart of American educational theory and
practice.

The large-scale entry of shame into the field of social psychology
had begun with Helen Merrell Lynd's *On Shame and the Search for Identity*
(1958), which argues for the importance of shame in modern life over and
above—if also in intimate dialogue with—the privileged affect of the psychoanalytic tradition, guilt.[13] In the standard understanding of these two
negative affects, guilt is a form of internal self-reproach for an act of trans-
gression, while shame stems from the exposure of the self to the negative
judgment of others. For Lynd, however, this formulation runs the risk of
missing how shame is a simultaneously external and internal phenomenon, capable of being elicited by even the notion—the prospective imagination—of exposure to negative judgment. For her the more salient
distinction between guilt and shame, and the one that makes shame so
central to modern life, is the "importance of the element of the unexpected" in the shameful experience, as evidenced in the sudden somatic
response of blushing. Thus, as Rita Felski puts it, "times of swift change
and social dislocation" not only impose the necessity of a "search for iden-

tity" on the part of the persons who endure them; they also subject these persons to the shameful experience of a "discrepancy between certain norms and values and others perceived as superior. The opportunities for experiencing shame increase dramatically with geographic and other forms of social mobility, which provide an infinite array of chances for failure, for betraying by word or gesture that one does not belong to one's environment."[14] One of these environments, needless to say, is the university classroom, which also understands itself—such is its complexity—as a source of pride.

Perhaps even more primary than the unexpectedness—more evocatively, the *unpreparedness*—associated with shame is the sense of existential vulnerability that it indexes. One most often feels guilt for deliberate or at least quasi-deliberate actions, such as lying and stealing, fucking and fucking over, not returning that call. Shame, by contrast, is an emotion associated with involuntary subjection to social forces, and marks the inherent priority and superiority of those forces to any given individual. Indeed, the real (external) or imagined (internal) "audience" of one's shameful diminishment, which is also the agent of that diminishment, can be understood as a personification of social forces in the abstract. It can be understood as an agent of "self-consciousness" in both the colloquial (negative) and the philosophical (positive) sense. This is why, in the systems-theoretical affect theory first developed in the 1950s and 60s by Silvan Tomkins and more recently revived in the work of Eve Kosofsky Sedgwick, shame is understood as the negative emotion, above all others, associated with the experience of selfhood as such. It is one form of the physicality of the cogito, a surplus of proprioception.[15] We say that a person's actions are regrettably "self-conscious" not simply when they act awkwardly, but when this awkwardness is produced and amplified by their consciousness of this potential-cum-actual awkwardness. Shame, in other words, is a fundamentally self-reflexive feeling, associated with negative feedback. We blush when we are unable to answer the teacher's question, and blushing embarrasses us further; we try to act cool in the cafeteria and, doing so self-consciously, act goofy.

But these of course are only some of the more dramatic moments in the larger and more or less continuous stream of "self-consciousness" in and through which we monitor our own behavior and adjust our relation, as we can, to an always potentially hostile and disapproving world. Indeed, as systems theory has made clear, processes of self-reflexive self-regulation are present in all organic systems, which relate to their environments via feedback loops.[16] What human self-consciousness adds to this process is on the one hand narrative: we not only observe our relation to the world, but we organize that relation, and to some degree predict its future, by representing it in and as an overlapping series of stories; and on the other hand a capacity for higher-order abstraction and introspection: this is how we create an internal realm, a mental theater of cruelty, where we are humiliated by "others" who are also "our own demons." What modernity, in turn, adds to the narrativizing and abstracting functions of human self-consciousness is the establishment of the bourgeois individual as the protagonist of what is now understood to be a modern social world consisting of millions and millions of ongoing, self-reflexively self-regulating "life stories."[17]

What I am calling lower-middle-class modernism is the meeting of all of these phenomena—social dislocation, affect, narrative, and the individual—in and around the scene of creative writing instruction in the postwar period, which formalizes and textualizes the modern "life story" in and as the production of self-reflexive fictions. Grounded in an affective dialectic of shame and pride, the autopoetic processing of experience as creative writing cashes out, in the literary marketplace, as a dialectic of "minimalist" and "maximalist" narrative forms.

LESS IS MORE, MORE OR LESS

The strength of postwar literature's connection to the postwar educational system can be seen not only in its association with creative writing programs, but in the way these programs echo, even as they substantially elevate, one of the more emblematic movements in educational theory and practice of the first three decades after the war. This was the enterprise known as "programmed instruction," which takes the programmatic aspect of the program, so difficult to reconcile with our persistently romantic conceptions of creativity, and literalizes it for use in the teaching of more basic, utilitarian skills like grammar and composition. One of the most prominent champions of what was also called "auto-instruction" was Wilbur Schramm, whom we met in Chapter 2 as the first director of the newly established Iowa Writers' Workshop. Leaving that post to the glory of Paul Engle, he eventually became director of the Institute for Communications Research at Stanford, where one of his chief concerns was the application of B. F. Skinner's behaviorist psychology to mass education.

In one of several texts he prepared on the topic, Schramm defined programmed instruction as a "learning experience in which a 'program' takes the place of a tutor for the student, and leads him through a set of specified behaviors designed and sequenced to make it more probable that he will behave in a given desired way in the future—in other words, that he will learn what the program is designed to teach him."[18] Often using crude "teaching machines" like the one devised by Skinner himself—today personal computers do this sort of work—programmed instruction also took the form of textbooks written as a progressive series of statements and repetitive fill-in-the-blank reinforcements, moving "frame by frame" through the "interactive" acquisition of a skill. Another of its promoters, William Deterline, argued in 1962 that, far from the bleakly impersonal enterprise it might seem to be, auto-instruction simply automated the interactivity of the ideally intimate educational form, the Socratic dialogue. It could thus, in his view, counteract some of the unfortunately depersonalizing effects of the population explosion in American schools: "The oft-voiced objection that auto-instruction might dehumanize education is simply not valid. The demands of mass education have already done this to a significant degree, and one of the attractive features of auto-instruction is its potential ability to provide mass instruction in a highly personalized manner."[19]

Later iterations of programmed instruction, incorporating a

"branching" structure that allowed further work in a given subset of the subject matter to be either pursued or bypassed, were uncannily precursive, in some ways, of early hypertext fictions created with the program Storyspace, though the latter would radicalize the branching of choices and remove the goal of utilitarian knowledge acquisition from the process. Branching instructional programs no doubt produced a more robust effect of "personalization" than the ones available when Deterline wrote, which reduced it to the question of pace: how fast are you able, or do you want, to work through the program? Since programmed instruction was by definition individual instruction, this could be allowed to vary considerably. It would be easy, and in some obvious ways correct, to dismiss this as a pathetically mean bit of "personality" to hand back to the student, strapped into the educational mechanism like a lab rat. But this would be to disregard how painfully shameful it is to be the "slow" student in a group learning context (and also, no doubt, how boring it is to be the "quick" one). Indeed, no less than in the Taylorized factory, the question of pace is important everywhere in the modern classroom, both as an organizing force of the curriculum, where certain levels of knowledge have to be disseminated by a certain grade, and as a mechanism for producing distinctions between students. However impoverished a notion of education it might seem to be founded on—i.e., education as conditioning—programmed instruction represents an interesting attempt to recognize and to some degree resist the tyranny of pace.

No wonder, then, that Gordon Lish—not yet the *Esquire* and Knopf editor, not yet the creative writing instructor and champion of American literary minimalism he would later become—took care to stress the temporal individualism of programmed education in the Teacher's Manual that accompanied his first major publication, the two-volume *English Grammar* (1964), which he wrote as an employee of Behavioral Research Laboratories in Palo Alto: "It is extremely desirable that you give each student, *individually,* the first test when he completes the first section. This method has the advantage of allowing faster students to proceed to the second section of the program when they are ready for it, while slower students will not feel that they are holding back the class."[20]

Even without the benefit of literary historical hindsight, Lish's *Grammar* is an interesting artifact, with traditionally bound volumes designed to be read straight through on the right-hand pages, then turned over and around and read back in the opposite direction, as though they aspire to the condition of a repetitive wheel mechanism or Möbius band. Beginning an auto-execution of Lish's program, the student who holds this strange text-object in her hands is brought into interaction, not with the rules of grammar immediately, but with a reflexive narrative that not only defines what grammar is but establishes the motive for the student's learning grammar in the first place. The following excerpt gives an example (the boldface is in the original text):

6. The growing tempo of modern life changes language. Because it saves time, and because time is increasingly valuable, people begin to spell the word **through** this way: **thru.** The spelling of words in a living language [does/does not] change.   (does)

7. The rules of proper usage change. For example, because it sounds awkward or affected to use the traditional form **It's I,** people increasingly say **It's me.** The attitude toward the rules of usage in a living language [does/does not] change.   (does)

8. These instances of change in vocabulary, spelling, and usage tend to bring [order/disorder] to our language. Grammar, however, brings order to our language because grammar deals with an unchanging law: **language creates information.**   (disorder)

9. Grammar is based on the unchanging law that language creates _____. Grammar does not deal with the changing laws of vocabulary, spelling, punctuation, and usage.   (information)

Grammar does deal with the [changing/unchanging] law that language creates information.   (unchanging)

[. . .]

12. Because it is undergoing great change, our language
tends toward [<u>disorder/order</u>].   (disorder)
You can cope with this disorder, however, if you understand
the system called _____.   (grammar)[21]

In a "modern life" characterized by hurry and disorder, grammar offers
the student access to the unchanging order of language, which, he soon
learns, can be broken into six interacting logical elements, including the
all-important noun. The rules governing these interactions are, the program later admits, flexible, overlapping, and sometimes confusing. Grammar, while logical, is not perfectly logical. But all of these complexities are
grounded and stabilized by the single "law" of language-as-information-
creation.

Dispensing with the problem of reference and representation from
the outset, this law defines language in notably pragmatist—we might
even call them productivist—terms. For Lish, language is a worker, working to produce information, somewhat like the future knowledge-workers
at whom his textbook is aimed. For these "tools" of the postwar economy, language itself is to be considered a tool: "Chief among the obstacles
to engaging a student's enthusiasm in the study of our language is his failure to view it as a *problem-solving mechanism*."[22] What is constructed here
is what we might call a popular or even populist formalism. Submitting
themselves to Lish's program, students are not taught proper usage, but
rather are conditioned to "rise above" the stream of historical change and
disorder and view it from the perspective of an ideal grammatical order.
From this perspective, not only can the once-proper "It's I" be seen for the
"affected" form it is now taken to be, but the student is given a perspective
on the very principle that produces such a potentially embarrassing drift.
Entering the program, the student comes out the other side prepared for
change, and thus protected from shame—in this case the shame of bad
grammar.

It would be wrong, I think, to lose sight of the "individual" who is
understood to persist in, and to be re-produced by, this textbook machine.

Not only is the person constructed as an individual disabled from see-ing himself as a member of an exploited social class who might assign blame rather than feel shame, but he is now prepared to move on to other tasks including, perhaps, the scripting of literary texts. As with the rela-tively humble acquisition of the types of knowledge we call "skill" or "technique"—the pianist doing scales or the apprentice painter practicing brushstroke technique—the question of individual creativity in the use of language on the student's part is not negated by the program but deferred while the primary skill is implanted in the body as habit.

But as if impatient for this more creative future, Lish's own "creative urges" begin to assert themselves in his textbook even as he dutifully sticks with the program. This curious feature of the text was noted by his fellow program textbook author, Leonard Wolf, a creative writing instructor at San Francisco State, in a brief introduction to the first volume: "The most unexpected gain the book provides is the gleaming thread of humor that weaves in and about the sober information. There is an unforgettable cast of unlikely words functioning as nouns. The student comes upon Hoagy, Chadwick, creebies, and mazzernicks doing unlikely things: Hoagy being attacked by a toothless mazzernick, for instance."[23] The occasional cute-ness of Lish's textbook can of course be read in any one of several ways. Most simply, it can be understood as a way of establishing the arbitrariness of the referents of the grammatical forms in question. More suspiciously, it could be read as a cynical indirection from the horrible normalization the program is performing on the brain of the student. Then again, and not at all implausibly, it could be read as a sort of encoded cry for help— I'm an employee of Behavioral Research Laboratories and they won't let me out!—from the authorial ghost in the textbook machine.

But perhaps most interesting is to read it as a modeling of the persis-tence of creativity even within the confines of extreme conventionality, whether it is the conventionality of grammar itself, which all but the most radically experimental writers tend to respect, or of the program textbook genre to whose rules Gordon Lish, as a writer-employee, must submit. This certainly is how Leonard Wolf suggests we understand it.[24] It's not such a large leap, really, from Lish's grammar textbook to his editorial sponsorship of literary minimalism, in the 1970s and 80s, and from there to the stories he published under his own name during the same period. One of them is called "Imagination" and begins like this: "X was a teacher of story-writing, and Y was a student of same. X was a remarkable teacher of story-writing. In the opinion of A to Z, exclusive of Y, X was the best there ever was. Still, Y sought out X for instruction—for although Y was not willing to hold X's skills in the very highest esteem, Y nevertheless held them in esteem high enough. . . . Then X met Z."[25] This is only the most extreme version of something one encounters throughout Lish's collection *What I Know So Far* (1983), and indeed throughout minimalist fiction in general, where characters frequently remain unnamed, reduced instead to pronouns or to their social functions (for example, "the wife"). And yet, for all its thematization of an empty formalism, a fiction of fill-in-the-blanks, the story manages to seem exceedingly "personal" and even narcissistic, inconceivable except as the product of Gordon Lish. Producing a reflexive collision of formality and personality, it recalls one of the examples from *English Grammar* demonstrating the function of the gerundive phrase, where the verb form functions as a subject: *"Becoming a first-rate lizard trainer requires nerve and cunning."*[26]

As an editor, meanwhile, Lish would always proclaim a grammarian's investment in the sentence as the most important unit of the narrative. The same was true of Mina P. Shaughnessy's classic text of composition theory for the era of the underprepared student, *Errors and Expectations* (1977), which spends the most time on the sentence and only belatedly moves "beyond the sentence."[27] This diminutive scale of concern is then redoubled at the level of genre: for minimalism, not just short stories but relatively short short stories are the favored form, as though echoing the processes that turn "through" into "thru." Lish is rightly credited with the relative badness, at least as compared to the rest of his oeuvre, of Carver's collection *What We Talk About When We Talk About Love* (1981) which Lish cut with too heavy a hand, converting his overbearing presence, by the logic of reversal, into an excess of negative narrative space.[28]

As a creative writing instructor, both at universities and, later, as an independent creative writing instruction entrepreneur, Lish has been remarkable for what he might have been expected to do but hasn't: write a creative writing textbook. Instead his teaching is "live," conducted in real time, usually over the course of many hours continuously. A participant in one of his private writing seminars described the experience: "You sat for six to eight hours without a stretch or a piss. You listened to the teacher and artist at work. . . . You accepted 12-gauge evisceration of your work and returned to the next meeting with something new, and you hoped better, to offer."[29] Shedding his textual carapace, the authorial ghost in the program textbook machine emerges to crack the whip for himself, training his lizards to become better writers by means of physical torture and shame. Thus he keeps faith with one of the pedagogical principles at the core of *English Grammar*, interactivity, while dispensing with its idea of shameless solitude. But even here, as in the student's self-empowering submission to the program, what we are observing is in fact a dialectic of shame and pride, since the shame of public "evisceration" of one's shamefully bad fiction is preparation for the eventual pride of publication.

To say that American literary minimalism is at least partially a product of the corporate educational technology and textbook business of the 1960s and 70s is not to deny that it might also be the singular aesthetic triumph of that enterprise. It is also simply a narrower version of the broader claim that, along with the emergence of the Program Era itself, minimalism is in part a product of the era of mass higher education. The arrival of the masses in the halls of academe is the unstated social referent of John Barth's idea, first proposed in 1986, that literary minimalism was somehow reflective of a "national decline in reading and writing skills, not only among the young (including even young apprentice writers, as a group), but among their teachers, many of whom are themselves the product of an ever-less-demanding educational system."[30] The assumption here is that, in league with television and movies, the orientation of that system toward the absorption of the social masses dumbs everybody down, and minimalism is one of the results. According to Barth, rarely in the work of minimalist writers "will one find a sentence of any syntactical complex-ity," which is unfortunate "inasmuch as a language's repertoire of other-than-basic syntactical devices permits its users to articulate other-than-basic thoughts and feelings." In short, "Dick-and-Jane prose tends to be emotionally and intellectually poorer than Henry James prose."[31]

To which the defender of minimalism could respond: yes, but *emo-tionally and intellectually poorer* in a deeper, more literal, but also more aes-thetically powerful sense than its detractors are prepared to credit.[32] Mini-malism was in any case founded on a skepticism of the idea that fiction is emotionally rich when it is emotionally "articulate," which sounds like an incipient violation of the aesthetic law that it almost always obeys: show don't tell. Minimalism had very little to say about emotion. That's because it was engineered as a way, not of explaining, but of beautifying shame. For the postwar student venturing into the hazardous space of the cre-ative writing workshop, the minimalist aestheticization of "Dick-and-Jane prose" is a re-performance, in a more elevated setting, of the original ac-quisition of the verbal self-control for which the children's primer was the program. Its impulse is toward something we could call autopastoral: an aesthetic appreciation of a simpler, slower, more controllable version of oneself. The excisions and understatements that are the hallmark of mini-malism—and that came to be seen, oversimplifying the case drastically, as the "house style" of the creative writing program—can be understood as analogous to the self-protective concealments, like shielding the eyes, triggered before, during, and after the fact of shameful exposure. The very shortness of the short forms associated with minimalism (and with cre-ative writing instruction in general) puts "mastery of form," a solid sense of completion, within visible reach of the student. The highly disciplined artifacts thus created are the work, simultaneously, of an externalization or expression of "authorial selfhood" as story and of the disciplined recon-figuration of the self through the patient labor of counterfactual fiction making. If the modern world is a world of risk, a "Risk Society," then min-imalism is an aesthetic of risk management, a way of being beautifully careful.[33]

The theme of risk management is already there in Raymond Carver's first professional publication, the story "Pastoral" (1963), which is inevitably, for the devotee of Hemingway, about a quietly moody young man's therapeutic fishing trip.[34] Arriving at the lodge after a long drive, the protagonist starts down the stairs to his cabin: "He held onto the banister and went slowly down the stairs" (35). And later: "The lights from the cafe showed him where he was walking, and he was careful" (37). One of the ways of being careful, of course, is to go slow: "He wasn't going to hurry. Not today" (39). This is the ultimate meaning, I think, of the effect of stasis so often produced in and by Carver's later, more mature fiction, such as "Night School": the situation might be bad, but if it is going slowly then it is under control and unlikely to produce nasty, shame-inducing surprises. Going slow is a way of keeping things, including one's aesthetic emotions, out of sight and under control. It is another way of being and staying—as contextualized so powerfully in Alan Liu's history of postwar corporate aesthetics—cool.[35]

And yet, these minimalist linguistic concealments have all the ambiguity of their physical analogues. As Silvan Tomkins observed, "shame is both an interruption and a further impediment to communication, which is itself communicated. When one hangs one's head or drops one's eyelids . . . one has communicated one's shame and both the face and self unwittingly become more visible, to the self and others."[36] This makes sense of the obvious way in which minimalism, even as it often stages itself as a quiet counter-spectacle, a form of resistance to the self-assertive blare of modern American gigantism, is also a way of soliciting a certain kind of attention—is even, as a kind of literary dropping of the eyelids, a form of seduction. As he heads up those stairs to the lodge, we find the protagonist of "Pastoral" nodding "to a young couple coming out. He noticed the way the man held her arm as they went down the stairs. He zipped up his coat and pulled it down as far as he could over his pants before opening the door" (33). Correct me if I'm wrong, but I believe the young man has just got an erection. This is indeed, from the reader's perspective at least, a coy concealment.

Hemingway is certainly the master figure here, and of American literary minimalism as a whole, though his legacy in Carver is subjected to an interesting inversion. Hemingway had been a privileged child of the upper middle class, the son of an outdoorsman medical doctor and a former opera singer; according to one of his biographers, he "associated intellect, art and culture with the aesthetes of the 1890s, with homosexuals and with the sissified music pupils of his mother."[37] Thus his own work as a writer was never set in self-consciously refined, stuffy places like his hometown of Oak Park, Illinois. More appealing, if no less founded on social privilege, was the family's vacation house in the Michigan woods, which sets the originary scene for literary representations of many kinds of hands-on craft labor in the stereotypically masculine mode.

In "Big Two-Hearted River," as any student of Hemingway knows, fishing is strongly associated with post-traumatic therapy, the healing of war wounds. In Carver's "Pastoral" it has the same therapeutic function, and is similarly gendered. What Carver adds to the formula, however, even as he removes the war referent, is precisely the thing that would come to be understood as the trademark and true source of power of his own work, to be imitated by legions of younger creative writers in their turn, whatever their class background might be. As the story unfolds, and the protagonist comes into conflict with some boys from a nearby labor camp, it becomes clear that this fishing trip is a small parcel of leisure stolen from the exhausting working life to which he has to return the following day. Shifting the class dynamics of Hemingway's retreat from the drawing rooms of the upper middle class into nature, Carver founds his own version of minimalism not on war wounds, but on the wounds of low-status employment—founds it, that is, on what Richard Sennett and Jonathan Cobb, in a best-selling work of sociology from the seventies, called *The Hidden Injuries of Class* (1973).

Thus the prideful attention to "craft" associated with literary minimalism can also be understood as the utopian return of unalienated labor in an economic order characterized by a large increase in jobs that are "white collar" in standard social definition but no less "alienated"—and often worse paid and less secure—than the unionized blue-collar jobs of the past. The model here is William Morris's Arts and Crafts movement and its American variants, which sought to reclaim ennobling, soul-satisfying labor from the mechanical jaws of industrialism. Another model is fishing, which any reader of Hemingway's "Big Two-Hearted River" or Raymond Carver's "Pastoral" will see can be pretty hard work. As a "recreational activity," though, it stands in a compensatory relation, as *good hard work,* to the loads of hurried shit work carried out in an office or retail environment.

BECOMING MAXIMAL

Of course, nobody does more work than Joyce Carol Oates. If Raymond Carver says too little, Oates says too much. The complaints habitually lodged against these two quintessential figures of the Program Era are strikingly complementary. His highly crafted minimalism is aesthetically empty, all too imitable, the corporate style of the creative writing program; her inimitable productivity is tacky, the sign of insufficient engagement in the meticulous rounds of revision that the master teachers of the creative writing establishment, like John Gardner, posited as the very basis of worthwhile literary achievement. "Fine workmanship," as he put it, "painstaking care, gives a sense of life's worth and dignity not only to the reader but to the writer as well."[38] Is there, as we might suspect, a unity underlying this opposition, these crises of aesthetic plenitude and privation? There is if we see the criticism of these two writers, where Oates is accused of "slop[ping] words across the page like a washerwoman flinging soiled water across the cobblestones" and Carver of exhibiting a "poverty of imagination," as the barely disguised symbolic class warfare that it is.[39] The objectivity of these insults is to be found not in their aesthetic judgments, which may or may not be accurate, but in their mostly unconscious apprehension of the importance of mass higher education in setting the scene of the careers of the minimalist and maximalist alike.

When Carver himself was asked, in 1973, who he thought was the

most important writer of his generation, he answered with notable conviction, and gained a lifelong friend: "To my mind Joyce Carol Oates is the
first writer of my generation, perhaps any recent generation, and we are
all going to have to learn to live under that shadow, or spell—at least for
the foreseeable future."[40] His own first collection of stories was still three
years away, while Oates at age thirty-five was already at this point the author of five very substantial novels, three collections of stories, two books
of poems, and a volume of academic literary criticism. She had been nominated for the National Book Award three times, and had won it in 1970 for
her multigenerational epic of a white working-class family in Detroit, the
novel *them* (1969). And yet, as Carver's equivocation, "at least for the foreseeable future," almost allows, the spell cast by Joyce Carol Oates would
soon be broken—or, rather, the nature of that spell would change. Publishing too many books under her name, asking for more attention than
the literary establishment can possibly give to any one writer, the symbolic value of shares of JCO in the market of literary prestige would start
to drop.

An early warning to this effect was issued in 1971, when Alfred Kazin
noted how even Oates's best fiction can seem an "impenetrably volumi-
nous history of emotions, emotions, emotions. You feel you are turning
thousands of pages, that her world is as harshly overpopulated as a sleep-
less mind."[41] He thought this effect of aesthetic overpopulation was "obviously related to the ease with which" she "transfers the many situations in
her head straight onto paper."[42] By 1982, James Wolcott's review of her fif-
teenth novel and thirty-seventh book would be entitled "Stop Me Before I
Write Again: Six Hundred More Pages by Joyce Carol Oates." The implication is that she writes the way a serial killer murders—maniacally, compul-
sively, although with disturbing regularity and efficiency. Losing control of
her own process, Oates "doesn't write books now, the books write her."
On these grounds, Wolcott suggests, she must be redefined as a producer
not of "literature," simply, but of a weird amalgam of high art and genre
fiction which is successful on neither account: "The novels of most so-
called serious writers are usually exercises of craft and care," complains

Wolcott, but this novel "seems a freak," a "word-goop with a ravenous case of the [munchies]."[43]

No less than with Carver, the minimalist, the question of class identity hovers everywhere around the maximalism of Joyce Carol Oates, whose life was altered when she left the near-poverty of her upbringing in upstate New York for an undergraduate career at Syracuse University. A private institution, it had grown from 5,000 students in 1942 to nearly 20,000 when she arrived in 1956, one of the "educationally hungry hordes" whose presence on campus, as one trustee put it, applied an "unremitting pressure of the giant force of need and demand."[44] Even amidst this tumult, her talent for writing was quickly perceived and nurtured by creative writing instructor Donald Dike. Thus began a lifelong affiliation with universities, first at Syracuse, later in and around Detroit, and finally at Princeton. While Carver's social ascent through education was a protracted patching together of college credits over the course of several years while he worked and raised two children, Oates seemed to soar upward from her humble beginnings on a blazing trail of straight A's and academic prizes and literary awards.

Thus it seems predictable that—as distinct from the virtually racialized post-ethnic stasis of Carver, and even more so from the strong, transgenerational racial identification of her colleague Toni Morrison—for Oates it is the dizzyingly swift malleability of class positionality that draws her attention, and becomes the explicit concern of one of the major works of her early period, *Wonderland* (1971), where a poor boy barely escapes being murdered by his suicidal father, only to be claimed by a family of rich eccentric intellectuals who put him through school and start him on his way to professional eminence.[45] Far from being resistant to change, as Carver's stories can seem to be, this novel, much like Oates's *them*, vaults through forty years of American history and yet seems to dwell with great narrative intensity in every moment, as though attempting to be equal, almost, to the force of historical time.

As we have seen, the various deprivations of Carver's represented worlds are set in counterpoint to the aestheticized inarticulacy of his highly crafted, paired-down sentences. Oates's narration, by contrast, drags the hidden injuries of class into the bright light of an agonized articulacy. Confirming Kazin's sense that her work narrates the history of emotions, emotions, emotions, the jacket copy of early editions of her books often quoted her as saying "All of my writing is about the mystery of human emotions." But to say that her work is "about" emotions suggests how it continuously explains, rather than sustains, their mystery. As a form of lower-middle-class modernism, then, Oates's maximalism represents a fundamentally different, if structurally complementary, form of shame management than one finds in Carver. In Oates, the hidden injuries of class meet their match in the form of a shameless rhetorical pride that often says "shame" but hardly ever shows it. Note how the opening of her story "Archways" could easily be describing a figure like Raymond Carver, but note also how unthinkable it would be to find it in a Carver story:

> Klein, a nervous young man whose overcoat in winter hung down far below his knees, felt shame that he was several years older than his fellow students, felt shame that he was seized often by an inexplicable panic, alone or with others, felt shame that he was poor. He was a graduate student in a state university that serviced thirty thousand students, having come to his life's work (he realized with shame) after having been frightened out of other, lesser tasks: clerking, work in the Railway Express, work at his father's filling station. He had slid from one job to another, one segment of his life to another, as if he had been loosed at the top of a great jagged hill and could not control his destiny.[46]

Stepping back to perform a socio-psychological analysis of Klein, but remaining closely tied to his experience and point of view, Oates's narration lays out the existential stakes of mass higher education with a verbosity alien to the minimalist mode.

And yet, even this project of propulsive narrative momentum is subject to its own encounter with stasis. Neither for Carver nor for Oates is

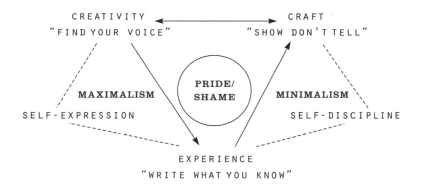

Literary maximalism can be thought of as a form of verbal pride, a way of being linguistically present, while minimalism is the aestheticization of shame, a mode of self-retraction. But with a further turn of the dialectic we can see how minimalist shame is a form of attention-getting, and how maximalist pride is also a way of shielding oneself with words.

upward mobility to be viewed, as the ideal of educational betterment would have it, as a sequence of steps up a ladder, a linear movement from low to high, from shame to pride. For Oates, the very swiftness of the social ascent enabled by education leaves the subject open to disorienting attacks from the internal demons of memory, as class identity (who you feel yourself to be) lags behind class positionality (where you currently stand) by a significant, though confusingly immeasurable, margin. Lower-middle-class modernism, as an offspring and elevation of mass educational practices, figures upward mobility as a continuing existential *process,* a *program,* a *working* of the shame/pride dialectic in the form of a textual memory-processing machine called fiction.

Consider another of Oates's early stories, "The Survival of Childhood" (1964), which simultaneously dramatizes and anatomizes the psychology of upward mobility in merciless detail: "Carl was tortured by memories of his childhood, which came to him as he drove home through the colorless day with a sharp, delicate pang of clarity. His life here in this

expanding industrial city, teaching grammar and literature to factory workers' children whose hard eyes showed distrust, was so different, so altered,
from his past life, that the reality of his link with those back-country people, with the back-country boy he himself had been, staggered his mind"
(*Upon the Sweeping Flood*, 31–32). Separated by the rural and urban places
of their origin, Carl and the college students he teaches are nonetheless
equally the products of the great transformation that has yanked so many
persons like themselves into unfamiliar educational territory, and we can
be sure that his students will have their own versions of their teacher's tale
of dislocation to tell. For Carl, meanwhile, a mind-staggering connection
to his former self is revived one day when he receives a letter in his departmental mailbox from hard-drinking, trouble-making Gene, the younger
brother he left behind when he went away to school all those years ago:

> As he opened it impatiently, visions of unhappiness and de-
> struction crowded his mind—fires, deaths, his father fallen
> with a stroke, his brother Gene maimed in a fight, the old
> house itself in which he and his five brothers and sisters had
> been born finally collapsing in, burdened by the incredible
> weight of time and suffering. His eye automatically scanned
> the letter for certain key words, signals of disaster, but found
> none.
>
> It began with a large HELLO CARL. (28–29)

Gene's shocking act of literate practice—he has never written to
Carl before—produces an uncanny amalgam of familiarity and strangeness for its recipient, as though the "illiteracy" of Carl's own past has found
a way to express itself in the medium of its own abolishment. The mysterious power of this communication from his brother eventually draws him
back home to what appears, in Carl's fevered visions, as a kind of lower-
class House of Usher, a place to contemplate the "mockery . . . blood
bondage" (38) makes to his proud sense of having "escaped the curse of
his family" (31). Meeting over beers in the local dive, his brother forces
him to see their separate fates as related by a zero-sum logic of inversion,

one brother gaining "ascendancy from hell" because the other dwells there permanently: Gene "had saved him from something." And in fact it turns out that Gene had had his own artistic talents as a child: "'Sometimes he'd draw all day long with charcoal or crayon, and I liked to watch,'" Carl tells his wife as he prepares for his journey. "'I was probably a little jealous'" (37). Gene had even gotten a job teaching art at the local high school— "'they had just begun offering art courses; it was something new'"—but had been fired for bad behavior. With this detail we are all but asked to see Gene's brief career as a teacher as a kind of stunted, back-country version of the artist-in-residency, the coupling of writing and teaching, that was coming to define the careers of writers like Carver and Oates.

In a story of such psychological intensity, it comes as no surprise when Gene takes the occasion of his brother's return to the family home to commit suicide with a shotgun. And it seems perfectly natural that Carl, feeling "lightheaded and absurd" (46) in the aftermath of this violent act, is compelled by an inner force to take his brother's place working behind the counter at the local country store for a day. Nor does it seem odd to him or to the narrator that he will be unquestioningly allowed to do this in a way that would be inconceivable if their fates were reversed, and uneducated Gene were to show up to teach Carl's classes at the university. But for Carl this brief stint at Gene's dead-end job becomes a kind of ritual performance of the immobility that persists even in the context of a successful academic career, even in the headlong narrative rush through time that characterizes Oates's fictions. This is the staccato stasis imposed by serial attacks of traumatic memory, which keep dragging Carl back to the swampy emotive life of the uneducated family from which he must separate himself again and again. Standing at the counter looking at the crappy stuff for sale in the store, Carl's "sense of the present was painful and analytical, and it seemed to him that he could pursue both past and present simultaneously, that one led inexorably into the other, that he was the focal point for their meeting" (47). Looking out the window at the rain, Carl could be staring into the heart of Carver Country, where social directionalities are never linear and the weather is always fairly bad. The rain falls "slowly, weightlessly dissolving into the earth, so that at times it seemed to move in both directions, lifting upward, sinking downward, a phenomenon of immobility—of entropy" (48).

Looking at these earlier, shorter versions of Oates's negotiations of the relation between class positionality and class identity—the first instantly changeable, the second only gradually, and perhaps always incompletely, so—we can begin to appreciate the source and power of the "spell," as Carver put it, cast by a massive novel like *them,* with its harrowing account of life in Detroit from the 1930s through to the novel's own present, the late 1960s, and which traces the disintegration of working-class community and the emergence of lower-middle-class deracination and aspiration. This was a period when, as one character sees it, the "world was pulling into two parts, those who were hopeless bastards and weren't worth spitting on and those who were going to get somewhere."[47] Seen in relation to this binary classification, the title of the novel could be said to condense an entire class politics into one pronoun. Written by an author who herself, as she often noted, came from severely straitened circumstances, but who at the time of her writing had become a literature and composition professor at the University of Detroit, it can seem a brutal act of performative distantiation between an author and her characters. *Them!* (1954) had after all been the title of a campy alien invasion movie only fourteen years earlier, and Oates's use of the title can seem literally to want to alienate her characters, to see them as though from an interplanetary distance.

Because it is an effect produced only after hundreds of pages of richly detailed social-historical realism, it is hard to describe in brief the astonishing impact of the moment, late in the novel, when the continuity of the long, feverish fictive dream it has been projecting is suddenly broken, and the character Maureen Wendall writes a long letter to her former night school teacher, never before mentioned in the text, a certain "Miss Oates": "I think I am writing to you because I could see, past your talking and your control and the way you took notes carefully in your books while you taught, writing down your own words as you said them, something that is like myself" (309).

One night you read something from *Madame Bovary,* which was our assignment, about the woman going for a walk in the field with her dog. You seemed to think that was important. Out in the field she looks around, she sees—I don't know what. I don't remember. . . . You read that passage to us and pointed out something about it, and I could tell you were thinking *That woman is something like me,* like you yourself, a stranger to us, and I sat there hearing myself think, *This is not important, none of this is real.* . . . Why did you tell us [books] were more important than life? They are not more important than my life. . . . Those things didn't happen and won't happen. None of them ever happened. . . . I am sitting with my heart beating steady and slow, writing all this down out of my hate, because it seems to me now that it's you I hate. . . . I hate you and no one else. (312–313; 319–320)

Rarely has "fiction" taken such a shocking revenge on "reality" as it seems to do in this sudden eruption of metafiction within an otherwise intensely naturalist narrative; and yet, the deeper point would seem to be that neither of these terms names a stable or separable domain of reference— "Miss Oates" in this context, exerting "control" over herself in the act of note-taking, is no less a fiction than the character Maureen, a composite of Joyce Carol Oates's actual students. In *them,* fiction and reality are brought together in a mental theater of cruelty where the writing self, working the dialectic of shame and pride, confronts its own demons— which is to say, enlists them in the autopoetic enterprise of making literature, a literary career.

THE REVENGE OF GENRE

Raymond Carver's career as a serious writer had been founded, according to his first wife, on a sudden and total rejection of the popular literary forms he had been learning to write with the help of a correspondence course offered by an outfit called the Palmer Institute of Writing, to which he would dutifully submit his apprentice efforts week by week. This was a forerunner of today's Internet creative writing instruction enterprises, which, in telling contrast to most creative writing instruction conducted on college campuses, teach their students to work within the conventions of highly specific genres, including market-tested popular genres such as "Science Fiction Writing," "Memoir Writing," "Romance Writing," "Screenwriting," and the like. One of these, The Gotham Writers' Workshop, claims six thousand students at a given time, and offers both classroom and online programs. In the latter, the virtual interactivity of programmed instruction and the sociality of the workshop come together in a striking way: "We call this process 'The Booth.' The writer listens to comments before responding. Each classmate begins with a positive comment about your writing. The idea is to identify what works and help you build upon your strengths. Then we move on to specific suggestions regarding what can be improved. Next, the teacher gives an extensive analysis of your writing. Finally, you exit the metaphoric 'Booth' with the opportunity to ask questions. The process leads to a structured dialogue, concrete suggestions, and a better understanding of your work."[48] Programs like this one are useful to think about not only for the commercial "democratization" of authorship they so boldly exemplify and enact, but also for the light they shed on what, if it weren't taken completely for granted, might seem the remarkable absence of "genre consciousness" in the course offerings of most university-based programs, which assume that the student is there to produce literature, and that literature is not generic.

The absence of genre consciousness in the program makes it clear how, even as the rise of the creative writing program was related to the parallel rise of mass higher education, it did not take its cultural bearings from the consumption habits of the lower middle class, but rather from the modernist tradition as it had been institutionalized in and as the New Criticism. When he took Gardner's creative writing class at Chico, Carver "stopped being interested in writing about little green monsters and the like," and began to work on stories "in a contemporary literary mode."[49] Replicating his mentor's general distaste for the "so-called experimental writing" associated with John Barth and the program at Johns Hopkins, or with Robert Coover and the program at Brown, Carver pursued a form of realism that understood itself to be elevated, literary, even self-reflexive to a degree, and yet responsive to what Gardner called the "normal" person's taste for character and story above feats of metafictional linguistic trickery.

So positioned, the aesthetic formation I'm calling lower-middle-class modernism enters into a fraught relation with a lower-middle-class readership as such, whose tastes it tends to find amusing and/or embarrassing but at times, especially in the form of the culturally uplifting domain of "middlebrow," too close for comfort to its own. If we don't know this from experience, we know it from lower-middle-class modernism itself, which frequently monitors the boundaries of cultural level. In the Introduction I showed how this worked in Jayne Anne Phillips's story "Home." Another version of this monitoring is found in Tobias Wolff's "An Episode in the Life of Professor Brooke," whose protagonist enters into a brief relationship with a nurse he meets at a regional meeting of the Modern Language Association, where he has traveled to take part in a panel discussion of Samuel Johnson.[30] The nurse has wandered into this arena of potential shame because she loves literature and is a member of a Literary Society, which is to say, a women's reading group on the model that would be magnificently massified by Oprah's Book Club. When she lists the poets she likes, they turn out to be "the sort who make Christmas albums, whose lines appear on the bottom of inspirational posters":

> "What do you do there?" Brooke asked. "At the Society."
> "We share."
> "You lend each other books?"
> "That," Ruth said, "and other things. Sometimes we read to each other and talk about life."
> "It sounds like an encounter group."
> "Isn't that why you write books?" Ruth asked. "To bring people together and help them live their lives?" (40–41)

The story is told from the perspective of Brooke, and written by a renowned memoirist and creative writing instructor—first as a colleague of Carver's at Syracuse, later as head of creative writing at Stanford. Yet it would be wrong to assume that the story simply expresses the squirming pathos of the scholar's encounter with an embarrassingly unprofessional reader. Rather, and much more interestingly, it silently claims the middle ground between them—between cynical professional jockeying for interpretive mastery, on the one hand, and the naïve pursuit of group therapy, on the other. This is the specific domain of creative writing as a discipline. For creative writing, as for criticism, literature is an object of professional, not amateur, knowledge. But for creative writing, as for reading groups, "literary value" in a traditional humanist sense is an all but non-negotiable quantity, the foundation of the entire enterprise. As such, the "middlebrow" is the proximate threat to creative writing, while genre or "trash" fiction, on the one hand, and academic literary criticism, on the other, are the more distant ones.

Against this backdrop, we can begin to understand the tremendous irony attached to the career of Joyce Carol Oates, which is that the emotional articulacy and narrative facility that characterize her narratives, product of a truly fearless command of language and the process of composition, would soon be taken as evidence of their convergence with the ways and means of disreputable genre fiction. Increasingly this prodigy of modern American letters would find herself freighted with an association to the "feminine" forms of the romance novel and the gothic thriller, and with the middlebrow sentimentality of women's realist fiction. And in fact Oates's fiction presents no neat separation between genre fiction, middlebrow fiction, and high literary fiction, as though the sheer speed with which she rocketed into the stratosphere of American literary prestige left insufficient time for the processes of disciplinary shaming that teach writers to police and self-police those boundaries.

Instead her career has conducted a fascinating dialogue with "low" fiction even from the time of her first novel, *With Shuddering Fall* (1964), which seems to shuttle between the modes of Dreiserian naturalism and the Harlequin romance novel as it pursues the theme of dangerous, helpless love.[51] The relation to genre fiction had become highly reflexive by the time of her "postmodern" gothic meta-romances of the 1980s, such as *A Bloodsmoor Romance* (1982), which, in a kind of feminist hyperbolizing of Jane Austen's *Northanger Abbey,* would simultaneously criticize and instantiate a low genre. It culminated in her decision, in 1991, to spin off a new pen name, "Rosamond Smith," in part to protect the increasingly uncertain reputation of "Joyce Carol Oates" from what had by then come to seem a gaudy over-productivity. According to Oates's biographer, during some periods of her career she has produced "forty to fifty pages [of fiction] each day," at which rate she could crank out a campus murder mystery like Rosamond Smith's *Nemesis* (1991) in under a week.[52] Many writers produce a "practice" novel or two before finally publishing a "real" one; Oates is said, during her high school and college apprentice period, to have written *twenty* practice novels. Discovering her ambitions as a poet, she once "turned out twenty-eight poems, some of them rather long," *in a single day.*[53] In the four years between 1966 and 1970 she wrote 70 stories, and by the early 1980s had published more than 300, a number that would climb to 392 by 1989 and now stands at well over 500 published stories, companion to the 40 or so novels and other books. And she did all this while usually carrying a full teaching load of composition, literature, and creative writing classes, often teaching summer school as well.

The nineteenth century had been more comfortable with such bulk production, and the word "prolific," which now almost automatically attaches to the name of Joyce Carol Oates, was not the subtle insult that it often is today. Only late in that century, when the novel presided with unquestioned power over a massively expanding book market, did a taint of many-ness begin to attach to the genre, inspiring its most adventurous and artistic practitioners to reestablish it as an object of noble scarcity. This was most consequential, of course, at the level of audience: increasingly, if always ambivalently, a large audience for a novel was taken as prima facie evidence that the novel might not count as literature. But literary overproductivity came under heavy suspicion as well, since that many-ness could easily be associated with the social kind. To publish huge numbers of books suggested a bending of literary labor to the model of assembly-line production, where each loose, baggy monster is mechanically produced to look much like the last. But it could also suggest a frighteningly grotesque process of organic reproduction, a mass birthing of books. Presented with such an outpouring of female creativity as one finds in Oates, it is predictable that her critics would begin to describe it as a horrible over-fecundity, a pathological displacement of biological reproduction into roiling, breeding masses of literary characters, and would attempt to shame her literary labor back into obedient submission to the program of painstaking craft.

This attitude can be partly accounted for by the fundamental bias in the postwar system of literary prestige against the entire category of "emotional" fiction by and for women. Whether in Oates, or in the notoriously "moving" middlebrow selections of Oprah's Book Club, which read one of her books in 1996, the specter of nineteenth-century sentimentalism was never far away. It was against sentimentalism that the modernist tradition in narrative as we know it—stretching as far back as Gustave Flaubert and Nathaniel Hawthorne, with his infamous dig at "scribbling women"—had first defined itself as a respectably "masculine" enterprise. As detailed in Oates's essay "(Woman) Writer: Theory and Practice," this has left the domain of "women's experience" curiously unclaimable for the purposes of establishing a high literary reputation: "So the (woman) writer has faith in the high worth of the craft to which she has dedicated herself, but she should not be deceived in gauging her relative position within it. Power does not reside with women—no more in the literary world than in the world of politics and finance—and power is never under the obligation to act justly. A writer may be afflicted by any number of demons, real or imagined, but only the (woman) writer is afflicted by her own essential identity."[54] The problem, as Oates perceives it, is that the woman writer, always brought back to the fact of her body, is not allowed to partake fully in the lofty value of "impersonality." But as we shall see, the problem more precisely is that she is afflicted with an "essential identity" of a certain kind, one that didn't happen to be negotiable for literary prestige.

Compare this to the situation of Carver, living with the consequences of his own, more conventional form of biological productivity. A dutiful essay on his literary influences—Hemingway, Chekhov—wends its course through the expected discussions but then takes a sudden and shockingly unsentimental turn: "I have to say that the greatest single influence on my life, and on my writing, directly and indirectly, has been my two children. They were born before I was twenty, and . . . there wasn't any area of my life where their heavy and often baleful influence didn't reach." Finding himself in a position of "unrelieved responsibility and permanent distraction," he "didn't have the time, or the heart, to think about working on anything very lengthy."[55] This is the minimalist as beleaguered lower-middle-class parent, stuck at the laundromat with the kids.

In Carver, the bond of family is not most importantly a "blood" bond, as in Oates, but rather an economic one, the aftermath of rashly passionate acts. Minimalism is the paradoxical attempt to give voice to the inarticulate embodiment of this parent, and the power of this aspiration is at least partly in its modesty—it is beautiful, but it doesn't scare anybody. The educational system played an important role in the discovery of the territory called Carver Country; the creative writing program did much to chart it, and even now it continues to place the stories of Raymond Carver near the top of the list of recent writers that creative writing students are encouraged to read. But while minimalist writing as Carver practiced it is evidently quite laborious, its results for critics like John Aldridge are nonetheless problematically unintimidating, leading legions of students in creative writing programs to follow the same path of "extremely modest intention" as the one taken by the master.[56] Thus, even though Carver himself was a model of slow and steady production, and never one to publish in bulk, an Oatesian air of excess reappears on the scene in the form of his tremendous influence over other writers, who together make minimalism seem, to its critics, like an "assembly-line" product, a formulaic genre, if not exactly "genre fiction" in its own right. This assumes, of course, that genre is a bad thing, something to be ashamed of.

Oates, by contrast, is essentially inimitable. Her output is staggeringly various in form and intent, ranging from high to low, from bizarrely experimental to extremely conventional, from very long to medium to short to very short. She has few literary progeny of note, even in the diffuse sense that Hemingway did (by Oates's own account, although Hemingway never set foot in a classroom as a teacher, he remains "very likely the most influential of American writers").[57] Indeed, a resistance to the very idea of progeny is built deep into her work. In the novel *Expensive People* (1968), she invented a fat young boy narrator who murders his mother, a writer uncannily like Joyce Carol Oates. She later commented, with some pride, that "not even Nabokov could have conceived of the bizarre idea of writing a novel from the point of view of one's own (unborn, unconceived) child, thereby presenting some valid, if comic reasons for it remaining unborn and unconceived."[58] Useless as a model, Oates's maximalism produces offspring only in the form of her own works. The endlessly articulate, uncanny, inimitable textual body emanating from Oates's study is "silent" only in the sense that it defies her mortal readers to keep up, to keep listening, and thus threatens to reduce itself to the pulp upon which it is printed. Only at that point, only when its audience begins to resist, when readers begin to duck for cover, does that output start to look like pulp fiction, like something shameful, something it would have been better to conceal.

Shame, we recall, occasions a personification of otherness as disapproving audience, literalized by Wolcott in the form of the mocking book critic. The emotion of pride, by contrast, could be understood to personify that otherness as self, as though we, and not society, can take credit for the form of our presence in the world, with all of its attractive protuberances and protrusions, extensions and excellences. In this sense, both shame and pride register our subjection to external social forces; but whereas shame is a feeling of the other's mocking resistance to us and our individual ends, pride is the sensation of that otherness being in some primordial sense *with* us, at once the source and vehicle of our existence and our will, "approving" of us because, strictly speaking, it is us. This is literalized in the pride of publication, which externalizes the self as printed text, but simultaneously exposes it to the shame of bad reviews. More than most writers, Joyce Carol Oates has filled the yawning emptiness of the air with her own proud corpus. It is the pride of the unalienated literary laborer, articulating a limitless self from the raw material of body, memory, and text. In an interview Oates described herself as one of those people "of peasant stock, from the country, who then come into a world of literature or philosophy. Part of us is very intellectual, wanting to read all the books in the library—or even wanting to *write* all the books in the library. Then there's the other side of us, which is sheer silence, inarticulate—the silence of nature, of the sky, of pure being."[59] It is indeed as a *force of nature* that Joyce Carol Oates presents herself to literary history, a "genius" in the technical, if not the honorific, sense.

Giorgio Agamben has noted the important distinction, in the history of art, between the figure of the "man of taste" who sets the agenda for the Kantian tradition in aesthetic theory, oriented to the experience of the spectator, and the figure of the genius who lives outside the laws of proportion and perfection. Already in the eighteenth century, in his account, the "refined sensibility" of the aesthete was being countered in the rise of a genre, the novel, "born to satisfy the exigencies of bad taste." At the end of that century "there even appeared a new genre, the gothic romance, which was based on the simple reversal of the criteria of good taste," regaining for art, "through disgust and terror, that area of the soul that good taste had deemed it necessary to exclude forever from aesthetic participation."[60] Understood in this context, we can see how a creative will as strong as Oates's can seem to pass out of the domain not only of good taste but of human individuality altogether, revealing itself as a sublime natural occurrence. She is, as a writer, the ultimate risk taker. And yet since she "risks" from what appears to be a bottomless well of labor capital, she can seem, to her critics, to take no risks at all: working all day, every day with something approaching total efficiency, she has time to try everything, to let loose an infinite number of literary progeny into the world, some of which, by the law of averages, are destined to win major literary awards.

Thus while hers is an educated, at times a self-consciously scholarly, literary project, unthinkable except in relation to the rise of mass higher education, there appears to be something untamed about it, something hard, ultimately, for the system to claim as its own. She is thus a fitting symbol of the human raw material, the "wetware," with which the educational system works, and whose lingering obduracy defines the limits of what that system can do. Joyce Carol Oates presents us with a paradox: she is a quintessential figure of the Program Era who will not get with the program.

AMOUNTING TO WHITE

Minimalism seems to have no politics, and it is, after all, despite a few exceptions, quite white. Critics of Carverian "Kmart realism" might well add that to the list of its deficiencies, echoing the long-standing distaste of intellectuals for lower-middle-class culture understood as a white culture, whose essential conservatism is understood to muffle calls for change in a blanket of sullen, suspicious, self-centered white noise. It's no wonder that lower-middle-class existence is the experiential category above all others that remains unclaimed in contemporary academic discourses of identity.

It is undeniably true that the political sphere as such—the sphere given lavish attention in Robert Coover's novel *The Public Burning* (1977) or Philip Roth's *Our Gang* (1973), for instance—is all but invisible in the lower-middle-class world of Carver Country, whose denizens seem utterly unaware of "the issues of the day," completely disconnected from the nexus of money and media, race and identity, personality and power, at the center of American public life in their time. Indeed, while we can write the history of Carver Country, its literary products have no History—no history to speak of, let alone monumentalize. This distinguishes them from the predominantly maximalist forms I have been calling technomodernism and high cultural pluralism, each of which is strongly prone to linking the individual experience of authors and characters to the kinds of things one finds in history textbooks, including war, slavery, the social displacements of immigration, or any other large-scale trauma. This lends them an aura of "seriousness" even when, as in Pynchon or Vonnegut, the work is comic.[61] Personal experience so framed is not *merely* personal experience, and in practice no amount of postmodern skepticism about the nature of historical knowledge (the emphasis of Linda Hutcheon's formulation of "historiographic metafiction" as a dominant postwar mode) is allowed to undermine that fact.[62]

If there is a politics of minimalism, in this public historical sense, it would appear to be a negative politics, a politics of silence—a resistance, perhaps, to media overstimulation or maybe just the silencing, by shame, of the voice of the lower-middle-class worker, trained to shut up and do his shit job and to feel lucky that he is a white person, if that in fact is what he is. According to Stephen Dobyns, in the years after Raymond Carver quit drinking and became a big success, he was known on a number of occasions to say, still somewhat dazed by it all, "This makes me feel just like a white man."[63] This formulation is interesting both for the lingering sense of inauthenticity it communicates, as though he might not actually be one, and for the outline it helps us draw around the relative invisibility of racial self-consciousness in his stories.

In this, as in so many of its dimensions, minimalism can seem to be a form of retreat or self-concealment, this time from the open and pervasive politicization of identity in 1960s literary culture into the smallness, privacy, and racial homogeneity of domestic life in the late 1970s and 80s. In this space the politics of gender relations—the personal as the political—is the single vestige of the idea of conflict between groups, between organized, or at least organizable, political interests, that we are ever asked to contemplate. Even here, though, this conflict is always condensed into an interpersonal relationship that threatens to contain and dehistoricize it, as when the out-of-work protagonist of Carver's quietly chilling story, "They're Not Your Husband," having nothing better to do with his time, polices his wife's body weight as she works at the local diner, forcing her to go on a diet, gauging her attractiveness to the other men she serves. As the low-status white worker defaults to pride in his race, here, it seems, is another insidious form of compensation, an assertion of the privileges of manhood. As a man and as a white man, the lower-middle-class worker, even when out of work, retains his privileged relation to the Universal, to the god-given dignity of Mankind.

My concern here is not to determine whether minimalism—whether any literary discourse, minimalist, maximalist, or otherwise—can be redeemed for a good politics, or must be consigned to the dust heap of the bad. Rather, I would like to work in the opposite direction, asking what the politics and/or non-politics of minimalism, however we care to judge it, can teach us about narrative fiction in the Program Era. In that field of endeavor, certainly, minimalism has mattered. But not only has it mattered; I would also argue that it manifests an ironic kind of "universality" after all, one that we would do well to keep in view if we want to understand the world which gave us mass higher education and the creative writing program at one and the same time. We can begin to do this by once again juxtaposing minimalism to the maximalism of Joyce Carol Oates, the paradoxically inimitable emblem of the productive power of lower-middle-class modernism, the one-woman literary labor force.

In stark contrast to Carver, Oates's fiction has been preoccupied by racial politics literally from the beginning. Her first published story, "In the Old World" (1959), which she wrote as a student at Syracuse and included in her first story collection, is the tale of a young white boy, racked with guilt, who turns himself in to the sheriff in town for blinding a black boy out in the countryside, only to find that the sheriff is not interested in holding him accountable for his crime. Her first novel, in turn, *With Shuddering Fall*, climaxes in a frothing riot of white rage and murderous racism. The theme of race relations and racial consciousness asserts itself again in the novel *them*, which climaxes with a depiction of the cataclysmic 1967 race riots in Detroit. Earlier in the novel, Oates takes care to delineate some of the psychological structures that will underlie that violence. When Maureen Wendall's mother Loretta visits a family member in the welfare section of the hospital with her son Jules, she "look[s] around pityingly": "She was so conscious of being white! And finally she did turn to Jules and say in a low voice, not quite a whisper, 'Jesus, how'd you like to be a nigger and sick on top of it? I did that much for you at least, kid.' Jules expelled his breath to show sympathy, humor. Actually, he was immensely grateful for being white. In Detroit being white struck him as a special gift, a blessing—how easy not to be white! Only in a nightmare might he bring his hands up to his face and see *colored* skin, *Negro* skin, a hopeless brown nothing could get off, not even a razor" (322–323). If Oates's literary maximalism is one that says "shame" but doesn't show it, here the urge to say everything serves to expose the white body as a racially marked body, amplifying the whisper of "white pride" until it can be heard clearly for what it is. Perhaps more than any other postwar American writer, Joyce Carol Oates has systematically sought to deprive the privilege of whiteness of the further privilege of presenting itself as an unmarked universality, the form of "selfhood" as such. In doing this she has made a significant literary contribution, *avant la lettre,* to what in the 1990s would come to be called, in imitation of "African American studies" and other minority-centered disciplines, "whiteness studies."

"How easy not to be white!" What's fascinating about Jules's understanding of his racial identity is how he associates it not with necessity, biological or otherwise, but rather with luck, with chance, as though the nightmare of being black might actually come true even now. Race, in other words, is yet another thing the individual cannot really control, and "white pride" comes tightly braided with a potential for shame. Thus if being white, in the context of 1960s Detroit, seems to Jules an unambiguous advantage, about the only thing he's got going for him, there are other contexts where it might suddenly be converted into a disadvantage.

This is what the character Calla almost realizes in Oates's 1991 novella, *I Lock My Door Upon Myself,* which tells a story of scandalous interracial love in early twentieth-century upstate New York. Calla, named by her dying mother for the funereal flower which is "white beyond white," is first constructed as a feminist heroine, somewhat along the lines of Edna Pontelier in Kate Chopin's *The Awakening* (1899); like her, Calla is a radical individualist compelled by social norms to do the last thing she wants to do: marry and have children. Openly neglecting these children, becoming a defiantly bad mother, she becomes an allegorical figure of the female artist, wandering alone through the countryside, following her own whim. Her relation to blackness, when she finally encounters it, is quite different from Jules's in 1960s Detroit. Here it entails the nascent perception, on her part, of the spiritual superiority that might be understood to attach to the "nightmare" of racial inferiority: "She felt a thrill of horror, amid the blacks. That their immediate ancestors had been *owned*. Not these blacks as individuals for most of them were young, many were children, but their blackness, their essence—that had been *owned*. And now in this city amid the heterogenous white population of the city they were so relatively few in number. . . . *Like me they are outcasts in this country. Not like me: they are true outcasts.*"[64] Echoing debates within academic feminism in the 1980s and 90s, the white feminist consciousness of Calla advances toward an identification with outcast blackness but is blocked by an acknowledgment of her relative social privilege as a white woman. Unable to identify with a transindividual, transhistorical community of racial outcasts, she is driven back into a position of free-floating individual alienation, disappearing into the attic (the madwoman in the attic) for fifty years, thinking "obsessively of the man who was her lover . . . a black man among white men in a world as steeped in racial injustice as in the unacknowledged breathable element of air" (68).

A few years later Oates would reach for almost the same formulation, and would complete the turn from Jules's gleeful sense of his own whiteness to a sense of her own impoverishment by that privilege. In an October 1993 letter to Robert Phillips, she reacted to the news that her colleague Toni Morrison had just been awarded the Nobel Prize in Literature: "Toni is so richly deserving of this award. . . . Not only a brilliant writer, magical, impassioned, but a woman with a mission; a vision; indefatigable energy & ambition. A model, for all her uniqueness. . . . I am only a *writer*—I have no socio/historical definition; no "constituency"; I represent no one & nothing—not even (I suppose) myself. My "self." The unjust advantages of a white skin . . . privilege . . . breathed in unknowing & uncontemplated as the very air."[65] Oates has often been rumored to be a candidate for the Nobel Prize in her own right; her reaction to Morrison's honor is a symptomatic blend of generous collegiality and agonized self-pity, giving credit where it is due but hastening to perform an analysis of the contemporary identity politics of authorship that now works, or so she believes, to her disadvantage.

An "unjust advantage" in the broader social world has thus in Oates's view come to stand as a sign of artistic disadvantage, a form of insignificance or emptiness, a radical loneliness beyond even the company of "self." But even as her analysis discovers a shameful lack on her part, that lack nonetheless obviously remains a point of individualistic—which is to say, in this context, "white"—pride. It is telling that a writer whose work is so intensely and thoroughly permeated by social history, and by her own relation to that history, should, for her own part, and to even herself, seem to "have no socio/historical definition." Among other things, it speaks to the condition of post-ethnicity of certain white immigrant groups, who at an earlier time might have seemed "different" enough from the white Protestant majority culture but no longer do. For Oates, as we have seen, her body is visible only as "afflicted" by gender, but this "essential identity" is not "thrilling," and does not tie it to a viable "constituency" which can be the fleshly vehicle of her pride.[66] In this sense, the modernist value of impersonality to which Oates wanted to adhere, against the insulting imposition of the essence of sex, comes back to haunt her in the form of the ghostly racial invisibility of her own massive corpus.

Minimalism, of course, as a discourse of beautiful shame, could never countenance such a protrusion of embarrassingly direct talk as one finds in Oates, and if a good politics must be a politics of expression, of truth-telling, it certainly does not measure up to her example. Preoccupied by its own socioeconomic deprivations, the white lower middle class in Carver's fiction does not feel shame for being white, as Oates's "white trash" Calla obviously—and to some degree anachronistically—does. Rather, one could say that Carver's characters, like their author, silently aspire to *become* "white," which is to say, actually and fully possessed of the inherited privileges that this term symbolizes in a racist society. It is in this aspiration, finally and ironically, that literary minimalism finds its objectivity and universality: not that everyone wants to be white, but rather they want to be fully human, prized for their very existence in the world and unalienated in the labor that enables them to survive in it.

Minimalism, then, is valuable to us in its very "colorlessness." Unredeemed by proud communal attachments except to the occupational category of "writer," it lays itself bare. It reveals the dependence of postwar American writing on the university, first and foremost, but it also lays bare the general condition of subjection of the majority of the postwar U.S. labor force, white and nonwhite, which owes its mobility, such as it is, to a system of mass higher education built to the specifications of the market. Whatever its disadvantages, political, aesthetic, or otherwise, the beauty of literary minimalism is in its artful unwillingness to *conceal the concealment* of its own dependency and weakness, which infuses it with an exquisitely shameful reflexivity. As an "embarrassingly" programmatic product of the program and unable, for all of its skills at understatement, to hide that fact from anyone very well, minimalism has the ironic advantage of revealing the systematicity of creativity in the Program Era in its starkest form. In doing so, it lays bare the recruitment of that creativity to the inhuman ends of the economic order we serve.

6

Art and Alma Mater: The Family, the Nation, and the Primal Scene of Instruction

> I knew then I had to have a house. A real house. One I could point to.
>
> SANDRA CISNEROS, The House on Mango Street

> The movements of the multitude designate new spaces, and its journeys establish new residences.
>
> MICHAEL HARDT and ANTONIO NEGRI, Empire

ANXIETIES OF AFFILIATION

While this book is not without its pretensions to novelty, in a way it is simply an assemblage of what used to be called "influence studies." Let's face it: whatever else it is, the creative writing program is also a medium of influence, a place where teachers exert themselves on students. One form of influence is traditionally textual, received through the conduit of the syllabus, and it certainly persists in the Program Era—consider the stylistic afterlives of Faulkner and Hemingway, who spent little time in the classroom but have been "teachers" to so many. But the program adds to this a more vivid sort of influence, the influence of the teacher at the head of the table, the professional author who, in his or her spare time, authors marginal comments on apprentice fictions. This form of influence has precursors in the relation between Stein and Hemingway, or Pound and Eliot, but it is far more formalized than those modernist mentorships, measured as it is in credit units and grades. It is similar to the editorial relation of, say, Maxwell Perkins and Thomas Wolfe, but stands at some remove from the direct end of publication, having more to do with producing writers than producing books. Such were the relations of, to name a few, Andrew Lytle and Flannery O'Connor; Verlin Cassill and Margaret Walker; Wallace Stegner and Ken Kesey; Yvor Winters and Scott Momaday; John Gardner and Raymond Carver.

But one must also speak in the Program Era of influence in a more unusual and original, because collective and institutional, sense. Program graduates, after all, have typically had several writing teachers by the time they earn their degree, as well as innumerable interactions with their influential peers, and together these teachers and students generate an influential social atmosphere that (no doubt) influences to some degree what the individual writes. Thus we find critics of the program sneering that so-and-so is such an "Iowa writer," so "Brown," so "Syracuse"—as though the mere attribution of institutionality is enough to disqualify the work—and thus we also find writers themselves squirming at the idea of their own institutionalization. It's at the level of the institution, in other words, that influence in the Program Era becomes an occasion for what Harold Bloom—envisioning something far loftier, an epic clash of strong poets with their poetic father figures—called the "anxiety of influence."[1]

Bloom's concept was always susceptible, with a little downward sociological pressure, to being re-envisioned in the crasser terms of professionalism, of position-taking in the struggle for career, and Sandra Gilbert and Susan Gubar have facilitated our appropriation even further by translating it into what they call the "anxiety of affiliation." For them this describes the condition of women writers in the early twentieth century, ambivalently eager to claim a maternal literary heritage but afraid that to do so would fatally compromise them in the eyes of a male-dominated and misogynist modernist literary establishment.² To the degree that "woman" still suggested being bound to biological reproduction and the limitations of the domestic sphere, as well as to the conventionalities of sentimental "women's" fiction, it remained tempting to reject this affiliation outright.

Tracing the term "affiliation" to its Latin roots in the *filia* and *filius* of family, the scene of childrearing, Gilbert and Gubar help us to see the potentially cloying and compromising side of something that can otherwise be a point of pride—institutional affiliation—and to appreciate once again the vexed intimacy, evident everywhere in postwar American fiction, of the writer, the family, and the school. Extending the etymology even further into the past, they find suggestive evidence that the origins of "affiliation" are in the Indo-European *dhei,* meaning "to suck," and connected with "she who suckles." If, then, the school in one respect plays the role of antidote to the family, offering the student his first real chance to disengage from those blood bonds and stand on his own, the direction of this link can be reversed. Moving in this direction, it becomes the anxiety of the institutionalized writer—the writer *feminized* and/or *infantilized,* in a way that Stein and Hemingway never were, by his or her humiliating affiliation with the "nurturing" institution of the school. This is more threatening, in some ways, than the institution conceived of as a "machine," although Ken Kesey's Big Nurse in *One Flew Over the Cuckoo's Nest,* as the emasculating agent of the maternal Combine, suggests how the two forms of horror can easily be brought together.

But in fact the psycho-dynamics of affiliation are even more complicated than this, because each of these institutions, the family and the school, are nested in and connected to others. As Henry James famously said in one of his Prefaces, "really, universally, relations stop nowhere," and once we begin to inventory our affiliations it is difficult to know where or when we can legitimately cut the cord and pronounce ourselves autonomous. For instance, Hemingway may have been safe from the school, but as a figure who came of age in the 1920s, he like so many American writers of the time (and like Henry James before them) felt called upon to consider his affiliation with the nation of his birth. There were of course many motives for the act of expatriation—Paris was a happening place, and it was relatively cheap—but one of them was an urge toward disaffiliation from a homeland that seemed crassly commercial, provincial, and (especially with the advent of Prohibition) hypocritical. And indeed, if there is one form of affiliation in modern literary history that stands behind all the others—an occasion for intense pride or bitter shame, and until recently the unquestioned basis of the literature curriculum—it is surely the national one. As nurturing institutions, the family and the school enter into a vexed relation to each other, and each of them relates, in turn, to the nation, with its root implication of the *common birthing* of a people. This has produced a sticky tangle of affiliations and attempted disaffiliations that literary historians have only barely begun to unravel.

Witness the anxiety of Ronald Sukenick, one of the most daring and accomplished of the radically experimental postwar writers and, partly for that reason, a longtime creative writing teacher. In his memoir of his youth in 1950s literary New York, *Down and In: Life in the Underground* (1987), the university hangs like a specter over his sense of artistic and intellectual independence. Shocked to discover that his teachers at Brandeis (Irving Howe, J. V. Cunningham) want him to get a Ph.D. in English (which he did) and "become a good academic" (which he delayed in doing), he describes his dilemma in the starkest terms:

> At stake here was that vague homunculus I chose to call my real self, independent of middle-class definitions of success and failure. This was the phenomenon vulgarized at the time as "identity crisis," but was a real issue and it will remain a real issue. Is the American personality simply the sum of success-driven responses to the network of cultural pressures? Or is it the stubborn assertion of a virtuous independence, however unexamined? Horatio Alger or the Lone Ranger? Is there such a thing as a real self, and if there isn't, what makes life

worth living? Consumption of products? Liberty and justice for clones? Social welfare for pods?[3]

Note how the question of Sukenick's affiliation with the university as an academic becomes, before long, a matter not only of masculine selfhood but also of national identity. If the "American personality" is unaffiliated then, for Sukenick, it is something that might well be proudly claimed in defiance of the schoolmarms. If instead it is conformist and success-driven, then perhaps "America" and the school must be rejected in tandem. And this (for a while) is what Sukenick did, disaffiliating himself from academe and hightailing it to what he calls "the underground." This is at once a state of mind and an urban space, and while it stands opposed to the campus it, too, is the scene of research, a place where "researchers in the risky discipline of living in contact with the deepest impulses" (7) can share their findings.

In light of his subsequent career as a founder of the creative writing program at the University of Colorado, it would be easy to dismiss the *avant-gardiste* pretensions of Sukenick's young manhood, and the facile tendentiousness of his (loosely psychoanalytic) assumptions about what our "deepest impulses" might be. (Apparently they are not impulses toward family life, or toward the organized social life of institutions.) Perhaps, though, this is only a boyish manifestation of one of the fundamental impulses of literature itself, and shouldn't be dismissed so quickly. To locate Sukenick's post-American non-success story in the speakeasies and poetry readings of the Lower East Side is one thing, that is, but hasn't the whole enterprise of literature as we have known it in modern times been driven by an impulse to artistic autonomy? Isn't this, for instance, part of what drove Henry James to leave the cloying family attachments of the United States behind and pursue his career abroad, and isn't it the force that drives the woman writer to find, in Virginia Woolf's famous formulation, a room of her own? That, too, was a space apart from *filia* and *filius,* and from the scene of suckling.

But then again, isn't an office on campus, in effect, a room of one's own?

WORLD REPUBLIC(S) OF LETTERS

According to Pascale Casanova's *The World Republic of Letters* (2004), the collective concern of literary artists across the centuries-long sweep of global modernity has been to "invent their literary freedom" by disengaging their work from the compromising contingencies of national politics and addressing themselves to the world.[4] "Denying their difference" and "assimilating the values of one of the great literary centers," modern writers have been rewarded for this sometimes painful process of national self-alienation with admittance to a notionally autonomous realm of notionally universal literary value. Here, then, it is the nation that plays the part of the family, the teat to which one is compromisingly attached, and it is into the abstract ideal of world literature that the writer flees.

Although Casanova does not pursue this link, the nation and the family have as we have seen often been tightly braided, the consanguinity of the one lending to the other a sense of its groundedness in nature. This is especially true in the context of ideological nativism, as in the 1920s U.S., where the work of essays like Charles Gould's *America, A Family Matter* (1922) was to exclude the immigrant on grounds of his inability to inherit American culture as a "birthright."[5] Then, too, the immigrant family could be understood as the vehicle of a resistance to assimilation to the cultural mainstream. Long in the making, the non-national, non-familial space that Casanova calls the "World Republic of Letters" was the domain into which putatively disinterested agencies like the Nobel Prize Committee belatedly emerged in the early twentieth century to give institutional recognition to the idea of transnational literary greatness, and to the literal and figurative arguments for *translatability* it carries in train. Presuming to speak for the world, the Swedish Academy began at this time to confer the status of classic upon authors who thereby became, like Shakespeare, Dante, and Cervantes before them, less national figures than part of the general cultural patrimony of humankind.

The fact that this autonomous realm had always, for Casanova, been an enchanted fiction masking a global structure of international domination did not alter its power to organize world literary space. Indeed, she notes, even during periods of intense international competition between European powers the *cultural* authority of a city like Paris (the most durable example of a world cultural capital) would typically remain uncontested, even unquestioned. Conferring transcendent value on a certain fraction of the artworks of the world, literary institutions in places like these were vested with the power to transmute the contingencies of history into something finer, something innocent, in theory, of the parochial political interests of the day. Thus, for instance, the translation of literary works from the global periphery out of their original tongues into one of the recognized languages of the international literary market could be understood as something other than the damning testament to global inequalities it in fact was. Rather, it could be taken as an innocently open-minded recognition of the greatness that sometimes arises, against all the odds, in culturally marginal places.

Despite its global focus, the model of world literary space constructed in Casanova's *World Republic of Letters* is useful to scholars of (merely) American literary history, allowing us to see more of what was entailed, for instance, in that fabled expatriation to Paris in the 1920s: it was not just a rejection of American hypocrisy and provinciality, but also an attempt to win recognition of the greatness of American writers from the only city really empowered at the time to judge this. By the 1950s, however, New York had begun to rate as an arbiter of global cultural value, and artists like Sukenick and his friends could afford to stick around stateside and wait to be recognized (or not) as the revolutionary geniuses they surely were. If it is still true, as Wai Chee Dimock has eloquently claimed, that "nowhere is the adjective *American* more secure than when it is offered as *American literature*," then there will be something undeniably revelatory for its readers in breaking the rigid national frames in and through which it has historically been understood, and seeing it in broader perspective.[6]

The cracks in Casanova's model become visible when one attempts to apply her model of world literary space to the present moment. Such is the timeliness of her intervention into contemporary critical discourse that one could easily fail to register her clear indication that the World Republic of Letters whose collective construction she has systematically explored may just now be collapsing all around us. Is the World Republic of Letters a *historical* construction in the cruel colloquial sense? Blaming the collapse of the Republic on the debasement, in postmodern times, of the very idea of aesthetic autonomy at the core of her study, Casanova infuses her otherwise tough-minded account of global literary politics with a nostalgia akin to Sukenick's nostalgia for the impulsive underground of his youth. However delusional that idea of autonomy might have been, for her the shameless penetration of commercial values into the farthest reaches and deepest depths of the literary field is worse, transforming Goethe's noble dream of "world literature" as the best literature of the world into a mere marketing gimmick, a kind of middlebrow literary tourism. Applying the tested modernist formula for criticizing such gimmicks, Casanova describes the breakdown of the World Republic of Letters into a globalized literary space increasingly dominated by multinational media corporations who sell "products based on tested aesthetic formulas and designed to appeal to the widest possible readership" (171).

A stronger, if no less critical, account of the contemporary situation in world literature is offered by James English, whose book *The Economy of Prestige* (2005) portrays a world in which, far from sacrificing the values of art to a sub-artistic reveling in commercial entertainment, cultural prizes on the model of the Nobel are in fact multiplying at a dizzying pace. Since these prizes are typically given in recognition of *artistic* merit, and not commercial success, this suggests the widespread persistence of an ideal of disinterested aesthetic value even now, in our hyper-capitalist age.[7] To which we might immediately add that, at least as a function of pedagogy, an investment in autonomous aesthetic value would appear, *contra* Casanova, to be still very much in evidence in the schools, which (*contra* also to the nightmares of the cultural conservatives) continue ardently to sing the praises of literature around the world.

The all but complete aversion to genre fiction in the creative writing program is incomprehensible except as an artifact of the lingering *pre-postmodernism* of the program and the larger world it inhabits, in which a concept of autonomous aesthetic value continues to circulate promiscuously. It's just that this value is no longer granted without argument to be in inherent conflict with market value, and is not negotiated within and between politically recognized nations, that task having passed into the untrustworthy hands of multinational media and publishing corporations. Even so, the professional unity that characterized Casanova's Republic of Letters has indeed fragmented to some degree, sacrificing what her teacher Pierre Bourdieu called the "corporatism of the universal" to an appreciation of difference.[8] This is rather the age of what James English calls "subnational" writing, in which one or another form of indigenous or local cultural value is translated and distributed to a world readership—as for instance when Kerri Hulme's *the bone people* (1984) is taken up and appreciated around the world as the quintessence of Maori (rather than New Zealand) culture, or (to supply our own example) when Toni Morrison is understood to speak for African America rather than the United States as a whole. Building on this idea, we could say that the market for contemporary world literature projects an ideological afterimage, or ghost, of the inexpensive labor power available to multinational corporations on the world periphery, and of the maternal labor that continually replenishes it.

Thus what has replaced Casanova's unified world literary space is what we might call a global literary pluralism, a World Pluribus of Letters. Here a writer is valued by readers in the developed world not for her transcendence of cultural particularity, but rather as a compelling aesthetic vehicle for its appreciation. These writers, and the cultures they are understood to represent, are thereby "given their due" of intercultural esteem in a way utterly undisruptive of the mechanisms of global capital, which are happy to organize world culture under the (as it turns out) profitable sign of "difference." Just as the international division of labor distributes different economic activities to different parts of the globe, so does world literature look to various regions and localities as reassuring repositories of cultural diversity and authenticity.

And here again, even after the fall of the Republic, a model of world literary space is useful to the study of merely American literature. In a way that any Paris-centric map of world literature like Casanova's would have trouble accounting for at full force, the U.S. has since the 1960s been the scene of a "cultural nationalist" rhetoric of a very particular kind, what English would no doubt want to call a "subnational" kind. While the citizen of the Republic of Letters disaffiliates from the nation in order to affiliate with art, the citizen of the World Pluribus of Letters disaffiliates from the empirical nation, the super-nation, in order to re-affiliate with a utopian sub-nation, whether that be African- or Asian- or Mexican- or (a particularly complex case) Native-America. This, in a way, is simply to recall the tremendous influence of the global wave of decolonization and nation building on the domestic U.S. liberation movements of the sixties, and to note the long half-life of this influence extending into the multicultural-transnational discourses of the present. Whether they have been the expression of formerly enslaved, immigrant, or indigenous populations, these subnational cultural interventions in the politics of American national culture have, through the years, sought to forge symbolic links to an international literary space which is not, however, the space of universal literary values but a pluralized space, a space of decolonized global cultural difference.

Although much changes with the collapse of the Republic and the rise of the Pluribus, note that each of them understands literature as, fundamentally, a technology of disaffiliation from empirical nations in favor of something more ideal. Unlike the bohemians of the fifties, who in Sukenick's account were brought together in a collective drive for extreme experience, the literary cultural nationalisms of the sixties sought to liberate U.S. minority writers from the assimilative coercions of the American mainstream by symbolically affiliating them with decolonized peoples engaged in more literal acts of nation building. Of course, to describe these subnational-to-international links as "symbolic" is to admit that in many if not most cases they have been as fictional, in their own way, as the fictions of innocent autonomous literary value that Casanova so ably strips away. This is what Toni Morrison recognized when, asked in a 1986 interview about the links between African and African American literature, she pointedly demurred, acknowledging that assertions of this link in the Black Nationalist period of the sixties and seventies "got very romantic."[9]

The same was no doubt true, though perhaps to a lesser degree, in the sub-nationalist context of the Chicano Movement, which was much closer in a literal geographic and demographic sense to the "other" nations, Mexico on the one hand, the quasi-mythical Aztlan on the other, to which it was transnationally linked but from which it was still, as a practical political matter, fairly far removed. What this meant, and what it still means, is that the literary technology of disaffiliation from the U.S. cultural mainstream can only really function if it has supplementary social institutional supports. Little magazines, urban-based cultural organizations, and small publishing houses have of course been crucial to this task. We owe to them the discovery and publication of works like Sandra Cisneros's *The House on Mango Street,* which before it was "colonized" for the mass market and made a ubiquitous offering of Vintage Paperbacks in the 1990s was put out by the small-scale enterprise dedicated to the publication of Latino authors, Arte Público Press. Appearing in the 1980s, Cisneros's novel was part of the decisive turn of Chicano letters from the masculinism of the Movement to its influential encounter with feminism.

But as the institutional position of Arte Público makes clear— housed by the University of Houston since shortly after its founding in 1970—it was above all the U.S. university that would sustain the symbolic connection of minority writers to a global pluralist space. To look at the contributors to important early anthologies of minority writing—from Ishmael Reed's *19 Necromancers from Now* (1971) to *Aiiieeeee! An Anthology of Asian-American Writers* (1974) to *This Bridge Called My Back: Writings by Radical Women of Color* (1981)—is to be struck by how many of the figures included in these volumes claimed an academic affiliation, the "day job" that enabled their editorial and literary pursuits, and it is to remember, in turn, how closely tied the anthology-genre is to the ways and means of the school.

As the material support of the dialectic of literary disaffiliation and affiliation, and thus to some degree a drag on the idea of pure spatial mobility, the university would hover as a discomfiting specter in the air above subnational cultural nationalisms, just as it had for young bohemians like Sukenick a few years earlier. In the case of the Chicano Movement, this might expose even the preferred term for Mexican American cultural authenticity and political agency, "Chicana/o," to the ironic charge of its inauthenticity. As Enrique Lamadrid put it, describing recent discussions surrounding the renaming of the Chicano Studies department at the University of New Mexico, "Unfortunately, the term 'Chicano,' with the newly ascribed meanings of the 1970s and 1980s, never made it very far past the walls of the university. The revisionist meaning of the term [it had once been a slur, but was reclaimed by sixties radicals as a badge of political honor] was never very widely accepted in most Mexican American communities."[10] That virtually all of the major figures of what is nonetheless invariably called "Chicano/a" letters—from Rudolfo Anaya to Arturo Islas to Rolando Hinojosa to Gloria Anzaldúa to Sandra Cisneros and Helena Viramontes, not to mention their most insightful critics—have been U.S. academics thus draws to the surface the institutional mediations entailed in the postwar aesthetic formation I have analyzed in this book as high cultural pluralism. This, as we have seen, is a model of narrative creation wedding the elevated aesthetic ambitions of literary modernism—which is to say, in Casanova's idiom, the search for autonomous literary languages—with the increasingly paramount value of cultural diversity in U.S. educational institutions.

Conceived primarily as a cultivation of diversity *within* the U.S.

nation-state, cultural pluralism as defined by Horace Kallen in the 1920s understood the ethnic group as a kind of "collective individual" or extended family, and the ethnos has figured ever since as a contested space of mediation between the liberal self-possessing individual on the one hand, and the notionally unmarked U.S. national cultural mainstream on the other. For instance, while both the ethnos and the mainstream assert the authority to make charges of disloyalty *to* the group—as when African American or Chicana or Asian American feminism is charged with gendered disloyalty—the ethnos and the individual alike assert the moral authority of their real or potential victimization *by* the numerically superior group that wants to assimilate them. As we saw in Chapter 2, Kallen's cultural pluralism, now known as multiculturalism, attempts to have it both ways, assimilating ethnic individuals to the mainstream *as other.* In this construction, the individual is both a member of one section in the multicultural "orchestra" of difference that is America, and also a kind of angelized observer (or auditor, to stick with Kallen's metaphor) of the nation's symphonic performance of a pluralized nationality.

But of course cultural pluralism has always referred, via the question of national origins, to the diversity of national cultures in the world at large. In recent years, as the appeal of metaphysical *belonging* in the United States of America has drastically diminished among the educated elite of the world, this conceptual pivot between internal and external difference from the nation has become an active site of cultural- and identity-political theorization. Hence the irresistible rise of critical discourses of cosmopolitanism, transnationalism, and diaspora in the U.S. academy, all of them geared, like the cultural nationalisms of the past, for spiritual and intellectual disaffiliation from what was once naïvely and unironically called "America." At the same time, of course, these discourses have become a new way of accumulating symbolic capital in the fervently globalizing U.S. academy, pointing scholars toward valuable bodies of expertise they might claim as their own and offering a rationale for the inclusion of certain creative writers in an emergent canon of world literature. In this context, the question posed to itself by fiction in the Program Era is whether and to what degree one can disaffiliate from the nation-state while still being affiliated with educational institutions located there.

TRANSLATED PEOPLE

Sandra Cisneros's account of her time as a graduate student in the Iowa Writers' Workshop in the late 1970s lays out some of the ironies attendant to the problem of affiliation with unusual clarity. Although the Workshop was early on invested in the value of cultural diversity, and had already helped produce a handful of prominent minority writers by the time Cisneros got there, who could doubt the intensity of her sense of alienation when she landed in the vast blankness due west of the "all brown all around" neighborhood of her working-class upbringing?[11] Eastern Iowa is not all that far from Chicago in geographic terms, but culturally it might well have seemed as far away as the moon. Lost in that bright white space, Cisneros could not at first resist the conversion of her difference into a sense of inferiority tied directly to the question of voice: "In Iowa, I was suddenly aware of feeling odd when I spoke, as if I were a foreigner. . . . I couldn't articulate what it was that was happening, except I knew I felt ashamed when I spoke in class, so I chose not to speak."[12]

How ironic that an institution dedicated to the discovery and cultivation of the literary voice of apprentice writers was instead experienced by Cisneros as a literal silencing of the speaking voice in the classroom. How ironic that a potentially prideful institutional affiliation (biographies of graduates rarely fail to mention Iowa's prestige) became in her case an occasion for shame. How ironic and yet—painfully predictable. Of course the social atmosphere of prestigious universities is typically quite different from that of inner-city minority communities, and often presents the sojourner from one to the other (or, rather, from the other to the one) with acute problems as well as opportunities. If shame and pride are the affective fuel of the school, the motive force of its everyday machinations, then unintended admixtures of the two are to be expected when school becomes the scene of an asymmetrical clash of cultures. By the same token, this cultural clash has been the *sine qua non* of some of the postwar period's most widely taught literary works.

Only somewhat less predictable than Cisneros's disaffection from Iowa is the fact that virtually every one of her classmates would have expressed a similar sense of alienation from the program. Not that we need assume that they were all equally justified in this emotion, or felt it as intensely as she did, but the feeling of alienation from institutions is all but endemic to the post-romantic artistic mentality, and educational institutions in the 1970s, in particular, still bore the effects of having been stand-ins for "the establishment" in the eyes of campus radicals only a few years earlier. The apprentice artist may in fact crave acceptance from institutions—will in this case have literally *applied* for it—but he will inevitably come into conflict with the judgmental social collectivities they represent. The threat of spectacular shame on the stage of the classroom has haunted virtually every student who has ever tread upon it, and this is perhaps particularly true for students in creative writing workshops. All of our efforts in the world are risky extensions of ourselves, and subject to the mortified recoil of shame, but our efforts at art, like our efforts at love, seem even more so. As a scene of self-exposure, the workshop offers an occasion not only for the "nurturing" of creativity but also, who could deny, for *Lord of the Flies*-style violence. Recall Francine Prose's campus novel *Blue Angel* (2000), where the creative writing teacher protagonist wonders, as the group discussion of a student story begins, "What maniac invented this torture, this punishment for young writers? . . . It's not an academic discipline, it's fraternity hazing."[13]

If, then, the opportunity presented by Iowa was ironically disabling to Cisneros as a minority student from the barrio, her painful situation presents us with the further irony that it was "representative" in the old-fashioned sense of being the best, because most impressive, example of a broader phenomenon, not merely an average one. Indeed, for Marcus Klein the alienated ethnic outsider is the most compelling figure for the dilemma of the modern American artist as such. In his well-known account of U.S. literary modernism, *Foreigners* (1981), he describes a situation in which "everybody was a foreigner, including the native-born and the millions of authentic foreigners."[14] This looks forward toward the postcolonialist recuperation of the transnational migrant as the representative figure of global postmodernity, a figure who, remaining vertiginously afloat on the world labor market, expresses the "globalized" existential condition even of the 98 percent of human beings who currently live in the country of their birth.[15]

But there is one further irony in these ironies of Cisneros's situation at Iowa, a kind of irony to the second power. And that is that the "disablements" of her cultural alienation on the prairie ultimately came to seem to her enabling, and her silencing by shame, as if by alchemy, became a viable literary voice. This is not to say that she simply got over it—got used to the fear and loathing and unbroken vistas of corn stubble. It was rather that she made canny use of an operational paradox involved in what Mark Seltzer has called the "wound culture" of the contemporary U.S., a paradoxically *enabling disablement*. At Iowa, Cisneros entered into the slipstream of this paradox and gradually turned it in the direction of a literary career:

> It wasn't until Iowa and the Writers' Workshop that I began writing in the voice I now write in, and, perhaps if it hadn't been for Iowa I wouldn't have made the conscious decision to write in this way. It seems crazy, but until Iowa I had never felt my home, family, and neighborhood unique or worthy of writing about. I took for granted the homes around me, the women sitting at their windows, the strange speech of my neighbors, the extraordinary lives of my family and relatives which was nothing like the family in "Father Knows Best." I only knew that for the first time in my life I felt "other." What could I write about that my classmates, cultivated in the finest schools in the country like hot house orchids, could not? My second-rate imitations of mainstream voices wouldn't do. And

imitating my classmates wouldn't work either. That was their
voice, not mine. What could I write about that they couldn't?
What did I know that they didn't?

During a seminar title[d] "On Memory and the Imagination" when the class was heatedly discussing [Gaston]
Bachelard's *Poetics of Space* and the metaphor of a house—*a
house, a house,* it hit me. What did I know except third floor
flats. Surely my classmates knew nothing about that.[16]

So Iowa was enabling after all, in a way. We could call it "negatively enabling," perhaps, since Cisneros's success there was by her account perfectly rebellious: "Each week I ingested the class readings and then went
off and did the opposite."[17] But this way of describing the agency of the
institution might distract us from the important positivity of her corporeal, if silent, presence in that seminar room.

Only when confronted with other students, students with different
bodies of experience to draw from in their writing, could Cisneros begin
to *compete* with them on the ground that she and they shared. This shared
ground was not the barrio, which in the context of Iowa was hers alone,
but the *literary field* as it was made concrete in the university classroom.
The most powerful actor in that space is of course the teacher, who has
proven by publication that she knows how to play the game, but that
teacher is the worldly representative of a more ideal observer, one with a
total command of the literary field. Cisneros's long journey to success in
this field began when she learned to convert her disabling sense of otherness into a valuable, because relatively scarce, form of cultural capital.

This was the beginning of a process of self-commodification, to
be sure, but the system of exchange to which it refers is not—at least not
initially—simply to be conflated with the publishing market. Not only
do almost all artistically ambitious authors in the postwar period "self-
commodify" in this sense—think of Tim O'Brien and his lifelong use of
nine months in Vietnam—but this would be too cynical by half, missing
an important stage in the process when what is at issue is not market value

but aesthetic value: How does one write good fiction? What interesting stories do I have to tell? Standing at some remove from "market forces" in the rawest sense, the classroom is the social space where the aesthetic practice of high cultural pluralism begins and to which, in the form of widely taught texts like Cisneros's own *House on Mango Street,* it often enough returns. Which is not to deny that when it does so—when a literary text gets canonized as a teaching text—its sales can increase dramatically.

Thus, while the childlike first person voice that speaks from the pages of *Mango Street* may indeed be, as Cisneros claimed, "very much an antiacademic voice—a child's voice, a girl's voice, a poor girl's voice, a spoken voice, the voice of a Mexican-American,"[18] this is not to say that this voice was in no sense a product of academia, which has been wise enough to hire the adult Cisneros (when she can stand it) to teach creative writing. "But it is precisely because I come from an anti-academic experience that I'm very good at teaching writing," Cisneros once said, demonstrating her subtle sense of the role of the artist-outsider as an enlivening liminal figure internal to the institution. This in fact, as we have seen, is the constitutive paradox of creative writing—that it wants to bring the metaphysical outside in.

So Cisneros, like all artists on campus, is the outsider inside, the *inside-outer,* if you will. Likewise, her most famous text is a classic instance of the postwar proliferation of the genre of the portrait of the artist as a student. James Joyce, in the original version, details the Irish Catholic upbringing that arrives at last at the consolidation of the triumphantly independent, masculine literary voice that speaks the text we have been reading, while Thomas Wolfe, in *Look Homeward, Angel* and *Of Time and the River,* gives an even more literal rendition, fictionalizing his experiences in writing classes at North Carolina and Harvard. Cisneros similarly details, in *Mango Street,* the reflexive formation of the Chicana artist subjectivity that authors *Mango Street.* As Felicia Cruz has put it, the "primary referent of Esperanza's collective tales might be the fictionalizing act itself."[19] The autopoetic circularity of this act of literary self-making is thematized in the chapter called "The Three Sisters," when an old lady admonishes the aspiring poet Esperanza: "When you leave you must remember to come back for the others. A circle, understand? You will always be Esperanza. You will always be Mango Street. You can't erase what you know. You can't forget who you are" (105). The question asked by some of the book's more cynical early critics is whether this "return" to Mango Street will be physical or merely figurative, a way of announcing a commitment to community betterment or of describing the expropriation of cultural materials for individualistic ends.[20]

Whichever (if either, or both) is the case, this text, fed by personal experience, was in a very real sense different from all of the other works that had been written at Iowa, and the hopeful aesthetic experience of urban poverty that it offers has been sufficient to make it a classic text of ethnic American literature. And yet it is in an equally real sense marked by the program. This can be seen even in the structuring of the text as a series of short, tightly crafted vignettes. Critics have noted the seeming similarity of this structure to one of the classic works of the Chicano Movement, Tomás Rivera's *y no se le trago la tierra* (1971), which is likewise a collection of vignettes, but we shouldn't miss how Cisneros's first person form echoes the pedagogical procedures of the classroom. These vignettes are the length of the typical creative writing workshop exercise and are very much akin to the short short story form which is, for a number of overlapping reasons, the privileged genre of the creative writing program. One thinks here of the proud tradition in American letters, stretching back to the nineteenth century, of achievement in the short story; and of the relatively short road the form offers to the status of "published writer." But primary among these reasons is doubtless that the short short story is, or at least seems, doable in the context of a busy schedule of classes. It offers the student the possibility of creating an aesthetic whole in the way that writing part of a novel does not. Indeed, as we have seen in and around Raymond Carver, we could say that the minimalist short story offers an occasion for aesthetic shame management: the text is small and simple, and the self shaped therein remains under control, dignified and unembarrassed. The psychological *and* aesthetic appeal of this form is summed up very well, ironically, in Bachelard's account of the miniature in *The Poetics of Space:* "The cleverer I am at miniaturizing the world, the better I possess it. But in doing this it must be understood that values become condensed and enriched in miniature."[21]

But the program is also projected into *Mango Street* at the level of theme. For instance, it seems uncannily like the author's future-anterior expression of her situation in Iowa, reading Bachelard with her more privileged classmates, when near the beginning of *Mango Street* a nun from Esperanza's school passes by her family's apartment building in Chicago:

> Where do you live? she asked.
>
> There, I said, pointing up to the third floor.
>
> You live *there?*
>
> *There.* I had to look to where she pointed—the third floor, the paint peeling, wooden bars Papa had nailed on the windows so we wouldn't fall out. You live *there?* The way she said it made me feel like nothing. *There.* I lived *there.* I nodded.
>
> I knew then I had to have a house. (5)

Something like this moment of shame through the agency of a schoolteacher may have been in Cisneros's past when she was at Iowa, but it was also by her own account a feature of her present. The repetition of the italicized deictic "there" in this exchange with a teacher—the language of pointing *at* but also *away*—recalls the shaming sensation of foreignness Cisneros felt at Iowa, a sensation of having been cast out from the national community, *alienated* in a literal sense. But this moment is also represented as giving Esperanza, as an observer, a new perspective on her home, one that allows her to see details she may never have noticed before. She is in other words alienated in a double sense, both from her family home and from the national community. Inhabiting a third place, the observation post of art, she experiences the recuperation of the painful self-consciousness of shame as the expansive individuality of artistic self-consciousness. In an aesthetic regime predicated on the demand to *write what you know,* these kinds of details—the peeling paint, the wooden bars

—will become the small change of authorial cultural capital that, invested wisely, add up to good writing. But it was at Iowa that Cisneros *came to know that she needed to write what she knows,* and it was at Iowa that the necessary presence of *an outside observer of her difference* was admitted into the core of her creative process.

Mango Street is a diminutive and geographically circumscribed text, a miniaturist text tightly tied to the small locality named in its title. It is, however, heavily committed to the virtues of upward mobility. "I knew then that I had to have a house"—a realization not in principle different from other forms of commodity lust, but here imbued with something finer by the sacrosanctity of homeownership in the American mythos of independence. An office on campus, however lovely, could never be an adequate substitute for this. At the same time, Cisneros's home is clearly some equivalent of Woolf's room: a space not just of autonomous property-holding but of artistic and creative autonomy. Thus much of the knotted interest of *Mango Street* is in observing its subtle rewriting of the thematic of escape—the familiar "escape from poverty" but also from the patriarchy—as a form of spiritual re-inhabitation of the impoverished space of girlhood. Here we can see how Cisneros's text already manifests in its narrow compass the expansionist logic that would drive its virtual rewriting, some fifteen years later, as a transnational narrative of some twenty times the length. I speak of the family saga *Caramelo* (2002), which is not literally a revision of or sequel to *Mango Street* but unmistakably continues its themes: girlhood, family, and the Mexican American community.

This is not to say that the growth of *Mango Street* into the saga *Caramelo* occurred in a vacuum, simply following an internal logic of upward and outward mobility. By the time she wrote *Caramelo* Cisneros had not only become a famous writer; she had also had time to absorb another kind of academic thinking, in some ways quite opposed to the New Critical craft aesthetic purveyed to her by the writing program at Iowa, where the drive was toward smaller and smaller forms. This was poststructuralism. If we know anything about "theory's empire" it is that it is expansive, a matter always of *larger* and *more.*

To many Program Era figures, and especially to the Carverian minimalists, the rise of theory among their scholar colleagues was disquieting, posing the threat of the "death of the author" in more senses than one. Not only did theory often not make much sense to these writers, but for a short while, during the boom, some people seemed to think that theory was more interesting than literature itself. Young writers were known to show up on campus bearing signs of its malignant influence, posing the threat of the death of the author in a more practical aesthetic sense. As Iowa graduate Tom Grimes pungently put it:

> [It is] impossible to apply Lacan's "language is what hollows being into desire"—say what?—to writing fiction. And, if anyone in the Workshop ever used the words "similarity is superinduced upon contiguity" to suggest a path to revision, there'd be unbridled pummeling of the unwitting semiotician.
>
> For the writer, literary theory not only is of no use but is detrimental to his progress and well-being. Once a writer starts believing that theory and not literature can be his guide through the labyrinth, he's doomed. His path always leads to literature, not theories about literature.[22]

But the rise of theory did more than inspire self-defenses against alien intellectual influences like these. While a given "postmodernist" or "ethnic" writer might or might not "do" theory, the general lesson in post-Enlightenment skepticism it seemed to be teaching was, on the whole, and within limits, enlivening and galvanizing. There arose "theory-head" fiction writer academics, such as Samuel Delany, who could talk the talk with the best of them, and an even greater number of writers who simply took inspiration from the vivaciously "creative" poststructuralist cognitive style. This was especially true insofar as the Derridean poststructuralist theme of "différance" came over time to be linked to the pluralist theme of cultural difference. For Chicana writers it was Gloria Anzaldúa's *Borderlands/La Frontera* (1987) that most influentially manifested the poststructuralist cognitive style, proposing with the concept of the "borderland" a cultural-geographical analogue to deconstruction and an appealing counter to the alleged rigidity of Enlightenment categories. (In theorist Walter Mignolo's recent conceptions of the "Colonial Difference" and "border thinking" and "bilanguaging," meanwhile, Anzaldúa's influence bounces back into high Theory in a kind of feedback loop.)[23]

For Cisneros, the advent and consolidation of theory's empire had three noticeable effects on her writing, which it is tempting to sum up simply as its "postmodernization." First, it committed her to the salutary nature of *fictionality*, which in *Caramelo* she calls "healthy lies," over and against the putatively oppressive and sickening Enlightenment concept of truth, and directed her to the potential cultural worth (though not without a remainder of irony) of the unrealistic, melodramatic *telenovelas* beloved by her non-literary family. Second, it committed her to the salutary nature of *numerousness*. This had been the practical issue of the floating value of difference since deconstruction, which the pluralist could take as insisting that sentences have *more meanings than one*, and that this is a *good thing*.[24] It also was aligned with the French feminist account of Woman as "this sex which is not one."[25] Allying itself with poststructuralist iterations of muchness and manyness, Cisneros's writing gradually abandoned the minimalist aesthetics of craft, which is an aesthetics of shame, evolving into a maximalist discourse of display and pride. One of the forms this pride takes is the figurative rediscovery, as in the romance tradition, of the formerly aristocratic Mexican lineage of a poor family very much like the one portrayed in *Mango Street*, whose humble characters might have worked as cleaning ladies but never conceivably employed one. The pride of the family in *Caramelo* is symbolized by a family heirloom, a shawl, the colorful and expensive *caramelo rebozo* of the novel's title, a garment that itself recalls one of the novel's many minor characters. She is the daughter of the family's cleaning lady in Mexico, and she has skin "of a color so sweet, it hurts to even look at her."[26] Finally, though, even as it reaches back to anchor itself in the sublime racial coloring of the indigene, the novel is propelled forward into a spatial and temporal *largeness,* a multi-generational, multi-racial geography of international extent.

As we have seen, part of what keeps a text like *Mango Street* circling in the barrio is the hovering threat of the white American disregard (and worse) beyond its borders. Its symbolic-geographic self-containment was the self-reparative achievement of a young woman torn painfully from the familiar by the call of the school. The book's initial publication by Arte Público Press in a sense redoubled that cultural self-containment in the virtual neighborhood of the small press. Beginning in 1991, however, with *Mango Street*'s publication by Vintage, it began to circulate as a marker of difference in a predominantly white national educational field. It's useful to think of this republication as analogous to the dynamic of translation in world literary space as described by Casanova. There the "removal" of a text from its original language situation signifies its conversion into the currency of autonomous art, art worthy of being read even by those with no particular knowledge of the cultural matrix from which the text emerged. In the U.S. pedagogical context, by contrast, such a removal signifies an attempt on the part of the educational system to recognize and promote the value of cultural diversity. When, a few years later, the text appeared in a Spanish translation as *La Casa en Mango Street* (Vintage Español, 1994), this process of expansion in a sense came full circle. Symbolically repatriated to Mexico by a Mexican translator, Cisneros's house of fiction is reconnected with the language from which it was (in theory) mournfully alienated even before the moment of its utterance in English.

The same dynamic of metaphorical back-translation is evident in *Caramelo,* where the force of disaffiliative desire moves in many interesting directions, not least in the novel's drive toward an aesthetic of "bilanguaging." In *Mango Street* Esperanza had been troubled by various kinds of numerousness and crowding. For her, hope for the consolidation of a viable artistic identity resides in the English language in a quite literal sense: "In English my name means hope. In Spanish it means too many letters" (10). When the novel was translated into Spanish, the "hope" that had previously resided in English (the language of escape from poverty) was symbolically (and somewhat confusingly) relocated to the "foreign" language, as "Esperanza," suggesting that Esperanza now means hope in Spanish, too. In any case, unlike the original *Mango Street,* but faithful to this translation, *Caramelo* thrives on the linguistic energy brought to it by Spanish, which erupts at various points to "deconstruct" the monological authority of English. In *Caramelo,* as if to announce at the outset the shattering of the shamed containment of *Mango Street,* an early chapter finds the Reyes family out on the road in three huge cars, "racing to the Little Grandfather's and Awful Grandmother's house in Mexico City" (5). On that trip, and on the dazzlingly many other trips the novel will take, linguistic numerousness is no longer a problem; it is rather a faithful compositional ally, a mark of existential plenitude. Reveling in numerousness, the novel also delights in cataloguing the commodious object matter of family life, as though its assemblage in print could reconstitute the wholeness of a people scattered to the winds of global commerce: "Aunty Licha, Elvis, Aristotle, and Byron are hauling things out to the curb. Blenders. Transistor radios. Barbie dolls. Swiss Army knives. Plastic crystal chandeliers. Model airplanes. Men's button-down dress shirts. Lace push-up bras. Socks . . ." (6).

Is it too early to declare the advent, in *Caramelo,* of a hemispherically integrated Latin American literary tradition, one that might genuinely include the writings of Chicanas and save them from the tediousness and terror of mainstream America? If so, it is not for lack of energy in the novel's attempts to imagine some of the conditions of possibility for such a thing. Even so, the playfully reflexive joke with which it closes might have serious implications. "You don't want people to think we're shameless, do you?" implores the narrator's father, hoping to keep the panorama of family secrets we have just observed as readers from becoming visible to strangers like us. "Promise your papa you won't talk these things" (430). "I promise, Father," she lies, owning up to the disturbing possibility that to celebrate one's family to the maximum, to put them proudly and visibly into print, might require betraying them to the eyes of an alien observer we might as well call "America." So, too, if the little girl with caramel-colored skin represents, for the narrator, an encounter with the redemptive beauty of indigenous color, one cannot miss how swiftly the onrushing narrative sweeps past this little girl into a future in which she has no future, certainly no future as a graduate of the prestigious Iowa Writers' Workshop. Thus it seems fair to wonder, in the spirit of Toni Morrison, what ghosts will be booking passage on these gleeful transnational journeys, which can never quite forget the educational institutions from which they were launched.

PLANTATIONS AND CAMPUSES

Critics—most of whom are also teachers—have made very little of the name given to the villain in Toni Morrison's widely taught novel *Beloved* (1987).[27] When "schoolteacher" is mentioned at all he is discussed merely, if accurately, as a practitioner of the nineteenth-century pseudoscience of race, that most suspect manifestation of the Enlightenment rationality to which Morrison's folk-modernist literary enterprise offers continuous symbolic resistance. The dehumanizing objectification perpetrated by schoolteacher's acts of *measurement, analysis,* and *classification* does not, we take it, extend only as far as the boundaries of the plantation, but is emblematic of a whole way of thinking in Western culture that must, according to Morrison, be countered by the mystical gnosis of love. To point out that schoolteacher is not only a racist rationalist but also a kind of capitalist—his advent on the scene of Sweet Home bears more than a little resemblance to a Reagan-era corporate restructuring, with a pursuit of efficiencies and liquidation of (human) assets—would already be to say something more specific about him than one typically encounters in the criticism, and understandably so. As a textbook example of what in high school English classes they still call, after E. M. Forster, a "flat" character, his presence in the novel is all but allegorical, a token not of the complexity of human motives but of an abstract set of values tending toward pure evil. Or rather it is structural, his simple badness functioning as a dialectical foil for the ethical complexity of Sethe's desperate act of infanticide. In turn the latter, in the elemental collision of competing imperatives it enacts, can be thought of as a kind of trigger to an interpretive perpetual motion machine, lending to this work the disturbing ethical undecidability and inexhaustible re-readability we associate with high narrative art.[28]

But what does it mean that the novel's literary descendant of Simon Legree, trading the latter's viciously unhinged licentiousness for the colder cruelties of plantation science, is called "schoolteacher," and that the bookish activities that earn him this name among the Sweet Home slaves are clearly in excess of business efficiencies? What does it mean for a reading of this novel, and for a reading of the Program Era as a whole, that schoolteacher's authorship-in-progress of what Sethe calls a "book about us" (44)—easily inferred to be one of those tracts "proving" the sub-humanity of the Negro—is pursued hard by the classroom where he instructs his white pupils in the finer points of their supremacy? What does it mean, in other words, that in this novel the roles of *author* and *teacher* and *slave-master* blend one into the other? What it means, for starters, is that to the long list of potentially relevant interpretive contexts for the novel *Beloved,* from the Middle Passage to the Reconstruction to the Moynihan Report, from the tradition of sentimental fiction to the psychology of trauma to the innovative narrative practices of postcolonial postmodernism and beyond, we must add another: education.[29]

The novel is preoccupied by it—so much so that we might accuse the ever-widening shelf of criticism on this work, having barely mentioned the fact, of staring into a blind spot even larger than the space occupied by schoolteacher. Is it perhaps the same blind spot that has kept critics from making an adequate assessment of the agency of the university in postwar American literary production as a whole? An alternative metaphor for the latter would be the screen which we learn not to see when we stare out of an otherwise open window into the distance, but which, if we make an effort to refocus our vision, reappears as a fine-meshed grid. In this case, however, owing to the jagged affective intensities of race, the resistance to institutional reflexivity is conducted with particularly high stakes, and with tensions not likely to be relieved by one of those funny campus novels—Nabokov's *Pale Fire* being the *ur*-version—where creative writers take satirical revenge on the scholars with whom they are now forced to consort as colleagues.

I would not be so bold as to claim that *Beloved* is a "campus novel"—that would be a stretch. It is rather an amalgam of slave narrative and plantation romance and gothic ghost story, and a kind of family saga to boot. I do however want to draw attention to the linkage it explores between slavery and schooling as two social institutions that have been particularly damaging to the psyche of African Americans, and the way this resonates with the contemporary scene of the novel's production. The latter, of course, is definable at a number of different scales, and that scalar variability will turn out to be important to the novel's meditation on the complexity of institutionality, where institutions are seen as nested one inside the other, interlinked and ambiguously contained by the nation, and where the lines of flight—escape routes—are no longer conceivable as linear. We first encountered slavery and the school in Chapter 2, where slavery was seen (with the prison) as the prime analogical exemplar of what was called bad institutionality—institutionality conceived as dehumanizing control and confinement.

The suspicion of school on these grounds reached its apogee of intensity in the 1960s, culminating in the publication of Ivan Illich's *Deschooling Society* (1970), but the potentially confusing proximity of empowerment *by* institutions to imprisonment *in* institutions was already evident in the nineteenth-century slave narrative. No reader of Frederick Douglass's *Narrative* (1845), to take the most canonical example, is likely to forget how, overhearing his master's discourse on the dangers of teaching a slave to read—"it would forever unfit him to be a slave!"—Douglass has only to take this "invaluable instruction" subversively literally, appropriating used primers for his use and "converting" as many white boys as possible into his "teachers."[30] Certainly by the 1960s, if not earlier, these interracial propinquities and intimacies had come to seem a more ambiguously beneficial affair. Not only might the tools of teaching be used against you, as they always have, but even to take hold and use them yourself is to risk a kind of recursive mental re-enslavement to the "white" norms they embody. This is to risk self-alienation at the point of self-observation—to take up the white point of view on oneself and suffer the fractures of double consciousness.

Morrison's novel represents this powerfully in a scene where Sethe overhears the master—more resonantly, the *overseer*—at work in the classroom, and is inadvertently hailed by his racist ideology. In stark contrast to the scene of overhearing in Douglass, here it is the occasion for bad interpellation and for lasting psychological damage:

> But I couldn't help listening to what I heard that day. He was talking to his pupils and I heard him say, "Which one are you doing?" And one of the boys said "Sethe." That's when I stopped because I heard my name, and then I took a few steps to where I could see what they was doing. Schoolteacher was standing over one of them with one hand behind his back. He licked a forefinger a couple of times and turned a few pages. Slow. I was about to turn around and keep on my way to where the muslin was, when I heard him say, "No, no. That's not the way. I told you to put her human characteristics on the left; her animal ones on the right. And don't forget to line them up." I commenced to walk backward, didn't even look behind me to find out where I was headed. (228)

Educational norms—their normativity is evident in Sethe's inability *not* to listen to schoolteacher's lesson—might not always lead to such a literal dehumanization of the would-be student (the shadow student) as they do here. But at a minimum, as Douglass's learning to "write a hand very similar to that of Master Thomas" (87) already portended, they are taken to pose a threat of inauthenticity.

As is well known, the literal "pre-text" of *Beloved* was a newspaper clipping Morrison encountered about a case of infanticide similar in its outlines to the one represented in the novel. But the pseudo-scholarly tract that schoolteacher is writing at Sweet Home might equally be considered the haunting pre-text upon which Morrison's own "book about us," *Be-*

loved, is written. As such, as one of the under-layers of a palimpsest, it is obliterated by Morrison's fiction but remains in a position to bleed into it from below. If, as she once said in an interview, "racism is a scholarly pursuit," then it makes sense to think that scholarly pursuits might be, for her, implicitly haunted by racism.[31] Her novel was also the work of a "schoolteacher," after all, and taking the character schoolteacher seriously as a schoolteacher leads us to a new interpretive context for Morrison herself as well as for her most widely taught work. Of course she was a different and (we can safely assume) more benign sort of schoolteacher than her character when she wrote *Beloved*. And "schoolteacher" would be a rather modest way of describing the occupant of the Albert Schweitzer Chair at the State University of New York at Albany, which Morrison assumed in 1984 after leaving her editorship at Random House and held until she left for a chair at Princeton in 1989.[32] But a teacher she was.

In the author's foreword to the Vintage edition of the novel (2004), she recalls how the character Beloved came to her in the happy "shock of liberation" from the editing job, and how this character's purpose, as she came to understand it, was to test the meaning of freedom for modern women (xvi). The implication is that freedom, however desirable, is not so simple and may indeed be haunted, Faulkner-like, by figures of one's own guilt. Morrison does not say whether her return to salaried employment the following year, this time as a professor, seemed like a return to professional "enslavement" as a teacher.[33] Certainly the novel, even as it was fated to return to the campus as a popular textbook, provides compelling evidence that resuming that role (Morrison taught in colleges for years before becoming an editor) reintroduced its author to the mother lode of ambivalence summed up by the word "school."

The disorienting power of this ambivalence is evident even in her otherwise flat characterization of schoolteacher, who sometimes seems to conduct himself, as we would expect, as a quintessentially un-progressive educator, centering the class on himself and reducing the educational experience to dictation: "He'd talk and [his pupils would] write. Or he would read and they would write down what he said" (226). Elsewhere, however, schoolteacher's teaching methods are revealed as proto-"progressive" in at least one of the term's original Deweyan senses. He may not nurture his pupils' individuality, but he does seem to be encouraging them to *learn by doing* when Sethe is horribly subjected to "two boys with mossy teeth, one sucking on my breast the other holding me down, their book-reading teacher watching and writing it up" (83). The *horror* of this event features prominently in several critical accounts of the novel, but not its *weirdness:* just what exactly is the yield of this educational experiment in suckling rape supposed to be? What sort of knowledge does schoolteacher believe himself and his students to be acquiring in the act? And what are we to make of the strange presence of Halle in the rafters, where, in another of the novel's several scenes of overhearing, he oversees the overseeing of this event? It seems at once a testament to the mobility of the point of view and a rebuke to the idea that a "superior" vision is necessarily a comforting one.

However schoolteacher might try to justify it as science, we might well suspect that this strange "research project" is at bottom simply a fig leaf for sadism. And we know for sure that it was, on Morrison's part, an excuse for some very strong symbolism—not only of the theft of black maternal labor by slavery, but of the widespread American use of black womanhood as a kind of bosomy existential battery, a thing from which to draw warm currents of moral authority and wisdom. Here, in an ironic reversal of the historical oppression of the African American female, this "liminal" figure becomes the imaginary anchor of that patriarchal system of oppression, its *alma mater.* Think, here, of the authority putatively granted to the mammies of the plantation romance, and in post-plantation romances like *Gone with the Wind* (1936).

We should keep this scene of suckling rape in mind when the idea of progressive "experimentalism" reappears later in the novel, but in a considerably more benign context: "When [Paul D] asked [Sethe's daughter Denver] if they treated her all right over there, she said more than all right. Miss Bodwin taught her stuff. He asked her what stuff and she laughed and said book stuff. 'She says I might go to Oberlin. She's experimenting on me.' And he didn't say, 'Watch out. Watch out. Nothing in the world more dangerous than a white schoolteacher'" (314). Even in the moment of Denver's bashful pleasure in books, there is a hovering threat. She, too, is being experimented upon. The strangeness in this instance, however, is not primarily thematic (what does schoolteacher think he's doing?) but formal; it is the oddness of Paul D's *not* saying, a not saying which is also the *narrator's* way of (not?) saying that white schoolteachers are dangerous. This is what ambivalence about the school looks like at the level of the sentence. On a larger scale, it might look something like the program Morrison founded when she got to Princeton, the Princeton Atelier. Disembedding the term "workshop" from its accreted associations by translating it into French, Morrison conceived and executed an educational program that would take the "performative" dimension that had always been crucial to the workshop and run with it. The result is not the usual workshop model that socializes and externalizes the act of writing in various ways, but a program where students and visiting artists of various kinds collaborate on projects leading to an actual public performance.

Morrison's ambivalence toward the formalities of schooling has been evident literally from the first page of her work as a published writer. In the epigraph to *The Bluest Eye* (1970), she stages an encounter with the same "Dick-and-Jane prose" that John Barth complained of in Carverian literary minimalism. But if minimalism returns to the simple language of the children's primer to reassert authorial self-mastery against the shame-inducing uncertainties of the information economy, then Morrison's epigraph does something quite different. Instead of simplifying, it gradually removes the spacing and punctuation between the lines and words of the children's primer to produce a recognizably "maximal" density and proto–high modernist illegibility:

> Here is the house. It is green and white. It has a red door. It is
> very pretty. Here is the family. Mother, Father, Dick, and Jane
> live in the green-and-white house. They are very happy. See

Jane. She has a red dress. She wants to play. Who will play with Jane? . . .

Here is the house it is green and white it has a red door it is very pretty here is the family mother father dick and jane live in the green-and-white house they are very happy see Jane she has a red dress she wants to play who will play with Jane. . . .

Hereisthehouseitisgreenandwhiteithasareddooritisverypretty-hereisthefamilymotherfatherdickandjaneliveinthegreen-and-whitehousetheyareveryhappyseeJaneshehasareddressshewant stoplaywhowillplaywithjane. . . .

The idea, we take it, is that the African American subject, as student, is shamed by the simplistic vision of domestic normality presented in the primer, no less than she is shamed before an audience of blue eyes. The link between this moment and Cisneros's representation of shaming by the schoolteacher nun in *Mango Street* should be quite clear. The first step toward pride, for Morrison, is an aggressive distancing of oneself from the normalizing apparatus of the school. At the same time, committing this act of symbolic violence against the school primer, Morrison commits herself to the intensely literary language and complex narrative structures for which she will be celebrated.

But these, too, as the conversion of her own novels into textbooks amply attests, can be found in the kinds of books one reads in school—though, admittedly, not until several years down the line, in high school or college or graduate school. In the case of Morrison's own education we are talking specifically about the legacy of literary modernism, her advanced knowledge of which was certified by the Master's thesis on William Faulkner and Virginia Woolf that she wrote at Cornell University. In 1983, when her reputation, though already large, had not yet scaled the heights it has reached today, her relation to the modernist legacy was a sticky issue. In an interview she felt constrained to resist the critical linking of her work to high modernism on the grounds that it was a way of not judging her work on its own terms—as though it needed the affiliation to modernism to be considered valuable. In the wake of the Nobel Prize this dependency is no longer conceivable, and it should be safe to point out how much Morrison learned from Joyce and Faulkner and Woolf when she studied them in school, turning their lessons in modernist narrative innovation to her own ends. Certain aspects of her work—think, for instance, of the sequence of chapters in *Beloved* where the free-floating voices of Beloved and Sethe and Denver meditate on the nature of kinship and belonging—are difficult to imagine without the models offered by such works as *As I Lay Dying*. Adopting Faulkner's form, however, she noticed a blind spot in it—what looked to her like an inability to see things from the African American point of view. Inhabiting this narrative blind spot, Morrison turns the high modernist tradition in narrative halfway around on its racial-perspectival axis, but she does not, as it were, leave the observation tower altogether. This is a dramatic reversal, and one of considerable literary historical import, but it keeps the American modernist machine humming.

What the aggression against the primer in *The Bluest Eye* misses, in other words, and what the second-level "haunting" of *Beloved* by a schoolteacher gradually remembers, is the lesson of the slave narrative: that for the purposes of a viable politics of liberation the meaning of school cannot be reduced to the bad institutionality of enslavement, although that sense of it might never go away. Even against the threat of psychic damage, it must be seized as a technology of liberation and put to use in what Antonio Gramsci famously called the "long march through institutions" toward justice. These competing imperatives—the urge to institutionalize versus the urge to flee from institutions—combine to produce Morrison's characteristically "implosive" narrative trajectories. For her, the "journey" outward that is education is in an important sense circular and endlessly self-questioning. Sethe's daughter Denver is the structural counterpart to schoolteacher's white students, and the question of her education runs like a background theme to the novel's more dramatic events. She is shown to inhabit a classroom quite happily for a year as a star pupil, only to be shamed out the door when a classmate asks her about her infamously infanticidal mother. Denver's brief sojourn in this educational paradise looks forward to her happy times with the Bodwins later in the novel. It also recalls, even as it dangerously formalizes, the 28 halcyon days of community education from which her mother Sethe benefited upon her arrival in Ohio: "One taught her the alphabet; another a stitch. All taught her how it felt to wake up at dawn and *decide* what to do with the day. . . . Bit by bit, at 124 and in the Clearing, along with the others, she had claimed herself" (111). This "school without walls" is a scene not of imprisonment but of self-making and self-possession. Its positive joys, which are also the joys of community, are the most proximate backdrop of the horror represented by schoolteacher's arrival to reclaim Sethe and her children for slavery— that is, for "education" conceived in quite the opposite terms, as *learning your place.*

But if we think that a positive educational experience can only be had, for Morrison, in the context of a homogeneous racial community like the one Sethe finds in her first days in Ohio, the handsome children's book of archival photographs of the school desegregation movement of the 1950s that Morrison put together indicates otherwise. *Remember: The Journey to School Integration* (2004) returns to the theme of memory so central to *Beloved,* but here instead of paralyzing trauma we get affirmative memories of the titular "journey" in which young black people so often featured as heroes. But this being a work of Toni Morrison, whose adult fictions are never in any simple sense affirmative, the situation appears upon closer inspection to be somewhat more complex. One of the culminating photographs of the book shows two girls, black and white, reaching out of the windows of what appears to be a school bus to hold hands.

Sure enough, a beautiful interracial connection is made on the journey to freedom, just as it is made when Sethe is aided in her flight from Sweet Home by the white girl Amy. But in this photograph the continuing bodily strain involved in this performance of sisterhood is plain to see.[34] So

School integration. Morrison's caption reads: "Anything can happen. Anything at all. See?" But we can also see the lingering physical discomfort of the children's bond. Toni Morrison, *Remember: The Journey to School Integration* (Boston: Houghton Mifflin, 2004), 70. Photograph: Corbis.

is the prisonlike rectilinearity of the public institution, represented by the steel window frames, that keeps the races together and apart. Not only is it unclear which direction the bus is moving, who is in back and who in front, but the black girl seems more than a little ambivalent about what is going on. If this linking of ebony and ivory is proof, as Morrison's caption has it, that "anything can happen" in a positive sense, it might also be given an alternative, "adult" reading. What we see from this perspective is not so much a triumphant journey toward racial comity in public institutions as a black girl dragged into a condition of *complicity* in her own socialization as the *internal* other of the system. What we see, that is, is the anxiety of affiliation, with its etymological origin in *filia* and *filius,* in "she who suckles."

And yet the journey—as they say—continues, and not only toward the destination of integrated schools (in fact, in the new millennium this is a receding destination). In a larger and multivalent sense it continues toward a destination whose openness to further specification—it is a better place, a promised land—portends a release from the confinement of the institutional "vehicles" moving toward it and makes that confinement provisionally tolerable. Thus, even when Morrison's imagination ranges far afield in time and space—into the nineteenth century in *Beloved;* to Europe and elsewhere in *Tar Baby* (1982)—it exhibits a complexity it is tempting to call "chaotic" in that neither the traditional immigrant drive to *belong* nor Cisneros's primary drive to *escape* will, alone, suffice to describe its route adequately.

Certainly this is true of Morrison's relation to the United States. There are no doubt several reasons why *Beloved* plays such an important role in Homi Bhabha's classic theorization of a poststructuralist postcoloniality in *The Location of Culture* (1994)—the two writers were, for instance, colleagues and close friends at Princeton when the book was being compiled. But, more substantively, one sees how what Bhabha describes as the novel's troubling "of the historical and discursive boundaries of slavery" can be made conversant with a postcoloniality in which, as was always implied by the term, the *legacies* of the colonial period persist into the present and litter the linear path to the future with torn spaces of recursion.[35] And this chain of influence goes both ways. Morrison's theorization of what she calls "American Africanism" in her critical work *Playing in the Dark* (1992) would seem to be playing off Edward Said's "Orientalism," sharing with that work the project of analyzing the role of a racial other in the literary imagination of a dominant culture. There are many fascinating things about Morrison's text—not least its unusually bold assertion of African American critical authority on the white mainstream literary tradition. It is indeed, not unlike the early novels of her colleague Joyce Carol Oates, a relatively early and powerful contribution to what would later be called Whiteness Studies.

Even more interesting for our current purposes is how forcefully Morrison positions herself in this work as a *non-scholar:* "I would like it to be clear at the outset that I do not bring to these matters solely or even principally the tools of a literary critic. As a reader (before becoming a writer) I read as I had been taught to do. But books revealed themselves rather differently to me as a writer."[36] Defining herself as a writer and claiming the specific authority of that point of view, Morrison, even as she in fact wields the academic idiom of theory with notable grace, is able to distance herself from the "arbiters of critical power in American Literature" who, from her perspective, "seem to take pleasure in, indeed relish, their ignorance of African-American texts" (13). In their melodramatic villainy (surely the ignorance of critics, circa 1990, would more likely have been experienced as a queasy embarrassment than something to relish?) these unnamed arbiters seem descended from the schoolteacher of *Beloved*. Except that, in fact, schoolteacher's pleasure in that novel was taken not in his ignorance of slaves, but precisely in acquiring (dubious) knowledge about them.

It is only by vilifying the scholars and critics, it seems, that Morrison can embrace white American fiction writers and celebrate their work as a "treasure trove" (xiii) of hard-won insight into the centrality of the racial other in the constitution of white American identity. In other words, the racism of writers is preferable, in its reality and honesty, to the blank denial of the literary critics, to the invisibility of African Americans in their accounts of American literature. Morrison's literalization of the thematic of racial invisibility as we have it canonically from Ralph Ellison—where the specificity of the black body is all too visible, a spectacle, while it is the common humanity of the black man that is invisible—arguably makes more sense as a description of the "subaltern" in the mind of Europe than it does as a description of Americanist criticism, where, as some have noted, inter-raciality has been a theme at least since Leslie Fiedler's *Love and Death in the American Novel* (1960).[37] So too Morrison's aspiration to "draw a map, so to speak, of a critical geography and use that map to open as much space for discovery, intellectual adventure, and close exploration as did the original charting of the New World" curiously positions her as an outsider to the nation, though one "without the mandate for conquest" (3). Thus, in a way precursive of theorizations of the Black Atlantic diaspora beginning a few years later, the *internal* difference of African America, with respect to the U.S. as a whole, is affiliated with the *external* difference of the transnational.

Nevertheless, set against the typical valorization of movement and spatial enlargement in postcolonial and transnational critical discourses, *Beloved* seems a strikingly static and "domestic" work, in both senses of that term. It is, after all, Sethe's explicit intention upon arriving at 124 Bluestone Road to stop moving: "'No more running—from nothing. I will never run from another thing on this earth'" (18). *Beloved* is a story of the will to stasis. It is an allegory of institutionalization, and of (domestic) establishment. Not for Sethe the joyously deconstructive mobility of the cosmopolitan; not for her the bracing modernity of the migrant or stateless refugee. The "border consciousness" expressed in this text is that of an *intra*-national border, the border between the Southern and Northern United States, and it does not offer the liberatory possibilities claimed, after Anzaldúa, for the international border in the Southwest United States. I believe Morrison's novel can be credited here with a prescient ability, in constructing this allegory of institutionalization, to see through subsequent, idealized conceptions of transnational motion all the way to their end, where they double back to confess their ambiguous similarity to the inhuman mobilities of the global market.[38] As so many slave narratives (not to mention *Uncle Tom's Cabin*) make clear, these include the vicious *defamiliarizations,* in a horribly literal sense, perpetrated by the slave trade, and they are in some sense the obverse, the dialectical counterpart, of the equally inhuman entrapments enacted by slavery in its located form, the plantation. If the novel finds the stasis of the plantation more interesting than mobility, the occasion of a haunting and not simply a very bad memory, it is because its commitment to stasis in better sorts of places—the household, the campus, the community—makes it so. This is why, in *Playing in the Dark,* the African American writer-critic might symbolically expatriate herself as a virtual "postcolonial" subject, but also why we will find her headed back toward inhabitation of the New World.

The ghost named Beloved is a figure for what catches up with you when you stop moving: an observer. One version was the overseer who can literally drag you back into slavery. In this case, it is a ghostly victim of murder empowered to make ethical judgments from the beyond. Her presence in the household on Bluestone Road represents a problem that arises eventually in all institutional structures of affiliation: complicity. In this novel the problem of complicity is enacted most obviously and awfully in Sethe's act of infanticide, which kills a child to preserve it from the soul-murder of slavery. But, as Naomi Mandel has pointed out, it is also condensed in Sethe's rueful observation toward the end of the novel that "I made the ink" (320) with which schoolteacher wrote his book, which suggests her complicity not in murder but in the dubious scholarly endeavors that justify enslavement.[39] This kind of complicity is not so much ethical—what was she supposed to do, not make the ink? make it badly?—as situational, having very little to do with bad intentions but everything to do with feeling bad. It arises whenever persons begin to share institutional spaces of any kind, including schools staffed by schoolteachers with damaging ideas. And it's enough, sometimes, to make you squirm in your seat and raise your arm and ask to be excused.

7

Miniature America; or, The Program in Transplanetary Perspective

and either I am nobody, or I am a nation.

DEREK WALCOTT, "The Schooner Flight"

REFLEXIVE AMERICANIZATION

Is the creative writing program an exceptionally *American* phenomenon? It's a loaded question, so put, and not only for the way it alludes to a formerly lively debate about the status of the United States in world history—whether it must be considered an exception to certain rules about how nations rise and fall. One of these was the rule that says that power corrupts. Was it possible that, uniquely possessed of Republican virtue and unburdened by too much history, the United States might erect itself as a perpetual beacon of liberty and justice for all? So it was hoped, but in recent years it is the exceptional size of its military expenditures, and not its fund of selfless virtue, that has loomed largest to scholarly observers of the United States, and the rule about the corrupting influence of power seems to them more generally applicable than ever. Another was the rule laid down by Marxism that said that capitalist exploitation would always produce a potent working-class radicalism. Here, however, the possibly exceptional case of the United States was not the fondest hope of patriots but a cause for frustration on the political left. Why, it was wondered, is the American worker so complacent? And yet the rise of a post-Fordist global economic order, the selfsame information economy we saw earlier as being at the base of the quietist minimalist aesthetics of Raymond Carver, has exposed this rule as a contingency of European industrial modernity, where conditions were, in retrospect, exceptionally favorable to organized labor. And complacency? It might be that, but it might also be a low-level, dysphoric sensation of suspended political agency that one perceives—one of those "ugly feelings" dragged squirming from the shadows by Sianne Ngai.[1] Whichever is the case, the general effect of quietude is the same. Rather than proving the rule, then, the American exception has in this case become the rule, and "globalization" is its unlovely name.

Thus, with no real competitors to capital in sight, and with the beacon of liberty and justice difficult to see through the smoke, the question of American exceptionalism has faded in recent years in favor of a more sober accounting of various differences and dominations on the world stage. In this context the creative writing program, to the degree that it must be admitted to be an American thing, might seem an even more dubious thing than it already did. Bad enough, as the broken record of romanticism keeps telling us, that it tries to institutionalize what should remain wild and free—creativity. But if it is also implicated somehow in a market-driven Americanism, then how could the citizens of the world possibly approve of it? Is the creative writing program, as some have said of "child-centered" progressive education in general, merely an academic adjunct to that consumerist apparatus, a sop to narcissistic desire? Is it further evidence of the corporate takeover of the university that so many commentators on the left have recently seen fit to decry?

That is no doubt an overstatement of the case, but an exceptional concern for the self-regard of students in the United States is one place to begin when trying to explain why creative writing happened here and not elsewhere. Of course all nations are, as Chris Looby has aptly said, "made, not born," but the creation of the United States was managed without plausible access to myths of its primordial rootedness in a certain place.[2] It was created in historical time in response to the urgent desires of an immigrant multitude. It was a settler nation, in other words, but having been settled it remained unsettled in a deeper sense—remained, as Gertrude Stein so compellingly put it, a space filled with moving. These simple facts of U.S. history, which are certainly unusual if not honorifically "exceptional," had a decisive influence on the nature and extent of the system of higher education that took hold and flourished there. And this unusual system was in turn the seedbed of educational innovations like creative writing. Higher education in the United States is a decentralized and diverse affair, with minimal federal oversight of administrative and curricular structures, and with an array of different kinds of schools comprising it. The relative ease and freedom granted in the founding of colleges in the United States, combined with the granting of tuition assistance to students themselves rather than institutions, ensures that most schools will have to compete for customers, bending all the more toward that quasi-erotic institutional-economic force known as "student demand." At the same time, the relative autonomy granted to colleges in setting standards assures an extraordinary flexibility in finding ways to meet that demand. Since what students most want (or what their families want for them) is a good job upon graduation, this has meant a gradual reorientation in U.S. higher education away from the liberal arts and toward the practical, pre-professional, and vocational courses of study.

But as if in compensation for the latter, the supremely impractical pursuit of literary authorship has become wildly popular in colleges as well. It is too early to announce the death of traditional literary studies, which offers excellent training to students entering the increasingly symbol-driven and fiction-laden postindustrial economy. But one can see by comparison to creative writing how literary studies has the disadvantage, in this economy, of being oriented toward the past, and of making students submissive to the genius of someone other than themselves. My extensive informal investigations over the last several years have yielded no instance where an undergraduate creative writing seminar has been less than fully enrolled; more typically, they are oversubscribed and restricted to admission by application to the teacher. Partly this is the result of the relatively small student-to-teacher ratio required by the workshop format, which creates a scarcity relative to lecture-format classes. Even so, one truth about creative writing instruction seems undeniable: the kids *love* the stuff. They love it suspiciously much, and on the graduate level, too, one rarely hears of a shortage of applicants to creative writing programs, most of them willing to go into debt for the privilege of attending one. This is partly why creative writing programs are a relatively easy sell to university administrators and also why—the odds of any one student making it as a professional writer being vanishingly small—they are subject to being criticized (sometimes fairly, but often not) as entrepreneurial exploitations of the American Dream of perfect self-expression.[3]

Creative writing is, in sum, as American as baseball, apple pie, and homicide. And yet there is evidence that after fifty years of standing more or less alone, this is beginning to change—evidence that writing programs are, like fast food and nuclear weapons and (perhaps more relevantly) mass higher education, beginning to proliferate abroad. Australia, Canada, New Zealand, the United Kingdom—with thirty or more graduate writing programs now located in these countries, the discipline is on the way to becoming a globally Anglophone phenomenon, at the least; and the recent programs in Israel, Mexico, South Korea, the Philippines, and elsewhere suggest an even broader reach.[4] Beginning with this widening of national reference, we could then reach for an even more expansive context in which to view creative writing and the larger creative economy of which it is a part.

We could call this the context of globalization, which in some quarters is called "Americanization" in any case, but a more fruitful term for it might be the one I used in the Introduction, "reflexive modernity." Unlike the more familiar "postmodernity," reflexive modernity as theorized by Ulrich Beck, Anthony Giddens, and others asserts a continuity with the disintegration of traditional communities *(Gemeinschaft)* into the impersonal, rationalized, and highly mediated collectivities *(Gesellschaft)* of modernity as the classical sociological tradition has conceived it.[5] It continues the process of disembedding individuals from aprioristic local determinations and setting them "free," as never before in human history, to make choices, indeed to conceive their lives as a series of choices, good and bad, which all told and interlaced with chance make a narrative, a life story. It refers, however, to the period when this very process has itself become a matter of reflection across broad swaths of social life, indeed a matter of constant *worry*. Are bureaucracies stifling? Are we heating up the planet? Will our own machines turn on us? This is the age of the "Risk Society" and of systematic risk management—and it is a fundamentally global phenomenon. "On a planet criss-crossed by 'information highways,'" notes Zygmunt Bauman, "nothing that happens in any part of the planet can actually, or at least potentially, stay in an *intellectual* 'outside.'"[6] But it is also an individualized and individualizing phenomenon, structuring the life of "free" persons as an endless process of self-monitoring—am I healthy? do people like me? have I found my voice?—and offering them a continuous stream of expert advice and consumer products designed to help them be who they want to be.

If, according to Max Weber, the freedoms of modern life assemble an "iron cage" of rationality in which individuality is trapped and slowly dies, then reflexive modernity is somewhat different: it is a hall of mirrors in which the subject engages in an endlessly entertaining but, on another level, frighteningly compulsory performance of self. "Perform or Else" is

Jon McKenzie's shorthand for the new dispensation in which, as he and Paolo Virno and others have described, the theatrical, technological, and management senses of "performance" have become all but indistinguishable.[7] A rich amalgam of compulsion and freedom, this kind of performance occasions a protracted state of half-belief in personal agency; and it is the role of creative writing, with its ritual suspensions of disbelief, to bolster this. What has been described throughout this book as "auto-poetics"—the routine reflexivity of literature embodied most explicitly in the literary genre of the portrait of the artist—is obviously nested in this larger reflexive-performative matrix. So is the quantitative scale of minimalist and maximalist aesthetics that, as we have seen, indexes the politics of literary labor. This no doubt is why the aesthetic products of the writing program, in reflecting on themselves, so often seem like parables of the modern social system as such.

Placing creative writing in this context, we can begin to work through the apparent incoherence produced in the "I hate the writing program" program when the charge of narcissism is made to share the docket with the other, more or less opposite, charge so often heard against it: conformity. Doesn't the imprisonment of artistry in the classroom indicate an excessive faith in institutions? Doesn't the mobocratic *work-shopping* of texts lay a blanket of defensively safe sameness upon their erstwhile originality? And doesn't the latter criticism suggest that the creative writing program, against all the empirical evidence to the contrary, could as plausibly be tagged as a weirdly un-American, well-nigh communist phenomenon as a quintessentially American one? In fact, proponents of the program since Iowa's Paul Engle have argued that it is only because the United States typically offers so little economic support or respect to its artistically ambitious writers, as compared to other countries, that the university must step forth to assume the compensatory function that it does. Perhaps we could say, then, that what is reflected in the invention of the discipline of creative writing in the United States is not narcissism alone but an unusually intense embrace of both sides of the faintly paradoxical task of *institutionalizing individuality*, a formulation that registers both the self-

expressive and the countervailing self-disciplinary elements of the program that we have been tracking in this book all along.

To the extent that this embrace is also an act of self-contradiction,
we could therefore say (in the tradition of Tocqueville) that the United
States is an exceptionally confused nation, one in which a regime of disciplinary individualism, supplying the ways and means of individuality from
without, constantly mistakes itself as the occasion for an individualism of
a wilder kind. It would be wrong, however, to overlook the symptom of a
more generally reflexive modernity embedded in this "American" confusion. In classical sociology the terminological correlates of individuality
and institutionality are "agency" and "structure," and for Scott Lash, at
least, reflexive modernity represents the "emergent demise of th[is] distinction altogether."[8] As he sees it, even the project of self-reflection recorded in the quintessentially modern Cartesian claim, "I think, therefore
I am," has in our day come to seem unnecessarily baroque, with that
wordy detour through pondering and logic. The more contemporary version, proper to reflexive modernity, dispenses with reflection in favor of
reflexivity in a more mechanical or twitching sense. "I am I" is his candidate for the (non-)cogito of our time, although we might, *contra* Lash, and
in the modern spirit of worry (I worry, therefore I am), insist upon concluding the statement with a question mark: "Am I me?" Really? That
would explain why Lash's new, streamlined cogito—his ego—still contains
a redundancy, an excess above the more nearly perfect "I am." The extra
"I" in "I am I" can be read as a defensive gesture of semantic completion, a
paranoiac sign that all is not well with reflexively modern subjectivity, as
though to say "I am" without further specification invites someone else to
finish the sentence unpleasantly: I am . . . a fool. I am worthless, fat, boring, a fraud. But I may or may not be American.

However justified, or not, the national limitations of this project
might be, the founding gesture of this book has been one of inclusion: the
idea has been to observe postwar fiction as a complex totality, substantially
widening the interpretive lenses through which it was typically viewed
and venturing a set of descriptions of the nature and function of its many

interacting parts. The medium of that totality has in turn been the U.S. system of higher education, a.k.a. "the university," understood as the axial institution of a postindustrial—which is also to say "information" and "creative" and "experience"—economy, and in particular the writing programs situated therein. The implication throughout has been that this more inclusive vision would yield, even against the omnipresent risk of oversimplification, insights that a narrower one could not. I have wanted to act on my belief that the ambitions of a big book like Hugh Kenner's *The Pound Era* (1971) might remain relevant (with one crucial substitution) even now, and have done so with results that you can see for yourself.

Now, however, as the material limits of the book I've called *The Program Era* have become visible on the horizon, it seems important to tack back in the direction of humility, and to admit the, in a sense, *smallness* of my concerns. The model for that humility is already latent in Kenner, who probably didn't expect anyone to start referring to the period of modernism, the modernist era, as the "Pound Era." *Pound?* Please. There was always something both plausible and risible in that period designation. True, Pound was an important poet and, even more so, a cultural figure, organizer, editor, and entrepreneur, but it can seem silly, in retrospect, to try to lord his name over an era that also included James Joyce, T. S. Eliot, Gertrude Stein, and so on—silly even to be playing this "great man" game. It's best, then, to think of the idea of the "Pound Era" as a heuristic device, a famously useful tool for entering into the study of literary modernism but not one that will give an adequately inclusive perspective on the whole.

The Program Era hasn't wanted to play the great man game, has played it reluctantly—wanting instead to track a period in which institutions, not individuals, have come to the fore as the sine qua non of postwar literary production. That is the difference that this book (and fifty more years of literary history) would make in our take on the history of modernism. And yet this perspective is in its own way limiting. We already know that it is troublingly American, but even within this all-too-narrow compass its gestures of inclusion exclude a great deal of what other critics might find crucial to understanding the American thing it tries to name. How could it not? We are in the orbit here of one of the truisms at the heart of systems theory: there is no inclusion that is not also exclusion. The act of "observation"—by which systems theory means much more than simply *looking at*—can only begin by making a distinction, a "cut" through the manifold that leaves a vast blankness beyond its purview.[9] You can't pay attention to everything all the time, and so you exclude most everything. You filter it out. In the present case, this has meant that a hundred pressing issues, and a hundred more interesting writers, from Joan Didion to E. L. Doctorow to Junot Díaz and Edwidge Danticat (to take only a few of the D's) have been mostly left out of consideration, as confirming (or not) as they might have been of the interpretive models I have tried to build.

What intrigues me about this dynamic of inclusion and exclusion, as I reflect upon the necessary limitations of this book, is that it is so similar to the fundamental dynamic of its subject, the creative writing program, and in particular to the modernist conception of narration it has institutionalized. The paradoxes of the observer are, in other words, strikingly similar to the paradoxes of narrative "point of view" in the Jamesian tradition. Meaningful experience can only begin in limitation, in the demarcation and narration of a distinct domain of concern. Observations are made by someone standing somewhere, even if it is "nowhere," and saying what they have seen; and the significance of what they say, the story they tell, is inextricable from the form their telling takes. This is the basic insight embodied in and systematized by a classroom classic like *Points of View: An Anthology of Short Stories* (1966/1995), which is structured as a sequence leading from the absolute intimacy of teller and told in the interior monologue through the progressive "distancing" enacted by first person and then various forms of third person narration.[10] I would like, then, as a way of getting one more perspective on the fiction of the Program Era, as well as some perspective on *The Program Era* itself, to examine two writers' attempts to adopt a "totalizing" view of the post-national domain—the planet earth—and a historical period—reflexive modernity—which they inhabit.

This examination will allow us to pay due respect to the aspiration to *self-transcendence* built into the practices of creative writing, where the effort is, by self-reflection, to free oneself from the system of identities in which we all move, and to look upon it from a point of remove. Here the project is not, as we saw it for Cisneros and Morrison in the previous chapter, to discover *who I really am* beyond the distortions of institutional affiliation. It is not to claim literary property rights in a certain domain of lived experience. It is rather to find a place to be *who I am really not,* a place to be free from the fixity of identity and to borrow the experiences of others. In James Alan McPherson's metafictional "Elbow Room" it is associated with the American landscape, and is the place the African American writer might go for some respite from the category "African American writer." Presented as if peppered with the queries of a writing teacher (which McPherson is) who has become involved in the writer's process, this text aligns the restrictions of story form in the craft tradition with the restrictions of identity itself:

> *A point of information. What has form to do with caste restrictions?*
> Everything.
> *You are saying you want to be white?*
> A narrator needs as much access to the world as the advocates of that mythology.
> *You are ashamed then of being black?*
> Only of not being nimble enough to dodge other people's straitjackets. . . .
> *A point of information. What is your idea of personal freedom?*
> Unrestricted access to new stories forming.[11]

This is an ambiguity at the heart of creative writing: does it allow you to be who you are? or to escape who you are? To the extent that fiction is a means of escape from determination, then fictional characters have an obvious reason for being: they are the vehicles of a therapeutic alienation, a movement from identity to otherness. If the risk of the first is the haunting discovery that the *person I really am* is the product of an American institution, the risk of the second is the discovery that the *person I am not* is the same—the product of an American institution. In this case, testifying to the limits of the imagination, the institutional other offers no plausible path of escape from its determinations, as the clinging of marginalia to McPherson's "Elbow Room" already portends.

Put these two together and you have the signature dilemma of reflexive modernity, one we might call, with apologies to Siegert and Seltzer, the dilemma of the *institutional apriori*.[12] Is there, after all, a space outside institutions for postwar American writers? Perhaps there is even now; perhaps this is what the great sprawl and effervescent verbal excess of literary maximalism are telling us: creativity will not be contained! At the same time, but in a different spirit, we could also observe that a system is never so completely closed as when it contains, within itself, a compelling representation of its own outside.

STUDY ABROAD

Published in the *New York Times Book Review* in 1988, Bharati Mukherjee's "Immigrant Writing: Give Us Your Maximalists!" has become infamous for its pointed criticism of the figure of the literary émigré, the writer who chooses to live in a kind of perpetual exile.[13] Blinded by nostalgia, unable to appreciate the finer textures of his present situation, all too often, according to Mukherjee, this sort of writer produces "mannered and self-referential" writing (28) ungrounded in close observation of the world around him. Far better to commit to a new country, trading the world-weariness of the émigré for the wide-eyed enthusiasm of the immigrants who, in a wave almost as large as the one seen in the late-nineteenth and early-twentieth centuries, have been fundamentally transforming American society since the 1960s. Mukherjee's idea is not that the immigrant writer in the U.S., of which she is one, should stop perceiving the world through the lens of her native culture. That culture is "in our eyes and ears and in some special categories of our brains," she claims, and for her own part she makes much of the profound influence on her writing of the Mughal miniaturist paintings she first saw as a child in Calcutta. The point, rather, is that the object of the immigrant writer's attention should be the contemporary American scene. The benefits in accepting it as such will not be the writer's alone. For Mukherjee, offering to the immigrant writer an unusually layered version of the call to "write what you know," the combination of perceptual habits acquired elsewhere with the immigrant's "hunger to belong" in a new country would revivify an American literary tradition that has been "sunk in a decade of minimalism" (28).

Mukherjee's timing in making such a pronouncement about the émigré, just as the assemblage of theories and themes known as "postcolonialism" was beginning to surge into prominence in the U.S. academy, could hardly have been worse—worse, at least, for her ability to find a secure place in an emergent postcolonial canon. Although her works bear many of the magical realist elements associated with central figures in that tradition like Salman Rushdie, and are as obsessed as anyone's with movements across national borders, her imagination turns out to have been moving, in some deeper sense, in the wrong geographical direction entirely. In Mukherjee, that is, "transnational movement" seems always to be headed, however indirectly, toward an inevitable destination in the United States. Having left India in 1961 to get an M.F.A. at the Iowa Writers' Workshop, Mukherjee had recently become a U.S. citizen when "Give Us Your Maximalists!" was published and was proud of it, and that sense of *arrival* subtly suffuses even her most peripatetic works. Plenty of postcolonial writers and thinkers (most of them, in fact) have seen fit to take up residence in the North American imperium, teaching at one U.S. university or another; Rushdie himself has recently signed on for an unlikely posting at Emory University in Atlanta. But none have been unstrategic enough, as Mukherjee has been, to name their object of desire "America." Partly, no doubt, this is simply a matter of the contingencies of biography:

arriving at age 21 in the American heartland in what was still effectively the 1950s, Mukherjee was formed as a writer well in advance of the aggressively intra-nationalist movements of the late 1960s and 70s, never mind the academic discourses of the 1980s and 90s. Thus it is not surprising that when she came into belated prominence with the publication of her prizewinning third book, *The Middleman and Other Stories* (1988), a strong hint of old-school immigrant Americanism was waiting to be detected beneath the superficial "postcoloniality"—if only by way of the author's national origin—of her body of work. Indeed, while her model of interesting *art* may have been the Mughal miniaturist painting, part of the many-layered indigenous traditions of her country of origin, her model of a successful *writer* was Bernard Malamud.[14]

Staking a claim to the signifier "America" in a way that book publishers and journalists could still appreciate but postcolonialist academics could not, Mukherjee in the 1990s would find herself casually dismissed by leftist thinkers like Aijaz Ahmad—in the context, ironically, of his own critique of postcolonial theory—as a typical example of the "right-wing people" that most immigrants from the global periphery to the metropolitan centers turn out to be.[15] Soon enough, with this blood in the water, a work like Mukherjee's *Jasmine* (1989), the story of one woman's odyssey from the Indian village of her childhood through a sequence of starkly different identities in the United States, would prove vulnerable to ingenious critical revelations of the retrograde conservatism lurking within its more readily apparent commitment to a self-consciously modern, implicitly Western feminist individualism. Naturally Mukherjee, who had always thought of herself as residing comfortably on the political left, was enraged by this rough treatment: "I find so many glaring errors in their so-called scholarship," she told one interviewer, speaking of the critics of her work influenced by her nemesis Gayatri Spivak; "I don't know how such shoddy work gets past a dissertation supervisor in any respectable university!"[16]

Amidst these fireworks, the other and equal object of Mukherjee's critique in "Give Us Your Maximalists!", the one implicitly addressed in its title, has been all but ignored in subsequent discussions of her ambiguous place in the postwar literary field. But the nature and shifting parameters of that field in the late 1980s and 1990s cannot be understood without restoring the presence of the sort of writers, led by Carver, who had come to such prominence in the seventies and eighties and who had created what many perceive as the "house style" of the creative writing program. Minimalism "is deft," Mukherjee conceded, but it is only "a shorthand of shared, almost coded responses to collective dread. Dread over what exactly? Well there's aging and there's fear of commitment and there are all sorts of variants on divorce and childlessness and dead-end jobs and midlife crises. . . . Minimalist techniques seem a healthy response to too much communication, too much manipulation and too much of everything . . . [but] I feel that minimalism disguises a dangerous social agenda. Minimalism is nativist, it speaks in whispers to the initiated. As a newcomer, I can feel its chill, as though it were designed to keep out anyone with too much story to tell" (28).

If, circa 1988, the émigré postcolonial theorists would be the bane of Mukherjee's near future, the more immediate targets of her ire were the minimalists, many of them associated with her own alma mater, Iowa. Accusing these writers of a purely *formal* nativism—it's not that they speak out against immigration, but that they speak in an "insider" code—Mukherjee sees a form of exclusivity silently framing their depictions of existential desperation, even the form of desperation most explicitly linked to lower-middle-class existence, that of "dead-end jobs." Whether or not this desperate exclusivity can or should be understood as a "privilege"—it sounds like a country club of the damned—Mukherjee's critical observation does throw into relief the undeniably intense Americanness, if not Americanism, of otherwise disaffected writers like Carver. For literary minimalism the question of nationality, like the question of race, is generally so obvious—so white American—as to never even arise. But the possibility that it might be lurking there silently is suggested by Maryann Carver's memory of how, having herself swung a scholarship for the Carver family to study abroad for a year in Tel Aviv, she saw Ray quickly became miserable there. She would hear her husband on the balcony "muttering America First, America First, which was pretty wild because this was 1968 . . . and all that was going on on the college campuses, the rallies and so forth." "I don't know what I'm doing in Asia," he would finally say, forcing the family to return to the U.S. after only four months.[17]

How galling it must have been for Mukherjee, taking a prominent public stand against provinciality like this on behalf of the progressive value of cultural difference, to discover a few years later that she had been outflanked on the left. Stranded in a suddenly untenable middle ground between postcolonial cosmopolitanism and an implicitly "white" American nativism, she was by default pushed into the nativist camp that she had set out in her article to criticize. Carver wanted to *stay* in America, Mukherjee to *arrive* there—the postcolonialists were not prepared to see a relevant difference between the two positions. How galling for Mukherjee, but how fine an opportunity for us to begin to take the measure of the "house style" of the creative writing program as it begins to interact with the pluralist values of cultural diversity. In this context, Mukherjee's "middling" position is useful as a literary historical marker, telling us something about "white" minimalism and "ethnic" maximalism alike. To the extent that any writer can be thought of as a product of his or her schooling, Mukherjee was a product of Iowa, living in the environs of the Workshop from a tender age and staying well beyond the two years needed to acquire an M.F.A. And yet, as a dark-skinned woman who had come of age in a culture utterly unfamiliar to Iowans, she was inevitably understood in classically Orientalist terms as an exotic presence there.

Mukherjee has given us one name for the literary mode, neither minimalist nor maximalist, that emerges from this collision of opposites— miniaturism. We have already seen it at work in Cisneros, whose Mango Street vignettes are small and self-contained but not linguistically parsimonious, seeded as they are with pockets of childlike poetry that would one day bloom into the exuberant maximalism of *Caramelo*. Cramming a great deal of detail into a small space, literary miniaturism might be described as maximalism in a minimalist package, or, in the Deleuzian idiom, as the becoming-maximal of Carverian minimalism. Its literary progenitors are writers like Jorge Luis Borges, whose story "The Aleph" offers a kind of metaphysics of the miniature, and Donald Barthelme, whose explosive smallness and overt (if surreal) politicality had never quite fit the minimalist mold. Its more recent inheritors include Nicholson Baker, George Saunders, and Lydia Davis, as well as the practitioners of "flash" or "sudden" or "micro" fiction, where the task for the writer is to do as much as possible within a very small space.[18] As we have it in the tradition of Hemingway and Carver, minimalism is an aesthetic of understatement, a literature of the unheroic, ordinary, and spare. The literary miniature, by contrast, as canonically described by Gaston Bachelard, is "automatically verbose," *even when* restricted to 1000 or 250 or 55 words. While the two forms are obviously subject to considerable overlap, as evidenced by the inclusion of some of Carver's shortest stories in flash fiction anthologies, miniaturism in its ideal form offers none of the brooding ellipses into the vast emptiness of the all-to-realistic beyond that we find in minimalism. Indeed, in Mukherjee's painterly account of miniaturism, the typical ornateness of the frame in Mughal miniaturist painting performs the crucial function of forcing the viewer not to look at the work "as a source of 'raw' sociological data, but as sociology *metaphorized;* that is, as a master-artist's observation on life/history/national psyche cast in the aesthetic traditions of the community and transmuted into art."[19]

It should be obvious by now what Mukherjee's miniaturist aesthetic, applied to her own literary production, owes to the creative writing program even in the self-conscious exoticism of its magical realism: for one thing, an appreciation of the small literary unit. As we've seen, whether it is minimalist or miniaturist, the point in writing a short story is for the student to delimit a small textual space and to master it. Unlike the sprawling maximalism toward which it is headed—which, never mind the rhetorical messiness of a Thomas Wolfe or a William Faulkner, in certain famous instances like Pynchon's *Gravity's Rainbow* flirts with nonsensical chaos—miniaturism, like minimalism, stays wholly within the Jamesian/New Critical regime of conscious craft and control. Indeed, in pointing so

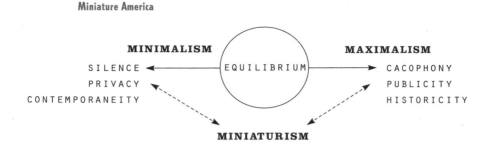

Stylistically and thematically, the development of postwar American fiction has been driven by a strong polarity of minimalist and maximalist compositional impulses that might alternatively be called the Hemingway / Faulkner dialectic. Its terms are divided by a primary allegiance either to the value of exclusion or inclusion; privacy or publicity; contemporaneity (a narrow span of story time) or historicity (the great sprawl of historical fiction); and finally to "less" or "more" verbiage or syntactic complexity. What we might then designate as the "neoclassical" position, since it exhibits the Aristotelian values of moderation, balance, proportionality, and so on, resolves into an equilibrium of "fine writing." One thinks here of the line leading from Fitzgerald through Stegner to John Updike—fine writers all, neither self-effacing nor overbearing. But Barthelme and Mukherjee are best described as "miniaturists" in that their short fiction condenses a maximalist relation to language into small forms. One could say the same for Thomas Pynchon's uncharacteristically short, but energetically wordy and history-obsessed, *Crying of Lot 49*.

obviously to the inherent restrictions of the medium that must be overcome in the execution of its designs, miniaturism could be said to intensify the commitment to craft that one finds in minimalism, or at least the commitment to *showing off* the intricate clockwork of its results. Its tensions mirror those of the standard Program Era career, which sometimes sticks with small forms, but often begins with a showcase collection of short stories (often enough written in workshop) and then moves on—as it did for Flannery O'Connor, Joyce Carol Oates, Philip Roth, Russell Banks, Sandra Cisneros, Denis Johnson, Junot Díaz, and so many others—to the big (or at least bigger) novel.

One would readily assent to Susan Stewart's claim that the miniature in art and literature is a figure for personal interiority—the dollhouse as bourgeois mind—if it weren't for the fact that the paintings Mukherjee takes as her aesthetic model are rather too "public" to be explained in those terms alone, already bearing, as they do, much of the "publicity" Stewart sees as characteristic of the gigantic.[20] Mukherjee's story "Courtly Vision," included in the collection *Sudden Fiction International* (1989), is written in the form of one continuous ekphrasis describing a tiny sixteenth-century painting from the Mughal court.[21] This painting condenses the dazzlingly colorful multiplicities of the Mughal world, centered on a glorious emperor setting forth from his palace into battle, and the story version needs only to add psychological interiority to the tiny figures represented therein. Like the typical Donald Barthelme story, and like the static medium of the painting it describes, "Courtly Vision" can barely be called a narrative, although such a lot is going on simultaneously in the painting that merely setting the scene and extrapolating on the states of consciousness of its human figures produces virtually narrative effects. Including the tiny hidden figure of one "Count Barthelmy," at whose grasping Western hands the empire will meet its demise, the whole display is energized by a kind of dramatic irony, a loose historical thread in the imperial tableau that will, with time, unravel it. And if "Barthelmy" seems to nod cleverly at Donald Barthelme as one of the progenitors of literary miniaturism, the little Christian priests visible in the painting can be read as Carverian minimalists *avant la lettre:* "What a comforting failure of the imagination these priests are offering," thinks a courtier, "What precarious boundaries set on life's playful fecundity" (197).

But so does miniaturism set a boundary on fecundity. It's just that, by contrast with minimalism, it allows that within this boundary, and subservient to the rules of precision and clarity, the imagination is free to embroider a world infinitely. Near the end of the story we are told that, in the painting, the emperor

> leaves his capital, applauded by flatterers and loyal citizens.
> Just before riding off the tablet's edge into enemy territory, he

twists back on his saddle and shouts a last-minute confidence
to his favorite court-painter. . . .

   Give me a total vision, commands the emperor. *His voice
hisses above the hoarse calls of the camels. You, Basawan, who
paint my [lady love] on a grain of rice, see what you can do with the
infinite vistas the size of my opened hand. Hide nothing from me, my
co-wanderer. Tell me how my new capital will fail, will turn to dust
and these marbled terraces be home to jackals and infidels.* (198)

The reflexive miniaturist vision, as a "total vision," is here literally figured
as an imperialist vision, and as such it is logically of a piece with the "Eye
of Apollo" that envisions the world from above—as on a flat map or a
globe or even, when NASA sends back photos of the Planet Earth from
outer space, in the form of the misty orb itself.[22]

   While the lower-middle-class modernist writer masters himself,
hoping thereby to ride out the unknowable uncertainties of his economic
future, the miniaturist attempts to cognitively master that world and that
future. He attempts to contain it not as the maximalist does, through the
prodigious expansion of textuality, but intensively, by means of a condensation that leaves the beholder in a position of specular mastery. If this
form of miniaturism represents psychic interiority, as Stewart claims, it is
the interiority of a distinctly *imperial,* distinctly *heroic* and *world-mastering*
subject, not the humble, wounded psyche of a Raymond Carver. And yet
it is an imperial subject wise enough, in Mukherjee's case, to factor into
his totalizing vision the absolute inevitability of his own decline. This, in
miniature, is the temporal sprawl so characteristic on the thematic plane
of literary maximalism, where, as with Faulkner, Pynchon, Oates, Vollman, and so many others, verbosity is associated with historicity. It is strikingly distinct from the typical matching of verbal understatement with a
relatively compressed story time in minimalism. And this is of course the
final irony of the powerful total vision insofar as it includes the march of
deep time in that totality: whereas minimalist stasis is a way of warding
off or managing change, the lesson of maximalism and miniaturism is that
nothing lasts forever, neither Mughals nor Romans nor Anglo-Americans,

and the ground upon which the observer stands is bound to break open and swallow him. In "Courtly Vision" (which already disorients postcolonial politics by remembering that empires come in non-Western versions, too) the inevitability of imperial decline is made real, made present, when, breaking the frame of the "painting" proper, the story ends with the copy that presumably accompanies it in a gallery or auction catalogue. Set against the majesty of the painting's historical referent, it turns out to have been an almost insultingly cheap offering: "'Emperor on Horseback Leaves Walled City.' Painting on Paper, 24 cms x 25.8 cms. Painter Unknown. No superscription. c. 1584 A.D. Lot No. SLM 4027-66. Est. Price $750" (198).

That the total vision represented in "Courtly Vision" can be had so cheap is significant of more than the decline of the Mughals or the rise of the West; it also suggests the rise of a more or less "democratic" distribution of a mediated experience of imperial subjectivity. To be sure, this painting costs quite a bit more than most Kmart shoppers could afford to spend on decor. But it costs much less, for all that, than a semester in a creative writing program. What I'm getting at is how even in this relatively luxurious form, so distinct from the down-market ordinariness of the minimalist aesthetic, the miniaturist story still bespeaks an intimacy with the mass pedagogical production of self-expressively "sovereign" individuals in the U.S., and with a wider culture in which the relatively long attention span required for reading a story is reduced to the absolute minimum (even the busiest person has time to read a story that is 55 words long). This is why it would be premature to dismiss the totalizing miniaturist aesthetic as ideologically "imperialist" without first noting how many layers of institutional mediation stand between this aesthetic practice and anything approaching actual world rule. It might be understood as part of a larger program of training in the imperialist mind-set, but it might just as easily be understood as compensatory—as a special effect of individual autonomy in a world dominated by massively trans-individual systems. In this sense, as Bachelard suggests, miniaturism has as much to do with feeling safe and calm as with feeling proud and powerful: "Miniature is an exercise that has metaphysical freshness; it allows us to be world conscious at slight risk. And how restful this exercise on a dominated world can be!"[23] A precious thing of the drawing room, this "exercise" in sublime safety has little to do with the call for vigorous manly exploit heard in the imperialism of a Teddy Roosevelt.

This is also why it is relatively easy, even as she distances herself from it on behalf of a maximal inclusion of cultural otherness, to trace the origins of Mukherjee's miniaturism in Program Era minimalism of the type she decries. The title story of her breakthrough collection, *The Middleman and Other Stories,* features a first person narrator who, in his romantic tough-guy cynicism, could easily be read as an extension of the cool minimalist persona into new demographic territory. He is not the ordinary lower-middle-class white guy this time, as he had been in Carver, nor even the taciturn veteran he had been in Hemingway. Alfie Judah is a U.S. citizen, but he is also a member of a Middle Eastern Jewish diaspora driven by the winds of global commerce, and when we meet him he has some business to attend to in Central America:

> There are only two seasons in this country, the dusty and the wet. I already know the dusty and I'll get to know the wet. I've seen worse. I've seen Baghdad, Bombay, Queens—and now this moldering spread deep in Mayan country. . . . I'll learn the ropes. . . .
>
> This place is owned by one Clovis T. Ransome. He reached here from Waco with fifteen million in petty cash hours ahead of a posse from the SEC. That doesn't buy much down here, a few thousand acres, residency papers and the right to swim with the sharks a few feet off the bottom. Me? I make a living from things that fall. That big fat belly of Clovis T. Ransome bobs above me like whale shit at high tide.[24]

Even as the narrator tells it like it is, even as he breaks it down, that hardboiled Chandlerian flourish of a too-good simile at the end of the passage already suggests an excess in style over and above the rigorous ordinariness of the Carver narrator. It suggests a tendency, even within Alfie's clipped syntax and short sentences, for a proto-maximalist display of linguistic wares. If Mukherjee's project is traceable back to minimalism, then, it is just as easily traceable forward to the characteristic maximalism of high cultural pluralism, a discourse not of shame but of the pride of voice.

As a kind of showing off of authorial skills in ventriloquism, stylistic excess in "The Middleman" enters into the story as if from above, as though from the gaudy hand of Basawan the court painter, and announces a principle of *authorial mobility* in relation to the hard facts of experience that runs contrary to the smallness of the material form. This is what it means to inhabit the superior perspective of the beholder of the miniaturist painting. In stark contrast to the sense of entrapment felt by the typical Carver character, as desperately stuck in himself as he is in his dead-end job, the authorial persona that unites Mukherjee's story collection roams the country entering different subjectivities at will, narrating each story in turn from a radically different sociological and ethnic perspective. In "Give Us Your Maximalists!" this mobility is claimed as the special property of the immigrant writer who, having "learned how to be two things simultaneously," is enabled "without difficulty to 'enter' lives, fictionally, that are manifestly not my own. Chameleon-skinned, I discover my material over and across the country, and up and down the social ladder."[25] That this claim is made contrary to facts of literary history that suggest otherwise— it is rather white writers like William Styron and Russell Banks and Robert Olen Butler and Neal Stephenson who have been most likely to assert the privilege of other-narration, and minority writers who have typically been asked to slot themselves into a single ethnos—makes it all the more interesting. The Carver character dreams, in the shadow of shame, of moving up the social ladder; the immigrant artist, in Mukherjee's account, moves in a higher dimension altogether, freed even from the predictable linearity of upward social advancement.

While *Middleman* sequences different subjectivities from story to story, demonstrating the imaginative mobility of their author, Mukherjee's best-known novel, *Jasmine,* published the following year, locates this sequence of identities in the life of one woman.[26] This is interesting because it drives Mukherjee, otherwise prone to idealizing the American dream of individual self-transformation, to acknowledge that there might be a psychological price to be paid for mobility and modernity alike. The titular figure is a woman born and raised in a small village in India but who, when we first meet her, is living as Jane Ripplemeyer, the wife of a small-time agricultural banker in Elsa County, Iowa. To marry a banker is not quite the same as marrying one's fellow student in the Iowa Writers' Workshop, as Mukherjee did when she married the Canadian Clark Blaise, but it is close. And remembering this similarity helps us to notice how insistently the novel places Jasmine in close proximity to universities, whether it is working as an au pair for a Columbia University professor, or working as a translator of Punjabi for scholars, or being mistaken for a student in Iowa.

With these situations, Mukherjee alludes to the important fact that, as in her own case, higher educational institutions not only serve as agents of upward social mobility for U.S. citizens, but also inspire the flow of social elites from nations on the periphery into metropolitan centers. The paranoid nativist view of this phenomenon is laid out in Neal Stephenson's *The Cobweb* (1996, written with his uncle under the pen name Stephen Bury), a campus novel in which Iraqi terrorists, posing as exchange students at an Iowa university, are discovered to have been acquiring knowledge for the manufacture of chemical weapons to be used against the U.S.[27] Mukherjee's version is less paranoid, but no less a reflection of some of the dangerous consequences of a globalized world: for her the "heartland" of small-town America, traversed by the laws of the market and a magnet for people like herself, is gradually losing its insularity, and not-too-profitable farmland is being converted into golf courses.

And this, we gather, is neither wholly good nor wholly bad. Certainly there is nothing simply Pollyannaish about Mukherjee's take on modernization here: it is a cruel thing, violently ripping people from the traditional life of the land, whether that land is in India or Iowa. But it also—especially for women—presents an array of possibilities for individual self-development unthinkable in a traditional society. Thus, even as Jasmine's liberation from village life is a cause for significant narrative exhilaration, her existential mobility approaches at times a state of schizophrenic dissociation or fragmentation, a "shuttl[ing] between identities" (77) with vertiginous lapses in continuity from self to self. The novel's horrible image of this fragmentation is the rotting body of a dog; encountered by Jasmine in the river flowing through her native village, it breaks into pieces and sinks. Finally, though, in something like a routinization of change, the woman named Jyoti, then Jasmine, then Jass, then Jane begins to *get used to it:* "It is by now only a passing wave of nausea, this response to the speed of transformation, the fluidity of American character and the American landscape. I feel at times like a stone hurtling through diaphanous mist, unable to grab hold, unable to slow myself, yet unwilling to abandon the ride I'm on. Down and down I go, where I'll stop, God only knows" (138–139). But we who have finished the novel know where she will stop: California. This is where Jasmine is headed—the state, and state of being, from which the novel is retrospectively narrated.

To arrive in California is of course to arrive in the state not so much of being as becoming, the place on the map where the American myth of self-making is by reputation least hampered by reminders of the heavy drag of history. What the postcolonialists can help us to see about Jasmine's arrival, which prophesies Mukherjee's own arrival in California as a professor at UC Berkeley a few years later, is that it is after all yet another arrival in "America." Accepting the United States as a whole world unto itself, buying into its pluralist self-conception as a nation of nations, Mukherjee would force Raymond Carver's nativist America to open itself to her outspoken otherness, and to accept it as one of the newer of many different forms of American sameness. But in doing so she has allowed that nation of nations to draw a heavily defended border around her literary ambitions. These ambitions did not begin, but always seem to end, in the United States. As she put it in an essay on her own work: "My theme is the making of new Americans."[28] To which the withering postcolonial response, exhaled in a cloud of cigarette smoke, might very well be: is that all?

SUPREME ALIENATION

Let us consider the creative writing workshop as seen from outer space.

This would be to see it in miniature, and in global context, where it is the concern of a relatively small number of people on planet earth but expresses, in condensed and institutionalized form, the aspirations of millions and millions more. They would make their lives meaningful, these humans, and they would make these lives more responsive to their desires. They are the denizens, if not the citizens, of reflexive modernity. Would the workshop look, from this vantage point, anything like the bus chugging through the night in Robert Olen Butler's novel *Mr. Spaceman?*[29]

Sitting at a console in a spaceship far above the earth, the large-eyed, eight-fingered ectomorph alien named (but only for the benefit of his temporary captives) Desi can see all the way down to and into the interior of this lesser vehicle, which happens to be on its way to a casino in Louisiana, U.S.A. Like the bus called Further, but without any Prankster zaniness visible on its carapace, this bus carries a group roughly the size of a typical seminar enrollment—or theater troupe; or saw gang; or army platoon; or therapy group; or, most pertinently, Last Supper party—any one of the long inventory of potentially analogical small groups and *small group meetings* that can help us understand the workshop as a social form. Granted, this group on the bus has no obvious affiliation to any school, and there are many things about the workshop experience it fails to register. But perhaps the problem is only that, in order to consider the creative writing workshop as seen *from* outer space, one must also consider it as being *in* outer space, and visible from a perspective even further alienated from the practice of creative writing than Desi's. From this vantage point it might appear obvious that Desi's "alienation" from the earth is in fact the hyperbolized image of an earthbound institutional relation. It is an image not of institutionality transcended, that is, but of transcendent institutionality.

And sure enough, when the passengers on the bus find themselves transported suddenly to a holding dock on the spaceship, they begin to point unmistakably to their origin in the world of creative writing down below. Of which world their author, Butler, is one of the more prominent inhabitants, being the Francis Eppes Professor of English holding the Michael Shaara Chair in Creative Writing at Florida State University, and a Pulitzer Prize winner to boot. Of which man Desi the friendly alien would seem to be some kind of fantastical self-projection.

Desi has beamed these people up to his ship so he can hear them tell their stories, one by one. He is the ultimate good listener, this alien, with a passionate desire to understand humanity humanistically. Having "the power to recall their voices and bring them inside me, to become the speakers," he will help his visitors to "find a voice to tell of the welter of things inside, to tell of the things that I intently hope will add up to the essence of the creatures of this place" (29). Can we read Desi's pseudo-psychoanalytical narrative elicitation procedures as a version of Butler's own teaching practices? The latter are distinctly therapeutic in flavor, envisioning the writing process as a kind of emotional daring, a valorous defeat of "defense mechanisms." In the teachings collected in the book *From Where You Dream: The Process of Writing Fiction* (2005), Butler instructs his students in ways of dis-identifying with that "part of your mind you've been rewarded for all through school," your "literal memory," and to start *"dreamstorming."*[30] The writerly voice that emerges from this methodically induced trancelike state will, he assures his students, be *"the embodiment in language of the contents of your unconscious"* (32), not the "garbagey analytical reflexive voice" (20) of the critic inside you. More simply, he tells them, good art does not speak with a "metavoice" (19). It "does not come from ideas" (13). This might be taken to confirm Lash's sense of the increasing outmodedness of the clunky cogito in self-reflexive modernity, trading the garbagey "I think, therefore I am" for the more dreamy "I am I."

Here, as so often, creative writing is imagined as an unruly antidote to the Enlightenment rationality that (in theory) governs the normal order of business of research institutions like Florida State, including, needless to say, the analytical efforts of literary scholars. It is imagined as a way of keeping the student-writer, and through him the institution itself, open to "the outside" which is the source of the unpredictable and new. More important, as with literary studies in general, it is a way of keeping the institution *human,* sanctioning efforts to understand the world on the scale of individual psychology—or, rather, the novelistic narration thereof— as opposed to the more specialized scales of attention that operate in, say, microbiology or cosmology or even sociology.[31]

And sure enough, as the abductees are sat down and brought into a trance one by one, they proceed almost immediately to *what really matters,* to the narration of the deeply embedded traumatic events that made them *who they are.* The model for their interactions with their teacher-confessor Desi is established early in the book when the alien replays the testimony he took from an abductee from Kitty Hawk, North Carolina, long ago. She was an elderly woman whose memories had stretched back to the very early part of the twentieth century:

> I think of her and I know she has gone from this life and I draw
> a quivering breath and my fingers wave before me, slowly, as
> if they are under water, like an anemone. I pass one of these
> grieving hands over the console and her voice comes forth and
> I put her inside me.
>
> I am Minnie Butterworth. *Papa would let me go off some days,*
> *just to walk and think and dream. He knew I took things hard.*
> *He wanted me to marry, but I was trying to feel right inside myself*
> *first.* (30–31)

Spoken now by Desi, Minnie's first person story continues until, taking a nap on a hillside, she is awoken suddenly by the sound of a strange machine with wings. *"And at that precise moment no human being had yet ever made a powered flight into the air and I saw the man lying prone in the center of the great lower wing and instantly I wished to be there in his place. Already, I wanted this act for myself"* (33). The essence of Minnie Butterworth's life is thus discovered in the pathos of gender, the early twentieth-century sexism that keeps her, a would-be Wright brother, earthbound, grounded. And as one proceeds to hear from several of the new batch of abductees in turn, various categories of social identity—the gay man, the black man, the working-class white woman, the white male veteran, the Vietnamese immigrant, and so forth—hover over the more or less poignant individuality of their voices. Obviously we are in the reflected presence, even up here in space, of the American system of cultural pluralism, with its familiar protocols of diversity and the proportional representation of identities.

But who could fail to see the link between Minnie's frustrated desire to see the world from on high—to transcend the limits imposed by her identity—and the symbolic satisfaction of that desire in the alien pedagogical figure of Desi? While Minnie voices a desire for self-transcendence, which Desi dutifully records, Robert Olen Butler, through the reflexive medium of his high-flying character, performs that self-transcendence in print. He performs it upon the "stuckness" of Minnie, who transcends herself through him. In fact, the more we look at it, the more it might seem that Desi's literary listening techniques are best understood not in terms of teaching students to express themselves, but as a description of Butler's own distinctly methodical writing process. It stands to reason that in the Program Era, the era of the writer-teacher, these activities would blend, and Robert Olen Butler is perhaps the best contemporary example of a figure in whom they do. If the rise of reflexive modernity occasions the imminent end of the distinction between agency and structure, Butler may be the writer in whom the long-held tension between the literary artist and the institution has likewise dissolved. Desi's activities at his computer-like "console" on the spaceship certainly seem related to Butler's fiction, which frequently takes the form of a more or less virtuosic ventriloquism enacted on the computer screen in his office.

The aesthetic high point of his fiction is *A Good Scent from a Strange Mountain* (1992), the Pulitzer-winner, a story collection in which a number of fictional Vietnamese immigrants to the U.S. speak their often very touching, and always rigorously dignified, personal narratives.[32] This is a fascinating inversion and miniaturization of the more typical Vietnam veteran novel, such as Tim O'Brien's *Going After Cacciato* (1978) or Butler's own *On Distant Ground* (1985), tracing a wholly new set of trajectories in the human fallout from that war. It is also an interesting reflection of Butler's own experiences as an U.S. intelligence officer in Vietnam, where, significantly, he served as a translator of Vietnamese.[33] The *reductio ad absurdam* of this miniaturist method is reached in Butler's recent *Severance: Stories* (2006), in which a flagrantly various series of beings—John the Baptist, Medusa, Cicero, a chicken, Nicole Brown Simpson, Maximilien Robespierre, Valeria Messalina, and the author himself—speak an internal monologue of precisely 240 words after being decapitated.[34] That all of these people and creatures sound somewhat alike—sound, in fact, in their paratactic stream-of-consciousness poeticity, something like William Faulkner characters—is telling, and not only of the imposing shadow of Faulkner that continues to fall upon the fiction of the Program Era. This is not the case with the voices of the Vietnamese in America in *A Good Scent*, whose experiences are seen from story to story to be richly textured and differentiated by age, gender, region, and especially religion. Here in *Severance* it is as though, ramping up the principle of other-inhabitation to such an outlandish extreme, the scaffolding of Butler's abundant artistic self-admiration begins to show through.

As a result of an interesting experiment conducted at Florida State in late 2001, soon after he arrived there from his previous posting in Louisiana, we know more about Robert Olen Butler's writing process than we usually do about such things. Held in Butler's campus office, the event was called "Inside Creative Writing," and it entailed making a video recording of every minute of his composition of a short story. The seventeen sessions, totaling some 30 hours of video, alternated between views of Butler's computer screen and his dreamstorming visage, or sometimes a split view of both at once. These apotheoses of process were broadcast on the local Florida PBS station, as well as posted to the Internet in real time, live, and left there for later discovery by literary historians.[35] As if this weren't "meta" enough, Butler bowed to the necessity of making some sort of show for his patient viewers by providing a running verbal commentary on his various compositional decisions as he went along. It was a veritable orgy of literary observation and self-observation, and the textual product of the event, the short story "This is Earl Sandt," has the distinct feel of a writing exercise designed to elasticize the sympathetic imagination. *Assignment: produce a narrative that fills in the backstory of a vintage postcard scrawled with a terse message penned long ago.*

In fact, something very much like this assignment is described by one of Butler's colleagues at Florida State, Wendy Bishop, whose book *Released into Language: Options for Teaching Creative Writing* (1990) is one of a small handful of systematic considerations of creative writing pedagogy. In a section of suggested exercises for use in the workshop, we find "Postcard Invention II: Figurative Description":

> In this exercise, students are encouraged not only to use what they see in the postcard, but also to use the postcard to trigger their imaginative prose or poetry. Again, I gather up a set of postcards. I try, this time, to find the most evocative set that I can: old postcards, hand-tinted postcards, foreign and regional postcards, cards that have been sent and contain enigmatic messages, and so on. . . .
>
> After finding a postcard that "talks" to him, the writer should write for about ten minutes and describe the scene. It may be the scene he sees in the card, or it may be a scene *evoked* by the card, the message on the card, and so on. He should use all his senses and feel free to add to what he finds on the postcard.[36]

Butler's link to this pedagogical program becomes readily apparent when "This Is Earl Sandt" is read in sequence with the other stories that were eventually collected in *Had a Good Time: Stories from American Postcards* (2005), where the methodical seriality of the whole dreamstorming enterprise becomes clear.[37] In all of these projects it is as though the radical formality and constraint-based creativity of writers like Samuel Beckett or the Oulipo group—in fact, as the viewer of "Inside Creative Writing" learns, Butler obsessively counts his own words as he composes a story—have been coated in homespun sentimentality. Perhaps the key term in Butler's pedagogical lexicon, and one that shows up constantly in his fiction, is "yearning," which is desire plus pathos.

As with Minnie Butterworth, the yearning for freedom from any one earthbound perspective is encoded in this story in the form of an encounter with the early days of aviation, which is itself a redoubling of the modern mobility embedded in and testified to by the postcard form as such. The black and white picture on its face shows a biplane in the sky with a rip in the wing, and the inscription on the back reads simply: "This is Earl Sandt of Erie Pa in his aeroplane just before it fell." Butler places the writer of these lines at the scene of the accident with a mass-produced Brownie camera (the assumption being that he had his own snapshot turned into a postcard), installing an apparatus of observation on the very *ground* of the story in several senses. Here, staring up into the sky, this camera prophesies the coming of the age of omnipresent mediation, the state of affairs Mark Seltzer has called the "media apriori":

> Then there was a movement on the wing. With no particular sound. Still the engine. But there was a tearing away. If I had been Earl Sandt, if I had been sitting in that rattan chair and flying above these bared heads, I might have heard the sound and been afraid.
>
> I lifted my camera. This had nothing to do with the thing happening on the wing. I was only vaguely aware of it in that moment. I lifted my camera and tripped the shutter, and here was another amazing thing, it seemed to me. One man was flying above the earth, and with a tiny movement of a hand, another man had captured him. (74)

Note how the narrator imagines himself momentarily taking Earl Sandt's elevated, Desi-like perspective, only to come safely back down to earth. That oscillation dramatizes the dialectical oscillation of the modern human being as subject and object of observations. As we have seen, the discipline of creative writing *works* this oscillation in the pedagogical making of literary texts. So, too, the "other amazing thing" about modernity that the narrator discovers in this moment of remote control is of a piece with the writing program's democratization of genius as the creativity of the multitude: that the unheroic proliferation of cheap recording technologies is the real story of modernity.

Bharati Mukherjee had attributed her own miniaturist narrative mobility across different domains of experience to her uprooted status as an immigrant. In Butler, we are presented with a different and I think more common kind of alien literary mobility, the "technicity" of the alienated white man. On the model of William Styron's *Confessions of Nat Turner*, but repeated on a small scale over and over again, Butler looses himself from that colorless category in an ostentatiously agile performance of other-inhabitation. Doing so, he testifies to his liberal sympathy with the other, and pledges fealty to the Internationalist ideal of peace through cultural exchange, but he also betrays a potentially aggressive, or at least self-serving, will-to-mastery of the idiom of the other. Consider the amazingly audacious and poignant story from *A Good Scent from a Strange Mountain*, "Mid-Autumn," which begins: "We are lucky, you and I, to be Vietnamese so that I can speak to you even before you are born. This is why I use the Vietnamese language. It is our custom for the mother to begin this conversation with the child in the womb, to begin counseling you in matters of the world that you will soon enter. It is not the custom among the Americans, so perhaps you would not even understand English if I spoke it. Nor could I speak in English nearly so well, to tell you some of the things in my heart. Above all you must listen to my heart. The language is not important" (95). Here, Desi-like, Butler tunes into and "ventriloquizes" the conversation of a Vietnamese mother with her unborn child, "translating" it into English.

It would be hard to imagine a more *culturally intimate* conversation than this one, which takes place "by custom" wholly within the Vietnamese maternal body. Which is of course a large part of the point, since it throws into relief the virtuosity of Butler's performance of narrative mobility, his ability to dive into difference and re-emerge speaking the universal language of the heart. When the mother recounts to her unborn daughter a traditional Vietnamese legend in which an Emperor conceives a "yearning" to go to the moon, we begin to see how this legend corresponds rather uncannily to the author's signature preoccupation with seeing things from above. Even so, the "respect for difference" in this story, as in the collection as a whole, is palpable, taking the form of a refusal of the presumption of interracial desire that had so enflamed critics of Styron's *Nat Turner.* It turns out that this Vietnamese mother once had a Vietnamese lover, only to lose him in the war. Her relation to the white man (presumably an American Vietnam vet with whom she now lives in the U.S.) who shows up at the end of the story is not pathological. It is not *Beloved's* nightmare of mossy teeth. But it is, we take it, merely practical, an accommodation to the traumatic displacements of history. The fictional addressee of this narrative is the "hybrid" child of the modern American present, but she can be expected, by the logic of the story, to become the bearer of the melancholy of a lost cultural wholeness.[38] This wholeness may never have been anything other than imaginary, but it is the state of the art of the system of high cultural pluralism that the emotional consequences of its loss are to be respected.

And Robert Olen Butler is nothing if not state of the art. That is his excellence, and also his averageness, and the source of his ultimate interest for us. Butler's Desi is a dream dreamed by a man of the system, and indeed could be said to personify himself *as* that system. The existential "systematicity" of Desi—the technicity that stands in for ethnicity—is evident in those qualities that have been popularly understood to attach to this particular kind of alien, the so-called "Grey": hairless grey-green skin, big eyes, superior intelligence, a body so small and slight, if excessively cranial and digital, that it is becoming disembodied.

If the crossing of man and machine looks like a robot, the evolutionary crossing of man and "technological system" in a more abstract sense might look like this, with skin like a dead television screen and only the most intelligent body parts, the head and fingers, looming large. We could see him as an insectoid update of that cruel apostle of Enlightenment

Supreme alienation. Illustration by Maxim Vdovichenko / Fotolia.

rationality and thief of mother's milk, Morrison's overseer-schoolteacher. Certainly the Grey alien stands in stark opposition to the earthiest of earthlings in the American racial imaginary, the bosomy black mother. But recoded as "friendly," he now personifies the educational system that, through the medium of creative writing instruction, and to the extent that it doesn't disrupt more important activities, would gladly have every human find her voice. This is the system that, apprised of its own potentially problematic institutionality, finds in creative writing an internal corrective to the impersonality of its technical operations. More specifically, Desi, perched above the earth, could be taken to personify the angelic and/or malefic *observer* native to that system, the imaginary being who confers a certain sameness upon the diverse stories of difference written under his watch. His is the view that sees the world below in reassuring, if intricate, miniature; he is an agent of shame—you live *there?* in *that* house?—but also a beacon of upward escape; to sit with him as he works the controls is to become complicit in what you see below.

But Desi is also simply *money:* that is one way to understand his pop iconicity, his genealogy in the sub-literary world of mass culture, even his grey-greenness. This would be to press our allegorical reading of Robert Olen Butler's alien toward an even greater level of abstraction. Neither a single author nor the creative writing program nor the entire educational system, he is a personification of the global information economy that contains all of them. Fredric Jameson has taught us how difficult it has become to envision social totalities believably, and the goofy ludicrousness of Desi as an alien Jesus might well be understood in this light.[39] This would explain the unaccountable narrowness of his range of vision, the short-circuiting of a truly global vision: in a position to see the whole earth and all of the peoples upon it, that is, Desi sees only America and takes it for the human whole, as if to be an American is no limitation at all. It would be a mistake, though, to think that the best way to critique and correct Desi's alien myopia must necessarily be from the vantage point of the transnational. Indeed, even in his defective universality, Desi points out how the "transnational" perspective is just as narrow, in some ways, as any other.

It would seem narrow, for instance, from the point of view of the *transplanetary* perspective that would subject the puniness of earthling pluralisms of all kinds to the test of the truly alien. If this hyper-cosmopolitan view seems an "unrealistic" perspective to take—or to think one could take—as a cultural critic, it is arguably not much more so, given the continuing claims of nation, than the transnational view. Modestly disclaiming any ability to see things from the universal (literally) perspective, the transplanetary perspective would merely recognize the statistical truth that there must somewhere be forms of intelligent being other than earthling ones.

The great visionary of this perspective is not Robert Olen Butler but Octavia Butler. She was a graduate of the anomalous Clarion Workshops in science fiction writing, begun at Clarion College in the late 1960s and continued as a six-week summer program at Michigan State University and other institutions since then. Not yet having found a space on the regular school year calendar, the Clarion Workshops hearken back in some ways to that forerunner of the creative writing program, the Bread Loaf Writers' Conference, founded in the 1920s as a way to bring established and aspiring writers together in the summer months and indicative of the, at that point, liminal status of creative writing as a scholarly pursuit. Clarion similarly draws attention to the marginality of genre fiction in general, and science fiction in particular, to the creative writing program, where gimmicky works like *Mr. Spaceman,* apart from being bad science fiction, are exceptions to the rule. As one of the more prominent graduates of the Clarion Workshop, and later one of its instructors, Octavia Butler was well placed to perceive how the formation of our individuality in and by the otherness of institutional relations could easily be radicalized in our relation to the truly alien.

Never mind the disorienting implications of a novel like *Kindred* (1979), in which a modern black woman must travel back in time to save the awful white slaveowner who is her ancestor. Butler's story "Bloodchild" (1984), imagining a future in which humans are used by aliens as carriers of their young, presents the theft of maternal labor in the starkest of terms, and the sheer disgust of the humans for the reproductive practices of their alien overlords looks ahead to the same feelings represented in Morrison's *Beloved.* The Xenogenesis trilogy—three novels from the 1980s collected in one volume as *Lilith's Brood* (2000)—takes this idea one step further: in order to survive the devastation wrought by themselves upon the earth, the humans here must begin to crossbreed with the disgustingly sluglike Ooloi who have taken an interest in them. These slimy creatures "have special organs for their kind of observation" that allow them to examine humanity at the cellular and even genetic level, all in preparation for the experimental hybridization of alien and human to create something new and different in the universe.[40] At one point, the heroine Lilith asks permission to look out from the Ooloi ship into space:

"'We're still beyond the orbit of your world's satellite,' it told her as she searched hungrily for familiar continental outlines. She believed she had found a few of them—part of Africa and the Arabian peninsula. Or that was what it looked like, hanging there in the middle of a sky that was both above and beneath her feet. There were more stars out there than she had ever seen, but it was Earth that drew her gaze. Nikanj let her look at it until her own tears blinded her. Then it wrapped a sensory arm around her and led her to the great room" (116). Seen from this perspective, the cultural differences between humans that led them to cataclysmic war look small indeed, and this classic NASA-like glimpse of planet earth cannot help inspiring nostalgia for earthling wholeness. And yet it is the destiny of this heroine to *overcome* her nostalgia for the old wholeness and her disgust for the new hybrid on behalf of a paradoxically posthuman human survival through the Ooloi. This, seen through the visionary magnifying lens of genre fiction, is what it really means to accept the necessity of the otherness of institutionality and of system: as Butler puts it in a sly comment on "Bloodchild": "I tried to write a story about paying the rent. . . . Sooner or later, the humans would have to make some kind of accommodation with their um . . . their hosts."[41]

But of course even Butler's visionary transplanetary perspective, should we succeed in adopting it as cultural critics, would ultimately be discovered to be a limiting one—necessarily so, because any and all perspectives are limiting. It may be the case, for instance, that the ultimate truth of the matter of the creative writing program is something we can only see by looking very closely—at some of its characteristic texts, yes, but perhaps also at its student bodies. What is it in people that makes them want to take classes in creative writing? We could chalk it up to the quality of *Americanness:* perhaps that is the thing, the gift, the affliction, that makes people want to study creative writing in school. Or we could, with Robert Olen Butler, answer it by reference to the universal human "yearnings"—to be loved, to understand ourselves, to have our say—that creative writing tries to satisfy. Or again we could strip away the pathos from this yearning and rediscover, underneath it, what the biologist or Octavia Butler might see: the restlessly seething diversifications of desire. Perhaps the true *subject of creative writing,* the person who can figuratively be said to speak to us from the million acts of self-expression of which the Program Era is the simultaneous product and occasion, is simply this *life force,* this maximal urge to live and create and differentiate.

If so, it will have to answer for the self-evidently disciplinary dimensions of the phenomenon that would seem to run contrary to any vision of unfettered fecundity. Creative writing might after all be a rebellious exercise of Eros, but it is also one that takes pleasure in the limitations of institutionalization. Can't we, if we squint hard enough in the direction of a writing work*shop,* see the afterimage (or rather the prevision) of the work*place* meeting in which the nervous student, like the office worker he is statistically destined to become, makes a presentation? One of the rituals of reflexive modernity, this presentation is always also a presentation of individual excellence, and it is a presentation as much to the presenter himself as to others, a plumbing of personal resources: Have I outstripped the rest? Am I a writer yet?

But it might finally be even simpler than that. To perform in the world is to say "I am," and to say "I am" is the most essential motive of every human performance, no matter how mundane. As an exercise of the imagination, creative writing supplies a special effect of personal agency in that performance, a way of saying not only "I am" but "I am whoever I want to be," which unfortunately I am not.

Afterword: Systematic Excellence

There are worse places for a phoenix to perform its fiery rite.

HUGH KENNER, "Classroom Accuracies"

Having figured out long ago that the point of view from which a story is told is crucially important to its meaning, scholars of literature have naturally been receptive to the insights of modern philosophical perspectivism—to the idea, put simply, that the truth of anything is relative to the position of its observer. And while that association may have been as dubious (since the point of view in fiction is a primarily aesthetic, and not rigorously philosophical, consideration) as it has been irresistible and overdetermined, it has helped to make literary studies an unusually reflexive enterprise, quick to turn on itself and question its own premises. No sooner have we generated a convincing reading of a text than we admit that its truth, its meaning, might look different from a different point of view, and contemplate a wholesale renovation of our methodologies. Perhaps the worst consequence of this elective affinity with perspectivism has been to instill in many literary scholars an aversion to the confident statement of fact, as though these statements could aspire to the authority of an iron law rather than being what they are: an invitation to correction, the sine qua non of lively and instructive debate. Its best consequence has been the unique restlessness with which literary scholars have searched for a rapport with other disciplines—history, linguistics, philosophy, sociology, and on and on—appropriating their insights (or what is taken to be their insights) and bringing them to bear on literature and other forms of cultural representation. Literary studies may be rather fragile at its foundations, but it is for this reason a remarkably agile vehicle for the interdisciplinary satisfaction of curiosity.

Given this constitutive open-mindedness, it is surprising that literary scholars have been so blind to the question of scale. What is the proper scale of literary analysis? As a question in essence of *quantity* and not simply *perspective,* perhaps it sounds too much like an incipient math test for them to care. The nearest we usually come to a direct consideration of the question of scale is in debates about close reading: is that practice, as one of the few competencies proper to literary studies, to be defended against the inattentive abstractions of the sociologists and historians? Or is it rather the outmoded vestige of a gentlemanly reverence for the literary text as an auratic object seeded with deep hidden meanings that only reveal themselves upon close—which is also to say, slow—inspection? Might it profitably be traded for what Franco Moretti has called "distant reading," by which he means, among other things, the subjection of many, many texts (databases) to various kinds of analytical counting, sorting, and explanation?[1] Is this approach too fundamentally at odds with literary experience, with the intimate commerce between reader and book, to really matter? Or is that alienation from literary experience exactly the point?

Questions of scale are also silently at issue in debates about the proper geographical frame of contextualization. As we saw in Chapter 6, since the rise of poststructuralist theory, literary scholars have generally been on the side of excess—not fewer meanings for the literary text but more, always more!—and this has found another expression in the recent rise to glory of the discourse of the "transnational." With its adjacent terminologies of transatlanticism, cosmopolitanism, diaspora, and the like, it offers itself as a critical response to the rhetoric (but also the facts) of capitalist globalization, and is founded on a recognition of the limits of the category that has always been the organizing force of the modern literature curriculum—the nation. Is there something necessary about just *this* frame of analysis of culture? Doesn't it impede our ability to trace the global flow of persons, ideas, and images, and institutionalize a certain narrow-mindedness on our part? Perhaps, but it is characteristic of the cognitive expansionism of literary studies—a panic response, it may be, to anxieties about its irrelevance in the world at large—that most of its energy has been invested in extending outward from the nation rather than inward to the regions and localities, not to mention the institutions, that are equally corrective to the thoughtless assumptions of disciplinary nationalism. The campus or classroom is after all a kind of geographical space, however small, and to contextualize a literary work in relation to one can be as telling as connecting it to the global cultural flow.

But whether it is as traditional as something like close reading, or as fashionable as something like transnationalism, the commitment to one scale of analysis over another on the part of any given literary critic is usually intense enough that the question of scale *as such* never even arises. Perhaps, if it did, it would seem absurd to want to grant one scale of analysis priority over another, as absurd as it would be to grant priority to microbiology over astrophysics, or vice versa. There is, in other words, no one proper scale of literary analysis. It's a fairly basic point, but one worth underlining: not only do different perspectives yield different appearances of truth, but different scales of analysis can be differently insightful. Here, too, just as with the question of narrative perspective, this is not something that literary studies needs to import wholly from without, but something already waiting to be discovered in literary texts themselves. Scale can first of all be considered as a spatio-temporal feature of aesthetic objects. The latter, as we have seen at various points throughout this book, may simply be a question of material form: what does it matter that short stories are relatively small while novels are relatively big? Or it may be a question of linguistic-representational mode: can we speak of the distribution of twentieth-century fiction along a scalar continuum from minimalism (understatement) to miniaturism (condensation) to maximalism (elaboration)? What links, if any, can be drawn between literary form and the work's presumed scale of address? Is the question of aesthetic scale attached in some meaningful way to the question of cultural minorities and majorities? Although none of them have been conclusively answered, these and other questions of scale have been worth asking.

Alongside and in addition to a consideration of these relatively "objective" quantities of culture, we might take them as an inspiration to meditate upon the question of scale as a matter of critical perspective. "Everything said is said by an observer," says systems theory.[2] If that observer is human, we know that he or she falls somewhere within a corporeal span of roughly one to seven feet, but we also know that this body is the seat of an extraordinarily elastic temporal and spatial *attention span*. If that observer is an institution—a corporate body larger and longer-lived than any one of its human members—that span can be even greater. Be it microcosmic or cosmic, a millisecond or a light year, a scene from distant childhood or a faculty meeting the day after tomorrow, the sheer variability of scales of attention in human life has been given short shrift in recent criticism, which errs when it thinks that one or another can claim an a priori privilege in the multi-scalar project of literary and cultural analysis. We can close-read or contextualize at various geographical scales; we can consider one text or many; we can track cultural developments in a certain "historical moment" or across the centuries: given that the attention span of criticism is highly variable, what might a self-consciousness of the question of scale bring to our critical practice?[3]

My approach to the question of scalar variability in the analysis of culture has been made abundantly evident in the preceding chapters, but it is also prefigured in the work of one of the premier minimalist writers of the second generation, George Saunders. Like Raymond Carver before him, Saunders teaches creative writing at Syracuse University, and his output of short stories, most of them published in the *New Yorker,* can be thought of as the crossing of Carver's lower-middle-class "loser" aesthetic with some of the surreal craziness and violent public-sphericity (if I may) of Donald Barthelme. Saunders's curious novella *The Brief and Frightening Reign of Phil* (2005) tells of the rise to power of a murderous, mediocre dictator in the nation of Outer Horner.[4] Nothing is surprising about that rise—his persecution of the neighboring people of Inner Horner, his demagogic manipulation of the national pride of the Outer Hornerites, his gradual descent into ungrammatical megalomania are all too familiar—except that the world in which it occurs is very, very small. Indeed it is absurdly small, as though something quite strange has been done to our usual conceptions of geographical scale. In fact, only one Inner Hornerite can stand in the nation of Inner Horner at a time, forcing the other handful of citizens of this country to stand in the Short Term Residency Zone in Outer Horner. Outer Horner itself, though larger, is not that all that large, fielding a militia that consists only of Freeda, Melvin, and Larry. No wonder, then, that the reign of the awful Phil will be a brief one: spatially and temporally, everything here has been compressed.

Part of Saunders's point in imagining this risibly small "geopolitical" arena is of course to produce an effect of simplifying estrangement, a Petri dish parable in which we can view the sinister spores of nationalist chauvinism beginning to grow. But it also radicalizes and thematizes the question of scale that had always attached to the project of literary minimalism in the Carver tradition, with its general preference for short-short stories about ordinary people and their strictly personal concerns. In doing so, Saunders is able to apply critical force in two opposing directions. On the one hand, he allows us to see in retrospect how each Carver character had in a troubling sense been a citizen in a nation of one, and how program fiction might expand its domain of concern and reclaim a properly political, or at least cultural-critical, consciousness. On the other hand, he engages the minimalist aesthetic with some of the absurd expansiveness of contemporary discourses of the global and the transnational, cutting these discourses, as we say, down to size. Indeed, as two huge hands descend from above at the conclusion of the novella to reshuffle the world and reshape its mechanical toy inhabitants, who awake in the soon-to-be-troubled land of New Horner, their world seems to be about the size of a desktop—the scene, that is, of the manual-intellectual labor of writing or typing. At this scale, revolution looks more like revision, and the limited purview of the observer (in this case the writer or the reader) becomes perfectly clear. So what is on the one hand an exercise in silly political surrealism is, on the other hand, a way of "getting real" by getting small.

Something of the same double motive has been at work in my attempt to locate postwar fiction in the university, where it cannot help engaging with the larger economies and histories that institution inhabits, but where it also cannot help being limited in that engagement. That limitation, in the form of the writer's protection from market forces, is part of the point, and it would be a given in any case. The assemblage of literary methodologies that have been brought together in this book to describe and explain this constitutive inside-outness, from the close reading of literary texts to the imposition of the transplanetary frame, from the more or less subtle registration of biographical individuality to the insulting simplicity of the diagram, has likewise been designed to avoid the literary critical version of what Bruno Latour identifies as the common mistake that social scientists make when they "use scale as one of the many variables they need to set up *before* doing the study." In doing so, they deprive themselves of the ability to range alongside the human behavior they wish to explain, which leaps in its domain of reference from "the whole of humanity, France, capitalism, and reason while, a minute later, [settling] for a local compromise."[5] It is thus with a keen sense of the arbitrariness of the question, the particularity of its scale, that I ask what, finally, does the discipline of creative writing mean to the university? I might just as easily have asked what it means to humanity, or to the state of California, or to certain kinds of writers, or to readers like you.

Inheritor of the New Critical positioning of aesthetic value as something that might be produced, as well as appreciated, in an academic environment, the discipline of creative writing is an odd but, to all appearances, healthy duck. With its penchant for specialized vocabularies and familiarity with the less-traveled regions of the library, literary scholarship is at least partly in sync with the scientism of its wider institutional environment, the research university. Creative writing, by contrast, might seem to have no ties at all to the pursuit of positive knowledge. It is, rather, an experiment—but more accurately, an exercise—in subjectivity. The very genre that would seem to bind the arts and sciences at the level of theme, science fiction, is only minimally represented in the creative writing program establishment. Privileging ideas and adventures over disciplined elevations of literary form, this genre is often brainy but is only rarely considered literary. Furthermore, commercially successful writers have little financial incentive to seek the patronage (that is, don the shackles) of the university. What role, then, is the creative writer playing there?

One way to answer this question is, first, to ask another question: If the sprawling modern university is an assemblage of centrifugal pluralisms—of splintered knowledges, divergent research agendas, and multiplying bureaucratic expressions of cultural and other forms of difference—how does the system hold together? Once it was supposed to be the domain of culture, the quasi-sacred Arts, which offered the secular institution an avenue back to the Unity of specialized knowledges in God, but no longer. Nor has a unity founded in national purpose, expressed in the intellectual exploration of a national culture, been the prize possession of the American university, even during the Cold War, when American Studies was at its strongest. The typically strong regional and state affiliations of American higher educational institutions—the U.S. does not even have a national university—and the tendency to oppositional liberal intellectualism confirmed in the rise of the "transnational" as a positive critical value have meant that their most impressive contributions to the nation *qua* nation have taken the form of technical assistance. (That assistance has of course been massive, and very well paid.) In his compellingly bleak and extremist analysis of the situation, *The University in Ruins,* Bill Readings suggests that the new God of the university is "excellence":

> Generally, we hear a lot of talk from University administrators about excellence, because it has become the unifying principle of the contemporary University. C. P. Snow's "Two Cultures" have become "Two Excellences," the humanistic and the scientific. As an integrating principle, excellence has the singular advantage of being entirely meaningless, or to put it more precisely, non-referential. [. . .]
>
> Today, all departments of the University can be urged to strive for excellence, since the general applicability of the notion is in direct relation to its emptiness.[6]

The University that Readings describes is one that has begun instead to behave like a corporation, integrating new management techniques and market valuations into its wholly self-referential, self-reproducing practices.[7] In this scheme, excellence is the "integrating principle that allows 'diversity' (the other watchword of the University prospectus) to be tolerated without threatening the unity of the system."[8] A "unit of value entirely internal" to that system, marking "nothing more than the moment of technology's self-reflection," it is a sign, above all, of bureaucratic efficiency, the smooth running of the pluralist machine.

Readings is right to see excellence as the new God of the university, and as a marker of institutional self-reflection, but he is crucially wrong, I think, in seeing it as a measure of bureaucratic efficiency alone. For one thing, as his own documentation shows, the rhetoric of excellence in the university tends to appear in contexts where what is at issue is competition—say, between one funding application and another—or reputation, as in the hierarchically arranged schools in the *U.S. News and World Report* rankings. If this is not yet "referential" to something wholly outside the educational system itself, it is nonetheless profoundly and importantly *relational,* a measure of relative "distinction" which, among other effects, cashes out in the workplace as the relative value of a degree from a given institution. In the early twentieth century Thorstein Veblen had a lot to say about the orientation of higher education toward business interests that resonates even now in Readings's account of the university in ruins; but Veblen, even more importantly, drew our attention to the excessive symbolic activity (that is, showing off) entailed in the creation and maintenance of such invidious distinctions. Knowing this, we should be on guard against assuming that appeals to excellence are, as Readings claims, a matter only of technocratic efficiency.[9]

On the contrary, taking off from his observation that the university increasingly functions as an "autonomous system" with little direct involvement in extracurricular agendas, we might say that the "excellence" of the university is an index not of its functional efficiency but of its more or less impressive capacity to waste. Excellence in this view is a primarily aesthetic term, the guise in which judgments of beauty-as-superiority reappear in an otherwise efficiency-oriented university environment. Readings is wrong, therefore, to say that the disappearance of a referential appeal to national culture has occasioned the "ruin" of the traditional university in our time, at least in the United States. Indeed, insofar as American culture has become a corporate culture, the rhetoric of excellence could be understood as a deep expression of that national culture, and seems for now to be holding educational institutions together fairly well.

It is safe to say, then, that creative writing in the university will exist as long as it seems simply too excellent to resist. The ideologues of science can make no effective arguments against this excellence, a form of beauty they worship every bit as fervently and irrationally as do the arts. Still less can academic administrators afford to be insensitive to the beauty of excellence; they often must judge the value of highly specialized research at second hand, by measuring the evidence of its relative prestige. Not only this, but an impressive creative writing program can be had for what amounts, as against particle accelerators and the like, to chump change, much of which is returned (as with Master's programs in general) in the form of healthy tuition payments. Thus, while creative writers in the university have often perceived themselves as outsiders to the institution that houses them, it is not hard to enumerate, as I have done throughout this book, their uses beyond the obvious one of teaching students something about writing. Inwardly, their job as teachers is to stand as inspiring exemplars of the unalienated laborer. In this sense, every artist on campus is half a performance artist: making his name, doing his job, owning the product of his labor of "self-expression," the artist or writer-in-residence is in a sense the purest version of the kind of worker, the white-collar professional, that so many college students are preparing to be.[10] Alternatively, but relatedly, they can be seen as offering a form of therapy to some of these students, the "creative types," in advance of their lifelong capture by the usual cubicle. Outwardly, the task of the academic creative writer is to produce, in her writings, unconscious allegories of institutional quality, aesthetically pure because luxuriously useless. More simply, these writers contribute a certain form of prestige to the university's overall portfolio of cultural capital, adding their bit to the market value of the degrees it confers. In this role they are somewhat like varsity athletes, but whereas varsity athletics typically symbolizes the excellence of competitive teamwork, creative writing and the other arts testify to the institution's systematic hospitality to the excellence of individual self-expression.

And isn't postwar American fiction, after all, unprecedented in its excellence? If I could, I would ask this concluding question with two voices in counterpoint, and only one of them sarcastic. The conservative modernism of T. S. Eliot and his ilk has ingrained in us the notion that art never improves; and judgments of postwar American literature, including critiques of the writing program, habitually see it in sad decline from the heroic heights of the as-yet-unprogrammed interwar modernist era.

But perhaps, in the interest of dislodging some tedious prejudices, and for love of the educational system that has made most of us what we are, or maybe just for the fun of it, it's time to resist this notion. One way to do so would be to crudely convert historical materialism into a mode of aesthetic judgment, putting literary production in line with other human enterprises, such as technology and sports, where few would deny that systematic investments of capital over time have produced a continual el-

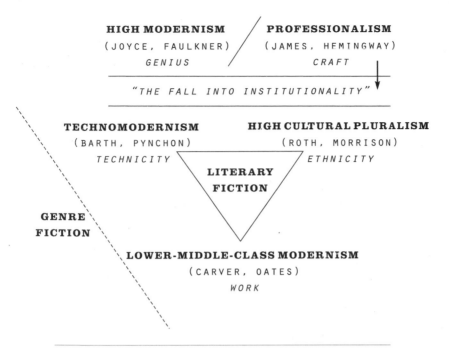

Modernism declines into the Program Era through the conduit of craft—but is this "fall" into institutionality really so unfortunate?

evation of performance. Granted, there is no way for a literary scholar, these days, to engage in strenuous aesthetic appreciation without sounding goofily anachronistic, so call the effort what you will. Call it a strategic triumphalism. Because of the tremendous expansion of the literary talent pool coincident to the advent of mass higher education, and the wide distribution, therein, of elevated literary ambitions, and the cultivation in these newly vocal, vainglorious masses of the habits of self-conscious attention to craft through which these ambitions might plausibly be realized, is it not true that owing to the organized efforts of the program—to the simple fact of our trying harder than ever before—there has been a system-wide rise in the excellence of American literature in the postwar period?

Of course, we can only measure literary excellence on our own terms, and the task of elevating individual authors high above their numerous accomplished peers has become increasingly difficult. This may have produced, as with the disappearance of the .400 hitter in professional baseball, a kind of optical illusion of encroaching mediocrity: being the dominant figure in Shakespeare's or even Pound's time was, by comparison to today, easy as pie.[11] But laying aside our anachronistic prejudices for the One over the Many Ones, moving our minds from the Pound Era into the Program Era, do we not bear daily witness to a surfeit of literary excellence, an embarrassment of riches? Is there not more excellent fiction being produced now than anyone has time to read?

What kind of traitor to the mission of mass higher education would you have to be to think otherwise?

Notes

Introduction: Halls of Mirror

1. Simon Karlinsky, ed., *Dear Bunny, Dear Volodya: The Nabokov-Wilson Letters, 1940–1971,* revised and expanded ed. (Berkeley: University of California Press, 2001), 300. Quoted in Brian Boyd, *Vladimir Nabokov: The American Years* (Princeton: Princeton University Press, 1991), 211. The novel was of course *Lolita* (1955). Vladimir Nabokov, *The Annotated Lolita,* ed. Alfred Appel, Jr. (New York: Vintage, 1991).

2. Karlinsky, ed., *Dear Bunny,* 293.

3. Nomi Tamir Ghez has shown how carefully Humbert's author ironizes his rhetoric "from behind." See Ghez, "The Art of Persuasion in Nabokov's *Lolita,*" in Ellen Pifer, ed., *Vladimir Nabokov's Lolita: A Casebook* (New York: Oxford University Press, 2003), 17–37.

4. D. G. Myers, *The Elephants Teach: Creative Writing Since 1880* (Englewood Cliffs, N.J.: Prentice-Hall, 1996).

5. Vladimir Nabokov, *Strong Opinions* (New York: Vintage, 1990), 114. Subsequent page references will be given in the text.

6. The example set by the Federal Writers' Project and other New Deal initiatives along that line was no doubt instrumental in establishing the legitimacy of its own form of institutional support for artistic production. On the latter see, for instance, Michael Szalay, *New Deal Modernism: American Literature and the Invention of the Welfare State* (Durham: Duke University Press, 2000).

7. Jakobson's apocryphal quip provides the epigraph (and title) to Myers's *The Elephants Teach.* A differently worded version is quoted in Boyd, *Vladimir Nabokov: The American Years,* 303.

8. See Robie Macauley, *The Disguises of Love* (New York: Curtis Books, 1952); Philip Roth, *The Professor of Desire* (New York: Vintage, 1994); Michael Chabon, *Wonder Boys* (New York: Villard, 1995); John L'Heureux, *The Handmaid of Desire* (New York: Soho Press, 1996); Francine Prose, *Blue Angel: A Novel* (New York: Harper Perennial, 2001). One could also include Nabokov's own *Pale Fire* (1962) in this list, since the scholarly activities of Kinbote are constantly shown to be compromised by his homosexual de-

sires, which Nabokov clearly wants us to see as further evidence of Kinbote's fundamental narcissism. See Vladmir Nabokov, *Pale Fire* (New York: Berkeley, 1968).

9. Rick Moody, "Writers and Mentors," *The Atlantic Monthly,* Fiction Issue (Summer 2005) *http://www.theatlantic.com/doc/200508/moody.*

10. Vladimir Nabokov, *Lectures on Literature* (San Diego: Harvest, 1982), 3. Subsequent page references will be given in the text.

11. His efforts to get his students to *see* what the text imagines—often by use of diagrams—should be placed against the backdrop of the increasingly bright blare of the mass visual culture so seductive to *Lolita*'s little girl.

12. The same caution guided Nabokov's most sustained scholarly project, an English translation of Pushkin's *Eugene Onegin* so literal as to make the poem all but unreadable. His aim, it seems, was not so much to translate the poem as to protect it from translation, that is, from the potentially competing artistry of the translator.

13. Nabokov operated on just such an assumption of the lucid self-knowledge of geniuses and famously despised psychoanalysis, the theoretical domain in which the idea and analysis of unconscious intentionality is most highly elaborated.

14. Vladimir Nabokov, *Bend Sinister* (New York: McGraw-Hill, 1974); Nabokov, *Pnin* (New York: Anchor-Doubleday, 1953).

15. Appel, Introduction to Nabokov, *The Annotated Lolita,* xxvi.

16. See, for instance, Terry Eagleton, *The Ideology of the Aesthetic* (Oxford: Wiley-Blackwell, 1991); Donald Barthelme, "Not-Knowing," in Barthelme, *Not-Knowing: The Essays and Interviews of Donald Barthelme* (New York: Random House, 1997), 11–26.

17. Quoted in Boyd, *Vladimir Nobokov: The American Years,* 218.

18. "Every man a king" was the slogan of Louisiana's populist governor, Huey P. Long.

19. Ulrich Beck, Anthony Giddens, and Scott Lash, *Reflexive Modernization: Politics, Tradition and Aesthetics in the Modern Social Order* (Stanford: Stanford University Press, 1994).

20. Ibid., 114.

21. C. Wright Mills, *White Collar: The American Middle Classes* ([1951]; New York: Oxford, 2002), 76; Christopher Newfield, *Ivy and Industry: Business in the Making of the American University, 1880–1980* (Durham: Duke University Press, 2003), 12.

22. See Andrew Hoberek, *The Twilight of the Middle Class: Post-World War II American Fiction and White-Collar Work* (Princeton: Princeton University Press, 2005), 6.

23. William R. Paulson, *The Noise of Culture: Literary Texts in an Age of Information* (Ithaca: Cornell University Press, 1988).

24. Thomas Frank, *The Conquest of Cool: Business Culture, Counterculture, and the Rise of Hip Consumerism* (Chicago: University of Chicago Press, 1998); see also Luc Boltan-

ski and Eve Chiapello, *The New Spirit of Capitalism,* trans. Gregory Elliott (London: Verso, 2007).

25. B. Joseph Pine II and James H. Gilmore, *The Experience Economy: Work Is Theatre and Every Business a Stage* (Boston: Harvard Business School Press, 1999).

26. Dean MacCannell, *The Tourist: A New Theory of the Leisure Class* (New York: Schocken, 1989), 23.

27. Anna Leahy, "Creativity, Caring, and the Easy "A": Rethinking the Role of Self-Esteem in Creative Writing Pedagogy," in Kelly Ritter and Stephanie Vanderslice, eds., *Can It Really Be Taught? Resisting Lore in Creative Writing Pedagogy* (Portsmouth, N.H.: Boynton/Cook, 2007), 56.

28. The complexities of Humbert's unreliability are laid out in James Phelan, "Estranging Unreliability, Bonding Unreliability, and the Ethics of *Lolita,*" *Narrative* 15:2 (May 2007), 222–238.

29. David Fenza, "About AWP: The Growth of Creative Writing Programs" (AWP, 2007), 2. *www.awpwriter.org/aboutawp/index.htm.*

30. Appel, *The Annotated Lolita,* lix.

31. John Irving, *The World According to Garp* (New York: Pocket Books, 1979), 457. One of the more interesting differences between John Irving and T. S. Garp is that the latter didn't attend, as Irving did, the Iowa Writers' Workshop, and never holds, as Irving briefly did, a professorship in English. To deprive his character of his own schooling is, we can surmise, to make him more interesting, less a product of the kind of institutions and more a product of "life itself."

32. Charles Caramello's way of putting this is to say that, while postmodern fiction sometimes questions the integrity of the book and the authorial self in a way that parallels the skeptical assertions of poststructuralism, it simultaneously "resists" that skepticism; as does, the literary historian needs to add, every other institutional agency in any way connected with literature. Charles Caramello, *Silverless Mirrors: Book, Self and Postmodern American Fiction* (Tallahassee: University of Florida Press, 1983).

33. Richard Florida, *The Rise of the Creative Class, and How It Is Transforming Work, Leisure, Community, and Everyday Life* (New York: Basic Books, 2002). See also John Howkins, *The Creative Economy: How People Make Money from Ideas* (London: Penguin Global, 2002).

34. Raymond Williams, *The Long Revolution* (London: Chatto and Windus, 1961), 19.

35. Alfred Kazin, *The Inmost Leaf: A Selection of Essays* (New York: Harcourt, 1956), 244.

36. Jay McInerney, "Raymond Carver: A Still, Small Voice," *New York Times,* August 6, 1989.

37. Fenza, "About AWP," 1.

38. The professional difficulties encountered by the Fugitive-Agrarians, who in fact harbored an intense bitterness toward the institution to which they are famously joined in literary history, is recounted in Paul K. Conkin, *The Southern Agrarians* (Knoxville: University of Tennessee Press, 1988).

39. David Fenza, "A Letter from the AWP's Director," in *AWP Director's Handbook: A Compendium of Guidelines and Information for Directors of Creative Writing Programs* (AWP, 2006), 1. *www.awpwriter.org/membership/dh_2.htm.*

40. As Myers notes, the formation of the AWP in 1967, coming some 80 years after the formation of the Modern Language Association, marks an important moment of professional consolidation in the history of creative writing programs. Founded in 1883, the MLA by contrast claims "over 30,000 members in 100 countries." See *www. mla.org/about.* By way of comparison to AWP's 305 graduate programs: in 2003–04 there was a total of 591 U.S. institutions offering either an M.A. (428) or a Ph.D. (143) in English literature. In 1991–92 that number had been 549. This represents an increase of 7 percent, as compared to a 39 percent increase in the number of creative writing programs over the same period. This picture of rapid numerical convergence looks much different on the undergraduate level. As of 2004 there were some 86 institutions that offered a B.A. in creative writing, while there were 1,222 offering a B.A. in English. These figures are made available by the National Center for Education Statistics: *nces. ed.gov/programs/digest/d05/tables/dt05_255.asp?referrer=report.*

41. Mainly focused on the six decades leading up to World War II, Myers's *The Elephants Teach* is to my knowledge the best account of the historical emergence of the ideas and institutions of creative writing instruction in the U.S., and has been of great help in establishing the background of my project here. Some initial steps toward an analysis of the postwar writer's relation to the university are taken in Ben Siegel, ed., *The American Writer and the University* (Newark: University of Delaware Press, 1989). A theoretically assertive account of the workshop is available in Donald Morton and Mas'ud Zavarsadeh, "The Cultural Politics of the Fiction Workshop," *Cultural Critique* (Winter 1988–89), 155–173, which argues that the writing program's commitment to realism betrays its efforts to "keep intact the legitimacy of bourgeois values" (159). The weakness in this left-formalist argument is not in the claim that the writing program is a bourgeois enterprise, which it most certainly is, but in the assumption that anti-realist fiction (hardly absent from the writing program establishment in any case) would necessarily be a "non-bourgeois" enterprise.

42. Tom Wolfe, "Stalking the Billion-Footed Beast: A Literary Manifesto for the New Social Novel," *Harper's Magazine,* November 1989, 49.

43. John W. Aldridge, *Talents and Technicians: Literary Chic and the New Assembly-Line Fiction* (New York: Scribner's, 1992), 28.

44. *www.uiowa.edu/~iww/bro-intr.htm.*

45. See for instance M. M. Bakhtin, *The Dialogic Imagination: Four Essays,* trans. Caryl Emerson and Michael Holquist (Austin: University of Texas Press, 1981).

46. Another limitation is methodological: although I have benefited from talking informally to individuals with direct experiences of the authors and programs of which I write, I decided early on to restrict at least this phase of my research to available documentary evidence, leaving a potentially very rich (and no doubt in many cases corrective) oral history dimension of this project for the future.

47. In recent years McCarthy has been affiliated with the quasi-academic Santa Fe Institute for the study of complex systems.

48. Langdon Hammer, "Plath's Lives," *Representations* 75 (2001): 61–88.

49. Kathy Walton, ed., *AWP Catalogue of Writing Programs,* 3rd ed. (Norfolk, Va.: Associated Writing Programs), 2.

50. Max Horkheimer and Theodor Adorno, *Dialectic of Enlightenment: Philosophical Fragments,* trans. Edmund Jephcott (Stanford: Stanford University Press, 2002), 182.

51. This may have been true since the founding of creative writing in Iowa in the 1930s, but one can measure in a more concentrated way the deflation of the spirit of 1960s and 70s experimentalism in the 1987 appearance of the second edition of Janet Burroway's popular textbook, *Writing Fiction: A Guide to Narrative Craft* (Boston: Little, Brown; first ed. 1982), in which she explains that she has "replaced about half the stories, generally in the direction of modern realism. Teachers and students alike consistently felt that the most useful stories for the purpose of this text were in that range, and that those which presented major problems of interpretation distracted from the concentration on technique. For that reason I have expunged some of the quirkiness and experimentalism that I admire" (ix).

52. T. Coraghessan Boyle, "This Monkey, My Back," in Frank Conroy, ed., *The Eleventh Draft: Craft and the Writing Life from the Iowa Writers' Workshop* (New York: HarperCollins, 1999), 9.

53. Quoted in Wendy Bishop and David Starkey, *Keywords in Creative Writing* (Logan: Utah State University Press, 2006), 60.

54. Some of the exceptions are: Joseph M. Moxley, ed., *Creative Writing in America: Theory and Pedagogy* (Urbana, Ill.: NCTE, 1989); Wendy Bishop, *Released Into Language: Options for Teaching Creative Writing* (Urbana, Ill.: NCTE, 1990); Wendy Bishop and Hans Ostrom, eds., *Colors of a Different Horse: Rethinking Creative Writing Theory and Pedagogy* (Urbana, Ill.: NCTE, 1994); Anna Leahy, ed., *Power and Identity in the Creative Writing Classroom: The Authority Project* (Clevedon, U.K.: Multilingual Matters, 2005).

55. Shirley Geok-lin Lim, "The Strangeness of Creative Writing: An Institutional Query," *Pedagogy: Critical Approaches to Teaching Literature, Language, Composition and Culture* 3:2 (2003), 159. But see David Morley's recently published *Cambridge Introduc-*

tion to *Creative Writing* (Cambridge: Cambridge University Press, 2007): if one book could justify the international spread of an academic discipline, this richly rewarding insider's account of what it all means, and how it should be done, might be it.

56. Eileen Pollack, "Flannery O'Connor and the New Criticism: A Response to Mark McGurl," *American Literary History* 19:2 (Summer 2007), 546–556.

57. Karl Shapiro, *Edsel* (New York: Bernard Geis, 1971), 116.

58. See Kelly Ritter and Stephanie Vanderslice, "Introduction: Creative Writing and the Persistence of 'Lore,'" in Ritter and Vanderslice, eds., *Can It Really Be Taught? Resisting Lore in Creative Writing Pedagogy,* xii.

59. John Barth, *Giles Goat-Boy; or, The Revised New Syllabus* (Greenwich, Conn.: Fawcett, 1966), xxii.

60. Ibid., xxii. Note also how the plot of Barth's arguably most important novel, *The Sot-Weed Factor* (1960) [London: Flamingo, 1993], is launched upon the proto-progressive education of its protagonist, who, falling under the influence of Master Burlingame, learns to disregard the "pernicious distinction between learning and other sorts of natural human behavior" (17).

61. Daniel Bell is quoted in Harold Perkin, "History of Universities," in *The History of Higher Education,* 2nd ed., ed. Lester F. Goodchild and Harold S. Wechsler (Boston: Pearson, 1997), 30.

62. John H. Roberts and James Turner, *The Sacred and Secular University* (Princeton: Princeton University Press, 2000), 75–122.

63. John Barth, *Further Fridays: Essays, Lectures, and Other Nonfiction, 1984–1994* (Boston: Little, Brown, 1995), 269.

64. Clark Kerr, *The Uses of the University* [1963], with a Postscript—1972 (Cambridge, Mass.: Harvard University Press, 1972), 136.

65. Hugh Kenner, *The Pound Era* (Berkeley: University of California Press, 1971).

66. Barth, *Further Fridays,* 269.

67. Hughes Mearns, *Creative Youth: How a School Environment Can Set Free the Creative Spirit* (New York: Doubleday, 1928).

68. Kerr, *Uses of the University,* 113; emphasis added.

69. Barth, *Giles Goat-Boy,* 731.

70. A less extreme version of this idea is condensed in the title of Barth's later novel, *Sabbatical: A Romance* (1982).

71. Neal Stephenson, *The Diamond Age; or, A Young Lady's Illustrated Primer* (New York: Bantam, 1995).

72. N. Katherine Hayles, "Flickering Connectivities in Shelley Jackson's Patchwork Girl: The Importance of Media-Specific Analysis," *Postmodern Culture* 10:2 (2000).

73. Shelley Jackson, "Stitch Bitch: The Patchwork Girl," *Paradoxa* 4 (1998), 528.

74. For Kenneth Womack, the satirical campus novel, in bringing together the ques-

tion of judgment and community, becomes an occasion for a post-poststructuralist ethical criticism. Kenneth Womack, *Postwar Academic Fiction: Satire, Ethics, Community* (London: Palgrave, 2002). As evidenced by the detective novels of Amanda Cross or the academic horror stories (literal ones) of James Hynes, the campus novel would also appear to be a genre well paired with other popular genre forms.

75. Mary McCarthy, *The Groves of Academe* (New York: Harcourt Brace, 1992), 225.

76. Saul Bellow, *The Dean's December* (New York: Harper and Row, 1982). What makes a work like Don DeLillo's *White Noise* particularly interesting in this regard—and what no doubt helps to bait so many college teachers into including it in the postwar novel survey—is the way it simultaneously instantiates and transcends this virtually "pre-modern" generic enclosure, representing the advent on the campus of exactly those outside forces—mass media, pollution, history as such—that make the campus novel seem too quaint a form to be taken seriously. While they have not to my knowledge received much attention from students, one could say the same for works like Ishmael Reed's *Japanese By Spring* (1993), Jane Smiley's *Moo* (1995), and Richard Russo's *Straight Man* (1997)—even, at a stretch, David Foster Wallace's "Westward the Course of Empire Makes Its Way" (1990): a fundamental component of each of their comic plots is the intrusion of wider economic realities into the formerly self-contained life of the university.

77. This term was coined by the neuro-physiologist Humberto Maturana to describe the self-making activities of the biological organism, which in his account lives in the solipsistic domain of its own structures of sense perception. See, for instance, Humberto R. Maturana and Francisco J. Varela, *The Tree of Knowledge: The Biological Roots of Human Undertanding,* rev. ed. (Boston: Shambala, 1992). Sociological systems theory borrows the term to describe the self-referential closure of all systems, biological, social, or otherwise.

78. See Niklas Luhmann, *Art as a Social System,* trans. Eva M. Knodt (Stanford: Stanford University Press, 2000), 149.

79. See Mark Seltzer, "The Crime System," *Critical Inquiry* 30 (Spring 2004), 557–583. Notice how, in Stephen King, an obvious desire to be thought "literary" coincides with the obsessive reflexivity of his best-selling horror oeuvre, where novelists are tortured in various ways by their popularity.

80. The utility of this coinage, which I first suggested in "The Program Era: Pluralisms of Postwar American Fiction," *Critical Inquiry* (Fall 2005), has since been independently confirmed by Ira Livingston's engaging *Between Science and Literature: An Introduction to Autopoetics* (Urbana: University of Illinois Press, 2006).

81. Franco Moretti, "Serious Century," in Moretti, ed., *The Novel, Vol. 1: History, Geography, and Culture* (Princeton: Princeton University Press, 2006), 364–400.

82. James Moffett and Kenneth R. McElheny, *Points of View: An Anthology of Short Stories,* rev. ed. (New York: Mentor, 1995).

83. Philip Roth, *The Anatomy Lesson* (New York: Vintage, 1996), 159. Subsequent page references will be given in the text.

84. Ross Posnock, *Philip Roth's Rude Truth: The Art of Immaturity* (Princeton: Princeton University Press, 2006), 21.

85. The reflexivity of Roth's enterprise is broached in S. Lillian Kramer, "Philip Roth's Self-Reflexive Fiction," *Modern Language Studies* 28:3,4 (Fall 1998), 57–72.

86. Other examples include the orthopedist in *The Anatomy Lesson;* Jimmy Herf in *The Counterlife;* and, most elaborately, the Roth-impersonating character Pipik in *Operation Shylock.*

87. Philip Roth, *Zuckerman Unbound* (New York: Vintage, 1996), 159.

88. Philip Roth, *I Married a Communist* (New York: Vintage, 1999).

89. Ronald Sukenick, *Up: A Novel* (New York: Dial, 1968); Joyce Carol Oates, *The Tattooed Girl: A Novel* (New York: Ecco, 2003).

90. The heterogeneous cluster of theoretical endeavors grouped under the term "systems theory" appears to encompass two opposed orientations toward the idea of the system: one emphasizes its self-referential closure and fundamental inability to communicate meaningfully with an environment that merely irritates it; the other emphasizes the fundamental interconnectedness of subsystems in the larger systems that are their shared environment, as popularized in the discourses of globalization and ecology. Since they stem from the same irresolvable paradox, it would be hard to take a principled stance in favor of one of these orientations over the other, though they do seem to lend themselves to distinct descriptive tasks depending on whether the observer, in a given case, sees a need to articulate a difference that makes a difference, or rather to recognize a necessary relation between putatively autonomous entities. Only an approach that oscillates between these two goals, I think, can do justice to the deep collusion of individuality (a form of difference) and institutionality (a structure of relation) in the discipline of creative writing.

91. Esther B. Fein, "Philip Roth Sees Double. And Maybe Triple, Too," *New York Times,* March 9, 1993.

92. Toni Morrison, *Beloved* (New York: Vintage, 2004); Cormac McCarthy, *The Road* (New York: Vintage, 2007).

93. The complex logic of this testimony is astutely analyzed in James Buzard's "On Auto-Ethnographic Authority," *Yale Journal of Criticism* 16:1 (2003), 61–91.

94. Philip Roth, *The Facts* (New York: Vintage, 1988), 59–60.

95. Sandra M. Gilbert and Susan Gubar, *No Man's Land: The Place of the Woman Writer in the Twentieth Century,* 3 vols. (New Haven: Yale University Press, 1988–1994).

96. Werner Sollors, *Beyond Ethnicity: Consent and Descent in American Culture* (Oxford: Oxford University Press, 1986), 174–207.

97. Flannery O'Connor, "The Regional Writer," in O'Connor, *Mystery and Manners: Occasional Prose* (New York: Farrar, Straus and Giroux, 1969), 56.

98. Flannery O'Connor, "The Fiction Writer and His Country," in *Mystery and Manners,* 28–29.

99. See my fuller discussion of this issue in Mark McGurl, "Faulkner's Ambit: Modernism, Regionalism, and the Location of Cultural Capital," *The Novel Art: Elevations of American Fiction after Henry James* (Princeton: Princeton University Press, 2001), 135–157. See also Andrew Hoberek, "Flannery O'Connor and the Southern Origins of Identity Politics," in Hoberek, *The Twilight of the Middle Class,* 95–112.

100. Elizabeth Tallent, "The Big X: Unraveling Mysteries in a Workshop for Fine Writing," *Stanford Today,* March/April 1996. *www.stanford.edu/dept/news/stanfordtoday/ed/9603/9603bigx.html.*

101. Tim O'Brien, *The Things They Carried* (New York: Penguin, 1990), 38.

102. For a sustained critique of the assumed separateness of postmodernism and multiculturalism in the broader theoretical senses of these terms, see Rafael Perez-Torres, "Nomads and Migrants: Negotiating a Multicultural Postmodernism," *Cultural Critique* 26 (Winter 1993–1994), 161–189, which is especially helpful in locating this negotiation in a specific social institution, the university. See also Phillip Brian Harper, *Framing the Margins* (New York: Oxford University Press, 1994), which argues for a convergence of postmodern and minority fiction in the idea of "fragmented subjectivity."

103. For Guillory, "technicity" is a linguistic phenomenon arising from intellectual specialization. See John Guillory, "The Memo and Modernity," *Critical Inquiry* 31 (Autumn 2004), 130. The term is also used by Martin Heidegger (or rather, his translator) in the essay "The Age of the World Picture," in Martin Heidegger, *The Question Concerning Technology and Other Essays,* trans. William Lovitt (New York: Harper, 1977), 115–154. The conjoining of universality and particularity in whiteness is brilliantly elaborated in Robyn Wiegman, "Whiteness Studies and the Paradox of Particularity," *Boundary 2* 26:3 (1999), 115–150.

104. Don DeLillo, *White Noise* (New York: Vintage, 1985), 10. On racial whiteness in the novel see Tim Engles, "'Who Are You Literally?': Fantasies of the White Self in *White Noise*," *Modern Fiction Studies* 45:3 (1999), 755–787. Turning to the scene of the author's upbringing in an ethnically specified, Italian-American neighborhood in the Bronx, and narrating its relation at once to the unmarked collectivity of the crowd and to avant-garde art, DeLillo's *Underworld* (1997) is ironically a more "mainstream" example of the high cultural pluralist aesthetic.

105. DeLillo, *White Noise,* 310.

106. Gordon Lish is quoted in Hal May, ed., *Contemporary Authors,* vol. 117 (Detroit: Gale, 2003), 262. This continued a trend begun earlier in the century, when the emergence of middlebrow institutions like the Book-of-the-Month Club signaled the expansion of a class of persons eager to acquire the habits of high cultural consumption not instilled in childhood.

107. Rita Felski, "Nothing to Declare: Identity, Shame, and the Lower Middle Class," *PMLA* 115; 1 (January 2000), 33.45.

108. Arno J. Mayer, "The Lower Middle Class as Historical Problem," *Journal of Modern History* (1975), 409–436.

109. John Irving, "Stories with Voiceprints," *New York Times,* September 30, 1979. nytimes.com/books/00/05/28/specials/phillips-black.html.

110. Laurie Clancy, "Jayne Anne Phillips," Jrank Biographies. *biography.jrank.org/pages/4660/Phillips-Jayne-Anne.html.*

111. See Jayne Anne Phillips, *Black Tickets* (New York: Vintage, 2001), 21; 11.

112. Hoberek, *The Twilight of the Middle Class,* 21.

113. George D. Stoddard, "Creativity in Education," in Harold H. Anderson, ed., *Creativity and Its Cultivation* (New York: Harper, 1959), 181–182.

114. Nabokov, *Bend Sinister,* 70.

115. Stoddard, "Creativity in Education," 188.

116. See Thomas S. Kuhn, *The Structure of Scientific Revolutions,* 3rd ed. (Chicago: University of Chicago Press, 1996).

117. Anderson, *Creativity and Its Cultivation,* xii.

1. Autobardolatry

1. Thomas Wolfe, *Look Homeward, Angel: A Story of the Buried Life* (New York: Scribner, 1995), 486. Subsequent page references will be given in the text.

2. Indeed, in an advance upon the merely cocksure self-nomination to the status of genius that we find in, say, Gertrude Stein's *Autobiography of Alice B. Toklas* (1933), well-born Eugene wonders in the end if that category isn't becoming a little too crowded for comfort. Muttering "over the names of 21 geniuses who wrote poetry, and 37 more who devoted themselves to the drama and the novel," he asks himself what "can I be, besides a genius? I've been one long enough. There must be better things to do" (494).

3. David Herbert Donald, *Look Homeward: A Life of Thomas Wolfe* (Boston: Little, Brown, 1987), 228.

4. The equal claims of the "bookish" and the free-form "experiential" in Wolfe's

educational formation as a novelist combine to produce the contradiction, first noticed by Wright Morris, that while his fiction would ground itself in the fundamental originality of personal experience, it records an experience that "in substance, was essentially vicarious. He got it from books. He gives it back to us in books." In this sense, one could say that Wolfe's writing is never so deeply, realistically autobiographical as when it is painfully, artificially rhetorical, the very form of his writing serving to redouble its thematic *Bildung* content. See Wright Morris, "The Function of Appetite," in Louis D. Rubin, ed., *Thomas Wolfe: A Collection of Critical Essays* (Englewood Cliffs, N.J.: Prentice-Hall, 1973), 91–96.

5. Harold Rugg, Foreward to Harold Rugg and Ann Shumaker, *The Child-Centered School: An Appraisal of the New Education* (New York: World Book Co., 1928), v.

6. Werner Sollors has argued that concerns for ethnic cultural difference are prefigured in American history by concerns for *regional* cultural difference. See Werner Sollors, *Beyond Ethnicity: Consent and Descent in American Culture* (New York: Oxford University Press, 1986), 174–207.

7. Younghill Kang, *The Grass Roof* (New York: Knopf, 1931), 3.

8. This project—the claiming of an experientially authenticated voice—has recently received a strong critical endorsement and theorization in Paula Moya's recognizably late-progressive (if nominally post-positivist realist), *Learning from Experience: Minority Identities, Multicultural Struggles* (Berkeley: University of California Press, 2002).

9. Hughes Mearns, *Creative Power: The Education of Youth in the Creative Arts* [1929] (New York: Dover, 1958), 5; 24.

10. John Dewey, *Democracy and Education* [1916] (New York: Free Press, 1997), 139, 351.

11. Obviously much of the substance of progressive educational theory has intellectual roots going farther back into the nineteenth century, both in Europe (e.g., Froebel) and the United States (e.g., Bronson Alcott). I refer here to the assembly and systematization of these ideas under the banner of "progressivism."

12. John Dewey, *The School and Society and The Child and the Curriculum* (New York: Dover, 2001), 7. Subsequent page references will be given in the text.

13. Patricia Albjerg Graham, *Progressive Education: From Arcady to Academe, a History of the Progressive Education Association, 1919–1955* (New York: Teacher's College Press, 1967), 9.

14. The potential for a large-scale reversal of the progressive commitment to assimilation in favor of cultural diversity can be located as early as 1916 in the work of Randolph Bourne, whose book-length account of the Gary schools celebrated William Wirt's reconception of classrooms as "workshops where children do interesting things

with their minds, just as in the shops they do interesting things with their hands." It was published in the same year as his prescient cosmopolitan pluralist critique of regnant melting-pot ideologies, "Trans-National America." See Randolph S. Bourne, *The Gary Schools* (Cambridge, Mass.: Houghton Mifflin, 1916), 28, and Randolph Bourne, "Trans-National America," *Atlantic Monthly* 118 (July 1916), 86–97.

15. Stanwood Cobb, *Discovering the Genius Within You* (Cleveland: World Publishing Company, 1932), 4. Subsequent page references will be given in the text.

16. I owe the term "countercultural capital" to Michael Szalay.

17. Greenlaw argues with Foerster directly in his brief for historical scholarly research, as against an insurgent, proto-New Critical emphasis on criticism and appreciation, in Edwin Greenlaw, *The Province of Literary History* (Baltimore: Johns Hopkins University Press, 1931), 16–18. The gist of Greenlaw's argument is pluralist: critics like Foerster, in his account, err by wanting to restrict literary study to one mode, pedagogical, and one manner, critical, while he would generously grant the value of criticism but argue for the additional value of meticulously acquired literary historical knowledge.

18. Koch is quoted in Donald, *Look Homeward,* p. 56. Wolfe was also inspired by the militantly anti-scientific, anti-scholarly teaching style of the charismatic metaphysician Horace Williams, whose classes largely dispensed with reading assignments in favor of *sui generis* discussions of philosophical and moral problems.

19. Richard Walser, *Thomas Wolfe Undergraduate* (Durham: Duke University Press, 1977), 105.

20. Of course, one of the stories implicitly told by every autobiography is "how I became the sort of person who would write an autobiography." The curious thing about a novelistic "portrait of the artist" such as *Look Homeward, Angel,* however, is that even as it claims an essential generic-ontological difference from the author's life, since it is "fiction," the autopoetic element of reflexive circularity is drawn in some ways even tighter than in the straightforwardly autobiographical text. This is true because, to begin with, the *act of writing* that produced the quasi-autobiographical text is not ancillary to an interest in the life, as for instance in the nonfictional memoir of the statesman, explorer, or actor, but rather is continuous with the very source of our interest in the life. Indeed, the task that a work like James Joyce's *Portrait of the Artist as a Young Man* or Wolfe's *Look Homeward, Angel* must set for itself is, by sheer force of narration, to produce literary interest from a relatively ordinary boyhood. This literary interest may then double back, after the celebrated success of the novel itself, to produce an increased interest in the biography, no detail of which is allowed thereafter to count as ordinary, and whose difference from the fiction, however slight, can now become a subject for interpretive debate and speculation. Certainly this is the case with

Wolfe, who, though he paid obsessive attention to the events of his own short life in the several million words of fiction he left behind, has been the subject of no fewer than five full-scale biographies and a handful of partial biographies.

21. What is called for, then, is a sympathetic rotation of the teacher into the mindset of the child, where, as one progressive teacher of the twenties put it, "'you have to feel the thing the child wants to do, to think his thoughts, in short, to become a child yourself'" (quoted in Rugg, *The Child-Centered School*, 229). At its farthest extreme, really only reached in the revival of militant progressivism in the 1960s, this line of thinking begins to undermine the rationale for the very existence of teachers and schools.

22. Which isn't to say that the "Creativists," as they sometimes called themselves, did not care at all for the quality of the works written by their charges; indeed, Hughes Mearns went to great lengths to publish the poetry of his students, promoting its high quality as evidence of the viability of creative writing as an educational endeavor.

23. Immanuel Kant, *The Critique of Judgement,* trans. James Meredith (Oxford: Clarendon Press, 1952), 191; 183.

24. See for instance John Barth, "Can It Be Taught?" in Barth, *Further Fridays: Essays, Lectures, and Other Nonfiction, 1984–1994* (Boston: Little, Brown, 1995), 22–34.

25. See Graham, *Progressive Education,* 24; Stanwood Cobb, *The New Leaven: Progressive Education and Its Effect upon the Child and Society* (New York: John Day, 1928), 3; Hugh Hawkins, *Between Harvard and America: The Educational Leadership of Charles W. Eliot* (New York: Oxford University Press, 1972), 80–119; 224–262.

26. D. G. Myers, *The Elephants Teach: Creative Writing since 1880* (Chicago: University of Chicago Press, 2006), 46; quoted on p. 49.

27. See Wisner Payne Kinne, *George Pierce Baker and the American Theatre* (Cambridge, Mass.: Harvard University Press, 1954).

28. A similarly vocational, if less overtly nationalistic, motive seems to have driven much of the creative writing instruction in fiction that began to appear sporadically in colleges across the U.S. in the early twentieth century, training students to make their living in the booming short story trade.

29. Thomas Wolfe, *Of Time and the River: A Legend of Man's Hunger in His Youth* (New York: Scribner's, 1935), 167–178. Subsequent page references are given in the text.

30. See Mark Seltzer's formulation of the "pathological public sphere" in his *Serial Killers: Death and Life in America's Wound Culture* (New York: Routledge, 1998), where the interaction of individual and group, private and public sphere, can only be represented as the violent opening up of the individual body to public inspection. Francine Prose, *The Blue Angel* (New York: Perennial, 2000), 199.

31. Actually, it's more complicated than that, since the intense attachment he felt to

his own experience was itself, upon close inspection, an attachment to disconnection. Wolfe's original title for *Look Homeward, "O Lost!"*, would have made clear his conception of experience as fundamentally a form of loss, since it must occur in linear time. Writing in this view becomes, not so much a mode of virtual retrieval—of *temps retrouvé*—but an almost physical act of memorialization somewhat akin to his father's "art," which was the engraving of tombstones.

32. Thomas Wolfe, "The Story of a Novel" [1935], reprinted with "Writing and Living" [1938] in Leslie Field, ed., *The Autobiography of an American Novelist* (Cambridge, Mass.: Harvard University Press, 1983), 116.

33. Wolfe, "The Story of a Novel," 40–41.

34. The sheer bulk of his textual production speaks to Wolfe's urge to monumentalize himself as a virtually physical textual presence—a *corpus*. It is perhaps no wonder, then, that critics tend to react not only critically but viscerally to the work, which succeeds uncannily well in simulating the presence of a horribly overbearing person.

35. See Henry James's Preface to *The Awkward Age* (1899): "I remember rejoicing as much to remark this, after getting launched in *The Awkward Age,* as if I were in fact constructing a play: just as I may doubtless appear now not less anxious to keep the philosophy of the dramatist's course before me than if I belonged to his order. I felt, certainly, the support he feels, I participated in his technical amusement, I tasted to the full the bitter-sweetness of his draught—the beauty and the difficulty of . . . escaping poverty *even though* the references in one's action can only be, with intensity, to each other, to things exactly on the same plane of exhibition with themselves. Exhibition may mean in a 'story' twenty different ways . . . and the novel, as largely practiced in English, is the perfect paradise of the loose end." Henry James, *The Awkward Age* (New York: Penguin, 1987), 14.

36. George Pierce Baker, *Dramatic Technique* (Boston: Houghton Mifflin, 1919), 4–5. In some of James's novels from the late 1890s, written just after he gave up trying to transfer his skills as a novelist to the potentially more lucrative London stage, we find narratives like *The Awkward Age* (1899) that, composed predominantly of dialogue, all but converge with the printed form of the play. In his late fiction more generally, as has been discussed by Seymour Chatman, David Lodge, and many others, one sees an attempt at a radical subtraction of the presence of the narrator as an independent personality except as it clings in the third-person narration of the experience of the central focalizing character. This is true even as—reclaiming the specific representational powers of the novel—that experience is internalized as the endlessly ruminative "action" of the character's thinking. While for Baker we "rather expect a novelist to reveal himself in his work" since the novel "may be, and often is, highly personal," the best dramatists "reveal singularly little of themselves" and "the best drama is impersonal" (7).

This is why we know so little about Shakespeare even with the evidence of the many plays. James would no doubt have assented to the claim that fiction—typically taking the form of a single narrative "voice" that he, like Baker, and against subsequent New Critical practice, assumed essentially to be the voice of the author—is highly personal. But the *achieved* "impersonality" of that personal narrative, while it was the inescapable rule of the theater, was for James equally important to good fiction. Neither do we learn much about the personal life of Henry James from the novels of Henry James, except perhaps (and it's not an unimportant exception) that he circulated in a transatlantic upper-bourgeois social milieu. While James adamantly opposed limiting authors to the representation of their own social class, the novelistic aesthetic of observational realism to which he subscribed made it predictable that he would mostly represent the high society that he knew from personal experience. Ventures into distinctly different social milieux, such as we see in *The Princess Casamassima* (1886), required him to do a more active form of research, which is another path to "writing what you know." See for instance David Lodge, Introduction to Henry James, *The Spoils of Poynton* [1897] (New York: Penguin, 1987), 1–16.

37. Quoted in Andrew Turnbull, *Thomas Wolfe: A Biography* (New York: Scribner, 1967), 274–276.

38. Bernard DeVoto, "Genius is Not Enough," *Saturday Review of Literature* xiii (April 25, 1936), reprinted in Rubin, ed., *Thomas Wolfe: A Collection of Critical Essays,* 72–79.

39. Wolfe, "The Story of a Novel," 3.

40. In fact, much of the manuscript of *Of Time and the River* was recast from first to third person at the last minute, and incompletely at that, Wolfe having careened into first person narration at some point during the drafting process.

41. Kang's position became, in effect, a practical embodiment of the Eliotic modernist one, where the authority of "Tradition" is prior to and necessarily frames the "Individual Talent" even as that talent speaks of and from personal experience. Wolfe instead turns this Eliotic structure inside out, imagining his relation to the literary tradition as consumer to consumed.

42. Although it would require a hopelessly naïve construction of biographical truth to do so, it would be interesting to think of individual works of fiction as all having a certain *coefficient of proximity*—greater or lesser—to that biographical truth, and even more interesting if one could then go on to map this information meaningfully onto other structuring elements of the field.

43. At length, this will produce the gothic pathos of the "dark half," as in Stephen King's 1989 novel of this title, where a would-be serious novelist is haunted by his own fantastically successful pen name, which has authored popular fictional killers who re-

fuse to die. A more "literary" example (although it is precisely this distinction that obviously drives Stephen King crazy) would be Philip Roth. After the huge commercial success of *Portnoy's Complaint* (1969), Roth records the experience of being haunted by his own famous alter-persona in the novel *Zuckerman Unbound* (1981).

44. Nella Larsen, *Quicksand and Passing* (New Brunswick, N.J.: Rutgers University Press, 1986), 4. Subsequent page references will be given in the text.

45. Alain Locke, ed., *The New Negro* (New York: Atheneum, 1992), xxv.

46. Robert R. Moton, "Hampton-Tuskegee: Missioners of the Masses," in Locke, ed., *The New Negro,* 325.

47. See for instance George Hutchinson, *The Harlem Renaissance in Black and White* (Cambridge, Mass.: Harvard University Press, 1996).

48. Ann E. Hostetler, "The Aesthetics of Race and Gender in Nella Larsen's Quicksand," *PMLA* 105, no. 1, Special Topic: African and African American Literature (January 1990), 35–46.

49. On Helga Crane as a frustrated (female) artist, see Linda Dittmar, "When Privilege is No Protection: The Woman Artist in *Quicksand* and *House of Mirth,*" in Suzanne Jones, ed., *Writing the Woman Artist* (Philadelphia: University of Pennsylvania Press, 1991), 133–154.

50. Another way to put this is to say that critics of this novel have put too little emphasis on the crossing of the novel's racial and gender themes with the (inter- and intra-racial) question of *class identity.* In this novel we see the complicated intertwining of two conceptions of class identity, a "modern" (post–nineteenth century) one which understands it to derive from the individual's educational, economic, or occupational position (whatever his or her "background"), and a traditional conception of class (tending toward the idea of "caste") where class is derived from the social status, or lack thereof, of one's family. Helga is upper class according to the first conception, but "lowly" according to the second, which in being defined by blood relations is proximate to the question of her racial identity.

51. Cobb, *The New Leaven.* The sixth of the "Seven Principles of Progressive Education" that appeared on the inside cover of the official journal of the Progressive Education Association, *Progressive Education,* from 1924 to 1929 was "Co-operation Between School and Home to Meet the Needs of Child Life." Quoted in Graham, *Progressive Education,* 30.

52. Ernest Poole's novel *His Family* (New York: Macmillan, 1917), winner of the first Pulitzer Prize for fiction, is among other things a sustained meditation on the elasticity and interpenetration of the categories of family, school, and city in the rapidly modernizing New York City of the early twentieth century. At one point the patriarch-protagonist and his progressive educator daughter have a "long talk . . . about her hope

of making her school what Roger envisaged confusedly as a kind of mammoth home, the center of a neighborhood, of one prodigious family" (77).

53. Cobb, *The New Leaven*, 8.

54. The logistics of this confusion of family and school are very similar to those of the "body-machine complex" as discussed in Mark Seltzer's *Bodies and Machines* (New York: Routledge, 1992), where late nineteenth-century American culture is described as simultaneously fascinated by biological and artificial modes of reproduction.

55. Reproduced in Walser, *Thomas Wolfe Undergraduate*, illustration section.

56. Gertrude Stein, *The Making of Americans* (Normal, Ill.: Dalkey Archive, 1995), 34.

57. Quoted in Thomas Clark Pollack and Oscar Cargill, *Thomas Wolfe at Washington Square* (New York: New York University Press, 1954), 40.

58. Matthew Wilson Black, "Creative Writing in the College," in Gertrude Hartman and Ann Shumaker, eds., *Creative Expression: The Development of Children in Art, Music, Literature and Dramatics* (New York: John Day, 1932), 243–252. Subsequent page references will be given in the text.

59. Bourne, *The Gary Schools*, 45.

60. Vardis Fisher, *Thomas Wolfe as I Knew Him and Other Essays* (Denver: Alan Swallow, 1963).

61. John Gardner, *The Art of Fiction: Notes on Craft for Young Writers* (New York: Vintage, 1984), 17.

62. Watt's only concessions to the artist were in the matter of scheduling, conveniently bunching Wolfe's eleven weekly hours of class time together in the afternoon, and in his assurances (in a different context they could easily become threats) that "association in the department here is like a trial marriage which can be annulled almost at will and without any of the disrepute that comes from divorce in social circles" (quoted in Pollack and Cargill, *Thomas Wolfe at Washington Square*, 40; what, if anything, Watt did to enable the writing career of Younghill Kang is unknown to me).

63. Wolfe, "The Story of a Novel," 39.

64. In fact Wolfe spent considerable time in Germany in the 1930s, where the successful translation of *Look Homeward, Angel* made him a celebrity; so did his friend and colleague Younghill Kang, who explained that he "was more popular than the high-nosed American in the Hitler thirties, because I could be mistaken for a Japanese, the only race descended from the gods outside the Aryans." Quoted in the chronological appendix to Younghill Kang, *East Goes West: The Making of an Oriental Yankee* (New York: Kaya, 1997), 406. In less heated moments Wolfe's narrator retreats from proto-genocidal ranting to a mocking sarcasm reminiscent of T. S. Eliot's Sweeney poems: "Would Herrick sing his sweet bird-song to Mr. Shapiro as he roared down to work

each morning in the Bronx Express? Would Miss Feinberg think of Crashaw as she ate her noonday cream-cheese sandwich in the drug store?" (477). That the ironic answer to these sneering rhetorical questions, confirmed by the rise of the New York Intellectuals, most of them Jewish, as the leading American literary critics of the immediate postwar period, would be "yes," could be gathered from Eugene's own reflection, later, that "all of them, even the most unlettered, seemed to have a completely natural unaffected interest and respect for the arts, or for scholarly and intellectual attainment" (497).

65. Wolfe's attitudes toward race are detailed in Paschal Reeves, *Thomas Wolfe's Albatross: Race and Nationality in America* (Athens: University of Georgia Press, 1968). The hateful erotics embedded in Wolfe's representation of teaching are further complicated by his long relationship with Aline Bernstein, whom he referred to as "my dear Jew." This relationship is fictionalized at length in *The Web and the Rock*. Bernstein, who was a successful set designer on Broadway, fictionalizes her relationship with Wolfe in her novel, *The Journey Down* (New York: Knopf, 1938).

66. Horace Kallen, *Culture and Democracy in the United States* (New York: Arno Press, 1970), 43. Subsequent page references will be given in the text.

67. The relation between family and nation in the United States has been explored in various contexts, including for instance Eric Sundquist, *Home as Found: Authority and Genealogy in Nineteenth-Century American Literature* (Baltimore: Johns Hopkins University Press, 1979), and Walter Benn Michaels, *Our America: Nativism, Modernism, and Pluralism* (Durham: Duke University Press, 1995).

68. Harold Loeb, *The Professors Like Vodka* (Carbondale: Southern Illinois University Press, 1974), 21. Subsequent page references will be given in the text.

69. For a fuller account of the logical entailments of identity by ascription, see Amy Gutmann, *Identity in Democracy* (Princeton: Princton University Press, 2003), 117–150.

2. Understanding Iowa

1. Flannery O'Connor, *The Habit of Being: Letters,* ed. Sally Fitzgerald (New York: Farrar, Straus, Giroux, 1979), 385. Subsequent page references will be given in the text.

2. Stanwood Cobb, *Discovering the Genius Within You* (Cleveland: World Publishing Company, 1932), 18.

3. From an unpublished autobiographical sketch written at Iowa, quoted in Jean W. Cash, *Flannery O'Connor: A Life* (Knoxville: University of Tennessee Press, 2002), 38.

4. Norman Foerster, "The Study of Letters," in Foerster et al., *Literary Scholarship:*

Its Aims and Methods (Chapel Hill: University of North Carolina Press, 1941), 26–27. Subsequent page references will be given in the text. On Foerster's role in the formation of the Workshop, see Stephen Wilbers, *The Iowa Writers' Workshop: Origins, Emergence, and Growth* (Iowa City: University of Iowa Press, 1980).

5. James Joyce, *A Portrait of the Artist as a Young Man* (New York: Signet, 1991), 217.

6. Paul Engle, "The Writer and the Place," in Engle, ed., *Midland: Twenty-five Years of Fiction and Poetry Selected from the Writing Workshops of the State University of Iowa* (New York: Random House, 1961), xxv. Subsequent page references will be given in the text.

7. Flannery O'Connor, *Mystery and Manners* (New York: Farrar, Straus and Giroux, 1970), 83; emphasis added.

8. Jeffrey J. Williams, "Introduction," in Williams, ed., *The Institution of Literature* (Albany: State University of New York Press, 2002), 2.

9. For an account of the quarrel between scholars and critics, see Gerald Graff, *Professing Literature: An Institutional History* (Chicago: University of Chicago Press, 1987).

10. As will become clear in what follows, this amounts to saying that more than a little "romanticism" remained in place even upon the rise to dominance of what we tend to think of as the anti-romanticist enterprise of New Criticism. For Wimsatt and Beardsley, "it is not so much a historical statement as a definition to say that the intentional fallacy is a romantic one." It is notable that, while their essay ends up addressing intentionality as a philosophical problem for interpretation, the more central motive of the essay is to question the relevance of intentionality in judging the aesthetic success or failure of the poem. The latter is embodied in workshop practice in the insistence on the author's remaining silent while the class discusses the story "on its own terms," without the author butting in to say "but I meant to . . ." etc. See W. K. Wimsatt and Monroe C. Beardsley, "The Intentional Fallacy," in Wimsatt's *The Verbal Icon: Studies in the Meaning of Poetry* (New York: Noonday, 1954), 6.

11. Caroline Gordon, *How to Read a Novel* (New York: Viking, 1957), 18–19.

12. O'Connor, *Mystery and Manners,* 128; 140.

13. Sarah Gordon, *Flannery O'Connor: The Obedient Imagination* (Athens: University of Georgia Press, 2000).

14. Michel Foucault, *Discipline and Punish: The Birth of the Prison,* trans. Alan Sheridan (New York: Vintage, 1979), 194.

15. O'Connor, *Mystery and Manners,* 170.

16. Ibid., 40. O'Connor is known to have read Richard Chase's *The American Novel and Its Tradition* (1957), which theorizes an American preference for the "romance-

novel" over the realist novel regnant in England. See Fitzgerald, ed., *Habit of Being*, 408.

17. Rosemary Magee, ed., *Conversations with Flannery O'Connor* (Jackson: University Press of Mississippi, 1987), 71.

18. Flannery O'Connor, *Collected Works* (New York: Library of America, 1988), 732. Subsequent page references to this story will be given in the text.

19. Wilbur Schramm, *The Story Workshop* (Boston: Little, Brown, 1938), 3.

20. Ibid., 4.

21. O'Connor, *Mystery and Manners*, 38.

22. See Cash, *Flannery O'Connor*, 80.

23. See Frederick Asals, *Flannery O'Connor: The Imagination of Extremity* (Athens: University of Georgia Press, 1982); Katherine Hemple Prown, *Revising Flannery O'Connor: Southern Literary Culture and the Problem of Female Authorship* (Charlottesville: University Press of Virginia, 2001), 41.

24. O'Connor, *Mystery and Manners*, 29.

25. Ibid., 100.

26. In response to an earlier and shorter version of these arguments, Eileen Pollack lays out this reading of the story—Miss Willerton as sexual fantasist—in exhaustive detail. Taking that level of meaning for granted, my purpose here to is to explore the opposite but corresponding erotics of the satirical rejection of this self-centered fantasy on the part of O'Connor as author. See Eileen Pollack, "Flannery O'Connor and the New Criticism: A Response to Mark McGurl," *American Literary History* 19:2 (Summer 2007), 546–556.

27. O'Connor, *Mystery and Manners*, 74, 98.

28. Alfred Kazin, "Flannery O'Connor: The Complete Stories," *New York Times Book Review* 28 (November 1971), 1; 22; reprinted in Melvin J. Friedman and Beverly Lyon Clark, eds., *Critical Essays on Flannery O'Connor* (Boston: G. K. Hall, 1985), 60–62.

29. R. V. Cassill, *Writing Fiction* (New York: Pocket Books, 1962), 206.

30. Cleanth Brooks and Robert Penn Warren, *Understanding Fiction*, 2nd ed. (New York: Appleton-Century-Crofts, 1959), x.

31. Wilbers, *The Iowa Writers' Workshop*, 3–18.

32. Ibid., 120.

33. Quoted in ibid., 86.

34. These positions correspond roughly to the "two separate paths" to the study of institutions in political science. The first identifies the institution as a "strategic response to collective action problems," while the second emphasizes the "role of prior choices, common norms, and culture" in laying out a framework for action. See Karol Soltan, Eric M. Uslaner, and Virginia Haufler, "New Institutionalism: Institutions and

Social Order," in Soltan, Uslaner, and Haufler, eds., *Institutions and Social Order* (Ann Arbor: University of Michigan Press, 1998), 3.

35. David Marion Holman, *A Certain Slant of Light: Regionalism and the Form of Southern and Midwestern Fiction* (Baton Rouge: Louisiana State University Press, 1995), 7–24.

36. Consider for instance the continued existence of the Fellowship of Southern Writers, whose mission is to "recognize and encourage literature in the South through commemorating outstanding literary achievement, encouraging young writers through awards, prizes and fellowships, recognizing distinction in writing by election to membership, and through other appropriate activities." See *http://thefsw.org/*.

37. Allen Tate, *Essays of Four Decades* (Chicago: Swallow Press, 1968), 535. Subsequent page references will be given in the text.

38. O'Connor, *Mystery and Manners,* 171. This paradox was the obverse of her often stated belief that a positive talent for writing, while it can be cultivated in school, is essentially God-given.

39. Ibid., 183, 193.

40. John Crowe Ransom, "Criticism Inc.," in Thomas Daniel Young and John Hindle, eds., *Selected Essays of John Crowe Ransom* (Baton Rouge: Louisiana State University Press, 1984), 94.

41. O'Connor, *Mystery and Manners,* 54; 52–53.

42. Ransom, "The Aesthetic of Regionalism," in Young and Hindle, eds., *Selected Essays,* 56.

43. Andrew Lytle, "The Subject of Southern Fiction," in Lytle, *Southerners and Europeans: Essays in a Time of Disorder* (Baton Rouge: Louisiana State University Press, 1988), 61.

44. Ibid., 120.

45. Allen Tate, *The Fathers* (Chicago: Swallow Press, 1960), 125.

46. Ibid., 128.

47. In O'Connor, *Collected Works,* 210–231; page references will be given in the text, preceded by "CW."

48. Not that the story is *simply* an endorsement of this racism: the distance between O'Connor's narrator and her characters is recorded in the switch from their "nigger" to the narrator's more polite, educated "Negro." Nelson's similarity to the statue, and his intense attraction to a black woman—a vision perhaps of the mother, the "mammy," he never had—at an earlier moment in the story furthermore suggests O'Connor's awareness of the constructedness—or, in the language of the story, *artificiality*—of racial divisions. That said, the infamous title of the story, floating free of quotation marks, would appear to be the author's responsibility alone. Her account of

its origin was that, upon hearing (at second hand) the phrase used by a rural white Southerner, she immediately committed herself to it as the title of a story and only then began to look for events to match it. In other words, the appeal of the titular phrase was as powerful and spontaneous to her as the horror for the figure itself would be to her characters. Charmed, perhaps, by the rural simplicity—the humble intellectual limitations—the title embodied, she drew a line in the sand and resisted Ransom's pleas to change it. See Magee, ed., *Conversations,* 20–21.

49. R. V. Cassill, *The Eagle on the Coin* (New York: Random House, 1950). Page references will be given in the text.

50. Margaret Walker, *Jubilee* (Boston: Houghton Mifflin, 1966), 486. Subsequent page references will be given in the text.

51. Margaret Walker, *How I Wrote Jubilee and Other Essays on Life and Literature* (New York: Feminist Press, 1990), 50. Subsequent page references will be given in the text.

52. See, for instance, James E. Spears, "Folk Elements in Margaret Walker's Jubilee" and many other contributions to Maryemma Graham, ed., *Fields Watered with Blood: Critical Essays on Margaret Walker* (Athens: University of Georgia Press, 2001), 225–230.

53. See also Lillian Smith's interracial romance novel, *Strange Fruit* (1944), and Harper Lee's *To Kill a Mockingbird* (1960).

54. Magee, ed., *Conversations,* 59.

55. William Styron, *The Confessions of Nat Turner,* with a new Afterword (New York: Vintage, 1993), 441. Subsequent page references will be given in the text.

56. John Henrik Clarke, ed., *William Styron's Nat Turner: Ten Black Writers Respond* (Boston: Beacon Press, 1968), 10. Subsequent page references will be given in the text.

57. Robert Dana, ed., *A Community of Writers: Paul Engle and the Iowa Writers' Workshop* (Iowa City: University of Iowa Press, 1999), 115.

58. Ibid., 124.

59. Paul Engle, ed., *On Creative Writing* (New York: E. P. Dutton, 1964), vii.

60. On the other hand, Engle himself had to report to the officials above him in the university hierarchy. While the prestige of the Workshop, and Engle's independent fund-raising efforts on its behalf, sufficed to assure him relative autonomy as director, the Workshop was (and technically remains) part of the English Department, a bureaucratic structure that occasionally produced tensions. See Wilbers, *Iowa Writers' Workshop,* 109–116.

61. Quoted in Wilbers, ibid., 88.

62. Paul Engle, *Always the Land* (New York: Random House, 1941), 10–11.

63. See, for instance, Franco Moretti, *Modern Epic: The World System from Goethe to Garcia Marquez* (London: Verso, 1996), 63–67.

64. As I will discuss at greater length in Chapter 3, Iowa graduate Wallace Stegner, founding the creative writing program at Stanford University in 1946, explicitly envisioned it as a place where returning veterans would learn to tell their stories. More accurately, this was how Stegner sold the idea of a creative writing program to the Texas oilman who donated the $75,000 needed to found it. See Diane Manuel, "Tending a Legacy: Mary Page Stegner on Life and Work," *Stanford Today Online,* March/April 1996, *http://www.stanford.edu/dept/news/stanfordtoday/ed/9603/9603mps02.html.*

65. On O'Connor's relation to the ideas presented in this symposium, see Jon Lance Bacon, *Flannery O'Connor and Cold War Culture* (Cambrige: Cambridge University Press, 1993), 41–60. Engle continues: "The following believed [in the alliance of businessman, artist, and university]: Northern Natural Gas Company of Omaha; Reader's Digest Foundation; The Fisher Foundation of Marshalltown, Iowa; W. Averell Harriman of Washington, D.C.; The Maytag Co. Foundation, Newton, Iowa; U.S. Steel Foundation; the John D. Rockefeller III Fund; Time Inc.; The Louis W. and Maud Hill Family Foundation of St. Paul; The Cowles Charitable Trust; The New York Foundation; The Fred Maytag Family Foundation; Quaker Oats Co.; Amana Refrigeration; Gardner Cowles, Jr.; Miss Lillian Gish; H. J. Sobiloff, New York; Mrs. John P. Marquand; *Esquire;* J. Patrick Lannan, Chicago; The Robert R. McCormick Foundation; Mrs. Loyal L. Minor, Mason City, Iowa; Mr. Joseph Rosenfield, Mr. Ed Burchette, and Iowa Electric Light and Power Co. . . . (Engle, *On Creative Writing,* viii).

66. Quoted in Wilbers, *The Iowa Writers' Workshop,* 134.

67. Paul Engle and Hualing Nieh Engle, eds., *Writing From the World: Poetry, Fiction and Criticism in translation and in original English by Members of the International Writing Program from the first Ten Years of Its Life* (Iowa City: University of Iowa Press, 1976), 1.

68. Ibid., 2.

3. The Social Construction of Unreality

1. *http://news-service.stanford.edu/stanfordtoday/ed/9603/9603mps02.html.*

2. Wallace Stegner, *On Teaching and Writing Fiction* (New York: Penguin, 2002), 54.

3. Lynn Stegner, Foreword to Wallace Stegner, *On Teaching and Writing Fiction,* xiii.

4. Eugene Burdick, "Rest Camp on Maui" [1946], in Wallace Stegner and Richard Scowcroft, eds., *Twenty Years of Stanford Short Stories* (Stanford: Stanford University Press, 1966), 12. Subsequent page references from this story will be given in the text.

5. Ironically, in its studied foregrounding of specifically "literary" effects, it's not hard to see the path from this story to the important "issue novels" Burdick would go on to write, where purely literary values would be skillfully subordinated to the ends of entertaining persuasion.

6. Hemingway's *The Sun Also Rises* had famously introduced this concept, though in the more leisurely context of bullfight appreciation, as "afición."

7. Wallace Stegner, "Saw Gang," in Stegner, *The Women on the Wall and Other Stories* (London: Hammond, 1952), 72.

8. Wallace Stegner, *Wolf Willow: A History, a Story, and a Memory of the Last Plains Frontier* (New York: Penguin, 2000), 219.

9. Wallace Stegner, *All the Little Live Things* (New York: Penguin, 1967).

10. Wallace Stegner, "The Book and the Great Community," in Stegner, *The Sound of Mountain Water* (New York: Doubleday, 1969), 282; 285.

11. Tom Wolfe, *The Electric Kool-Aid Acid Test* (New York: Farrar, Straus and Giroux, 1968), 87. Subsequent page references will be given in the text.

12. Thomas Pynchon, *The Crying of Lot 49* (New York: HarperPerennial, 1999), 82–83. Subsequent page references will be given in the text.

13. However unrealistic it may be in other ways, *The Crying of Lot 49* is arguably as deeply grounded in the landscape and folkways of California as O'Connor's stories are in small-town Georgia, and its determination to explore the Nocal/Socal cultural polarity keeps it from lingering on campus too long. That said, it spends more than a little time at large in the Bay Area, either in Oedipa's fictional hometown of Kinneret-Among-the-Pines, somewhere on the San Francisco Bay Peninsula, or among the broken souls of downtown San Francisco, or across the Bay in Berkeley.

14. Barrett Watten, "The Turn to Language and the 1960s," *Critical Inquiry* 29 (Autumn 2002), 140.

15. For a fine analysis of the "retro" aspects of this novel see Andrew Hoberek, *The Twilight of the Middle Class: Post–World War II American Fiction and White Collar Work* (Princeton: Princeton University Press, 2005), 120–125.

16. Pynchon's declined opportunity to teach creative writing is reported in Matthew Winston, "The Quest for Pynchon," *Twentieth Century Literature* 21:3 (October 1975), 284.

17. John Barth, "Four Forewords: Lost in the Funhouse," in Barth, *Further Fridays: Essays, Lectures, and Other Nonfiction, 1984–1994* (Boston: Little, Brown, 1995), 274.

18. Thomas Pynchon, *Slow Learner* (New York: Bantam, 1985), xii.

19. For J. Peter Euben, *Lot 49* is an anti-textbook, the opposite of those works that "present . . . the world as easily comprehensible and directly available," but if this is true then all literary works on the syllabus should be considered anti-textbooks. While

it does not do entirely without textbooks in the traditional sense, literary studies as a discipline could be said to be entirely dedicated to the proposition that the world is not "easily comprehensible and directly available" without the labor of interpretation. See J. Peter Euben, *The Tragedy of Political Theory* (Princeton: Princeton University Press, 1990), 281.

20. Brian McHale, *Postmodernist Fiction* (New York and Lond: Methuen, 1987) 23. The title of this chapter is adapted from one of the chapter headings of McHale's fine formalist account of postmodern narrative as driven by an ontological pluralism, i.e., by the idea that there are many realities, not one. In deploying this "classically modernist" narrative form, Pynchon seems, like Stegner, a product of the New Critical hegemony, a paragon of showing without telling whose respect for the dramatic method is embodied not only in the novel's narrative form but in its fascination with the text of an old play. Thinking about the novel in this context adds another layer of significance to the emblem of the Tristero that appears throughout the book, confirming Oedipa's sense that she has stumbled upon a conspiracy. Rather than a simple negation of official postal services in favor of marginal ones, the *muted* post-horn might be understood to posit an ideal of curtailed or disciplined expressivity as a form of high literary removal from the major chords of the mass cultural mainstream. The muted post-horn is at any rate an odd model of cultural production in the sixties, which might better be described as an attempt to seize the post-horn from the powers that be and blow on it as hard as possible.

That Oedipa's research efforts are historicist as well as New Critical may however suggest a nascent resistance to these New Critical values in favor of a kind of externalist "relevance" more akin to the discipline of history than literature. Pynchon is, after all, an importantly historical novelist, and the historical novel must be counted among the most important postmodern genres, a vehicle for the various para-scholarly efforts not only of Pynchon, but of writers like Stegner and Barth and DeLillo and Doctorow and Morrison and—most imposingly—William T. Vollman.

21. Kenneth Boulding, *The Meaning of the Twentieth Century* (London: George Allen, 1965), 137.

22. Norbert Wiener, *The Human Use of Human Beings: Cybernetics and Society* [1950/1954] (New York: Avon, 1967), 58.

23. W. Richard Scott, *Organizations: Rational, Natural, and Open Systems,* 2nd ed. (Englewood Cliffs, N.J.: Prentice-Hall, 1987), 82.

24. Albert O. Hirschman, *Exit, Voice, and Loyalty: Responses to Decline in Firms, Organizations, and States* (Cambridge, Mass.: Harvard University Press, 1970), 43; italics in the original.

25. Charles Reich, *The Greening of America* (New York: Random House, 1970), 137.

26. Ivan Illich, *Deschooling Society* [1970] (New York: Harper, 1983).

27. Scott, *Organizations*, 82.

28. Walter J. Ong, "The Barbarian Within: Outsiders Inside Society Today," in Ong, *The Barbarian Within* (New York: Macmillan, 1962), 260.

29. The key text here is Richard Slotkin, *Regeneration Through Violence: The Mythology of the American Frontier, 1600–1860* (Middletown, Conn.: Wesleyan University Press, 1973), and its sequel *Gunfighter Nation: The Myth of the Frontier in Twentieth-Century America* (New York: HarperPerennial, 1992).

30. John Gardner, *Grendel* (New York: Vintage, 1989), 67–68.

31. Hirschman, *Exit, Voice, and Loyalty*, 108.

32. *Indian Voices: The First Convocation of American Indian Scholars* (San Francisco: Indian Historian Press, 1970), 71.

33. The same had been true of congruent theorizations such as Edward De Bono's "lateral" (creative) and "vertical" (logical) thinking, discussed in my Introduction, which are admitted to be "complementary" processes. See Edward De Bono, *Lateral Thinking: Creativity Step by Step* (New York: HarperPerennial, 1990), 14.

34. Victor Turner, *The Ritual Process: Structure and Anti-Structure* (Chicago: Aldine, 1969), 129.

35. Michel Foucault, "Of Other Spaces" (1967), trans. Jay Miskowiec; originally published in French as "Des Espaces Autres," *Architecture/Mouvement/Continuité* (October 1984), *www.foucault.info/documents/heteroTopia/foucault.heteroTopia.en.html*.

36. Further was also, at times, depending on who had done the most recent paint job, spelled "Furthur."

37. Tony Tanner, "Edge City (Ken Kesey)," in *City of Words: American Fiction 1950–1970* (New York: Harper and Row, 1971), 32.

38. Stanley Elkin, *A Bad Man* (New York: Random House, 1967); John Cheever, *Falconer* (New York: Knopf, 1977). A key sociological text in this vein would be Erving Goffman's *Asylums* (1961), with its account of various forms of resistance to the "total institution" whose preeminent example is the prison, while a key literary precursor would be Franz Kafka.

39. Ken Kesey, *One Flew Over the Cuckoo's Nest* (New York: Viking, 1964), 26. Subsequent page references will be given in the text.

40. Stephen L. Tanner, *"One Flew Over the Cuckoo's Nest,"* in Harold Bloom, ed., *Ken Kesey's One Flew Over the Cuckoo's Nest*, Modern Critical Interpretations (Philadelphia: Chelsea House, 2002), 124.

41. Lish is quoted in Paul Perry, *On the Bus: The Complete Guide to the Legendary Trip of Ken Kesey and the Merry Pranksters and the Birth of the Counterculture* (New York: Thunder's Mouth Press, 1990), 38.

42. Quoted in Robert Faggen, "Ken Kesey: The Art of Fiction CXXVI," *The Paris Review* (Spring 1994), 64.

43. James Baker Hall, "Ken," in Ed McClanahan, ed., *Spit in the Ocean #7* (New York: Penguin, 2003), 148.

44. John Daniel, "The Prankster Moves On," in McClanahan, ed., *Spit in the Ocean #7*, 135.

45. Ibid., 135.

46. Quoted in Ken Kesey and John Clark Pratt, *One Flew Over the Cuckoo's Nest: Text and Criticism* (New York: Viking, 1996), 337.

47. Wallace Stegner, "Get Out of That Story!" *The Writer,* December 1942, quoted in Jackson J. Benson, *Wallace Stegner: His Life and Work* (New York: Viking, 1996), 141.

48. Wallace Stegner, *The Potter's House* (Muscatine, Iowa: Prairie Press, 1938).

49. For a more thorough discussion of Bromden as narrator, see M. Gilbert Porter, "The Plucky Love Song of Chief 'Broom' Bromden," in Bloom, ed., *Ken Kesey's One Flew Over the Cuckoo's Nest,* 103–105.

50. Terry G. Sherwood, *"One Flew Over the Cuckoo's Nest* and the Comic Strip," in Bloom, ed., *Ken Kesey's One Flew Over the Cuckoo's Nest,* 12.

51. Perry, *On the Bus,* 123.

52. Ruth Sullivan, "Big Mama, Big Papa, and Little Sons in Ken Kesey's *One Flew Over the Cuckoo's Nest,*" in George J. Searles, ed., *A Casebook on Ken Kesey's One Flew Over the Cuckoo's Nest* (Albuquerque: University of New Mexico Press, 1992), 60.

53. Quoted in an interview with Robert Faggen, *The Paris Review* 130 (Spring 1994).

54. Quoted in Perry, *On the Bus,* 89.

55. Of course, the very existence of the Prankster Archive was a concession to the melancholy joys of the Stegnerian backward glance, and strong evidence that the group can be seen as a kind of institution.

56. Robert Stone, "The Boys' Octet," in McClanahan, ed., *Spit in the Ocean #7,* 200.

57. Faggen, "Ken Kesey," 60.

58. Donald Barthelme, *60 Stories* (New York: Penguin, 1981), 53. Subsequent page references from "The Balloon" will be given in the text.

59. Jerome Klinkowitz, *Keeping Literary Company: Working with Writers Since the Sixties* (Albany: SUNY Press, 1999), 125; Kathleen Fitzpatrick, *The Anxiety of Obsolescence: The American Novel in the Age of Television* (Nashville: Vanderbilt University Press, 2006).

60. Leslie A. Fiedler, "The End of the Novel," in Fiedler, *Waiting for the End* (New York: Stein and Day, 1964), 174.

61. Daniel J. Boorstin, *The Image: A Guide to Pseudo-Events in America* (New York: Vintage, 1992), 5.

62. Philip Roth, "Writing American Fiction," in Roth, *Reading Myself and Others* (New York: Vintage, 2001), 167; 170. See also Raymond Olderman, *Beyond the Waste Land: The American Novel in the Nineteen-Sixties* (New Haven: Yale University Press, 1972), which credulously claims that the "unreality" of American life required of novelists a paradoxical return to romance in order to be realistic.

63. Roth, "Writing American Fiction," 177.

64. Ishmael Reed, ed., *19 Necromancers From Now: An Anthology of Original American Writing for the 1970s* (Garden City, N.J.: Anchor, 1970), xiii–xiv.

65. Ishmael Reed, *Yellow Back Radio Broke-Down* (Normal, Ill.: Dalkey Archive, 2000), 9. Subsequent page references will be given in the text.

66. Bruce Dick and Amritjit Singh, eds., *Conversations with Ishmael Reed* (Jackson: University Press of Mississippi, 1995), 63.

67. Ibid.

68. Ishmael Reed, *Shrovetide in Old New Orleans* (New York: Atheneum, 1978), 226–227.

69. Quoted in Joan Mellen, *Kay Boyle: Author of Herself* (New York: Farrar, Straus, 1997), 464. Subsequent page references will be given in the text.

70. Kay Boyle, *The Long Walk at San Francisco State and Other Essays* (New York: Grove, 1970), 4–5.

71. Ibid., 6–7.

72. Kay Boyle, *The Underground Woman* (Garden City, N.Y.: Doubleday, 1975), 205; 9.

73. Zimbardo's documents are available at *http://www.prisonexp.org.*

4. Our Phonocentrism

1. Philip Roth, *Portnoy's Complaint* (New York: Vintage, 1994), 274. Subsequent page references will be given in the text.

2. "'I could tell you a tale,'" says a seafaring raconteur near the beginning of John Gardner's *The King's Indian* (New York: Vintage, 1974), as though apologizing for his violation of New Critical protocols, "'if ye'd understand from the outset that it has no . . . shape or form or discipline but the tucket and boom of its high-flown language.'" Gardner inserts opening quotation marks at the beginning of almost every paragraph of this novel's 140 pages, reminding us again and again that our "listening" to his tale is mediated by its telling to someone else, a fictional addressee who can actually (fiction-

ally) hear what we can only see on the page. The strenuous efforts of a storyteller are visible everywhere in this tale, and yet—technically—this telling is not direct but is "shown" along approved Jamesian (or in this case Conradian) lines.

3. Walter J. Ong, *Orality and Literacy: The Technologizing of the Word* (London: Routledge, 1982), 21.

4. Albert B. Lord, *The Singer of Tales,* 2nd ed. (Cambridge, Mass.: Harvard University Press, 2000), 4. Subsequent page references will be given in the text.

5. Marshall McLuhan, *The Gutenberg Galaxy: The Making of Typographic Man* (New York: Signet, 1969), 9.

6. Wayne C. Booth, *The Rhetoric of Fiction,* 2nd ed. (Chicago: University of Chicago Press, 1983), 16.

7. Dorothy J. Hale, *Social Formalism: The Novel in Theory from Henry James to the Present* (Stanford: Stanford University Press, 1998), 67.

8. Walter J. Ong, "The Jinnee in the Well-Wrought Urn," in *The Barbarian Within and Other Fugitive Essays and Studies* (New York: Macmillan, 1962), 20.

9. For a systematic critique of the personification of texts in postwar American literature, see Amy Hungerford, *The Holocaust of Texts: Genocide, Literature, Personification* (Chicago: University of Chicago Press, 2003).

10. Commenting on Gates's editorial decision to include a cassette tape of oral performances along with the text of the *Norton Anthology of African American Literature,* Barbara Johnson would manage the rapprochement of McLuhanite and Derridean thinking thusly: "Trained as I am in deconstruction, I have always been suspicious of the privileging of the spoken word as a sign of presence or authenticity. But this attitude clearly cannot account for the *signifying* dimensions (precisely, the inflection) of performance." See Barbara E. Johnson, "Response" to Henry Louis Gates, in Houston A. Baker and Patricia Redmond, eds., *Afro-American Literary Study in the 1990s* (Chicago: University of Chicago Press, 1989), 43.

11. Walker Gibson, "The 'Speaking Voice' and the Teaching of Composition," in Peter Elbow, ed., *Landmark Essays on Voice and Writing* (Mahwah, N.J.: Hermagoras Press, 1994), 11–17.

12. Albert Guerard et al., *The Personal Voice: A Contemporary Prose Reader, Shorter Edition* (Philadelphia: Lippincott, 1968), iii–iv.

13. This context is reflected in one of the selections made available to students in *The Personal Voice,* Robert J. Oppenheimer's essay "Prospects in the Arts and Sciences," which takes the importance of science and technology research as a given but also, in a way bound to delight writer-teachers like Guerard and Hawkes, speaks of the "growing recognition that the creative artist is a proper charge of the university, and the university as proper home for him" (138).

14. Alice Hoffman, Introduction to *Ploughshares Fiction Issue #91* (Fall 2003).

15. For a systematic discussion of sixties anti-realism as self-assertion, see Manfred Putz, *The Story of Identity: American Fiction of the Sixties* (Munich: Vilhelm Flink, 1987).

16. Carol Gilligan, *In a Different Voice: Psychological Theory and Women's Development* (Cambridge, Mass.: Harvard University Press, 1993), xix. Interestingly enough, Gilligan's research has little to do with voicing per se, dealing rather with the different learning styles of girls and boys, which suggests the excessive appeal of the trope of voice in this period.

17. N. Scott Momaday, "To Save a Great Vision," in *The Man Made of Words* (New York: St. Martin's Press, 1997), 27.

18. See Franz Boas, *Anthropology and Modern Life* [1928] (New York: Norton, 1962), 13.

19. See Henry Louis Gates, Jr., *The Signifying Monkey: A Theory of African-American Literary Criticism* (New York: Oxford University Press, 1988), 170. For an extended analysis of the widespread importance of the trope of voice in 1930s literature—the most immediate precursor to what we find in the 1960s—see Helen Choi, "Vox Pop Modernism: Technology, Ethnicity and Community," dissertation, UCLA English Department, 2006. A fine examination of the American dialect tradition is available in Gavin Jones, *Strange Talk: The Politics of Dialect Literature in Gilded Age America* (Berkeley: University of California Press, 1999).

20. Karl Kroeber, "Technology and Tribal Narrative," in Gerald Vizenor, ed., *Narrative Chance: Postmodern Discourse on Native American Indian Literatures* (Norman: University of Oklahoma Press, 1993), 18.

21. Larry Landrum, "The Shattered Modernism of Momaday's *House Made of Dawn*," *Modern Fiction Studies* 42.4 (1996), 764. Subsequent page references will be given in the text.

22. Tom Wolfe, *The Electric Kool-Aid Acid Test* (New York: Farrar, Straus and Giroux, 1968), 48–49. Subsequent page references will be given in the text.

23. Ken Kesey in the *Paris Review,* interviewed by Rogert Faggen, "The Art of Fiction No. 136," Issue 130 (Spring 1994), 65.

24. See my "Learning from Little Tree: The Political Education of the Counterculture," *Yale Journal of Criticism* 18:2 (Fall 2005), 243–267.

25. Shari M. Huhndorf, *Going Native: Indians in the American Cultural Imagination* (Ithaca: Cornell University Press, 2001); Philip J. Deloria, *Playing Indian* (New Haven: Yale University Press, 1998).

26. N. Scott Momaday, *The Names: A Memoir* (Tucson: University of Arizona Press, 1976), 25.

27. As Stegner put it, "I have seen him gradually comprehending, accepting, even

asserting his Indianness. Actually, of course, his Indianness is as much assumed as inborn." Quoted in Matthias Schubnell, *N. Scott Momaday: The Cultural and Literary Background* (Norman: University of Oklahoma Press, 1985), 11.

28. Sam Deloria is quoted in *Indian Voices: The First Convocation of American Indian Scholars* (San Francisco: Indian Historian Press, 1970), 34.

29. English was also, ironically, the lingua franca of sixties Pan-Indianism, the only way to knit together one hundred or so living Native languages into a self-conscious Native American cultural whole.

30. Momaday had been inspired by the man himself when, spending a year studying law at the University of Virginia, he was able to sit in on the many audiences Faulkner held there during the year he was a writer-in-residence in Charlotte.

31. Ernest Hemingway, "Indian Camp," in *In Our Time* (New York: Scribner's, 1986), 16; 19.

32. N. Scott Momaday, *House Made of Dawn* (New York: HarperPerennial, 1999), 52.

33. See Marvin Harris, *The Rise of Anthropological Theory: A History of Theories of Culture,* updated ed. (Walnut Creek, Calif.: Altamira Press, 2001), 568–604.

34. Kesey in the *Paris Review,* "The Art of Fiction No. 136," 66.

35. Fredric Jameson, *Archaeologies of the Future* (New York: Verso, 2005), 164. See also Stephen Greenblatt, "Towards a Poetics of Culture," in *Learning to Curse: Essays in Early Modern Culture* (New York: Routledge, 1990), 115.

36. "The Playboy Interview: Marshall McLuhan," *Playboy Magazine,* March 1969.

37. If, for Hawkes, the Voice Project responded to the recognition that "nothing less than a revolution in present literary taste and values as well as in our ideas about language is needed if higher education is not to become increasingly remote from life itself and increasingly meaningless to younger people," one happy consequence of this revolution might be larger readership for his own relentlessly bleak novels, where nothing so hopeful as "personal growth" could ever conceivably occur.

38. John Hawkes, "The Voice Project: An Idea for Innovation in the Teaching of Writing," in Jonathan Baumbach, ed., *Writers as Teachers, Teachers as Writers* (New York: Holt, Rinehart and Winston, 1970), 92. Susequent page references will be given in the text.

39. Certainly it is not surprising to read Hawkes's admission, in the copious debriefing document he delivered to the Education Department at year's end, of the Project's general "inability to develop forms of [physical] expression" meaningfully analogous to writing in the time that they had, even though he remained convinced by the connection. See John Hawkes et al., *Voice Project: An Experiment in Teaching Writing to College Freshmen* [ERIC Accession Number ED 018 422], 98.

40. The "inhibitions" generated by the impulse to revise-as-you-go are what motivates Peter Elbow's signal contribution to composition pedagogy, the exercise he calls "freewriting," a kind of automatic writing designed to loosen the student up. See Peter Elbow, *Writing Without Teachers* (New York: Oxford University Press, 1973).

41. John Hawkes et al., *Voice Project,* xxii.

42. Indeed, even as the conditions of recording in the Yugoslavian countryside could not help conditioning the "authenticity" of the performances he captured, Parry is reputed to have been an extraordinarily gifted and resourceful sound technician as well as classicist.

43. Hawkes et al., *Voice Project.*

44. One of these teaching assistants, Francelia Mason, would go on to become an academic specialist in oral literary tradition; another, Zeese Papanikolas, who kept the log cited above, would become a progenitor of academic ethnic studies in Utah; and still another, Stephen Dixon, would go on to a celebrated career as a short story writer and creative writing professor at Johns Hopkins.

45. Leo Litwak and Herbert Wilner, *College Days in Earthquake Country: A Personal Record* (New York: Random House, 1971), xiii.

46. Jackson Benson, *Wallace Stegner: His Life and Work* (New York: Penguin, 1997), 259.

47. Al Young, *Snakes* (New York: Dell, 1970), 18–19.

48. It has been argued that, in fact, much first person fictional narration is observably "double voiced" in that many things that the character-narrator says can only really be understood as issuing from an Implied Author fulfilling what James Phelan calls a "disclosure function." Henrik Skov Nielsen goes even further, arguing that this aspect of first person narration should be understood as impersonal, that is, as issuing from nobody, not even an Implied Author. See James Phelan, *Living to Tell About It: A Rhetoric and Ethics of Character Narration* (Ithaca: Cornell University Press, 2005), and Henrik Skov Nielsen, "The Impersonal Voice in First-Person Narrative Fiction," *Narrative* 12, no. 2 (May 2004).

49. Charles T. Davis and Henry Louis Gates, *The Slave's Narrative* (New York: Oxford University Press, 1985), xxiii.

50. And yet, as many have pointed out, in a further turn of the screw this investment in "diversity" can itself become another, more supple technology of assimilation to the status quo, especially as aided by the romantic individualism that helps to cordon off the student's fascination with his or her difference from broader social movements to which it might become attached.

51. Ishmael Reed, ed., *19 Necromancers from Now: An Anthology of Original American Writing for the 1970s* (Garden City, N.J.: Anchor, 1970), xv.

52. For a meticulous account of the antinomies of individualism in the postwar period see Cyrus R. K. Patell, *Negative Liberties: Morrison, Pynchon, and the Problem of Liberal Ideology* (Durham: Duke University Press, 2001).

53. In his informative study of the neo-slave narrative, Ashraf Rushdy restricts the term to a small group of texts, including Johnson's, published in the 1980s. But this restriction puts his account at odds with the currency of the term in the 1960s, and forces him into an unjustified neglect of works like Ernest Gaines's *Autobiography of Miss Jane Pittman* (1971), which it is hard to describe as anything other than a neo-slave narrative in his terms but which doesn't fit into his periodization of the genre. This is partly why what Rushdy describes in this book as the "neo-slave narrative" would more accurately (if less gracefully) described as the "neo-neo-slave narrative" or, as I suggest here, the "meta-slave narrative." See Ashraf H. A. Rushdy, *Neo-slave Narratives: Studies in the Social Logic of a Literary Form* (New York: Oxford University Press, 1999). A larger structure of self-consciously black literary reflexivity is theorized by Madelyn Jablon in *Black Metafiction: Self-Consciousness in African American Literature* (Iowa City: University of Iowa Press, 1997).

54. Charles Johnson, *Oxherding Tale* (New York: Penguin, 1995), 152; emphasis in the original. Subsequent page references will be given in the text.

55. Charles Johnson, *Middle Passage* (New York: Simon and Schuster, 1990), 171.

56. Kenneth W. Warren, *So Black and Blue: Ralph Ellison and the Occasion of Criticism* (Chicago: University of Chicago Press, 2003), 29.

57. Richard Yarborough, "The First Person in Afro-American Fiction," in Baker and Redmond, eds., *Afro-American Literary Study*, 114–115.

58. W. D. Winnicott, *Playing and Reality* (New York: Routledge, 2005), 3. Thus the concept of "creativity" relevant to creative writing as we know it has two overlapping, but in theory separable, meanings: on the one hand, of course, by contrast to most of the writing done in the utilitarian composition class, it suggests that this writing will be fictional. But the recent emergence of "creative nonfiction" as a subcategory of creative writing instruction suggests, in the form of a contradiction in terms, that the "creativity" in creative writing perhaps even more basically signifies the personal freedom of the student engaged in it. In *Creative Nonfiction: How to Live It and Write It* (Chicago: Chicago Review Press, 1996), x, Lee Gutkind promotes this curricular activity as a "genuine three-dimensional experience [that] provides many more outlets for satisfaction and self-discovery, flexibility, and freedom" than writing fiction does, but as one which like fiction "encourages the writer to become a part of the story or essay being written." Granted, it is hard to see "creative nonfiction" apart from the historical context that would also produce "reality TV" and other panic reflexes of postmodern over-mediation at the turn of the current century. But in a sense it merely makes ex-

plicit the real-world payoff in liberated subjectivity that had always been understood to underlie the student's production of fictions.

59. See Richard De Mille, *Castaneda's Journey: The Power and the Allegory* (Santa Barbara: Capra, 1976); and Richard De Mille, *The Don Juan Papers: Further Castaneda Controversies* (Santa Barbara: Ross-Erikson, 1980).

60. See, for instance, the author bio on the final page of Ernest Gaines, *The Autobiography of Miss Jane Pittman* (New York: Bantam, 1971); Ernest Gaines, "Miss Jane and I," *Callaloo* no. 3, Ernest J. Gaines: A Special Issue (May 1978), 28. Subsequent page references to *The Autobiography* will be given in the text.

61. B. A. Botkin, ed., *Lay My Burden Down: A Folk History of Slavery* (Chicago: University of Chicago Press, 1969), ix. Octavia Butler's *Kindred* (1979), in which a modern African American woman finds herself transported through time to the days of slavery, was, Butler tells us, motivated precisely by this conundrum as it emerged in the classroom. When a fellow student at Pasadena City College didn't seem to her to have the requisite feeling for what their slave ancestors had been through, fictional transport into a personal experience of slavery seemed the only answer. Thus while Gaines, inventing a just-plausibly-real link to the distant past with an extremely elderly woman, deploys a realist technology for the production of that empathic immediacy in students, Butler the science fiction writer would manage it in the literal, if unrealistic, form of time travel.

62. This recalls the early drafts of the novel, which Gaines had at first intended to write in the form of a collective porch narrative of the life of Jane Pittman by those who knew her, only to find her first person voice asserting itself in his writing.

5. The Hidden Injuries of Craft

1. John W. Aldridge, *Talents and Technicians: Literary Chic and the New Assembly-Line Fiction* (New York: Scribner's, 1992), 48.

2. Raymond Carver, *Will You Please Be Quiet, Please?* (New York: Vintage, 1992), 94–95. Subsequent page references to stories in this volume will be given in the text.

3. Robert Rebein, *Hicks, Tribes, and Dirty Realists: American Fiction after Postmodernism* (Lexington: University Press of Kentucky, 2001), 29. See also Phillip E. Simmons, *Deep Surfaces: Mass Culture and History in Postmodern Fiction* (Athens: University of Georgia Press, 1997), 106.

4. Maryann Carver quoted in Sam Halpert, *Raymond Carver: An Oral Biography* (Iowa City: University of Iowa Press, 1995), 67.

5. Ibid., 67.

6. Bob Adelman, *Carver Country: The World of Raymond Carver* (New York: Scribner's, 1990).

7. Arno J. Meyer, "The Lower Middle Class as Historical Problem," *Journal of Modern History* 47:3 (September 1975), 409–436.

8. Rebein, *Hicks, Tribes, and Dirty Realists,* 24.

9. Ibid., 137.

10. Clark Kerr, *The Great Transformation in Higher Education, 1960–1980* (Albany, N.Y.: SUNY Press, 1991).

11. Daniel Bell is quoted in Harold Perkin, "History of Universities," in Lester F. Goodchild and Harold S. Wechsler, eds., *The History of Higher Education,* 2nd ed. (Boston: Pearson, 1997), 30.

12. Langdon Hammer, "Plath's Lives: Poetry, Professionalism, and the Culture of the School," *Representations* 75 (Summer 2001), 61–88.

13. Helen Merrell Lynd, *On Shame and the Search for Identity* (New York: Harcourt Brace, 1958).

14. Rita Felski, "Nothing to Declare: Identity, Shame and the Lower Middle Class," *PMLA,* vol. 115, no. 1 (January 2000), 39.

15. See for instance Silvan S. Tomkins, *Affect, Imagery, Consciousness,* 2 vols. (New York: Springer, 1963).

16. See for instance Humberto Maturana and Francisco Verela, *The Tree of Knowledge: The Biological Roots of Human Understanding,* rev. ed. (Boston: Shambhala, 1992).

17. This summarizes the account of modernity laid out in Anthony Giddens, *Modernity and Self-Identity: Self and Society in the Late Modern Age* (Stanford: Stanford University Press, 1991).

18. Wilbur Schramm, *Programed Instruction Today and Tomorrow* (Fund for the Advancement of Education, 1962), 1.

19. William A. Deterline, *An Introduction to Programed Instruction* (Englewood Cliffs, N.J.: Prentice-Hall, 1962), 6.

20. Gordon Lish, *English Grammar Teacher's Manual* (Palo Alto: Behavioral Research Laboratories, 1964), 3; emphasis in the original.

21. Gordon Lish, *English Grammar,* 2 vols. (Palo Alto: Behavioral Research Laboratories, 1964), 2–3.

22. Lish, *English Grammar Teacher's Manual,* 7; emphasis in the original.

23. Lish, *English Grammar,* vol. 1, iv.

24. Although, as someone who would become one of the world's foremost experts on *Dracula* and its cultural offspring, and perforce knowledgeable about writing technologies and generic conventions both, he may have been uniquely prepared to appreciate the inevitable "horror" of the crossing of technology and creativity.

25. Gordon Lish, "Imagination," in *What I Know So Far* (New York: Holt, Rinehart and Winston, 1983), 44–50.

26. Lish, *English Grammar,* vol. 2, 33.

27. Mina P. Shaughnessy, *Errors and Expectations: A Guide for the Teacher of Basic Writing* (New York: Oxford University Press, 1977).

28. Ground zero of the (considerably overblown) controversy surrounding Lish's editorship can be found in D. T. Max, "The Carver Chronicles," *New York Times Magazine,* August 9, 1998.

29. George Carver, "Lish, Gordon: Notes and Reflections of a Former Student," *Pif Magazine,* May 31, 2005, *www.pifmagazine.com/SID/6921.*

30. John Barth, "A Few Words About Minimalism," *Further Fridays: Essays, Lectures, and Other Nonfiction, 1984–1994* (Boston: Little, Brown, 1995), 70–71.

31. Ibid., 71.

32. For a vigorous defense of minimalism on different grounds, see Cynthia Whitney Hallett, *Minimalism and the Short Story: Raymond Carver, Amy Hempel, and Mary Robison* (Lewiston, N.Y.: Edwin Mellen Press, 1999).

33. In this it is a variation of the Depression-era "insurance aesthetic" laid out in Michael Szalay's *New Deal Modernism: American Literature and the Invention of the Welfare State* (Durham: Duke University Press, 2001). The "risk society" is a concept influentially explored in Ulrich Beck, *The Risk Society: Towards a New Modernity* (London: Sage, 1992).

34. Raymond Carver, "Pastoral," *Western Humanities Review* 17:1 (Winter 1963), 33–42. Subsequent page references are given in the text.

35. Alan Liu, *The Laws of Cool: Knowledge Work and the Culture of Information* (Chicago: University of Chicago Press, 2004).

36. Tomkins, *Affect, Imagery, Consciousness,* 136.

37. Jeffrey Meyers, *Hemingway: A Biography* (New York: Da Capo, 1985), 17.

38. John Gardner, *On Becoming a Novelist* (New York: Norton, 1983), xxiii.

39. James Wolcott, "Stop Me Before I Write Again: Six Hundred More Pages by Joyce Carol Oates," *Harper's,* September 1982, 67–69; Aldridge, *Talents and Technicians,* 48.

40. Raymond Carver, *Call If You Need Me: The Uncollected Fiction and Other Prose* (New York: Vintage, 2001), 178.

41. This predicts, in a more literal way than he intended it, James Wood's invention of the term "hysterical realism" to describe what he perceived as the limitations of the maximalist books of the 1990s, which pursue "vitality at all costs." Wood contrasts the unfortunate "sociology" of contemporary maximalist fiction with works that more humbly tell us "how somebody felt about something." But one can argue that—as his

own term "hysterical" already suggests—maximalist works *are* telling us how somebody felt about something: curious, excited, zany, frazzled. See James Wood, "The Smallness of the 'Big' Novel: Human, all too Inhuman," *The New Republic,* July 24, 2000.

42. Alfred Kazin, "[On Joyce Carol Oates]," in Linda W. Wagner, ed., *Critical Essays on Joyce Carol Oates* (Boston: G. K. Hall, 1979), 157–160.

43. Wolcott, "Stop Me Before I Write Again," 69; 67.

44. James E. Allen, "An Uncommon Man: The Story of Dr. William Pearson Tolley and Syracuse University" (New York: Newcomen Society Monographs, 1963), 10.

45. Joyce Carol Oates, *Wonderland* (Greenwich, Conn.: Fawcett Crest, 1971).

46. Joyce Carol Oates, *Upon the Sweeping Flood and Other Stories* (Greenwich, Conn.: Fawcett Crest, 1966), 147. Subsequent page references from this volume will be given in the text.

47. Joyce Carol Oates, *them* (New York: Fawcett Crest, 1983), 12. Subsequent page references will be given in the text.

48. See, for instance, *www.writingclasses.com.*

49. Halpert, *Raymond Carver,* 61.

50. Tobias Wolff, "An Episode in the Life of Professor Brooke," *In the Garden of the North American Martyrs* (New York: Ecco, 1981), 27–43. Subsequent page references will be given in the text.

51. Joyce Carol Oates, *With Shuddering Fall* (Greenwich, Conn.: Fawcett Crest, 1964).

52. Rosamond Smith, *Nemesis* (New York: Penguin, 1991).

53. Greg Johnson, *Invisible Writer: A Biography of Joyce Carol Oates* (New York: Plume, 1999), 148.

54. Joyce Carol Oates, *(Woman) Writer: Occasions and Opportunities* (New York: E. P. Dutton, 1988), 31–32.

55. Raymond Carver, "Fires," in *Call If You Need Me,* 97; 98; 100.

56. Aldridge, *Talents and Technicians,* 56.

57. Oates, *(Woman) Writer,* 301.

58. Quoted in Johnson, *Invisible Writer,* 160.

59. Ibid., 10–11.

60. Giorgio Agamben, *The Man Without Content* (Stanford: Stanford University Press, 1999), 21.

61. Think here of the importance of major historical reference in the recent rise of the graphic novel to artistic respectability, whether it be Art Spiegelman's highly reflexive *Maus* (1986) or Marjane Satrapi's *Persepolis* (2001) or even Alan Moore's *Watchmen* (1986–87).

62. Linda Hutcheon, *A Poetics of Postmodernism: History, Theory, Fiction* (New York:

Routledge, 1988). Witness the outrage that surrounds acts of imposture in autobiography: whether it is Forrest Carter the not-Indian or Danny Santiago the not-Chicano or James Frey the lying betrayer of Oprah, these scandals remind us of the lingering pre-postmodernism of contemporary literary ideas about historical experience, identity, and authenticity.

63. Halpert, *Raymond Carver,* 114.

64. Joyce Carol Oates, *I Lock My Door Upon Myself* (New York: Plume, 1991), 40.

65. Quoted in Johnson, *Invisible Writer,* 396.

66. Hence the tremendous irony of Oates's recent discovery, explored in her novel *The Gravedigger's Daughter* (2007), that her grandmother was in fact born of Jewish parents but hid that affiliation from everyone around her, including her granddaughter.

6. Art and Alma Mater

1. Harold Bloom, *The Anxiety of Influence: A Theory of Poetry* (New York: Oxford University Press, 1973).

2. Sandra M. Gilbert and Susan Gubar, *No Man's Land: The Place of the Woman Writer in the Twentieth Century,* Vol. 1, *The War of the Words* (New Haven: Yale University Press, 1988), 165.

3. Ronald Sukenick, *Down and In: Life in the Underground* (New York: Morrow, 1987), 97. Subsequent page references will be given in the text.

4. Pascale Casanova, *The World Republic of Letters* (Cambridge, Mass.: Harvard University Press, 2004), xiii. Subsequent pages references will be given in the text.

5. Cited in Walter Benn Michaels, *Our America: Nativism, Modernism, and Pluralism* (Durham: Duke University Press, 1995), 6.

6. Wai Chee Dimock, "Scales of Aggregation: Prenational, Subnational, Transnational," *American Literary History* 18.2 (2006), 219.

7. James English, *The Economy of Prestige: Prizes, Awards, and the Circulation of Cultural Value* (Cambridge, Mass.: Harvard University Press, 2005).

8. Pierre Bourdieu, *The Rules of Art: Genesis and Structure of the Literary Field,* trans. Susan Emanuel (Stanford: Stanford University Press, 1992), 337.

9. Danielle Taylor-Guthrie, ed., *Conversations with Toni Morrison* (Jackson: University Press of Mississippi, 1994), 227.

10. See "Lamadrid Proposes Name Change for Chicano Studies," in University of New Mexico's *UNM Today* (October 26, 2004). *www.unm.edu/~market/cgi-bin/archives/000363.html.*

11. Sandra Cisneros, *The House on Mango Street* [1984] (New York: Vintage, 1991), 28. Subsequent page references will be given in the text.

12. Author's introduction to the 1994 edition of Cisneros, *Mango Street,* xii–xiii.

13. Francine Prose, *The Blue Angel* (New York: Perennial, 2000), 199.

14. Marcus Klein, *Foreigners: The Making of American Literature, 1900–1940* (Chicago: University of Chicago Press, 1981), x.

15. This figure of 98 percent—based on the generous estimate of 125 million persons living outside the country of their birth in a global population approaching 6 billion—is the smallest of a range cited in Peter Kivisto, *Multiculturalism in a Global Society* (Oxford: Blackwell, 2002), 3. One could even say, by this logic, that the dilemma of the ethnic artist magnifies the existential dilemma of the "individual" as the latter has been understood in the Liberal tradition since the seventeenth century—understood, that is, as the predicate of social institutions, not their product. And yet, as Cisneros and many other (especially female) ethnically marked writers have attested, the structural threats to artistic individuality come at them from at least two directions, from the cultural mainstream and *la raza* both, each of them capable of a large and intimidating disapproval. See, for instance, Pilar E. Rodriquez Aranda, "On the Solitary Fate of Being Mexican, Female, Wicked and Thirty-three: An Interview with Writer Sandra Cisneros," *The Americas Review* 18:1 (Spring 1990), 66: "You're told you're a traitor to your culture. And it's a horrible life to live. We're always straddling two countries, and we're always living in [a] kind of schizophrenia."

16. Sandra Cisneros, "Ghosts and Voices: Writing from Obsession," *The Americas Review* 15 (Spring 1987), 72–73.

17. Author's introduction to *Mango Street,* xv.

18. Ibid.

19. Felicia Cruz, "On the 'Simplicity' of Sandra Cisneros's *House on Mango Street,*" *Modern Fiction Studies* 47:4 (Winter 2001), 937.

20. Ibid., 917.

21. Gaston Bachelard, *The Poetics of Space,* trans. Maria Jolas (Boston: Beacon Press, 1994), 150.

22. Tom Grimes, ed., *The Workshop: Seven Decades of the Iowa Writers' Workshop* (New York: Hyperion, 1999), 14.

23. See Walter D. Mignolo, *Local Histories/Global Designs: Coloniality, Subaltern Knowledges, and Border Thinking* (Princeton: Princeton University Press, 2000), esp. 250–277. An earlier registration of the border concept in scholarship occurs in Jose David Saldivar, *Border Matters: Remapping American Cultural Studies* (Berkeley: University of California Press, 1997).

24. The politics of Cisneros's narratology in *Caramelo* is taken up in James Phelan, "Rhetoric, Politics, and Ethics in Sandra Cisneros's *Caramelo*," in Amy Schrager Lang and Cecilia Tichi, eds., *What Democracy Looks Like: A New Critical Realism for a Post-Seattle World* (New Brunswick, N.J.: Rutgers University Press, 2006), 114–122.

25. See Luce Irigaray, *This Sex Which Is Not One,* trans. Catherine Porter and Catherine Burke (New York: Cornell University Press, 1985).

26. Sandra Cisneros, *Caramelo* (New York: Vintage, 2003), 37. Subsequent page references will be given in the text.

27. Toni Morrison, *Beloved* (New York: Vintage, 2004). Page references will be given in the text.

28. This is why so many readers of the novel, conditioned by the book's cultural framing as a selection of Oprah's Book Club to expect something more sentimentally affirmative, are surprised (pleasantly or unpleasantly) by what they find.

29. See, for instance, Caroline Rody, "Toni Morrison's *Beloved:* History, 'Rememory,' and a 'Clamor for a Kiss,'" *American Literary History* 7:1 (Spring 1995), 92–119; James Berger, "Ghosts of Liberalism: Morrison's *Beloved* and the Moynihan Report," *PMLA* 111:3 (May 1996), 408–420; Nancy Armstrong, "Why Daughters Die: The Racial Logic of American Sentimentalism," *Yale Journal of Criticism* 7:2 (1994), 1–24; Rafael Perez-Torres, "Knitting and Knotting the Narrative Thread: *Beloved* as Postmodern Novel," *Modern Fiction Studies* 39:3/4 (Fall/Winter 1993). Of course, my list of themes doesn't begin to exhaust the interpretive contexts that have been found for the novel. One essay that begins to plum the significance of "schoolteacher," understanding him as an allusion to Nathaniel Hawthorne, is Caroline M. Wodat's "Talking Back to Schoolteacher: Morrison's Confrontation with Hawthorne in *Beloved*," *Modern Fiction Studies* 39:3/4 (Fall/Winter 1993), 527–546. An essay that reads the novel in relation to the question of education is Satya Mohanty's "The Epistemic Status of Cultural Identity: On *Beloved* and the Postcolonial Condition" (in Paula Moya and Michael R. Hames-Garcia, eds., *Reclaiming Identity: Realist Theory and the Predicament of Postmodernism* [Berkeley: University of California Press, 2000], 29–66), but there it is reduced to the question of Paul D.'s learning not to stand in judgment of Sethe's act of infanticide. I would argue that Morrison wants us to consider her act as horrible and possibly criminal, and that not to do so is to trade away some of the tragic power of the work for progressive pluralist therapy.

30. Frederick Douglass, *Narrative of the Life of Frederick Douglass, An American Slave* (New York: Penguin, 1986), 78; 82; 87.

31. Taylor-Guthrie, ed., *Conversations with Toni Morrison*, 258.

32. An online dialogue with the author conducted in 1998 makes clear her sense of

kinship with the tribe of schoolteachers, and the way *Beloved* has returned to the class-room near which it was written:

> *Timehost* presents question #1030 from Beatle4: "I just got finished reading 'Beloved' for my 12th grade AP English class. I have to give a seminar on it next week and am working on it now. What do you think are some good activities that my group and I can do with 'Beloved'?"
>
> *Toni Morrison* says, "I remember once an honors class complained that there were no Cliff notes of 'Beloved' and I suggested to them that they make them. And at the end of the semester, this class sent me the projects that they had done, which were designed to be like Cliff notes. The teacher was as excited as the students were by how effective the project was in analyzing the book as well as the history that prompted the book."

www.time.com/time/community/transcripts/chattr012198.html, January 21, 1998.

33. In the foreword she links the conflicting demands of editing and writing explicitly to the conflict between teaching and writing, but only to express her sense of the tiresome and dubious predictability with which she hears them invoked. Since creative writing professors are hired at least in part to write—that is the "research" component of the job—we can probably assume that the conflict was not as severe as it had been in the "9 to 5" (but more typically 9 to 7, and with innumerable additional hours spent at home reading manuscripts) job of book editing.

34. Toni Morrison, *Remember: The Journey to School Integration* (Boston: Houghton Mifflin, 2004), 70.

35. When Bhabha later offered a class at the University of Chicago in 1998 called "Global Fictions," he placed three of Morrison's novels on the syllabus and brought the author herself—on campus that year as a visiting professor—into the classroom as a discussant. See Jenny Adams, "Bhabha Teams Up with Toni Morrison to Explore Global Fictions Through Discussion," *The University of Chicago Chronicle* (18:4), November 12, 1998. *chronicle.uchicago.edu/981112/morrison.shtml*.

36. Toni Morrison, *Playing in the Dark: Whiteness and the Literary Imagination* (New York: Vintage, 1992), 3.

37. See, for instance, Wendy Steiner, "Clearest Eye," *New York Times,* April 5, 1992.

38. See Yogita Goyal's discussion of Morrison's "ambivalence" with respect to various conceptions of diaspora and transnationality in Goyal, "The Gender of Diaspora in Toni Morrison's Tar Baby," *Modern Fiction Studies* 52:2 (Summer 2006), 393–413.

39. Naomi Mandel, "'I Made the Ink': Identity, Complicity, 60 Million, and More," *Modern Fiction Studies* 48:3 (Fall 2002), 581–612. For Mandel, arguing in a deconstructive vein, the relevant institutional medium of complicity is language.

7. Miniature America

1. Sianne Ngai, *Ugly Feelings* (Cambrige, Mass.: Harvard University Press, 2005).

2. Christopher Looby, *Voicing America: Language, Literary Form, and the Origins of the United States* (Chicago: University of Chicago Press, 1996), 1.

3. See, for instance, the controversy surrounding the conversion of the venerable one-year M.A. program at Hollins College in Virginia into a more expensive two-year M.F.A. program, prompting its director of 32 years, Richard Dillard, to resign in protest. See *The Chronicle of Higher Education* 50:21 (January 30, 2004), A8.

4. A fairly comprehensive listing of graduate writing programs abroad is available in Tom Kealey, *The Creative Writing MFA Handbook: A Guide for Prospective Students* (New York: Continuum, 2005), 206–212.

5. See, for instance, Ulrich Beck, *Risk Society: Towards a New Modernity* (London: Sage, 1992), and Anthony Giddens, *The Consequences of Modernity* (Stanford: Stanford University Press, 1991).

6. Zygmunt Bauman, *Liquid Times: Living in an Age of Uncertainty* (Cambridge: Polity, 2007), 5.

7. Jon McKenzie, *Perform or Else: From Discipline to Performance* (New York: Routledge, 2001); Paolo Virno, *A Grammar of the Multitude* (Cambridge: Semiotext(e), 2004).

8. Scott Lash, "Reflexivity as Nonlinearity," *Theory, Culture & Society* 20:2 (2003), 49.

9. See, for instance, William Rasch, "The Limit of Modernity: Luhmann and Lyotard on Exclusion," in William Rasch and Cary Wolfe, eds., *Observing Complexity: Systems Theory and Postmodernity* (Minneapolis: University of Minnesota Press, 2000), 199–214.

10. James Moffett and Kenneth R. McElheny, *Points of View: An Anthology of Short Stories,* rev. ed. (New York: Mentor, 1995).

11. James Alan McPherson, "Elbow Room," in *Elbow Room: Stories* (New York: Ballantine, 1983), 262.

12. This term is derived from Mark Seltzer's "media apriori," by which he designates a condition in which there is no outside to mediation; he in turn is borrowing from Bernhard Siegert's "postal apriori," which names the virtual presence of the postal system as the condition of possibility of and in the rise of the (epistolary) novel. See Mark Seltzer, *True Crime: Observations on Violence and Modernity* (New York: Routledge, 2006); Bernhard Siegert, *Relays: Literature as an Epoch of the Postal System* (Stanford: Stanford University Press, 1999).

13. Bharati Mukherjee, "Immigrant Writing: Give Us Your Maximalists!" *New York Times Book Review,* August 28, 1988. Page references to this article will be given in the text.

14. See Clark Blaise, introduction to Bharati Mukherjee, "Saints," in Tom Grimes, ed., *The Workshop: Seven Decades of the Iowa Writers' Workshop* (New York: Hyperion, 1999), 163.

15. Aijaz Ahmad, *In Theory: Classes, Nations, Literatures* (New York: Verso, 1992), 209.

16. Tina Chen and S. X. Goudie, "Holders of the Word: An Interview with Bharati Mukherjee," *Jouvert: A Journal of Postcolonial Studies,* 1997. *http://social.chass.ncsu.edu/jouvert/v1i1/bharat.htm.*

17. See Sam Halpert, *Raymond Carver: An Oral Biography* (Iowa City: University of Iowa Press, 1995), 72.

18. See, for instance, James Thomas, Denise Thomas, and Tom Hazuka, eds., *Flash Fiction: Very Short Stories* (New York: Norton, 1992); Robert Shapard and James Thomas, eds., *Sudden Fiction* (Gibbs Smith, 1983).

19. Chen and Goudie, "Holders of the Word," 4.

20. Susan Stewart, *On Longing: Narratives of the Miniature, the Gigantic, the Souvenir, the Collection* (Durham: Duke University Press, 1993), 71.

21. Bharati Mukherjee, "Courtly Vision," in Robert Shapard and James Thomas, eds., *Sudden Fiction International* (New York: Norton, 1989), 215–219. Subsequent page references will be given in the text.

22. For an analysis of this iconography, see Denis Cosgrove, *Apollo's Eye: A Cartographic Genealogy of the Earth in the Western Imagination* (Baltimore: Johns Hopkins University Press, 2003).

23. Gaston Bachelard, *The Poetics of Space,* trans. Maria Jolas (Boston: Beacon, 1969), 161.

24. Bharati Mukherjee, *The Middleman and Other Stories* (New York: Grove, 1999), 3.

25. Mukherjee, "Immigrant Writing," 30.

26. Bharati Mukherjee, *Jasmine* (New York: Grove, 1999). Page references to this novel will be given in the text.

27. Stephen Bury, *Cobweb* (New York: Bantam, 1997).

28. Bharati Mukherjee, "A Four Hundred Year-Old Woman," in Janet Sternburg, ed., *The Writer on Her Work: New Essays in New Territory* (New York: Norton, 1997), 37.

29. Robert Olen Butler, *Mr. Spaceman* (New York: Grove, 2000). Page references to this novel will be given in the text.

30. Robert Olen Butler, *From Where You Dream: The Process of Writing Fiction,* ed.

Janet Burroway (New York: Grove, 2005), 19; 31. Subsequent page references will be given in the text.

31. The latter is in fact importantly inter-differentiated, is either more or less "literary," depending on the scale of the social aggregates to which it draws attention, from the notoriously arid grand theories of Talcott Parsons and Niklas Luhmann to the dramatistic "group dynamics" studied by Kurt Leuwen, Erving Goffman, and others.

32. Robert Olen Butler, *A Good Scent from a Strange Mountain* (New York: Grove, 2001).

33. The question being whether the performance of other-narration in *A Good Scent* should be seen as the ideological reversal of Butler's conscription to the war machine, a belated flower in the barrel of the rifle, or, more suspiciously, as the continuation of white American imperialism in a softer medium. That it wants to be the former is clear enough from Butler's earlier novel, *On Distant Ground* (1985), in which an American soldier returns to Vietnam in the final days of the war determined to find the child he has become convinced he left in the womb of a woman he fell in love with there. "'Do you really think my purpose in coming to Vietnam was to be a spy?'" the protagonist asks incredulously, arrested by the victorious Vietcong at the novel's conclusion.

34. Robert Olen Butler, *Severance: Stories* (San Francisco: Chronicle Books, 2006).

35. "Inside Creative Writing" is archived at *http://www.fsu.edu/~butler/*, accessed March 12, 2008.

36. Wendy Bishop, *Released into Language: Options for Teaching Creative Writing* (Urbana, Ill.: NCTE, 1990), 93.

37. Robert Olen Butler, *Had a Good Time: Stories from American Postcards* (New York: Grove, 2004). Page references will be given in the text.

38. See Anne Anlin Cheng, *The Melancholy of Race: Psychoanalysis, Assimilation, and Hidden Grief* (New York: Oxford University Press, 2001).

39. See, for instance, Fredric Jameson, *The Geopolitical Aesthetic: Cinema and Space in the World System* (Bloomington: Indiana University Press, 2001).

40. Octavia Butler, *Lilith's Brood* (New York: Grand Central, 2000), 22. Subsequent page references will be given in the text.

41. Octavia Butler, afterword to *Bloodchild: And Other Stories* (New York: Seven Stories Press, 2005), 31–32.

Afterword: Systematic Excellence

1. Franco Moretti, "Conjectures on World Literature," *New Left Review* I, January-February 2000. See also Moretti, *Graphs, Maps, Trees: Abstract Models for a Literary The-*

ory (New York: Verso, 2005). An informative introduction to the history of close reading is available in Andrew DuBois, "Close Reading: An Introduction" in DuBois and Frank Lentricchia, eds., *Close Reading: The Reader* (Durham, N.C.: Duke University Press, 2003), 1–40.

2. Humberto R. Maturana, "Biology of Language: The Epistemology of Reality," in George A. Miller and Elizabeth Lenneberg, eds., *Psychology and Biology of Language and Thought: Essays in Honor of Eric Lenneberg* (New York: Academic Press, 1978), 31.

3. The branch of systems theory most attentive to questions of scale has been called "hierarchy theory"; it is introduced in Valerie Ahl and T. F. H. Allen, *Hierarchy Theory: A Vision, Vocabulary, and Epistemology* (New York: Columbia University Press, 1996). There is also a highly developed consideration of the importance of scale in the discipline of geography. See, for instance, David Harvey, *The Condition of Postmodernity* (Cambridge, Mass.: Blackwell, 1996), esp. Part III; Andrew Herod and Melissa W. Wright, *Geographies of Power: Placing Scale* (Malden, Mass.: Blackwell, 2002).

4. George Saunders, *The Brief and Frightening Reign of Phil* (New York: Riverhead, 2005).

5. Bruno Latour, *Reassembling the Social: An Introduction to Actor-Network Theory* (New York: Oxford University Press, 2005), 183; 185.

6. Bill Readings, *The University in Ruins* (Cambridge, Mass.: Harvard University Press, 1996), 22–23.

7. Bill Readings, "For a Heteronomous Cultural Politics: The University, Culture, and the State," *Oxford Literary Review 15* (1993), 163–199.

8. Ibid., 168.

9. The relevant texts are Thorstein Veblen, *The Higher Learning in America: A Memorandum on the Conduct of Universities by Business Men* [1918] (New York: Transaction, 1992), and *The Theory of the Leisure Class* [1898] (New York: Dover, 1994).

10. A few of these students, of course, will become professional writers, the creative writing instructors of tomorrow.

11. See Stephen Jay Gould, *Full House: The Spread of Excellence from Plato to Darwin* (New York: Harmony, 1996). Granted, literature has nothing as convenient as baseball's numerical batting average to measure "excellence," the very definition of which, in literature, is subject to dispute.

Index